Linux for the Oracle DBA
The Definitive Reference

Oracle In-Focus Series

Jon Emmons

This book is dedicated to my parents Bruce and Rachael. Thank you for encouraging me in all my different interests and for teaching me that there is no limit to what I can accomplish!

Jon Emmons

Linux for the Oracle DBA
The Definitive Reference

By Jon Emmons

Copyright © 2010 by Rampant TechPress. All rights reserved.
Printed in the United States of America.
Published in Kittrell, North Carolina, USA.
Oracle In-focus Series: Book 40
Series Editor: Donald K. Burleson
Production Manager: Robin Rademacher and Jennifer Stanley
Production Editor: Valerre Aquitaine
Cover Design: Janet Burleson
Printing History: June 2011 for First Edition

ISBN 10: 0-9823061-9-9
ISBN 13: 978-0-9823061-9-2
Library of Congress Control Number: 2011920068

Table of Contents

Using the Online Code Depot

Purchase of this book provides complete access to the online code depot that contains sample code scripts. Any code depot scripts in this book are located at the following URL in zip format and ready to load and use:

rampant.cc/linux_dba.htm

If technical assistance is needed with downloading or accessing the scripts, please contact Rampant TechPress at rtp@rampant.cc.

Conventions Used in this Book

It is critical for any technical publication to follow rigorous standards and employ consistent punctuation conventions to make the text easy to read. However, this is not an easy task. Within database terminology, there are many types of notation that can confuse a reader. For example, some Oracle utilities such as STATSPACK and TKPROF are always spelled in CAPITAL letters, while Oracle parameters and procedures have varying naming conventions in the database documentation. It is also important to remember that many database commands are case sensitive, are always left in their original executable form and never altered with italics or capitalization. Hence, all Rampant TechPress books follow these conventions:

- Parameters: All database parameters will be lowercase italics. Exceptions to this rule are parameter arguments that are commonly capitalized (KEEP pool, TKPROF); these will be left in ALL CAPS.

- Variables: All procedural language (e.g. PL/SQL) program variables and arguments will also remain in lowercase italics (*dbms_job*, *dbms_utility*).

- Tables & dictionary objects: All data dictionary objects are referenced in lowercase italics (*dba_indexes*, *v$sql*). This includes all *v$* and *x$* views (*x$kcbcbh*, *v$parameter*) and dictionary views (*dba_tables*, *user_indexes*).

- SQL: All SQL is formatted for easy use in the code depot, and all SQL is displayed in lowercase. The main SQL terms (select, from, where, group by, order by, having) will always appear on a separate line.

- Programs & Products: All products and programs that are known to the author are capitalized according to the vendor specifications (CentOS, VMware, Oracle, etc.). All names known by Rampant TechPress to be trademark names appear in this text as initial caps. References to UNIX are always made in uppercase.

Acknowledgements

This type of highly technical reference book requires the dedicated efforts of many people. Even though I am the author, my work ends when I deliver the content. After each chapter is delivered, several Oracle DBAs carefully review and correct the technical content. After the technical review, experienced copy editors polish the grammar and syntax.

The finished work is then reviewed as page proofs and turned over to the production manager, who arranges the creation of the online code depot and manages the cover art, printing distribution, and warehousing.

In short, the author plays a small role in the development of this book, and I need to thank and acknowledge everyone who helped bring this book to fruition:

- **Robin Rademacher and Jennifer Stanley** for the production management including the coordination of the cover art, page proofing, printing, and distribution.

- **Valerre Q Aquitaine** for help in the production of the page proofs.

- **Janet Burleson** for exceptional cover design and graphics.

- **John Lavender** for assistance with the web site, and for creating the code depot and the online shopping cart for this book.

- **Don Burleson** for providing me with the opportunity to write this book.

With my sincerest thanks,

Jon Emmons

Getting Started with Linux

A Short History

Having a little background on Linux helps to understand why things are the way they are. Originally written in 1991, Linux is a relatively young operating system compared to its UNIX counterparts that have their origins in the late 1960s. The Linux kernel, the core of any Linux operating system, was conceived, created, and named after Linus Torvalds.

Linus' intent was to create a free operating system for himself and other hobbyists. Soon after Linus announced his project, several other software developers started to contribute code to the Linux kernel and port software to compile it to work with the Linux kernel.

Interest in the project skyrocketed and many formal releases of Linux followed. Linux gained popularity as more tools and capabilities were introduced, especially among educational institutions. Today Linux has found applications from education to industry and in devices ranging from supercomputers to television remote controls.

A fairly early version of the Linux kernel has been distributed under the GNU (General Public License) that allows it to be used at no cost for free or commercial projects. Linus Torvalds still oversees code changes to the Linux kernel, but today Linux development goes far beyond the kernel.

The Linux kernel is typically packaged into a distribution, often referred to as a distro, of Linux to provide a full set of tools for a specific purpose. The tools shipped with a Linux distro vary quite a bit and include compilers, web servers, graphical interfaces and an array of command line tools. Of the hundreds of Linux distributions, only a few are appropriate for running Oracle databases and those are the ones that will be focused on in this book.

Through the years, UNIX operating systems, e.g. Solaris, AIX, and HP/UX, have enjoyed considerable popularity with servers due to their stability and inherent ability to serve multiple users and multiple applications simultaneously. Linux shares these features, but is referred to as a UNIX-like operating system as it is not certified as or necessarily completely compliant with the standard tools and interfaces defined within the Single Unix Specification.

Choosing the Right Linux

A top-down approach is best for choosing the right Linux for your application. Start with the requirements of the software that will be used on the system, then consider the requirements of the appropriate database version, which is probably dictated by the application.

There are three layers to be concerned with when configuring a system: the platform, which refers to the type and capability of the server hardware, the distribution (distro) of Linux, and the version. Oracle supports a small handful of options for each of these layers.

Choosing the Hardware Platform

The first concern is the hardware platform you intend to use. The most popular hardware platforms are the x86 and x86_64 platforms that use hardware derived from the popular Intel series of PC processors. The x86_64 platform represents hardware capable of more advanced 64-bit processing. x86_64 has become popular in servers and is gaining popularity in desktop systems.

> Historically, 32-bit platforms were limited to addressing 4 GB of memory. There are acceptable workarounds that allow the DBA to address up to 64 GB of memory, but 64-bit Linux can natively address these larger memory sizes and offers other performance advantages.

Older versions of Oracle that support Linux are on several other hardware platforms including PowerPC, Itanium and zSeries, but as of the writing of this book, Oracle 11g on Linux is only supported on the x86 and x86_64 hardware platforms.

Choosing a Distribution of Linux

Oracle 11g currently supports Red Hat Enterprise Linux, Oracle Enterprise Linux, SUSE Linux and Asianux. Of these, Red Hat Enterprise Linux (RHEL) probably has the most name recognition. It is widely used and supported by an extensive variety of applications.

Oracle Enterprise Linux (OEL) is a relatively new offering from Oracle Corporation. It is largely based on Red Hat's offerings but with the added advantage that support for OEL is available through Oracle, thus consolidating database and operating system support with one vendor.

Though less recognized than Red Hat, SUSE Linux predates it by many years. Originally developed in Germany and other parts of Europe, the distribution is now maintained by Novell, Inc.

The Asianux distro is a collaboration between several vendors in Asia. Several Asian languages are supported and local assistance is available to Asian customers.

Choosing the Linux Version

Oracle 11g supports RHEL 4 or 5, OEL 4 or 5, Asianux 2 or 3 and SUSE SLES10. Oracle occasionally changes their supported versions. An up-to-date list of platforms, distros and versions can be found in Oracle Support (formerly Metalink) note 169706.1. This note also lists supported Linux versions, distros and platforms for older Oracle versions.

Between Oracle's limitations and any additional requirements, other software may only have a few viable choices for platform, distribution and version. Budget, support and experience will further contribute to these choices, but when possible, it is best to lean toward the latest version that will meet your requirements.

Where to Get Linux

If a new system is being bought, Red Hat Linux may be preinstalled by the hardware vendor. This will save the time of installing it and the system will come with appropriate drivers for all the hardware preinstalled.

If the intent is to install Red Hat on an existing system, then buy it from a software vendor, but it is probably easiest to purchase it directly from Red Hat at www.redhat.com. There, a license can be purchased for RHEL support, disks, or download disk images of the software to burn disks. The site includes detailed instructions that describe how to burn these disk images to CDs or a DVD in order to install it on a system. Depending on the licensing, there may be access to several different versions and platforms of RHEL. Make sure to download the appropriate version for the chosen hardware.

Oracle Enterprise Linux (OEL) is available directly from Oracle. The software can be purchased in disk form from the Oracle store or disk images can be downloaded so that disks can be burned. To download OEL, go to the same page that is used to download other Oracle software: http://www.oracle.com/technology/software/index.html. OEL is listed under "Enterprise Linux". This leads to a page where Enterprise Linux can be downloaded or where a choice can be made from several Oracle VM options.

Under most circumstances, it is preferable to download Enterprise Linux. The Oracle VMs are for use with virtualization servers and offer operating system installations with popular software packages such as Oracle Database or Oracle Application Server preinstalled. To purchase a license and support, talk to the Oracle sales representative. If you are only looking to learn about or try out OEL, download it from oracle.com for free! This is a great opportunity to learn more about Linux without the expense of a license.

Installing Linux

Every distribution and version of Linux has different installation steps, but this section will highlight some of the common installation steps for setting up the Linux system for use with Oracle Database. The following steps and screenshots were produced using RedHat Enterprise Linux 5.3.

In choosing a system to use for Linux, it is recommended to use a system with nothing else on it. If this is just a testing system, consider creating a virtual system; see *Building One's Own Virtual Test System* later in this chapter. It is possible to install Linux on a system and preserve an existing operating system, but this is an advanced and somewhat risky prospect that will not be covered here.

The first step is to obtain installation media. As mentioned in the last section, this can either be purchased or downloaded and written to blank disks. Both methods should yield a bootable disk or set of disks that can be used for installation. Once this is achieved, then it is time to start up a soon-to-be Linux system with the disk in the optical drive, and the installer will launch.

If the installer does not launch, there may be hardware problems or just a need to change the order in which the system looks at disks to boot. This is usually a setting in the system's BIOS. If something troubling appears, consult the hardware documentation.

Once the installer has been successfully launched, there is a prompt to choose either a graphical installation mode or text installation mode.

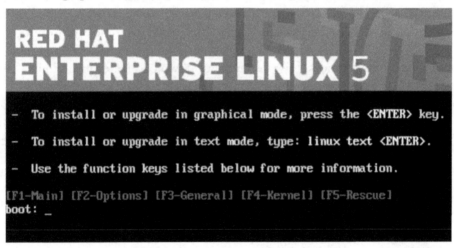

Figure 1.1: *Linux Installer Option – Graphical or Text Mode*

Either mode goes thorough basically the same steps. The graphical mode is used for this installation, but in some instances, graphical mode may not work on the DBA's hardware.

After choosing the graphical mode, enter the Red Hat installer. Choose Next at the first screen and a series of choices for the installation is presented. The first choices are for region and keyboard settings. For the machine used in this book, English and U.S. English have been chosen, respectively.

Red Hat Linux typically asks for a subscription number at this point in the installation process. This step may be skipped, but if there is a subscription number, it is best to enter it.

Setting Up Disks

The next step of most Linux installations is to format and configure the hard drives. Unless Linux has been previously installed on the system, a warning appears that the following steps erase all data from the hard disk.

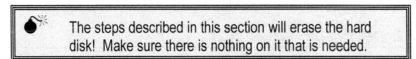

The steps described in this section will erase the hard disk! Make sure there is nothing on it that is needed.

There are several ways the disks can be laid out on the Linux system, depending on your need. The easiest way to get started, but still have some flexibility, is to choose the option to "Remove all partitions on selected drives and create default layout". In order to customize the default layout, choose the option to "Review and modify partitioning layout".

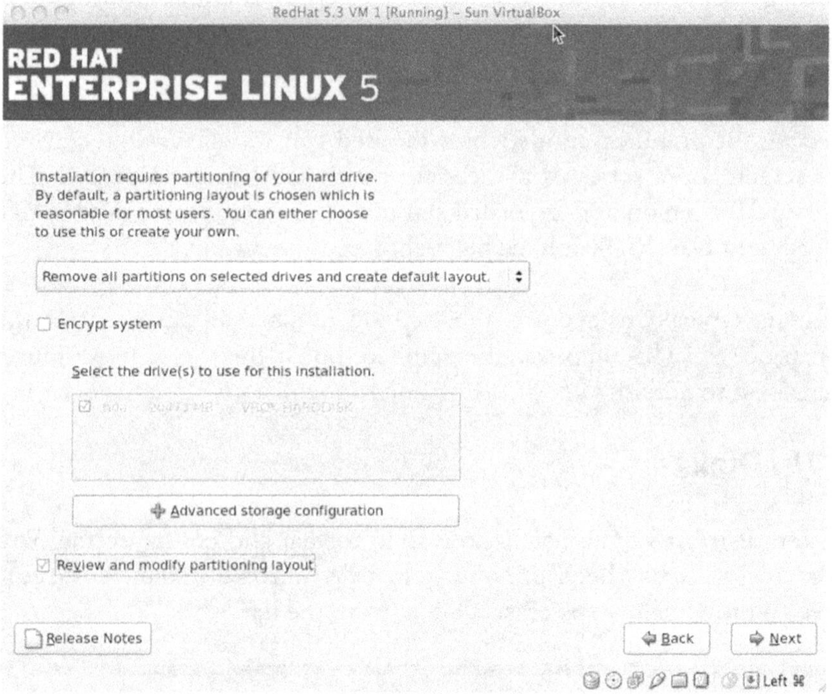

Figure 1.2: *Disk Layout*

> 🔔 If the system has multiple disks or is attached to a SAN, there will be quite a few more options to consider. See the chapter on file systems for details on more complex disk configurations.

When Next is clicked, there is again a warning that the existing partitions are about to be removed. Think carefully, and then click Yes if it is best to continue.

Since the choice to review and modify was made in the last screen, the installer now displays the default partition layout. It is important that the layout is modified to meet specific needs.

Figure 1.3: *Default Partition Layout*

There are two main concepts that can be seen in play on this screen. Hard Drives represent physically separate disks; in this case, only one disk is shown, referred to as */dev/hda* that is divided into partitions. Partitions represent different areas of the physical disk divided to serve different purposes.

By default, the installer configures a handful of volumes. There is a small boot volume, listed above with the mount point of */boot*. This is a special partition that contains the Linux kernel, which is the core of the OS, and other items needed early in the startup process.

A larger volume is created with the mount point of /, referred to as slash or as the root volume. This volume is typically at least 8 GB and contains the majority of the operating system and much of the software installed on the system.

Finally, there is a swap volume which does not have a mount point listed. Fortunately, it is easily identified by the type swap. This partition is used as virtual memory for the system. When more memory is needed than is installed in the machine, the operating system moves some of the contents of memory to this partition.

The Logical Volume Manager

LVM volume groups represent a logical construct managed by the Logical Volume Manager (LVM). An LVM volume group may be made up of a single disk partition, as with the device VolGroup00 in the previous configuration (Fig. 1.3), or may contain several physical devices aggregated into one logical construct.

LVM presents disks to the operating system for use in the form of logical volumes. These are what will become your disk mount points, such as '.' (slash), /*tmp* or /*u01*.

> To simplify, the Logical Volume Manager sits between the disks and the operating system. Its job is to manage the physical disks and to present usable space to the operating system. Having this extra layer of abstraction allows much greater flexibility when dealing with disks.

The boot partition is kept as a physical partition, i.e. not managed by LVM, so it can be made available immediately at startup without the overhead of LVM.

Configuring Disks for Oracle

At this point, it is good to consider the requirements of the Oracle product that will be installed on this system. The system in this example has been set up with a 20 GB disk and will be used for Oracle database 11g.

The root partition has, by default, taken up most of the disk. To make room to resize the swap partition and add other partitions, choose the root partition listed with the mount point of / and click Edit. Since the root partition is part of a LVM volume group, the installer will open a window where the entire LVM volume group can be modified.

In the list of volume groups, again choose the root partition and edit it. For this system, the root partition was changed to 10 GB (10240 MB). This should be safe enough to contain the operating system, but will free up the other 10 GB on the disk for other purposes. Next, edit the swap partition. In this screen there may be nothing identifying it as swap, but it will likely be the only partition without a mount point listed. Again, select the partition and edit it.

This system has 1 GB of RAM. With this configuration, Oracle recommends the swap to be at least 1.5 times the amount of RAM; in this case, 1.5 GB. To allow some extra overhead, the size of the swap volume was changed to 2 GB (2048 MB.)

> 🔔 The disk requirements for Oracle database on a specific platform can be found in document ID 169706.1 on metalink.oracle.com.

Finally, you need space for the Oracle software and database system. Oracle requires at least 2 GB of space. To accommodate that space with some room to spare, a 3 GB /*u01* partition is created by clicking Add, entering /*u01* as a mount point, leaving the file system type and logical volume name as their default values, and entering 3072 in the size field.

To create additional volumes for data files, archive logs and other Oracle files, a 3 GB /*u02* partition was also created and a /*u03* partition using the remaining space. The final layout, seen in the following image, should be appropriate for a small test system.

🖧 **User ID = book, password = reader**

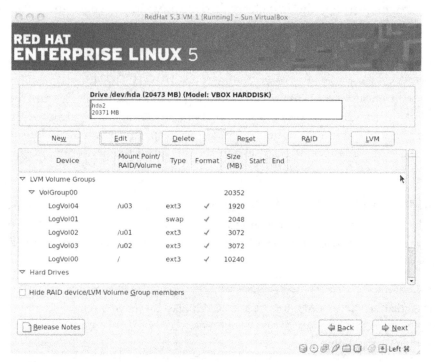

Figure 1.4: *Disk Layout Final*

When a system is set up for a specific application, consider the requirements of that application in addition to Oracle's requirements. When you are satisfied with the disk layout, click Next.

The Boot Loader

The boot loader is a small piece of software that allows selecting from the different operating systems installed on a machine and initiates the loading of that operating system. In most installations, Linux is the only operating system on a machine, but the boot loader is still needed to initiate the operating system startup. For most purposes, the default GRUB boot loader is sufficient. It is best not to install a boot loader unless you really know what you are doing.

At this point, the boot loader can be configured to launch other operating systems, e.g. Windows or another Linux distribution. It is also possible to choose to configure a boot loader password for additional security. These options are often unnecessary but offer additional flexibility and security in some circumstances.

Network Setup

In this step, choose what network devices Linux will use. By selecting a device and clicking Edit (Fig. 1.5), Linux can be told to get network information from a DHCP server or enter an IP address provided by the network administrator.

Also choose if a host name should be provided by the DHCP server, or enter one given to by the network administrator. These and the other settings in this window determine how this system will interact with the network.

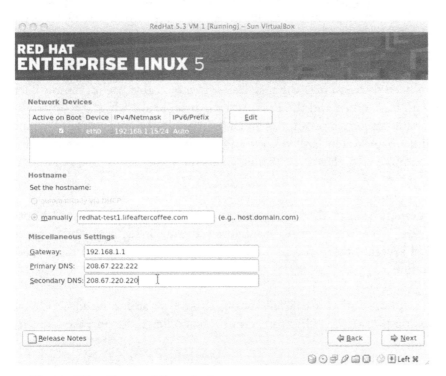

Figure 1.5: *Choosing Network Devices*

If a test box is only being configured for personal use, then DHCP configuration may be sufficient. If a server or a test box is being configured for multiple users, then specify many of these values manually.

Your network setup depends a lot on how your local network has been configured. Consult your network administrator for help with this step. Keep in mind that to connect to this system from another computer, either use the IP address specifically or have it added to the DNS server.

Final Steps

The final few steps of the Linux installer ask the system's time zone to be set up, set a password for the root account, and customize additional software to be installed. Particular attention should be paid to setting a root password that is known only to the DBA and is complex enough not to be guessed. A good root password should be at least eight characters long and contain both upper- and lower-case letters as well as numbers.

There is no need to customize the installed software at this point. Simply click Next through this screen and the next, and the installation will start. When the installation is complete, a prompt is given to remove the installation disk and click Reboot. The system will reboot and go through several screens, some text, and some GUI. Then go through several setup steps to prepare the system for use.

When the system restarts, there is a prompt to set up several options. Choose to set up the system's firewall, configure advanced security and logging settings, and several other options. For the most part, the defaults for these settings are fine.

The one exception is that a firewall setting should be added to allow Oracle connections on port 1521. On the firewall screen click Add, and then specify port 1521 and TCP.

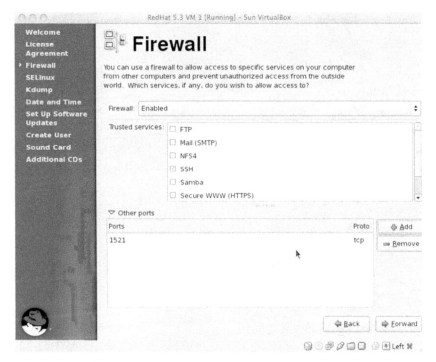

Figure 1.6: *Firewall Configuration*

This will save a step later on when the Oracle listener is set up.

There is also an option given to set up software updates and register the system. Choose to set this up now, but only if successfully connecting to the network is possible. There is also an option that allows for creating additional users on this system. This is a good time to create a user so connecting to the system as someone other than root can be accomplished, but do not create an oracle user here. That will be done in the next section.

Logging On to the System

If the system has just been set up, then there is probably a keyboard, mouse and monitor attached to it. There are ways to set up a Linux server without this, but that is a more advanced topic than will be covered here.

When the system starts up, a login screen appears.

Figure 1.7: *Linux Login*

From here, log in as root or as another user that has been created on this system. Logging on as root is generally discouraged, but when a system is first being set up, it can be the most convenient way to log on and work.

When a username and password has been entered, the Linux desktop appears.

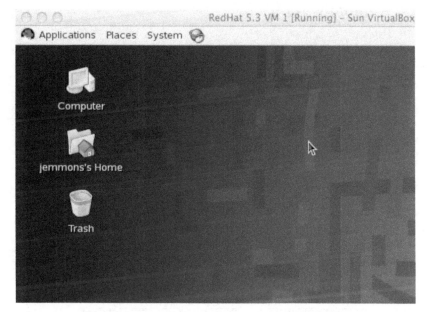

Applications Places System

Computer

jemmons's Home

Trash

Figure 1.8: *Linux Desktop*

Even if you have never worked with Linux or UNIX before, some familiar ground will be found here. The icon labeled Computer is similar to My Computer on Windows. The home directory is similar to My Documents but also contains configuration files for this account.

In the top menu, access some of the applications that are installed on this system including a web browser, disk utilities and under Accessories, the Terminal application. Settings and system options can be found under the System menu as well as options to lock this system, log out, or shut down.

These are the options that should be of the most concern for now. More of what is available on the Linux desktop will be explored in Chapter 5.

Connecting Remotely via SSH

Most of what needs to be done on Linux systems can be done remotely in one way or another. The most common method for connecting remotely to a Linux system is using the Secure Shell Protocol, commonly referred to as SSH.

By using an SSH application like PuTTY on Windows or command-line SSH from another Linux or UNIX system, commands can easily be issued on the Linux system, software can be set up, and just about anything that could be done while standing in front of the actual system can be done.

To connect via SSH, the Linux system should be configured to receive SSH connections. Most distros of Linux, RedHat and Oracle included, will automatically configure SSH when installed. Connecting via hostname is possible if the system has been added to DNS or the IP address to the Linux system.

> 🔔 There are several SSH clients available for each platform. While there are several commercial options available, it is recommended to start with the free ones. If Linux or UNIX is being used, including Macintosh OS X, bring up a terminal window and use SSH from the command line. If Windows is being used, download PuTTY from http://www.chiark.greenend.org.uk/~sgtatham/putty/.

When connecting remotely, there is a chance to enter a username and password just like at the login screen. Once logged in, a command prompt is seen, just like if the Terminal application was brought up from the Linux desktop. For most purposes, there is no difference between using the Terminal application and connecting remotely through SSH.

If command line Linux is a new concept, do not panic. The next chapter will introduce a lot of the basics and more advanced topics will be examined throughout the rest of this book.

Build A Virtual Test System

With the free software called VirtualBox and a free download of OEL, creating a virtual test system can be both free and easy.

Having your own test system allows you to try out settings, commands, scripts, and other system changes in a safe environment before using them on systems to which others will connect. Even if there is a dedicated system for your own use, it may be useful to also have a virtual test system.

There are many types of virtualization, but this section concerns a virtual system that exists as a guest system within another fully functional operating system. This allows running an operating system like Linux on a desktop computer without having to overwrite the existing operating system.

This type of virtualization makes some resources, like memory and processor, available by using some special sharing capabilities now common in PC hardware. Additional resources like hard disk, network and a video card are emulated by software. Through this combination of techniques, an entire virtual system is available to install an operating system and run software on.

There are a handful of software packages available that allow virtualization on Windows, Mac OS X and Linux systems. The most popular options are VMware (vmware.com), Parallels Desktop (parallels.com) and VirtualBox (virtualbox.org.) Each of these have their advantages and deserve consideration, but at this time, VirtualBox offers the most robust set of tools within a free software package and is available for all major desktop operating systems. For this reason, VirtualBox is being used as an example in this chapter, but the steps are similar for other virtualization software. The following steps outline how to prepare a VirtualBox virtual system for Linux. Once this setup is complete, proceed through all the steps described in the section Installing Linux.

The first step, of course, is to download and install the VirtualBox software for your operating system. It is available from virtualbox.org and installs like any other software. When VirtualBox is started, the VirtualBox home screen opens up. The home screen has two systems already configured.

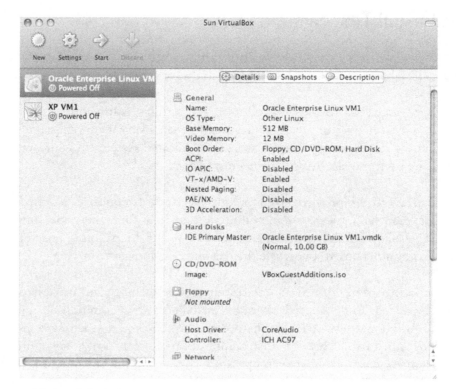

Figure 1.9: *VirtualBox Home Screen*

To start setting up a new virtual system, click the New button near the top. VirtualBox will go through several steps to create and set up the new virtual system.

First, set a name for the system. This is the name that identifies it on the VirtualBox home screen. There is also a prompt to choose the type of operating system to use on this system. Choose Linux for the operating system. For vendor, choose Red Hat if Red Hat Enterprise Linux is being installed or Linux if Oracle Enterprise Linux is being installed.

Then select the amount of memory allocated to this virtual system. There is a limit to the amount of memory available on the system, but it is good to give a virtual machine 512 MB of memory (1 GB if possible).

Next, there is the option to set up the hard drive for the new virtual system. This hard drive will actually be a file on the operating system. Set a size and location for this hard disk image. For a basic Oracle test system, it is recommended to start with around 20 GB. The hard drive file will only grow as space is used up on the drives, so there is no harm in setting a higher limit.

Figure 1.10: *Setting Up Hard Drive of Virtual System*

With the new virtual machine configured and the hard drive file set up, it is almost time to start up. The one remaining step is to make install media available. If there is an install disk, it can be put into the drive now, or if there

---

Build A Virtual Test System   **23**

is an ISO disk image, tell the virtual machine to open that as if it were a real disk.

Choose the machine that was just created at the VirtualBox home screen and click on Settings. Choose Storage from the top of this window and options related to the hard drive and other media are seen. Choose the option for CD/DVD-ROM and select the Mount CD/DVD Drive checkbox.

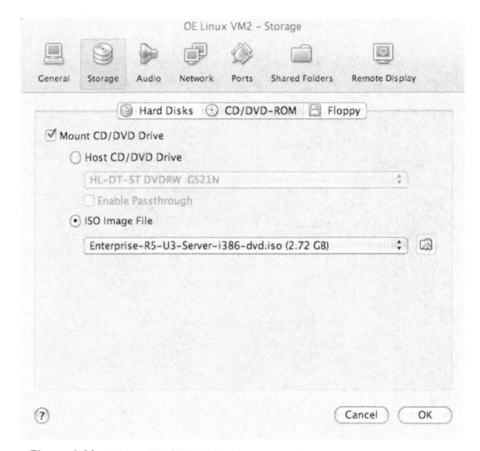

Figure 1.11: *Mount CD/DVD Drive*

Here, you can choose to mount the host CD/DVD drive if media has been installed in the computer's drive, or choose to mount an ISO image file from your hard drive.

With all these settings in place, choose the machine and click Start.

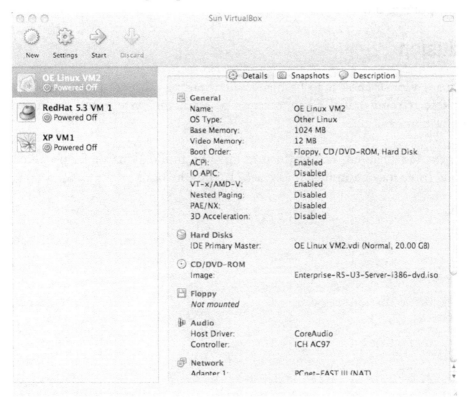

Figure 1.12: *VM2 Ready to Go*

The virtual machine starts up from the install media and the same installation steps can be followed as would be done with a normal system. Installation and setup are basically the same as with a standalone system. With a virtual machine, it is easiest to use DHCP for the network settings (this is typically the default) as the virtual machine is sharing the network interface with the host system. Other configurations are possible, but this can always be changed later.

When the installation is complete and a prompt is given to restart the system, unmount the install media from the Devices menu and restart the system. You now have a virtual system that can be changed, started up, shut down or deleted at any time desired. Virtualization software will even let you easily clone a system or take a snapshot so that the entire system can be restored to a specific point in time.

Conclusion

There are a lot of choices to be made when starting out with Linux. With the right research and initial setup, starting to learn the system and setting up Oracle can now begin.

The next few chapters will go further into the foundations of Linux before tackling some major administration tasks later in the book.

Command Line Basics

About the Command Line

Much of what is needed for managing the Linux system and the databases on it is best done on the command line. The commands available there are often the most powerful, flexible and consistent ones available. If there is already familiarity with the Linux command line, this chapter may be largely review; however, it might be worth the time to skim through the content here to be assured nothing has been missed.

To use these commands, the DBA should already be connected to the system via SSH or logged on to the system directly and in the Terminal application.

Commands, Options, Arguments and Input

Many Linux commands will be detailed in this book and it will be helpful to define some language that will be used. Many people use these terms interchangeably, but for the sake of this book, this is how I will describe command syntax.

There are three parts that generally make up the commands that will be used.

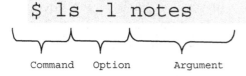

```
$ ls -l notes
```
    Command   Option   Argument

The first part is referred to as the command, and it describes what to do. This does introduce some ambiguity, and the term 'command' is used to refer both to this first part as well as all three; in practice, there will be little confusion.

The second part of a command is the option or options. Typically beginning with a dash (-), options change the behavior of the command being called. Sometimes a command will be used with no options, and other times there will be several options.

> **The third part of the command syntax is the argument or arguments. These typically describe what the command should act upon. In the code listing example above, the _ls_ command is being told to list the contents of the directory called notes.**

After a command is started, it may need additional information entered or it may take information from a file or files. This is referred to as input and, as will be seen later in the book, input can come in many forms.

Finding Your Way Around

The first thing that you need to be able to do on Linux is to navigate through the directories and files on the system. Here are a few commands to help determine where you are and how to get around the system.

pwd

To check what directory you are currently in, use the _pwd_ command.

```
$ pwd
```
```
/home/jemmons
```

The _pwd_ command prints the current or working directory that the DBA is in at any point in a command-line session. In this case, it is in the directory _/home/jemmons_. This is what is referred to as the home directory for this user, and it is the directory to typically start in when a new session is opened.

ls

To view the contents of this directory, use the _ls_ command.

```
$ ls
```
```
Desktop   notes   to_do.txt
```

The output of the *ls* command shows the name of everything in the current directory, but does not tell much more than that. To see more details, add the −*l* option to *ls*.

```
$ ls -l

total 24
drwxr-xr-x 2 jemmons jemmons 4096 Sep 16 13:19 Desktop
drwxrwxr-x 2 jemmons jemmons 4096 Sep 17 10:36 notes
-rw-rw-r-- 1 jemmons jemmons   53 Sep 17 10:50 to_do.txt
```

This provides much more information including the permissions, the owner and group associated with these items - in this case, jemmons for both - and the modification date and time. These details will become more significant as more is learned about files and directories. It is good to note that the first letter in each line is *d* if the item is a directory.

If you want to look into a directory that you are not currently in, provide it as an argument to the *ls* command.

```
$ ls notes

chapter1.txt   chapter2.txt   chapter3.txt
```

Files beginning with a period are typically excluded from *ls* output, but they can all be viewed by adding the option -*a*.

```
$ ls -a

.               .dmrc           .gnome2          .mozilla
..              .eggcups        .gnome2_private  .nautilus
.bash_history   .emacs          .gstreamer-0.10  notes
.bash_logout    .esd_auth       .gtkrc-1.2-gnome2 .redhat
.bash_profile   .gconf          .ICEauthority    to_do.txt
.bashrc         .gconfd         .lesshst         .Trash
Desktop         .gnome          .metacity        .viminfo
```

The hidden files shown above are created automatically on Oracle Enterprise Linux (OEL). Most of them control how things behave either at the command line or in the Linux GUI. Setting up some of these files will be covered later in the book.

There are two special directory entries that are in every directory on the system, but are always hidden; these entries are shown in the output above for '.' and '..'. These represent the current directory and the directory one level up

---

Commands, Options, Arguments and Input   **29**

from the current directory, respectively. How these entries are used for navigation will be seen in the next section.

cd

To move between different directories, use the *cd* command and provide the directory to be moved to as an argument.

```
$ cd notes
$ pwd

/home/jemmons/notes
```

Here, the *pwd* command has been used to confirm that directories were changed into the notes directory. To go up one level to the parent directory of this one, use the hidden '..' directory entry.

```
$ cd ..
$ pwd

/home/jemmons

$ cd ..
$ pwd

/home
```

This allows moving into and out of directories one at a time. If moving through more than one level of a directory needs to be accomplished, give a more complex argument to the *cd* command like this:

```
$ pwd

/home

$ cd jemmons/notes
$ pwd

/home/jemmons/notes
```

This method of moving around uses relative path names, path names which are only applicable to where you are now or which may have different results if in a different location. For instance, if there is a directory called *notes* in the directory */home/areader*, then execute the command *cd notes* from the working directory of */home/areader* and you end up in the directory */home/areader/notes*.

Yet if the exact same *cd* command is executed from */home/jemmons*, ending up in */home/jemmons/notes* is the result.

There are times when you want relative path names, but when you want to be more specific and refer to a single location without ambiguity, use absolute path names.

 After changing directories, you may return to the last directory you were in by entering *cd -*. This leads to the previous directory and the location will be printed to the screen.

The / Directory and Absolute Paths

At the base of all the directories in Linux is the / or *slash* directory. This is the highest level on the system and, from a logical standpoint, contains all the other directories.

Because it is the highest level on the system, use it as an anchor point to refer to any other directory path on the system without ambiguity. As an example, using the *cd* command to change the directory to */home/jemmons/notes* always takes the user to that directory no matter where they started from.

```
$ pwd

/home/jemmons

$ cd /home/jemmons/notes
$ pwd

/home/jemmons/notes

$ cd /tmp
$ pwd

/tmp

$ cd /home/jemmons/notes
$ pwd

/home/jemmons/notes
```

Whenever there is a path beginning with a slash, it is considered an absolute path. This type of path is also seen in the output of the *pwd* command when the command outputs the exact path the DBA is in on the system.

The Home Directory

When each command line session is started, always begin in the user's home directory. This location is specified when an account is created and is the place where user-specific configuration files are kept. It is also a good place to keep files that belong to that user.

By default, a user's home directory is a subdirectory of the */home* directory with the same name as the username, e.g. */home/jemmons* for the examples so far in this book. As will be seen when an account for Oracle is set up, a different location can be specified if so desired.

There are a few ways referring to this home directory can be achieved. If its specific location is known, it can be referred to by its absolute path, like */home/jemmons*.

```
$ cd /home/jemmons
$ pwd

/home/jemmons
```

An alternative way to refer to the home directory of the user you are logged in as is by using the *tilde* (~) character. This is shorthand for the current user's home directory.

```
$ cd ~
$ pwd

/home/jemmons
```

 Another way to get to the current user's home directory is to simply enter the *cd* command with no arguments at all. Just type *cd* and hit enter! This is different from MS Windows where entering just *cd* will print the current working directory.

If the home directory of another user needs to be located on the system, it is still possible to use the tilde but it must be followed by the username for that user.

```
$ cd ~areader
$ pwd
```

```
/home/areader
```

 The permissions set on a given directory, especially another user's home directory, may prevent a specific operation like the *cd* above. Typically, these will result in a "Permission denied" error. Permissions will be examined extensively later in this book.

Viewing the Command History and Repeating Previous Commands

As you navigate around and start making changes to your system, it is sometimes helpful to see what commands have been run recently and sometimes repeat selected ones. There are a couple of easy ways to do that in Linux.

If the bash shell is being used, which is the default in most Linux distros, use the up and down arrow keys to navigate through recent commands. Pressing the up arrow displays the next older command at the prompt, and the down arrow displays the next newer command.

When the command that you are in is found, then edit it or press Enter to execute that command again. If it is decided that none of these commands should be executed again, press the down arrow until a blank line appears or delete the contents of the line you are on.

history

If a list of recently executed commands needs to be viewed, use the *history* command.

```
$ history

        1  pwd
        2  ls
        3  ls -l
        4  ls notes
        5  ls -a
        6  cd notes/
        7  pwd
        8  cd ../
        9  pwd
       10  cd ..
       11  pwd
       12  cd jemmons/notes
       13  pwd
       14  cd /home/jemmons/notes
       15  pwd
       16  cd /tmp
       17  cd /home/jemmons/notes
       18  pwd
       19  cd /home/jemmons
       20  pwd
       21  cd ~
       22  pwd
       23  history
       24  history
```

This can be very useful for documenting the steps that have been taken. As seen on line 23 of the history output above, *history* displays all commands entered, even ones that did not run successfully.

After a while, the output of *history* can get very long. If only a few commands need to be displayed, call *history* with a number of lines as an argument.

```
$ history 5

       21  cd ~
       22  pwd
       23  hisotory
       24  history
       25  history 5
```

The history can also be cleared and you can start over again by executing *history -c*. There is a limit to how many commands are kept in the history. The default is 1000, but this may vary by implementation. Another way to repeat previously executed commands is by using the exclamation point (!) followed by a history number. After using history to look up the command's number, the syntax looks like this:

```
$ !22
```
```
pwd
/home/jemmons
```

This is referred to as history expansion. There are options that will allow previous commands to be repeated while substituting some of the text of the command, but to get started, just use history expansion to repeat previous commands. Great care must be taken when repeating previous commands, especially when used with commands that make changes. Commands that make changes will be covered in the next section.

Changing Things

Once navigating around at the command line feels comfortable, the next thing to master is how to make changes.

mkdir

To create a new directory in the current directory, use the *mkdir* command.

```
$ mkdir lists
$ ls
```
```
Desktop  lists     notes  to_do.txt
```

> 🔔 If you want to create more than one directory at a time, list multiple directories separated by spaces after the *mkdir* command.
>
> 🔔 If you want to make multiple directories within one another, use the -*p* option and separate the directories with a slash (/).

mv

Now that there is a new directory, move an item into it with the *mv* command.

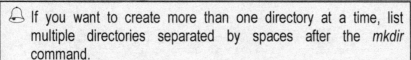
```
$ mv to_do.txt lists/
$ ls lists
```

```
to_do.txt
```

The *mv* command requires two arguments in the order of source, then destination. *mv* can be used with files, as seen above, or directories. *mv* can also be used to rename a file.

```
$ cd lists
$ ls

to_do.txt

$ mv to_do.txt to_do_list.txt
$ ls

to_do_list.txt
```

touch

In some instances, it is useful to make an empty file as a place keeper or for editing in the future. Use the *touch* command to create an empty file.

```
$ touch shopping_list.txt
$ ls

shopping_list.txt   to_do_list.txt
```

This creates a new empty file. The *touch* command can also be used on an existing file to update its modification time.

```
$ ls -l

total 12
-rw-rw-r-- 1 jemmons jemmons  0 Sep 20 07:34 shopping_list.txt
-rw-rw-r-- 1 jemmons jemmons 53 Sep 17 10:50 to_do_list.txt

$ touch to_do_list.txt
$ ls -l

total 12
-rw-rw-r-- 1 jemmons jemmons  0 Sep 20 07:34 shopping_list.txt
-rw-rw-r-- 1 jemmons jemmons 53 Sep 20 07:35 to_do_list.txt
```

This can be useful when a file needs to appear to be updated even if it has not been, or if there have been issues with the system clock and the timestamp for the file needs to be reset.

rm and *rmdir*

Oftentimes, files or directories that are no longer needed need to be removed. To remove files, use the *rm* command.

```
$ ls

shopping_list.txt   to_do_list.txt

$ rm shopping_list.txt
$ ls

to_do_list.txt
```

Similar to *mkdir* and many other commands, list multiple files to be removed by separating them with spaces.

The command *rmdir* can be used to remove empty directories, but it will not work if the directory still has something in it.

```
$ cd ../
$ ls

Desktop   lists   notes

$ mkdir empty_dir
$ ls

Desktop   empty_dir   lists   notes

$ rmdir empty_dir
$ ls

Desktop   lists   notes

$ rmdir lists

rmdir: lists: Directory not empty

$ ls

Desktop   lists   notes
```

If you want to remove a directory and its contents, add the *-r* flag to the *rm* command.

```
$ ls

Desktop   lists   notes

$ rm -r lists
```

```
$ ls

Desktop   notes
```

 Before using *rm -r*, or any other form of *rm* for that matter, be sure that what is about to be deleted is no longer needed! There is no undo, and no easy way to recover deleted files!

While the examples in this section have been using relative paths, they can also be used with absolute paths.

Commands like *mkdir, rm, touch* and even *ls* can act on multiple files or directories at once. To do this, simply list the files or directories that should be acted on with spaces separating them.

Commands like *mv* and *cp* that require a source and destination pair will almost always require them in that order. Multiple sources can be listed but only if the destination provided is a directory.

Viewing Files

Viewing and changing the name and location of a file have already been covered. Now the contents of a file will be examined. There are many more methods available than can be covered here, so focus will be only on the most commonly used ones.

cat

To simply see the contents of a file, use the *cat* command.

```
$ cat chapter2.txt
```

Much of what is needed to manage the Linux system and the databases is best done on the command line. The commands there are often the most powerful, flexible and consistent ones available.

The *cat* command prints the contents of the file to the screen, but *cat* is actually designed to concatenate multiple files and display them as if they were one, hence the name. To use *cat* this way, give *cat* multiple file names as arguments.

```
$ cat chapter2.txt chapter3.txt
```

Before installing Oracle, the Linux system needs to be customized to meet certain requirements. This involves installing software and customizing some settings. Another thing to note is as it just prints the entire file to the screen without any control to page through it, *cat* becomes less useful when viewing large files. One of the most popular commands to view larger files is *more*.

more

The *more* command allows viewing files too big to fit in a single window by showing them one page at a time.

```
$ more chapter1.txt
```

After the *more* command is executed, the first page is displayed. The bottom of the screen shows a percentage of how far you are through the file that is currently being viewed. Within *more*, moving forward or backward in the file or searching for a string of text can be done. Here is a quick reference for the *more* commands that are most likely to be used:

Command	Action
h or ?	Display help screen with a short summary of common commands
Space	Display the next page of text
b	Go back one page of text
Return	Move one line forward in the file
v	Edit this file using the default editor
control-l	Redraw the current screen (useful when the screen size has been changed)
q	Quit *more* and return to the command prompt

Table 2.1: *Common more Commands*

While *more* only allows viewing the contents of a file, use the *v* command to open this file in an editor. More about vi, the default editor in Linux, will be shown later in this book.

Another popular command for viewing files is *less*. The *less* command offers all the functionality of *more*, but with some additional features, many that are geared specifically to programmers. For most file browsing, *more* does everything that is needed by it; however, if preferred, most of the *more* commands will work in *less*.

head and *tail*

Often, especially with large log files, your only interest is in seeing the end of a file. To view just the last handful of lines in a file, use the *tail* command.

```
$ tail required_packages.txt

elfutils-libelf-devel-0.97.1-5.i386.rpm
glibc-headers-2.3.4-2.41.i386.rpm
glibc-kernheaders-2.4-9.1.103.EL.i386.rpm will be required as a prerequisite
glibc-devel-2.3.4-2.41.i386.rpm
gcc-3.4.6-10.i386.rpm
libstdc++-devel-3.4.6-10.i386.rpm
gcc-c++-3.4.6-10.i386.rpm
libaio-devel-0.3.105-2.i386.rpm
sysstat-5.0.5-19.el4.i386.rpm
unixODBC-devel-2.2.11-1.RHEL4.1.i386.rpm
```

By default, *tail* displays the last 10 lines of a file. This is a great way to look at recent entries in Oracle database alert logs. If more than 10 lines need to be seen, specify a number of lines as an option. For example, *tail -15 required_packages.txt* will show the last 15 lines of the file *required_packages.txt*.

When a log file is being actively written to, like with an alert log, displaying new lines on the screen as they are written to the file may be preferred. To do that, add the *-f* option to the *tail* command like this: *tail -f alert_TEST.log*. This allows the monitoring of a log in near real time, though sometimes lines may appear too quickly to read.

Of course, there will be times where the beginning of a file rather than the end needs to be seen. For this, use the *head* command.

```
$ head required_packages.txt
```

```
REHEL4, OEL4:
Refer to Note 880211.1

binutils-2.15.92.0.2-25
compat-libstdc++-33-3.2.3-47.3
elfutils-libelf-0.97.1-5
glibc-2.3.4-2.41
glibc-common-2.3.4-2.41
libaio-0.3.105-2
libgcc-3.4.6-10
```

The *head* command defaults to displaying the first 10 lines of the specified file. Like with *tail*, the default can be overridden and more lines or fewer lines can be displayed by adding a number as an option. For example, *head -5 required_packages.txt* will display only the first five lines of the file.

grep

Sometimes only specific lines of a file with certain text on it need to be seen. The *grep* command examines a file and only display lines that contain a certain string.

```
$ grep gcc required_packages.txt

libgcc-3.4.6-10
gcc-3.4.6-10.i386.rpm
gcc-c++-3.4.6-10.i386.rpm
```

This example displays all the lines in the *required_packages.txt* file which contain the string *gcc*. In this usage, *grep* matches the string *gcc* in only its given lowercase form. To search for a string without case sensitivity, add the *-i* option.

Occasionally, you may want to reverse this search and look for lines which do not contain a given piece of text. In that case, use the *-v* option for *grep*.

```
$ grep -v -i rpm required_packages.txt
REHEL4, OEL4:
Refer to Note 880211.1

binutils-2.15.92.0.2-25
compat-libstdc++-33-3.2.3-47.3
elfutils-libelf-0.97.1-5
glibc-2.3.4-2.41
glibc-common-2.3.4-2.41
libaio-0.3.105-2
...
```

In this example, the two options *-v* and *-i* have been combined to search without case sensitivity for lines that do not contain the string *rpm*. When using multiple options, most Linux commands will let you combine them after a single hyphen. Entering *grep -i -v* is the same as *grep -iv*.

These are the most common ways file contents may be viewed. In the next chapter, how to edit files with the popular, though often maligned, vi editor will be shown.

Searching for Files

Even before installing additional software is started, there are literally tens of thousands of files on a Linux system. Thankfully, the *find* command can help with locating what is needed.

find

The *find* command is a very flexible and powerful command. Later in the book it will be shown how it can be used to search for files by age, size and many other properties. For now, just focus on finding files by name.

The *find* command uses a somewhat more complicated syntax than the other commands that you have been given so far. It first takes an argument that specifies where to search, and then one of several options can be given to specify what criteria to search by.

```
$ find ./ -name required_packages.txt
```

```
./notes/required_packages.txt
```
Here the *-name* option is shown that tells *find* to search for files with the name given. The *find* command returns the location of the path to every file with that name, but only within the specified search area. In this example, the search area will be all directories beneath the current working directory as noted by the ./ value.

When first starting out, it is best to limit the searches to small areas. In the case above, it has been limited to only searching within the current working directory.

Learning More

This book focuses on the commands that are most useful to the Oracle DBA, but there are many more commands available and other options that may be useful in specific circumstances. Thankfully, help is not far away. There is a way to look up more information on a command right at the Linux command line.

man

The best way to learn more about a command is usually its man page. The *man* command is a Linux command that searches several locations on the system for manual pages, or documentation that is distributed electronically with most Linux software.

To access the man page for a specific command, enter the *man* command and provide the command you wish to learn more about as an argument.

```
$ man ls

LS(1)                           User Commands
      LS(1)

NAME
      ls - list directory contents

SYNOPSIS
      ls [OPTION]... [FILE]...

DESCRIPTION
      List  information  about the FILEs (the current direc-
      tory by default).  Sort entries alphabetically if none
      of -cftuvSUX nor --sort.

      Mandatory  arguments to long options are mandatory for
      short options too.

      -a, --all
            do not ignore entries starting with .

      -A, --almost-all
            do not list implied . and ..

      --author
            with -l, print the author of each file

      -b, --escape
            print octal escapes for nongraphic characters
...
```

The man pages are typically displayed on the screen in the *less* file viewer, very similar to *more*, in which the arrow keys can be used to navigate, or 'space' used to move a page down and 'b' to move a page up. The man pages are typically displayed in the format shown above. First, there is the command name with a short description, then a synopsis that shows the order of options and arguments that can be used with this command.

Next is a more detailed description of the command followed by all the valid options for the given command. It is not unusual for a command to have dozens of options. This can be quite overwhelming at first, but the more these commands are used, the more comfortable one will become with their options.

Knowing how to read and interpret the man pages is essential to learning about commands, but without a firm foundation they will have little meaning. Hopefully, at this point parts of the man pages are better understood, and by the end of the next chapter, most of what the man pages have to offer should also be understood.

whatis and *info*

Two other commands that give information about other commands are *whatis* and *info*. Both accept an argument much like the *man* command.
The *whatis* command prints just a short description of the command in question.

```
$ whatis ls

ls                      (1)  - list directory contents
ls                      (1p) - list directory contents
```

The *whatis* command is dependent on a database which has to occasionally be rebuilt to include new software, but as can be seen in the output above, it offers a nice succinct description.

The *info* command is similar to *man* but uses a different set of files to display command documentation.

```
$ info mkdir

12.3 `mkdir': Make directories
```

```
================================
```

`mkdir' creates directories with the specified names.   Synopsis:

```
    mkdir [OPTION]... NAME...
```

If a *NAME* is an existing file but not a directory, `*mkdir*' prints a warning message on stderr (standard error) and exits with a status of 1 after processing any remaining *NAMEs*. The same is done when a *NAME* is an existing directory and the *-p* option is not given. If a *NAME* is an existing directory and the *-p* option is given, `*mkdir*' ignores it. That is, `*mkdir*' does not print a warning, raise an error, or change the mode of the directory, even if the *-m* option is given, and will move on to processing any remaining *NAMEs*.

The program accepts the following options. Also see **Note Common* options:

`-m MODE'
`--mode=MODE'

Set the mode of created directories to *MODE*, which is symbolic as in *chmod* and uses *a=rwx* (read, write and execute allowed for everyone) for the point of the departure.

Most commands have more documentation in the man page than is available in *info*, but there are occasional exceptions, so it is worth keeping *info* in mind. Unlike the *man* and *whatis* commands, *info* can be called without any arguments. That displays a list of commands for which *info* pages are available.

Examining the System

The upcoming chapters will go into great detail on monitoring many aspects of the system, but here are a few easy-to-use commands that are useful for getting a bird's eye view of the system.

hostname

When you connect to several systems, it is easy to lose track of what system to which you are connected. The *hostname* command is the quickest way to check the system.

```
$ hostname
```

`oelinux-test1.lifeaftercoffee.com`

 Before running dangerous or destructive commands, it is good practice to make sure you are on the right system by running *hostname*.

whoami

When setting up Oracle and other products, start using multiple Linux accounts. To check what user is currently being worked on, use the *whoami* command.

```
$ whoami

jemmons
```

The *whoami* command prints the name of the user you are working as currently. This will be very useful as multiple accounts are starting to be used as well as the *su* command to switch between them.

uname

Another command which will give some information on the system's configuration is *uname*.

```
$ uname -a
Linux oelinux-test1.lifeaftercoffee.com 2.6.18-128.el5 #1 SMP Wed Jan 21
07:58:05 EST 2009 i686 i686 i386 GNU/Linux
```

With the *-a* flag, some detailed system information can be seen. There is the kernel name, the hostname, additional information about the kernel, the hardware platform and the operating system. This information is often useful when requesting OS support or when trying to determine compatibility.

top

The *top* command gives a live report of several key aspects of the Linux system. *top* continuously refreshes the output on the screen every three seconds by default.

```
$ top

top - 13:01:21 up 7 min,  1 user,  load average: 0.01, 0.31, 0.24
Tasks:  83 total,   1 running,  82 sleeping,   0 stopped,   0 zombie
Cpu(s):  3.4%us,   6.2%sy,  0.0%ni, 80.1%id,  9.5%wa,  0.5%hi,  0.3%si,  0.0%st
Mem:   1035244k total,   366408k used,   668836k free,    21412k buffers
Swap:  1048568k total,        0k used,  1048568k free,   266792k cached

  PID USER      PR  NI  VIRT  RES  SHR S %CPU %MEM    TIME+  COMMAND
    1 root      15   0  2064  620  532 S  0.0  0.1   0:00.66 init
    2 root      RT  -5     0    0    0 S  0.0  0.0   0:00.00 migration/0
    3 root      34  19     0    0    0 S  0.0  0.0   0:00.00 ksoftirqd/0
    4 root      RT  -5     0    0    0 S  0.0  0.0   0:00.00 watchdog/0
    5 root      10  -5     0    0    0 S  0.0  0.0   0:00.02 events/0
    6 root      10  -5     0    0    0 S  0.0  0.0   0:00.01 khelper
    7 root      10  -5     0    0    0 S  0.0  0.0   0:00.00 kthread
   10 root      10  -5     0    0    0 S  0.0  0.0   0:00.14 kblockd/0
   11 root      20  -5     0    0    0 S  0.0  0.0   0:00.00 kacpid
   48 root      20  -5     0    0    0 S  0.0  0.0   0:00.00 cqueue/0
   51 root      13  -5     0    0    0 S  0.0  0.0   0:00.00 khubd
   53 root      10  -5     0    0    0 S  0.0  0.0   0:00.00 kseriod
  110 root      16   0     0    0    0 S  0.0  0.0   0:00.00 pdflush
  111 root      15   0     0    0    0 S  0.0  0.0   0:00.00 pdflush
  112 root      11  -5     0    0    0 S  0.0  0.0   0:00.00 kswapd0
  113 root      11  -5     0    0    0 S  0.0  0.0   0:00.00 aio/0
```

In the first line of the *top* output, see the system time and the amount of time since system startup; in this case, seven minutes. The load average is shown. Load average is a good big-picture indication of how busy a system is. A lower number indicates a more idle system. In the following lines, information on the tasks (processes) that are running on the system, how busy the processor or processors are, and memory usage and swap (virtual memory) usage can be seen.

After this system-wide information, there are several lines with information about the busiest processes on the system by CPU usage. This can be useful in finding processes that are using more than their share of the system's resources.

Each of these topics will be examined further in later sections of this book. For now, just keep *top* in mind as a good way to get a quick overview of what is happening on the system.

df

The *df* command is used to report on the space available and in file systems. By default, *df* reports space in kilobytes; by using the *-h* flag, *df* to report in kilo-, mega- or gigabytes can be obtained as appropriate.

```
$ df -h

Filesystem                            Size  Used Avail Use% Mounted on

/dev/mapper/VolGroup00-LogVol00       9.7G  2.0G  7.3G  22% /
```

```
/dev/mapper/VolGroup00-LogVol03                    3.0G   69M  2.7G   3% /u02
/dev/mapper/VolGroup00-LogVol02                    3.0G   69M  2.7G   3% /u01
/dev/mapper/VolGroup00-LogVol04                    1.9G   35M  1.7G   2% /u03
/dev/hda1                                     99M   12M   82M  13% /boot
tmpfs                                        506M    0  506M   0% /dev/shm
```

In the output, the filesystem can be seen, which refers to the physical disk or LVM volume the data is on, the size of the partition, how much is used and available and what percent of the disk is used. The final column shows where the disk is mounted, also known as the mount point.

Any files or directories within a mount point will take up space on that filesystem unless they fall under another lower level mount point. As an example, everything on the system will fall under the / mount point unless it is a subdirectory of /u01, /u02, /u03, /boot or /dev/shm.

Conclusion

This chapter has gone through the basics of navigating, modifying and investigating the Linux system. The next chapter will expand considerably on these topics.

An understanding of the material presented in this chapter is essential to understanding the rest of the book. If you are not comfortable with some of the topics presented so far, go back and reread them or get some help if necessary.

Advanced Command Line Use

In the last chapter, some basic command line navigation and manipulation was covered. This chapter starts to show the power and flexibility of the command line. Also how the command line environment can be customized will be seen.

Variables

The command line shell allows the use of variables, much like a programming language. Some variables will affect the behavior of the shell itself, and others will be used to help control Oracle or store some values, thereby allowing for some programming within the shell.

Setting, Viewing and Clearing Variables

Setting variables at the command line is as simple as giving the variable name, followed by an equal (=) and the value that is desired put in the variable. Here is an example:

```
$ chapter=3
```

To retrieve the contents of a variable, the variable name must have a dollar sign ($) in front of it. This example uses the *echo* command, which is a common method to check the contents of a variable.

```
$ echo $chapter
```

3

The *echo* command simply prints to the screen what it receives as an argument. In this case, the variable *$chapter* is replaced by its value, which is then printed to the screen on the next line.

Whenever choosing to retrieve the contents of a variable, precede the variable name with a dollar sign as shown previously. If the variable is being manipulated by either setting it, changing it or unsetting it, then do not use the dollar sign.

Variable names are case sensitive, so the variable *chapter* is different from the variable *Chapter*, which is different from the variable *CHAPTER*. Each of these variables may have different contents, so be careful to use consistent capitalization with the variables.

 Using multiple words in a variable name can make the contents more clear. Two common methods to create multiple word variable names are to use an underscore (e.g. *chapter_number*) between the words, or to capitalize the first letter of each word after the first (e.g. *chapterNumber*). My preference is to use underscores as they are found to be easier to read, but both methods are acceptable.

Variables can be updated in the same way they are set. When a new value is assigned to a variable in use, the old value is discarded.

```
$ chapter=4
$ echo $chapter

4
```

Variables in most shells are un-typed, meaning they do not require you to specify what kind of information will be stored in them. Variables may contain numbers or text. It will be up to the program using them to determine how they should be handled.

The *set* command can be used to view all variables set in the current session. There will likely be more variables than will be expected since *set* returns variables set by the shell as well as ones that have already been set.

```
$ set

PWD=/home/jemmons/notes
SHELL=/bin/bash
TERM=xterm-color
UID=501
```

```
USER=jemmons
chapter=2
...
```

If a variable is no longer needed, it is good practice to unset it. The *unset* command removes a variable's name and contents.

```
$ unset chapter
$ echo $chapter
```

Variables are all unset when the current command line session is exited unless you provide for them to be set again at login. This will be covered further when customizing the environment is explained.

Exporting Variables

When a variable is set, it becomes available for use in the current session, but sometimes a variable may need to be made available for other programs that are run from the current session. To accomplish this, use the *export* command.

A good example of this is setting the *ORACLE_SID* variable.

```
$ ORACLE_SID=TEST
$ export ORACLE_SID
```

By exporting the *ORACLE_SID* variable, other programs that are called from this session to retrieve the contents of the variable are allowed. This variable is used to specify what database to connect to if SQL*Plus is started without specifying one.

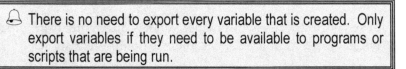

There is no need to export every variable that is created. Only export variables if they need to be available to programs or scripts that are being run.

A list of all the currently exported variables can be obtained using the *env* command.

```
$ env
```

```
HOSTNAME=oelinux-test1.lifeaftercoffee.com
TERM=xterm-color
```

Variables

```
SHELL=/bin/bash
HISTSIZE=1000
USER=jemmons
ORACLE_SID=TEST
PATH=/usr/kerberos/bin:/usr/local/bin:/bin:/usr/bin:/home/jemmons/bin
PWD=/home/jemmons/notes
PS1=$
HOME=/home/jemmons
. . .
```

Above is a partial list of the exported variables that are likely to be seen in a command line session. It can be seen that the variable that was just exported, *ORACLE_SID*, is listed. The shell automatically sets many of the other variables listed. Several of these will be shown in the next section.

Environment Variables

Environment variables are a set of variables that affect the behavior or describe the condition of the current command line session or other programs on the system. Like other variables, they can be listed using *set* or viewed individually using *echo*.

```
$ echo $SHELL

/bin/bash

$ echo $PS1
$
$ echo $HOME

/home/jemmons

$ echo $ORACLE_SID

TEST
```

Some shells set and retrieve environment variables differently from other shell variables, but in bash and Bourne shells, there is no differentiation.

> ⚠ *Environment* variables, variables that will have an effect on more than the current shell session, typically have names that are all UPPERCASE. Variables such as counters, which are only used in the current session typically, have lowercase names. This is a convention, not a steadfast rule, but it is good practice, especially when you begin shell scripting.

Some *environment* variables, like *PATH* or *ORACLE_SID*, will need to be updated. Others like *HOME* or *PWD* are set by, and should only be updated by, the system. Following is a list of some of the more important shell variables.

Variable	Contains	Update Notes
ATH	The *binary search path*	The location of additional installed software may be added to the *PATH*, but be careful when removing a location.
MANPATH	The *man page search path*	Additional locations where man pages can be found may be added. If not set, the system-wide *MANPATH* will be used.
PS1	The command line prompt. This is displayed at the beginning of each command line.	This can be changed to the preference, but extremely long prompts may become cumbersome.
PS2	The secondary prompt. This is displayed when multi-line commands are entered.	This can be changed to the preference but should be kept short and different from *PS1*.
HISTSIZE	The number of commands to track for retrieval by the *history* command.	Typically defaults to 1000. Can be set to another number if desired.
HOME	The location of the current user's home directory	Do not update. Set by shell.
OLDPWD	The previous working directory set before the last *cd* command.	Do not update. Set by the *cd* command.
ORACLE_SID	The SID of an Oracle database to be connected to.	Can be set and exported, or set using the *oraenv* script.
ORACLE_HOME	The location where the database binaries are installed for the current database	Should only be set or updated by the *oraenv* script.

Table 3.1: *Some Important Environment Variables*

There are many more environment variables available and often software like Oracle will require certain settings. More information about other environment variables can be found in the man pages for the specific shell.

Viewing and Controlling What is Executed

When a command is executed at the command line, there is a lot more going on than meets the eye. While the whole process is very complex, what is described below should provide a functional understanding of how commands are parsed. Some of these terms may be new to you, but they will be examined, one at a time, later in this section.

Steps to Command Execution

After a command is typed at the command line and the enter key is pressed, the shell goes through the following steps to execute the command.

1. The string of text that makes up the command, including options and arguments, is broken up into words based on where spaces are in the command text. The first word of the command text is considered the command name and the remaining words will be used as options and arguments.

2. If the command contains one or more slashes, the shell executes the command based on the path described in the command providing the options and arguments described in the remaining words. Steps 3, 4 and 5 will be skipped.

3. If the command does not contain slashes, the shell checks to see if an alias is defined that matches the command name. If a matching alias is found, the value of the alias is substituted for the command line.

4. The shell checks through its library of shell built-in commands. These are commands that are part of the functionality of the shell itself, as opposed to part of the operating system or software that has been added on. As an example, the *history* command covered in the last chapter is a command built into the shell, whereas the *ls* command is not. If a built-in is found, it is executed with the options and arguments given in the remaining words and Step 5 is skipped.

5. The shell searches through the directories described in the *PATH* environment variable for a program matching the command name given. If one is found, it is executed with the options and arguments given in the remaining words.

This is a lot to digest, but it can be very useful in understanding how things are executed at the command line. It may be helpful to review these steps again after reading the following sections on the *PATH* and aliases.

The *PATH* Variable

When most commands are executed, the shell is being told to run a program from a file on disk. Since Linux does not keep all its programs in one location, use the *PATH* variable to list the locations where programs can be found. This is typically referred to as the binary search path.

The current contents of the *PATH* variable can be examined using *echo*.

```
$ echo $PATH
```

```
/usr/kerberos/bin:/usr/local/bin:/bin:/usr/bin:/home/jemmons/bin
```

The *PATH* variable is a list of locations on disk separated by colons. The example above is a typical default path for Linux. This one includes a path within the user's home directory *(/home/jemmons/bin)* where the user can keep their own commands and scripts.

There are several common locations where programs are kept in Linux, but as software is added, it would be good to expand on the *PATH* variable to allow Linux to find the newly installed software. To add these locations, simply update the *PATH* variable.

```
$ export PATH=$PATH:$ORACLE_HOME/OPatch/bin
```

In this example, the current values for the *PATH* variable are included and *$ORACLE_HOME/OPatch/bin* is added. This, of course, also requires that the *ORACLE_HOME* variable be set.

Like other variables, the *PATH* only remains set for the current session. To make the change more permanent, update it in the user's profile. How to do that will be shown as the system for Oracle is customized.

When a command is called, the shell steps through the paths in the binary search path one at a time until it finds a matching command. Once it finds a match, it stops searching. In some cases, there may be more than one command that matches, but whichever one is found first in the binary search path is executed.

Most entries in the binary search path are absolute paths, paths that begin with / and describe a unique location on the system. One common exception to this is to include the current working directory in the *PATH* variable.

There are a few ways to include the working directory in the binary search path. The first, and clearest way, is to add an entry for '.'.

```
$ export PATH=$PATH:.
$ echo $PATH
```

/usr/kerberos/bin:/usr/local/bin:/bin:/usr/bin:/home/jemmons/bin:.

Since the binary search path is searched in order, this causes the current directory to be searched only if a command is not found in any of the previous entries.

The current working directory can also be indicated if the first or last character of the *PATH* variable is a colon. If the colon is the last character of the *PATH*, the behavior is exactly as above; however, if it is the first character, this causes the current working directory to be searched before all other directories.

Indicating the present working directory should be searched last:

```
$ echo $PATH
```

/usr/kerberos/bin:/usr/local/bin:/bin:/usr/bin:/home/jemmons/bin:

Indicating the present working directory should be searched first:

```
$ echo $PATH
```

:/usr/kerberos/bin:/usr/local/bin:/bin:/usr/bin:/home/jemmons/bin

Finally, anywhere in the binary search path that a double colon is found (::), the present working directory will be searched.

Present working directory in the middle of a search path:

```
$ echo $PATH
```

```
/usr/kerberos/bin:/usr/local/bin:/bin:/usr/bin::/home/jemmons/bin:.
```

 Since the present working directory changes each time you change directories, it can have unexpected and sometimes undesired results and can even pose a security risk. For this reason, I recommend not having the present working directory as part of the search path.

Checking What is Executed

Depending on what is installed, the *PATH* variable can grow quite long. It will occasionally be useful to check what directory a given command is being executed from. To do this, use the *which* command.

```
$ which grep
```

```
/bin/grep
```

If the command is found within the binary search path, the *which* command returns the full path where the command resides on disk. If there is more than one command within the binary search path with the same name, the *which* command only returns the location of the first one found. This is the same one that would be executed if that command were called.

There are two other ways that *which* may react. If an alias is set, *which* returns the alias definition in addition to the command which this alias will eventually execute.

```
$ which ls
alias ls='ls --color=tty'
```

```
/bin/ls
```

Aliases will be delved into more in a few pages.

If *which* cannot find a command, it returns an error like this:

```
$ which history
```

```
/usr/bin/which: no history in
(/usr/kerberos/bin:/usr/local/bin:/bin:/usr/bin:/home/jemmons/bin)
```

This indicates one of a few things. Since it is known that the *history* command works, this states that this command is not an installed program, but rather a shell built-in command. Since they are part of the shell program itself rather than being individual programs on the disk, shell built-in commands do not appear in a *which* search.

This output of the *which* command may also indicate that a command is not installed on the system. If you want to see if the software is installed somewhere on the system, use the *find* command to search for it by name.

If the software is installed on the system but *which* cannot find it, then the software's location probably needs to be added to the *PATH* variable. That should allow *which* to find it and allow it to be found by the shell when the command is executed.

Another way to search for programs is using *whereis*. The *whereis* command searches a set of standard locations for Linux executables and man pages.

```
$ whereis ls

ls: /bin/ls /usr/share/man/man1p/ls.1p.gz /usr/share/man/man1/ls.1.gz
```

Unlike *which*, *whereis* lists multiple entries if more than one program is found by a given name. It also gives the location of the man pages for that command which can be useful for setting the *MANPATH* variable.

Aliases

The shell has the ability to assign an alias, a shortcut to a command. Aliases can refer simply to commands or to commands and options. As an example, if a DBA has a lot of experience working in DOS, they may want to make an alias for the *ls* command called *dir*.

```
$ alias dir='ls'
$ dir -l

total 16
drwxr-xr-x 2 jemmons jemmons 4096 Sep 16 13:19 Desktop
drwxrwxr-x 2 jemmons jemmons 4096 Sep 20 10:39 notes
```

When the previous command is parsed, it compares the command name *dir* to the list of known aliases. A match is found, so it substitutes the *ls* command for *dir*. The resulting command, *ls -l*, is then executed as normal.

By using the *which* command, it can be seen that there is an alias in place for the *dir* command.

```
$ which dir

alias dir='ls'
     /bin/ls
```

Many modern Linux variants now come with a command called *dir* which is a clone of *ls*, but some older versions do not. To remove the alias that was just created, use the *unalias* command.

```
$ unalias dir
$ which dir
/usr/bin/dir
```

To see all the aliases assigned in the current session, execute the *alias* command with no arguments.

```
$ alias

alias l.='ls -d .* --color=tty'
alias ll='ls -l --color=tty'
alias ls='ls --color=tty'
alias vi='vim'
alias which='alias | /usr/bin/which --tty-only --read-alias --show-dot --
show-tilde'
```

The aliases in the output above are the ones typically set by default in Linux. An alias is used for the *ls* command which, instead of changing the command called, simply adds an option. This is a good example of how an alias can be used to change the behavior of a command rather than changing what command is being called.

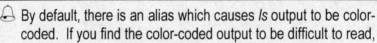 By default, there is an alias which causes *ls* output to be color-coded. If you find the color-coded output to be difficult to read, turn it off by executing *unalias ls*.

Becoming Another User with *su*

As the system is administered, there are a lot of things that need to be done as different users. The root user is particularly instrumental in setting up the system and directories that will be needed. When switching users temporarily in a shell session is needed, use the *su* command.

```
$ whoami

jemmons

$ su - areader

Password:

$ whoami

areader

$ exit

logout

$ whoami

jemmons
```

There are a few ways that eventually lead to using *su*, but for now this is the most common. Here, the name of the user whose identity is to be assumed is provided as an argument for *su*. The *su* command has an option that is provided as simply a dash (-), which causes the settings to be applied for the user you are becoming.

If *su* is called without providing a username, it assumes that the DBA wants to become the root user. This is useful when making changes to the system. Since the root user is the administrator for the whole system, it gets a special exception for *su*, and is able to become any user on the system without being prompted for a password. This is a great troubleshooting tool, but also highlights one more reason the root password must be kept secure.

File and Directory Ownership

In Linux, every file and directory has an owner and a group associated with it. To view the owner and group for a given file, use *ls -l*.

```
$ ls -l

total 32
-rw-rw-r-- 1 jemmons jemmons 1027 Sep 20 08:24 chapter1.txt
-rw-rw-r-- 1 jemmons jemmons  216 Sep 20 08:26 chapter2.txt
-rw-rw-r-- 1 jemmons jemmons  163 Sep 17 10:36 chapter3.txt
-rw-rw-r-- 1 jemmons jemmons  708 Sep 20 10:39 required_packages.txt
```

The third and fourth columns of the *ls -l* output indicate the owner and group, respectively. In this case, the group name that matches the owner name can be seen. By default, when a user is created in Linux, a group is created with the same name. Though not the most flexible configuration, this is a good security measure for typical users.

chown

The *chown* command allows for changing the ownership of a file. Changing ownership typically requires root permissions.

```
$ su -

Password:

# cd ~jemmons/notes
# ls -l

total 32
-rw-rw-r-- 1 jemmons jemmons 1027 Sep 20 08:24 chapter1.txt
-rw-rw-r-- 1 jemmons jemmons  216 Sep 20 08:26 chapter2.txt
-rw-rw-r-- 1 jemmons jemmons  163 Sep 17 10:36 chapter3.txt
-rw-rw-r-- 1 jemmons jemmons  708 Sep 20 10:39 required_packages.txt

# chown areader chapter1.txt
# ls -l

total 32
-rw-rw-r-- 1 areader jemmons 1027 Sep 20 08:24 chapter1.txt
-rw-rw-r-- 1 jemmons jemmons  216 Sep 20 08:26 chapter2.txt
-rw-rw-r-- 1 jemmons jemmons  163 Sep 17 10:36 chapter3.txt
-rw-rw-r-- 1 jemmons jemmons  708 Sep 20 10:39 required_packages.txt
```

The arguments for *chown* are a username, then the file or files that are desired to be changed. The resulting output shows that the owner has been changed to areader.

chgrp

The *chgrp* command is similar in syntax and function to the *chown* command but is used to change the group associated with a file or directory.

```
# chgrp areader chapter1.txt
# ls -l

total 32
-rw-rw-r-- 1 areader areader 1027 Sep 20 08:24 chapter1.txt
-rw-rw-r-- 1 jemmons jemmons  216 Sep 20 08:26 chapter2.txt
-rw-rw-r-- 1 jemmons jemmons  163 Sep 17 10:36 chapter3.txt
-rw-rw-r-- 1 jemmons jemmons  708 Sep 20 10:39 required_packages.txt
```

Here, it can be seen that the group ownership has been changed to areader.

A shortcut with *chown* allows for changing both the owner and group at the same time. Instead of simply providing the owner as the first argument to *chown*, an owner/group pair is provided separated only by a colon.

```
# ls -l chapter1.txt

-rw-rw-r-- 1 areader areader 1027 Sep 20 08:24 chapter1.txt

# chown jemmons:jemmons chapter1.txt
# ls -l chapter1.txt

-rw-rw-r-- 1 jemmons jemmons 1027 Sep 20 08:24 chapter1.txt
```

Since it is common to change both the owner and the group at the same time, this syntax will be used often.

File and Directory Permissions

File permissions are also displayed as part of the *ls -l* output, but they are a little more cryptic than ownership.

```
$ ls -l

total 32
-rw-rw-r-- 1 jemmons jemmons 1027 Sep 20 08:24 chapter1.txt
-rw-rw-r-- 1 jemmons jemmons  216 Sep 20 08:26 chapter2.txt
-rw-rw-r-- 1 jemmons jemmons  163 Sep 17 10:36 chapter3.txt
-rw-rw-r-- 1 jemmons jemmons  708 Sep 20 10:39 required_packages.txt
```

The first column of the output shows permissions for the given files. The first character indicates the type of file which is being viewed. Most commonly, a dash (-) indicates a normal file and *d* indicates a directory.

The next three characters of the first column indicate the permissions given to the owner of the file, the following three indicate permissions for the group, and the last three permissions to anyone on the system who is not the owner or part of the group.

Each of these sets of three characters typically indicate permission to read (r), write (w) or execute (x) the given file. Read and write permissions are most commonly associated with files that contain data while execute is commonly used to allow users to run programs and scripts.

chmod

The *chmod* command is used to update permissions on both files and directories. There are several ways to manipulate file permissions, but the safest way is to provide a set of symbols to *chmod* to indicate what permissions should be changed.

```
$ ls -l chapter1.txt

-rw-rw-r-- 1 jemmons jemmons 1027 Sep 20 08:24 chapter1.txt

$ chmod g-w chapter1.txt
$ ls -l chapter1.txt

-rw-r--r-- 1 jemmons jemmons 1027 Sep 20 08:24 chapter1.txt
```

The symbols given as the first argument for the *chmod* command are composed of a single character indicating the permission level to modify either user, aka owner (u), group (g), other (o), or all (a); an arithmetic sign indicating if the given permission should be added (+), removed (-) or modified to match (=); and finally, what permissions should be modified, r, w or x. This can be a bit confusing at first, but some examples should help make this clear.

The first example used here performed *chmod g-w* which removed the write permission from the group. This example will remove the read permission from other users on the system.

```
$ chmod o-r chapter1.txt
```

```
$ ls -l chapter1.txt
```

```
-rw-r----- 1 jemmons jemmons 1027 Sep 20 08:24 chapter1.txt
```

Using the plus operator, you can add permissions to the file.

```
$ chmod g+w chapter1.txt
$ ls -l chapter1.txt
```

```
-rw-rw---- 1 jemmons jemmons 1027 Sep 20 08:24 chapter1.txt
```

Even combining multiple changes into a single *chmod* command can be done by providing multiple operations separated by a comma. This example sets the permissions for other users to read only and adds execute to the owner.

```
$ chmod u+x,o=r chapter1.txt
$ ls -l chapter1.txt
```

```
-rwxrw-r-- 1 jemmons jemmons 1027 Sep 20 08:24 chapter1.txt
```

These commands will become more clear and familiar with use. More information and a reference for setting file permissions can be found in the chapter on file management.

The *chown*, *chgrp* and *chmod* commands can all be used on files or directories. The behavior on directories may be a little different than is expected. This is also examined further in Chapter 12 about file management.

Editing with vi and vim

When administering the system and databases, configuration files often need to be edited, logs searched through and shell scripts written. For a long time, the vi edit has been one of the most popular editors for manipulating text files on UNIX and UNIX-like systems because of its consistency and ubiquity.

In most modern Linux distros, vi has been replaced by vim, an improved text editor based on vi (the name vim is an acronym for Vi IMproved.) An alias for vi is set up by default in both RedHat and OE Linux, so for those used to using vi, the command will still work. For most purposes where this may be a concern, vim is identical to the vi editor found on many UNIX systems, but it does offer several advantages, particularly for programmers. Where vi is mentioned in this book, consider it synonymous with vim, especially since the *vi* command that is included with Linux is often just another copy of vim.

vi is a very powerful text editor, but it will seem cumbersome at first if you are not used to it. While it is unlikely you will start using it for all your text-editing needs, it is invaluable to be able to make quick changes on the system without having to transfer files to your workstation and back to the server.

Invoking vi

The *vi* command is typically started with a file name as an argument. An existing file name or the name of a file that needs to be created can be provided.

```
$ vi chapter1.txt

Having a little background on Linux helps us understand why things are the
way they are.

Originally written in 1991, Linux is a relatively young operating system
compared to its UNIX counterparts that have their origins in the late 1960s.

The Linux kernel (the core of any Linux operating system) was conceived,
created, and of course named after Linus Torvalds.

Linus' intent was to create a free operating system for himself and other
hobbyists.

Soon after Linus announced his project several other software developers who
were interested in the project started to contribute code to the Linux
kernel and additionally to port software to (compile it to work with) the
Linux kernel.

Interest in the project skyrocketed and many formal releases of Linux
followed.

@                                                                          @
"chapter1.txt" 13L, 1027C                        9,1            Top
```

In the example above, two @ symbols can be seen near the bottom of the screen. This indicates that there are more lines present that will not fit completely on the current screen. If a short file is being edited, tilde (~) will be seen, indicating lines past the end of the file that is being edited.

Different Modes in vi

vi has two primary modes, insert and command. For the most part, insert mode can be thought of as the mode where text can be entered into the document and command mode as the mode where just about everything else will be done.

Pay special attention to the case of the commands in this section. Like other commands in Linux, *vi* commands are case sensitive.

Command Mode

When vi is first invoked, the starting point is in command mode. In command mode, use the arrow keys to move up and down or left and right through the text. This is also the mode where searches are executed from as well as being able to copy and paste from. Even saving changes and exiting vi must be done in command mode.

There are a lot of ways to get out of command mode, but to get back into command mode at anytime, all that is needed is to press Escape. In command mode, one line at a time or several can be moved around. Moving around can also be accomplished by words or skipping directly to a specific point. Here are some popular commands for moving around in command mode:

Command	Action: Move the Cursor
←, →	left or right one character
↑, ↓	up or down one line
h	left one character
l	right one character
j	down one line
k	up one line
$	to the end of the current line
^	to the beginning of the current line
w	to the beginning of the next word
b	to the beginning of the previous word
G	to the end of the file
25G	to line 25 (any number can be used instead of 25)
enter	to the beginning of the first word on the next line

Table 3.2: *Cursor Movement Commands*

Under some circumstances, depending on what is being used for a ssh program or terminal, it may be found that the arrow keys do not work. Instead, the letters h, j, k, l will have to be used to move around. Though not as easy as using the arrow keys, this can help in a pinch.

The *G* command can be particularly useful to jump to the end of a file or to a specific line number. In fact, many of these commands, including the arrow keys, can have a number entered before them to move more quickly. As an example, entering the number 20 and then the right arrow would move you 20 characters to the right, or 5 and the w key would move you to the right 5 words.

Insert Mode

Insert mode allows entering text into your file. There are several ways insert mode can be entered depending on where the text should be put, but the most common is using the i key. This starts inserting text at the position of the cursor, pushing any text after the cursor to the right.

When insert mode is entered into, -- INSERT – appears at the bottom of the screen to indicate being in insert mode. Then enter text where the cursor is or move around using the arrow keys and enter text elsewhere in the file. There are several ways to enter insert mode depending on where entering the text is desired. Below is a list of some of the more useful ways to switch to insert mode and how to get back out.

Command	Action
i	Insert text to the left of the cursor position
a	Insert text to the right of the cursor
I	Insert text at the beginning of the current line
A	Insert text at the end of the current line
o	Start inserting on a new line below the current line
O	Start inserting on a new line above the current line
escape	Return to command mode

Table 3.3: *Common Commands for Entering and Exiting Insert Mode*

Making and Undoing Changes

There are a lot of ways to change, remove or replace text in vi. The following commands allow specific changes to be made, and perhaps most useful, undo changes that have been made.

Command	Action
x	Delete one character
r	Replace one character with the next character typed
dw	Delete from the cursor position to the end of the current word
dd	Delete the current line
D	Delete from the current character to the end of this line
cw	Same as *dw* then enter insert mode
cc	Clear the text on this line and enter insert mode
C	Delete from the current cursor position to the end of the current line and enter insert mode
J	Join the next line to the current line
u	Undo the last change. Can be repeated to undo the past several changes.
.	Repeat the last edit command at the current cursor position

Table 3.4: *Commands for Changing Text and Undoing Changes*

Like the cursor movement commands, many of these commands can be preceded with a number to repeat the given command. Even the *undo* command can be preceded by a number to undo several recent commands.

Copying and Pasting

vi offers many options for copying and pasting including the ability to copy and paste from multiple buffers (a buffer is similar to the clipboard in Windows or Mac OS), but the basic copy and paste commands will only be touched upon. The following commands allow you to copy and paste.

Command	Action
yy	Copy the current line into the default buffer
7yy	Copy the current line plus the next six lines to the default buffer
p	Paste the contents of the default buffer below the current line
P	Paste the contents of the default buffer above the current line

Table 3.5: *Common Copy and Paste Commands*

If multiple lines are copied with the *yy* command, the number of lines does not need to be specified when pasting. The *paste* command automatically pastes the entire contents of the default buffer.

Searching and Replacing

Searching for text and replacing text in vi can be very handy, but it is not as easy as you might think! Here are some of the more useful search and replace commands in vi:

Command	Action
/search text	Find and move the cursor to the next occurrence of *search text*
?search text	Find and move the cursor to the previous occurrence of *search text*
n	Repeat the last search
N	Repeat the last search but in the opposite direction (previous occurrence instead of next or next occurrence instead of previous)
:%s/search text/replace text/g	Find all occurrences of *search text* and replace it with *replace text*
:noh	Turn off highlighting of searched for text

Table 3.6: *Some Search and Replace Commands*

When these commands encounter the end of the file, they wrap around to the beginning and continue searching. If searching backwards, they wrap from the beginning to the end. It has probably been noticed that the find and replace command is very complicated. There are ways of making it even more complicated and having it search only specific lines, but that level of complexity is not particularly needed.

Saving and Exiting

Work should be saved often and when all is done, exit vi. As with other things in vi, there are several ways to save and exit. Here are a few common ones:

Command	Action
:w	Save changes
:w filename.txt	Save changes to *filename.txt* instead of the file opened
:q	Exit vi (changes should have already been saved)
:q!	Exit vi without saving changes
:wq	Save changes and exit vi
ZZ	Save changes and exit vi (same as *:wq*)
:w!	Write changes despite read-only permissions (must be file owner)

Table 3.7: *Commands for Saving and Exiting in vi*

This short section is only a brief introduction to vi, but it should be enough to do basic editing and some shell scripting. vi allows text to be manipulated in just about any way imaginable, so if there is something specific that is to be done in vi, take a look through the help documents available by entering *:help* within vi or in an easier-to-navigate form on the Web at http://vimdoc.sourceforge.net.

Listing Multiple Commands on One Line

Sometimes, listing more than one command on a single command line may be desired. To do this, simply end the first command with a semicolon and start the next command immediately after. This is common practice when setting, then exporting, a variable.

```
$ ORACLE_SID=TEST;export ORACLE_SID
```

Commands entered using this method are executed in order from left to right, and a command will only be executed after the one to its left has completed. More than just two commands can be combined in this fashion by putting additional semicolons, but it is important to remember if a command in a list like this is slow or hangs up for some reason, it can delay the subsequent commands.

Continuing a Long Command on Another Line

Commands with multiple or large options and arguments can quickly grow quite long. To make the commands easier to understand, use the shell escape character, which is a backslash, to continue a command on the next line.

```
$ cp /home/jemmons/notes/chapter1.txt \
> /home/areader/notes/backup/chapter1.txt
```

This is useful for long and complex commands and can be used as well when executing multiple commands. The escape character is being used to tell the shell to ignore the special meaning typically associated with the enter key and instead, treats it as just a line feed.

Escaping Special Characters

The escape character, which in bash is backslash, can be used to ignore the meaning of several key characters. For instance, typically when the shell encounters a dollar sign followed by text, it tries to replace that with the contents of a variable. If there is no variable by that name, an empty string is returned.

```
$ echo v$session

v
```

To tell the shell to ignore the special meaning normally associated with the dollar sign, put a backslash in front of it.

```
$ echo v\$session

v$session
```

 Using this method, file names with special characters in them can be easily created. This is generally discouraged as the files will be more difficult to reference and manipulate.

If several special characters in a string of text need to be ignored, use quotes instead. Depending on the specific needs, there are a few types of quotes that can be used.

Single and Double Quotes

Quotes are used at the command line to cause certain special characters to be ignored. Quotes allow characters to be used like ampersands as part of a sentence and multiple words are treated as a single argument for commands.

Single Quotes

Single quotes can be used around text to prevent the shell from interpreting any special characters. Dollar signs, spaces, ampersands, asterisks and other special characters are all ignored when enclosed within single quotes.

```
$ echo 'All sorts of things are ignored in single quotes, like $ & *
; |.'
All sorts of things are ignored in single quotes, like $ & * ; |.
```

When handling strings of text, this is a very efficient way to prevent the shell from interpreting special characters or trying to substitute variables. Even semicolons are ignored when placed between single quotes.

Since the newline character is not interpreted between single quotes, a string within single quotes can easily be made to span multiple lines.

```
$ echo 'Text within single quotes can
> span multiple lines
> because the newline character
> is not interpereted'
Text within single quotes can
span multiple lines
because the newline character
is not interpreted
```

The only thing that cannot be put within single quotes is a single quote. Fortunately, there is another type of quote that can be used for that.

Double Quotes

Double quotes act similarly to single quotes, except double quotes still allow the shell to interpret dollar signs, back quotes and backslashes. It is already known that backslashes prevent a single special character from being interpreted. This can be useful within double quotes if a dollar sign needs to

---

be used as text instead of for a variable. It also allows double quotes to be escaped so they are not interpreted as the end of a quoted string.

```
$ echo "Here's how we can use single ' and double \" quotes within double
quotes"
```

Here's how we can use single ' and double " quotes within double quotes

It may also be noticed that the apostrophe, which would otherwise be interpreted as the beginning of a quoted string, is ignored within double quotes. Variables, however, are interpreted and substituted with their values within double quotes.

```
$ echo "The current Oracle SID is $ORACLE_SID"
```

The current Oracle SID is test

Like single quotes, text within double quotes can span multiple lines. Though double quotes are more flexible in what they display, there are times that the use of single quotes to eliminate the need for escape characters may make a script easier to understand.

The Back Quote

Back quotes are wholly unlike single or double quotes. Instead of being used to prevent the interpretation of special characters, back quotes actually force the execution of the commands they enclose. After the enclosed commands are executed, their output is substituted in place of the back quotes in the original line. This will be clearer with an example.

```
$ today=`date '+%A, %B %d, %Y'`
$ echo $today
```

Monday, September 28, 2009

Here the value of the variable *today* has been set to the output of the *date* command. The shell executes the command *date '+%A, %B %d, %Y'* which prints the day, date and year as output. The shell then places that output in place of the back quoted string and sets the value of the variable *today*.

A command within back quotes can be used nearly anywhere in the shell. These are evaluated and substituted before the rest of the line is executed.

Tab Completion

The bash shell offers tab completion as a way to reduce the amount of typing needed to complete long file and path names. When a path is being entered, start typing the name of the next element in the path (both directory and file names work) and press Tab. If enough information has been entered so that there is only one possible match, bash fills in the rest of the name. In this example, only *cd n* is entered and Tab is pressed:

```
$ cd n[tab]otes/
$ pwd

/home/jemmons/notes
```

Bash checked through the current directory and finding only one thing that started with the letter n, it filled in the rest.

If there are multiple things that match the name, a slightly different behavior is seen. In this example, *more ch* has been entered and *tab* has been pressed. This first tab caused the rest of the word *chapter* to be completed, but since there are multiple files beginning with this word, it could not complete any further. Then *tab* was entered twice more, which displays all the files in this directory matching what has been entered so far.

```
$ more ch[tab]apter[tab][tab]

chapter1.txt   chapter2.txt   chapter3.txt

$ more chapter1[tab].txt
```

More of the file can then be entered manually and *tab* used to complete the rest of the file. While this may seem frivolous in this small example, when navigating long path names and managing files with large names, it can be a real time saver.

Wildcards and Pattern Matching

Another time saver at the shell is wildcards. Wildcards can be used in two different ways. They can be used to specify a single location or file by using a wildcard to represent a character or characters, or they can be used to reference multiple files with a single command.

There are several wildcards that can be used in the bash shell. The most common wildcards are * and ?. The wildcard * can represent 0, 1 or more of any string of regular characters. The wildcard ? represents exactly 1 of any character.

In this use of a wildcard, a single location is being specified.

```
$ cd /home/je*/notes
```

Since there is only one directory in */home* that starts with *je*, the wildcard is translated to fill in the rest of the directory name and the *cd* command succeeds.

In this example, use the same wildcard to specify multiple files which match a pattern.

```
$ ls chapter*
```

```
chapter1.txt   chapter3.txt   chapter5.txt
chapter2.txt   chapter4.txt
```

There are multiple matches, but the *ls* command is capable of handling multiple files, so the command again succeeds.

The *?* wildcard can be used in a similar way, but only matches a single character in the file name. To demonstrate the difference, a file has also been created called *chapter10.txt*.

```
$ touch chapter10.txt
$ ls
```

```
chapter10.txt   chapter2.txt   chapter4.txt   required_packages.txt
chapter1.txt    chapter3.txt   chapter5.txt
```

```
$ ls chapter?.txt
```

```
chapter1.txt   chapter3.txt   chapter5.txt
chapter2.txt   chapter4.txt
```

Since the *?* wildcard will only match a single character, the file *chapter10.txt* is not included in the results.

With range substitutions, you can get even more specific and give a set of characters or a range of characters within brackets.

```
$ ls chapter[123].txt

chapter1.txt   chapter2.txt   chapter3.txt

$ ls chapter[3-5].txt

chapter3.txt   chapter4.txt   chapter5.txt
```

The first example above matches the character 1, 2 or 3 in place of the bracketed text. The second matches anything from 3 to 5 inclusive.

These sets or ranges can work with letters also. A range of letters are case sensitive, so [a-z] would match any lowercase letter while [A-Z] would match any uppercase letter.

 Wildcards and range substitutions are very powerful, but must be used with caution. The * wildcard is especially dangerous when combined with destructive commands like *rm*.

Redirecting Input and Output

The shell has some very powerful features that allow for redirecting both input (the text or data required by a command) and output (the text or data that results from a command) to another command or a file. Combined with the broad array of tools available at the command line, redirecting input and output allows for some very sophisticated tasks. This can be somewhat confusing at first, but with some good examples and a little experimenting, it should quickly become clear.

A Brief Description of Input and Output Streams

As text is entered and the results are viewed during a command line session, something called standard streams is being utilized. Streams are simply channels on which text can be passed. The text that is typed is sent to a program, e.g. the Bash shell or SQL*Plus, over the stream called standard input (abbreviated stdin). This stream is automatically set up when a program is started, so most of the time not much thought needs to be given it.

When the result from a command appears, the output of that command is being displayed through a stream called standard output (abbreviated stdout). Text sent to standard output will, by default, be printed to the terminal application.

Another stream called standard error (or stderr) exists only for error text. By default, this will also be printed to your terminal and will appear exactly like the output of stdout. When programming, it is possible for there to be more streams, but typically you need to only be concerned with these three standard ones.

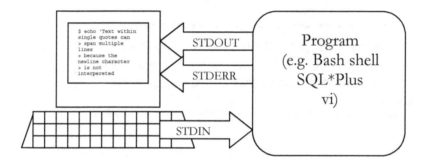

Figure 3.1: *Default Behavior of the Standard Streams*

Standard in, standard out and standard error are sometimes referred to by their stream numbers, 0, 1 and 2 respectively. These streams are what will be manipulated in the next few sections to allow for writing and reading from files and other commands.

Sending Command Output to a File

Sometimes it is more useful to write the output of a command to a file than to view it on the screen. This can allow for further manipulation of the output in the file or for making a record of the output of a command.

To redirect the standard output, use the greater-than sign (>) after the command and give the name of the file that the output should be written to. It is easiest to think of this as an arrow showing which way the information will flow. In this example, the output of the uptime command is written to the file *uptime.log*.

```
$ uptime > uptime.log
$ cat uptime.log

 12:24:07 up  1:01,  1 user,  load average: 0.08, 0.02, 0.01
```

When dealing with files, the > symbol replaces the entire contents of the file given with the output of the command, but this behavior can be overridden by providing the double greater-than symbol(>>).

```
$ uptime >> uptime.log
$ cat uptime.log

 12:24:07 up  1:01,  1 user,  load average: 0.08, 0.02, 0.01
 12:26:22 up  1:04,  1 user,  load average: 0.06, 0.04, 0.01
```

The greater-than symbol will redirect standard output, but not standard error. A workaround for this is to add an additional redirection of '2>&1' which tells the shell to redirect stream 2 (standard error) to stream 1 (standard output.)

```
$ uptime >> uptime.log 2>&1
$ cat uptime.log

 12:24:07 up  1:01,  1 user,  load average: 0.08, 0.02, 0.01
 12:26:22 up  1:04,  1 user,  load average: 0.06, 0.04, 0.01
 12:32:45 up  1:10,  1 user,  load average: 0.01, 0.05, 0.01
```

Now any errors which happen during the execution of the *uptime* command are also written to the *uptime.log* file. These errors could also be captured to a different file by redirecting 2 to the file name with either > or >>, depending on whether the file needs to be overwritten or appended with each execution.

```
$ uptime >> uptime.log 2>>uptime.err
```

This can be an effective way to track output and errors on commands that run for a long period of time or cannot be monitored in real time.

Reading Input From a File or From the Terminal

Redirecting input is similar to redirecting output. To redirect input from a file, use the less-than symbol (<). The example here uses the *sort* command which simply sorts the input in order.

```
$ more required_packages.txt

glibc-2.3.4-2.41
glibc-common-2.3.4-2.41
libaio-0.3.105-2
libgcc-3.4.6-10
libstdc++-3.4.6-10
make-3.80-7.EL4
pdksh-5.2.14-30.6
elfutils-libelf-devel-0.97.1-5.i386.rpm
glibc-headers-2.3.4-2.41.i386.rpm
libaio-devel-0.3.105-2.i386.rpm
sysstat-5.0.5-19.el4.i386.rpm
unixODBC-devel-2.2.11-1.RHEL4.1.i386.rpm

$ sort < required_packages.txt

elfutils-libelf-devel-0.97.1-5.i386.rpm
glibc-2.3.4-2.41
glibc-common-2.3.4-2.41
glibc-headers-2.3.4-2.41.i386.rpm
libaio-0.3.105-2
libaio-devel-0.3.105-2.i386.rpm
libgcc-3.4.6-10
libstdc++-3.4.6-10
make-3.80-7.EL4
pdksh-5.2.14-30.6
sysstat-5.0.5-19.el4.i386.rpm
unixODBC-devel-2.2.11-1.RHEL4.1.i386.rpm
```

The shell reads the contents of the *required_packages.txt* file into the standard input of the *sort* command which then orders the text and displays it on standard output.

Another way that input can be redirected is to move it from standard input using file markers and the double less-than symbols. Though less frequently used at the command line, this is a useful technique for scripting.

```
$ sort << EOF

> charlie
> delta
> bravo
> alpha
> EOF
alpha
bravo
charlie
delta
```

After the <<, a file marker is named, in this case EOF. Any name can be used, but EOF is often used to stand for End Of File. When the shell sees this, it continues to read from the standard input until it encounters a matching file marker alone on a line. Once it sees that, it will take the input given and pass it to the standard in for the given program.

Redirecting from One Command to Another

Using the tools that were just covered, you could easily send the output from one command to a file to be manipulated by another command; but in most cases, the middleman can be cut out and streams redirected straight from one command to another.

The pipe (|) allows connecting the standard output from one command to the standard input of the next. This practice is called pipelining. Say, for example, that only the lines in the *required_packages.txt* file that contain the string *lib* need to be seen, but they should be seen in alphabetical order. Use *grep* to display only the lines that contain the string *lib*, then pipe the output of *grep* directly into the input of the *sort* command.

```
$ grep lib required_packages.txt | sort
elfutils-libelf-devel-0.97.1-5.i386.rpm
glibc-2.3.4-2.41
glibc-common-2.3.4-2.41
glibc-headers-2.3.4-2.41.i386.rpm
libaio-0.3.105-2
libaio-devel-0.3.105-2.i386.rpm
libgcc-3.4.6-10
libstdc++-3.4.6-10
```

Like other methods that have more than one command on a line, this set of commands is interpreted from left to right. The output is also fed from left to right, from the standard output of the *grep* command into the standard input of the *sort* command, which is then displayed on the screen.

Redirection and pipelining can be confusing, especially when more than one method is used in a single command. If there is trouble in identifying what is going on, simply work from left to right and interpret one symbol at a time.

Shell Scripting

Shell scripting is a method of programming which will allow you to utilize the tools used at the command line in a more automated way. Scripts can be written to monitor aspects of the system, clean up log files, start and stop processes and much more.

A shell script can be as simple as a few commands strung together in a file, or it can be a complicated program that repeats tasks, makes decisions and provides feedback. The last section of this book will address some of the more complicated tasks that can be tackled with shell scripts, but often a simple script is all that is needed.

A shell script is simply a text file, and if you can fight your way through some vi commands, all the tools already exist to create one. To start out, the classic "Hello World" program is a good recommendation.

Using vi, create a file named *hello.sh* with the following contents:

```
#!/bin/sh

echo "Hello World!"
```

The first line of this file is what is referred to as the shebang. Though not necessary in all circumstances, under certain conditions it will be used to identify what program to use to run the script.

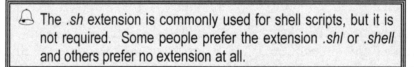

> 🔔 The *.sh* extension is commonly used for shell scripts, but it is not required. Some people prefer the extension *.shl* or *.shell* and others prefer no extension at all.

With the *hello.sh* script created, it is now time to make it executable. Using the *chmod* command, add execute permissions for the owner of the file.

```
$ chmod u+x hello.sh
$ ls -l hello.sh

-rwxrw-r-- 1 jemmons jemmons 30 Sep 29 13:28 hello.sh
```

Now the script can be run. To call it, run ./*hello.sh*. The ./ tells the shell that this script can be found in the current directory.

```
$ ./hello.sh
```

```
Hello World!
```

If the script did not yield the expected results, go back and check that there are not any typos and that the permission change worked properly.

Once your *hello.sh* script works, the basic steps needed to create a shell script have been done. Commands can be run in a shell script just like it is done at the command line. Commands in shell scripts are run in order and, unless the DBA has been redirected, the output is displayed on the screen. Here is another example of a basic script that could be tried which incorporates many of the tools that have been covered in this chapter.

🖫 hello.sh

```
#!/bin/sh
# A short script to provide some system information
# By Jon Emmons

echo "Hello $USER!"
echo "Welcome to `hostname`"
echo "--- Current Disk Usage ---"
df -h
echo "--- Current uptime, users and load averages ---"
uptime
echo "--- Load average numbers represent the 1, 5 and 15 minute load
averages ---"
echo "--- Lower numbers are better for load averages ---"
```

Lines that begin with a pound symbol (#) in a shell script are ignored when the script is run. These are comments that should be used to document things about the script.

The *status.sh* script uses *echo* extensively to provide additional output to the screen. When run, the output should look something like this:

```
$ ./status.sh
```

```
Hello jemmons!
Welcome to oelinux-test1.lifeaftercoffee.com
--- Current Disk Usage ---
Filesystem            Size  Used Avail Use% Mounted on
/dev/mapper/VolGroup00-LogVol00
                      8.6G  2.0G  6.3G  24% /
```

```
/dev/hda1              99M   12M   83M  13% /boot
tmpfs                 506M    0  506M   0% /dev/shm
--- Current uptime, users and load averages ---
 13:44:08 up  2:22,  1 user,  load average: 0.00, 0.00, 0.00
--- Load average numbers represent the 1, 5 and 15 minute load averages ---
--- Lower numbers are better for load averages ---
```

Remember that shell scripts can be very simple like this. Whenever there are repetitive or complicated tasks to do at the command line, this is probably a good candidate for a shell script. Simple things can often be tackled just by writing a series of commands like the script above.

Conclusion

This chapter covered some of the key aspects of Linux and the command line. The concepts and tools examined here form the foundation that will be needed to configure and administer the system. As more complicated administration topics are introduced, these tools will be combined in various ways.

Graphical User Interfaces

Graphical User Interfaces

While most of the system and database administration can be done through the command line, certain things require or are easier to do through a graphical user interface (GUI). Installing Oracle, creating databases and managing an Oracle Wallet are just a few tasks that may need to be done through a GUI.

As with other tasks covered in this book, there are several ways to access a GUI on a Linux system. In this chapter, the most straightforward ways to access a GUI from a keyboard and monitor attached to the server or from a workstation in another location will be examined.

For most Oracle related tasks, the GUI is used in conjunction with the command line. Commands that are started at the command line open windows to work in the GUI, and the command line is used to review logs and changes made through the GUI interface.

Each of these methods employs what is called the X Windows System to display windows on a screen (also known as X11 or just X.) The X Windows System is typically a process or set of processes running on the system called an X Windows Server.

The *DISPLAY* Variable

When dealing with any of the methods in this chapter, the *DISPLAY* environment variable plays a key role in telling the programs that are launched where to display their interfaces. In most cases, it will be automatically set, but in some cases, it may need to be overridden.

The *DISPLAY* variable is made up of a hostname, X server number and screen number. Remember that an X server is a running X Windows server process. The *DISPLAY* variable can be viewed using *echo*, and if necessary, can be set like this:

```
$ export DISPLAY=hostname:0.0
```

The hostname may be blank if the X server is on the local system. The server number is typically 0 if a GUI is being used directly on the system, or may be a higher number if the display is being sent over SSH or to another X server process. The second number indicates a screen number and is typically set to 0.

The Built-in Display

Most modern Linux distros, including Red Hat and OE Linux, offer a graphical user interface that you can log into and use somewhat like MS Windows. If you have physical access to your Linux system, meaning it is not in a server room or hosting facility that cannot be accessed, then take advantage of this when a GUI needs to be used.

Both Red Hat and OE Linux come with the GNOME desktop. GNOME desktop is an open-source desktop environment designed to be both intuitive and flexible. The interface is different from MS Windows, but since it is largely icon and menu-driven, it should be easy to navigate around it without much trouble.

The GNOME desktop appears by default when logging into a Linux system directly on the server.

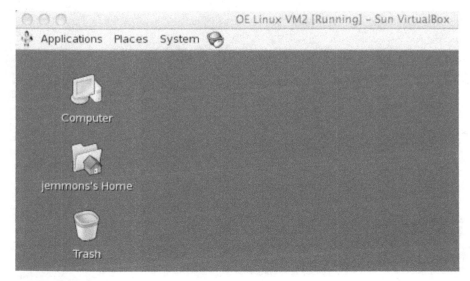

Figure 4.1: *The GNOME desktop*

GNOME offers several features like a web browser, a file browser, easy access to popular Linux desktop applications and even preference panels for changing system settings.

Most of the tasks that are of interest are initiated from the command line. To access the command line from GNOME, choose Applications->Accessories->Terminal.

Figure 4.2: *Starting the Terminal Within GNOME*

A terminal session in GNOME is basically the same as a terminal session from a SSH client. Start multiple terminal sessions if needed by selecting Terminal again.

In the terminal session, the *DISPLAY* variable can be examined to see what X server will be used when commands are called.

```
$ echo $DISPLAY
```

```
:0.0
```

Since the hostname is blank, new windows come up on the local system. Server 0 is used, which is the default server you are logged into. The easiest way to test the X Windows setup is to launch a small, simple program. Linux typically includes the xclock program, which is a perfect candidate for testing X Windows. To launch it, simply type *xclock* in the terminal.

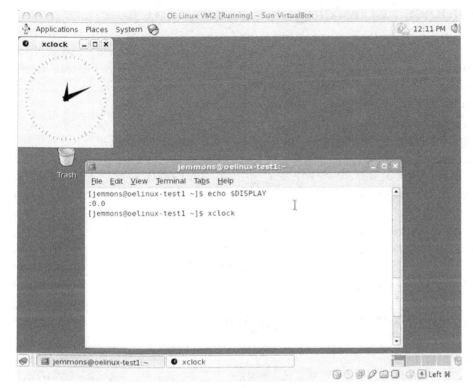

Figure 4.3: *Xclock Running in the GNOME Desktop Environment*

The analog clock should appear on the screen. It can be closed by clicking on the x in the upper right corner of the clock's window.

It is noticed that while most processes are running in an X Windows server, the command line session that they were started from is unresponsive. When the process completes and closes, continue to use the session or an ampersand (&) can be added after the process when it is first started.

```
$ xclock &
```

The ampersand forces the process to run in the background and allows continual use of the command line session while it is running.

X Windows Forwarding

There are several factors that may inhibit the user from using the built-in display in Linux. Linux servers are often in a fairly inhospitable server room. Furthermore, to save money, space and power, they are rarely connected directly to a keyboard, mouse and monitor.

Thankfully, the X Windows system is flexible enough to allow windows for processes running on one system to be displayed on another system, whether it is in the next room, the next town, or even another country. This practice is called X Windows forwarding.

To set up X Windows forwarding, three things are needed: a remote system that the processes can be run on, a workstation or local system that the windows should appear on, and a method to send the X Windows information between these systems.

Tunneling X Windows Through SSH

The ability to pass information from a remote system to a local server is built into the functionality of X Windows, but it is inherently insecure. For that reason, the X Windows information is tunneled through the secure shell (ssh.)

The secure shell encrypts the X Windows information being passed between the servers. It also sets the *DISPLAY* variable, automatically making setup even easier.

X Windows Forwarding on MS Windows

To use X Windows on an MS Windows workstation, first a Windows compatible X server is needed. There are several options available in different price ranges. My preference is for the free Xming X Server. Xming can be found at http://sourceforge.net/projects/xming/.

Once downloaded, Xming installs like most other Windows software. To start the Xming X Windows server, choose All Programs->Xming->Xming. Xming then starts and places a small x icon in the notification area of the Windows Taskbar.

With Xming Server running, there is now a local X Server and assuming there is already a remote system that could be connected to and processes run on, all that is needed is a method to send the X Windows information between the two systems. Thankfully, PuTTY has this ability built into it.

Assuming that PuTTY is already downloaded, (Chapter 1 has information on downloading PuTTY) it can be launched and the connection can be set up as normal. Before connecting, X11 forwarding must be enabled. This setting is in Connection->SSH->X11. Make sure the checkbox next to "Enable X11 forwarding" is checked.

Figure 4.4: *Enabling X11 Forwarding in PuTTY*

If X Windows forwarding will be regularly used, this setting can be saved by checking this box and saving the change in the Session section.

> 🔔 If new sessions to enable X11 forwarding by default are desired, check the "Enable X11 forwarding" box, return to the Session screen, select Default Settings in the stored sessions box and click Save.

With X11 enabled, the SSH session to the remote system can now be started normally. Once connected, the *DISPLAY* variable can be examined. It should be set to something like ':10.0' When the SSH session is started with X Windows forwarding enabled, the SSH session is assigned an unused X Server number on the remote system, but information sent to this server number is forwarded through SSH to a X Windows server on the other end.

With Xming running and a PuTTY session open with X11 forwarding enabled, test the X Windows configuration by launching xclock.

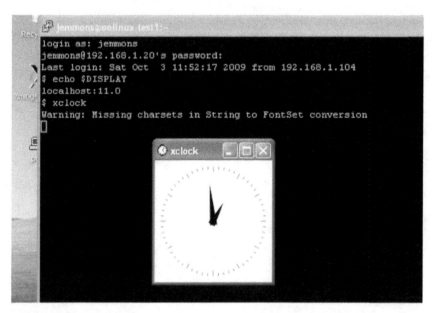

Figure 4.5: *Xclock Running on the Server, but Displaying in Windows*

The analog clock should appear on the screen. It may appear behind the PuTTY session, at which point it can be selected from the taskbar to bring it to the front.

Xming comes with a minimal amount of fonts, so you will likely get a warning about fonts or characters. Additional fonts are available to support Xming, but the default ones are sufficient for most purposes.

With the configuration tested, xclock can be closed, the PuTTY session can be exited and Xming is quit by right clicking on the system tray icon. When another X Windows session needs to be started, simply launch Xming and make sure X11 forwarding has been enabled in PuTTY.

X Windows Forwarding on Mac OS X

The X Windows server and SSH client built into Mac OS X can be used to do X Window forwarding. On the latest versions of OS X, all the tools are installed by default, but users of older versions may need to add X11 from the install media.

To forward X Windows on OS X, start in the Terminal application. Terminal can be found in the Utilities folder within the Applications folder. When opened, the Terminal application starts a command line session on the Mac. This is similar to when Terminal was started within GNOME. From here, the *ssh* command can be called as usual, but add a *-X* option to enable X Windows forwarding.

```
Last login: Sat Oct  3 15:54:02 on ttys001

$ ssh -X jemmons@oelinux-test1.lifeaftercoffee.com

jemmons@oelinux-test1.lifeaftercoffee.com's password:
Last login: Sat Oct  3 12:58:55 2009 from 192.168.1.104

$ echo $DISPLAY

localhost:10.0
```

When *ssh* is started with the *-X* option, another application, X11, is started automatically. That is the X Windows server on the local system. With the SSH session started, test the forwarding with xclock.

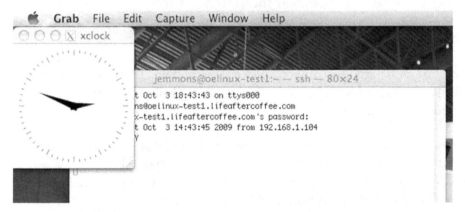

Figure 4.6: *Xclock Running on the Server, but Displaying in Mac OS X*

The xclock display opens in the X11 application. It may be covered by other applications, so if it is not seen, try selecting the X11 application. Closing the xclock window closes the program on the server.

If all the SSH sessions should have X11 enabled by default, set up an alias for *ssh* with the *-X* flag.

```
$ alias ssh='ssh -X'
```

When you are done with X Windows, quit the X11 application.

X Windows Forwarding on Linux and UNIX

If a Linux or UNIX system is being used as the chosen workstation, take advantage of the built-in X Windows server. From the Terminal application, *ssh* to the remote host as usual, but the *-X* option can be added to enable X Windows forwarding.

```
$ ssh -X jemmons@redhat-test1.lifeaftercoffee.com

jemmons@redhat-test1.lifeaftercoffee.com's password:
Last login: Sun Oct  4 07:10:01 2009 from 192.168.1.20
/usr/bin/xauth:  creating new authority file /home/jemmons/.Xauthority

$ echo $DISPLAY

localhost:10.0
```

Like with other operating systems, examine the *DISPLAY* variable to check the current setting. In this instance, it can be seen that the host is listed as localhost. This is the equivalent of it being blank.

After checking the *DISPLAY* variable, launch xclock to confirm that the X Windows forwarding is working.

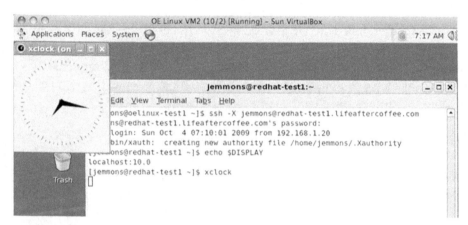

Figure 4.7: *Xclock Running on the Server but Displayed on a Local Linux System*

Xclock is now running on the remote system, but the display is being shown on the same X Windows server that is showing the local GNOME desktop. Closing the xclock window quits xclock and allows the shell session to continue being used.

If all the SSH sessions should have X11 enabled by default, set up an alias for *ssh* with the *-X* flag.

```
$ alias ssh='ssh -X'
```

VNC Server

Another option for accessing a GUI on a remote server is using Virtual Network Computing (VNC). VNC is an open source system that allows viewing a remote desktop session on your local workstation. Unlike X Windows forwarding, VNC does not require having an X Windows server running on your local system. Instead, the X Windows server runs on the remote system and a VNC client on your local system allows the display output to be viewed on the remote system.

One big advantage of VNC over X Windows forwarding is that a VNC Server will retain its state, even if the SSH connection is lost. This is useful for long installs, especially over unreliable network connections.

To use VNC, there needs to be a VNC server process running on the remote system and a VNC client on the local workstation. Both RedHat and OE Linux come with a VNC server pre-installed. Free and commercial VNC clients are available for all platforms. Below are a couple of popular free options for Windows and Mac.

VNC Clients

RealVNC maintains a free edition of their commercial VNC client for MS Windows. It can be downloaded from http://www.realvnc.com/products/free/4.1/index.html. The application installs like other Windows applications, but there is the option to install and configure VNC server as well. If just the client is wanted, uncheck these options.

On Mac OS X, there is an open source VNC client called Chicken of the VNC. It can be downloaded from http://sourceforge.net/projects/cotvnc/ and includes only the VNC client (Mac OS X actually has a VNC server built into it.)

Starting the VNC Server

To start the VNC server on the Linux system, execute the command *vncserver.* If it is the first time VNC has been started, a password is requested for VNC.

```
$ vncserver

You will require a password to access your desktops.

Password:password
Verify: password

New 'oelinux-test1.lifeaftercoffee.com:1 (jemmons)' desktop is oelinux-
test1.lifeaftercoffee.com:1
```

```
Creating default startup script /home/jemmons/.vnc/xstartup
Starting applications specified in /home/jemmons/.vnc/xstartup
Log file is /home/jemmons/.vnc/oelinux-test1.lifeaftercoffee.com:1.log
```

Once the password is set, *vncserver* displays the server connection information. Make a note of the server number after the hostname. This is needed to set up the VNC connection as well as to stop the server.

More than one VNC server can be started by running the *vncserver* command more than once. Each VNC server starts on its own port with its own server number. This allows multiple users to run their own VNC server at the same time without interfering with each other.

Tunneling VNC through SSH and Connecting

With the VNC server up and running, it would be possible to make an exception in the Linux firewall rules to allow the workstation to connect to the VNC server, but an easier and more secure solution is to tunnel the VNC traffic through SSH. This encrypts the traffic to and from the VNC server as well as prevents VNC from being exposed to hackers.

Tunneling VNC and Connecting on MS Windows

To tunnel VNC traffic to a MS Windows workstation, add a port configuration to pass traffic on the VNC port to the local system through the SSH connection. To do this, launch PuTTY and enter the system connection information, then choose Connection->SSH->Tunnels.

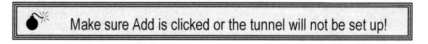

Figure 4.8: *The PuTTY Tunnels Configuration Screen*

In this screen, a source port can be entered, the port which might be 'listened' to on the remote system, and a destination, where the port could appear on the local system. If the VNC server started on server number 1, the port is 5901, if it started on 2 the port is 5902 and so on.

Enter the information as seen in the illustration and click Add.

Make sure Add is clicked or the tunnel will not be set up!

Once the tunnel has been added, connect and log into the system. Your tunnel is established at the same time as the SSH connection and is only available as long as the SSH session is open.

With the SSH session running, now launch VNC Viewer on your workstation. In the connection dialog, enter localhost and the port number for the server/tunnel that has been set up.

Figure 4.9: *VNC Viewer: Connection Details Screen*

The format for the server setting is hostname:port, as seen above. When you click OK, a prompt shows up for a password. This is the password you set when the VNC server was first started. After entering the password, the VNC screen should appear.

Figure 4.10: *VNC Viewer Connected to the VNC Server*

Tunneling VNC and Connecting on OS X

You can take advantage of the built-in SSH client on Mac OS X to set up a tunnel for VNC. To do this, use the *-L* option for *ssh* and provide the ports to connect to.

```
$ ssh -L 5901:localhost:5901 jemmons@oelinux-test1.lifeaftercoffee.com

jemmons@oelinux-test1.lifeaftercoffee.com's password:
Last login: Mon Oct  5 13:23:57 2009 from 192.168.1.104

$
```

If the VNC server started on server number 1, the port is 5901, if it started on 2 the port is 5902 and so on. The tunnel is established with the SSH session and persists until the session is ended.

With the tunnel set up, Chicken of the VNC can now be launched. If it is not selected automatically, choose New Server and enter the connection information.

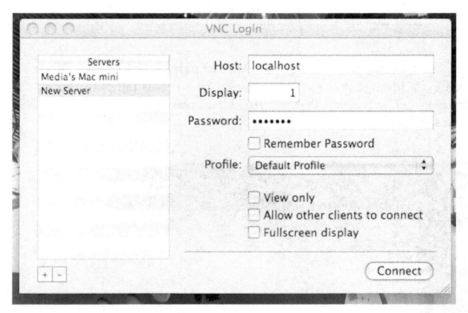

Figure 4.11: *Chicken of the VNC Connection Screen*

Since the SSH tunnel set up is done, use localhost as the host name. If a standard port is being used, enter the display number and the port is configured automatically. If a non-standard port number is being used, enter the host:port pair in the Host field. The password required here is the password that was set when starting the VNC server for the first time. With that entered, click Connect and the VNC Server screen appears.

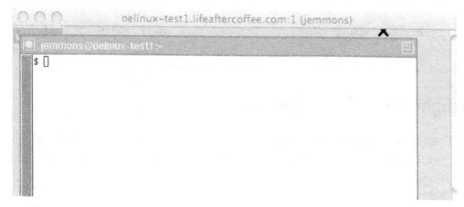

Figure 4.12: *Chicken of the VNC Connected to the VNC server*

Closing and Reconnecting VNC Sessions

To close out of VNC Viewer or Chicken of the VNC, just close the VNC window. This will perform a disconnect from the VNC server but anything that is left open within the VNC session continues to run as long as the VNC server is running. Windows left open in VNC will still be there if there is a reconnect, even if connecting from a different workstation.

Any tunnels set up through SSH are closed out when the SSH session is terminated. They can be reestablished using the same steps used to establish them. Reestablishing tunnels will not affect the VNC server.

By default, the VNC screen may not be pretty, but it is functional enough to perform an Oracle install or a quick Wallet Manager setup. Later in this section, how to change VNC to display a more standard desktop will be shown.

Stopping the VNC Server

To stop the VNC server, use the *vncserver* command with a -*kill* option. A server number is provided as an argument.

```
$ vncserver -kill :1

Killing Xvnc process ID 2695
```

Killing the VNC server closes all windows and stops processes that were running in that VNC session. If more than one VNC server is running, each one has to be explicitly killed using its server number.

Changing the VNC password

The VNC server password is set the first time the server is started. If the password needs to be changed after that, use the *vncpasswd* command.

```
$ vncpasswd

Password:
Verify:
```

This replaces the VNC password for the current user. Each user can have a different password for his or her own VNC servers.

Customizing VNC to Use the GNOME Desktop

The default VNC desktop is sufficient for doing basic tasks but is not pretty. If VNC is being used a lot, it is worth changing the configuration to use a more standard configuration. When *vncserver* is run for the first time, it creates a hidden directory called .*vnc* in the current user's home directory. This directory has configuration files, logs and the password file. Specifically, the file *xstartup* within this directory controls is what happens as the VNC server is started.

The *xstartup* file is just a shell script and can be edited with vi. To cause VNC to launch the standard desktop (usually GNOME) when *vncserver* is started, remove the pound (#) from the two lines shown in bold below.

```
#!/bin/sh

# Uncomment the following two lines for normal desktop:
```

```
unset SESSION_MANAGER
exec /etc/X11/xinit/xinitrc

[ -x /etc/vnc/xstartup ] && exec /etc/vnc/xstartup
[ -r $HOME/.Xresources ] && xrdb $HOME/.Xresources

xsetroot -solid grey
vncconfig -iconic &
xterm -geometry 80x24+10+10 -ls -title "$VNCDESKTOP Desktop" &
twm &
```

With that change made, stop and start the VNC server and when reconnected, the Linux desktop should be seen as if you logged into the system directly.

Setting VNC Server Number or Screen Size

When *vncserver* is started, specify the server number that VNC should start up by adding an option of a colon and number. This example will start the VNC server on port 5.

```
$ vncserver :5
```

This can be useful if the VNC server should be started consistently on the same port.

The screen size can also be adjusted to give additional working space or to avoid scrolling. The *-geometry* option allows screen size to be specified in pixels for the resulting VNC server.

```
$ vncserver -geometry 800x600
```

The geometry parameters are given in the form of *widthxheight*. The example above causes the VNC server to have a screen size of 800 pixels wide by 600 pixels high.

Conclusion

While it may not be done daily, many Oracle tasks require access to a graphical interface. With the tools in this section, a graphical interface can be opened right on the system or miles away from it.

If everything that has been covered thus far in the book is understood, it is now time to work on setting up an Oracle server. In the next chapter, meeting the prerequisites and setting up Oracle will be the topic.

Meeting Oracle Requirements and Installing Oracle

Before installing Oracle, make sure all the software and settings on the system that Oracle needs to run are available. In some cases, software may need to be added to the system, and other times it will be sufficient to just confirm that the required software is already installed.

The exact prerequisites for Oracle are different with each version but the overall steps will always be very similar. The examples here are based on Oracle Database 11g Release 1.

Oracle Requirements

Before packages are installed, it is best to collect as much information on the requirements as possible. A good place to start is the Oracle Database Quick Installation Guide for the platform. There is a different version of the Quick Install Guide for 32-bit or 64-bit Linux, so make sure the correct one is obtained.

> Oracle documentation can be found in many places, but the easiest is tahiti.oracle.com. Documentation is available there for all recent releases of Oracle Database and Application Server.

If you are not sure which platform (32- or 64-bit) you are on, you can check it using the *uname* command.

```
$ uname -m

i686
```

The *uname* command returns either *i686* or *i686_64* which represent 32-bit and 64-bit Linux, respectively. In documentation titles and content, 32-bit Linux is often referred to as *Linux x86* and 64-bit is referred to as *Linux x86-64*.

While the Quick Installation Guide provides details on how to examine the system and confirm prerequisites, My Oracle Support note 169706.1 offers a condensed overview of requirements by platform. This note offers an easy way to look up hardware and software requirements and provides links to many other useful notes pertinent to the given platform.

Hardware Requirements

Many of these hardware requirements, especially memory and disk, are considered minimum requirements for installing Oracle database. Also consider the requirements of the applications that will be using Oracle. In addition, it is good to plan for some database growth and possible additional requirements of future versions of Oracle and other software.

Memory

Oracle requires a minimum amount of physical RAM be installed in the system before Oracle is installed. While some performance monitoring tools like *top* report total memory, it is best to check the system maintained *meminfo* file. There is a lot of information in that file, but *grep* can be used to check the physical memory specifically.

```
$ grep MemTotal /proc/meminfo

MemTotal:      1035244 kB
```

Oracle 11g requires 1GB of RAM, which, in this case, exists. If there is not enough RAM, then install more physical memory in the system. Also, confirm that enough swap is available for the Oracle installation. Again, this can be found in the *meminfo* file.

```
$ grep SwapTotal /proc/meminfo

SwapTotal:     2097144 kB
```

Swap is disk that is used to augment physical memory. Oracle makes the following recommendations for swap on Linux systems:

- For systems with 1-2 GB of RAM, swap should be 1.5 times the amount of RAM.

- For systems with 2-16 GB of RAM, swap should be equal to the amount of RAM.

- For systems with over 16 GB of RAM, swap should be 16 GB.

Again, these are minimum recommendations. Other programs running on this system may result in the need for more swap.

If the system does not meet or exceed these recommendations, then allocate additional swap space. If free space is available in the volume group, extending the swap space using the Logical Volume Manager should be possible.

These steps must be performed as root, so first use *su* to become the root user. With root permissions, *grep* the */etc/fstab* file to determine what device is being used, then issue *swapoff* to temporarily disable swap on this partition.

```
$ su -

Password:

# grep swap /etc/fstab

/dev/VolGroup00/LogVol01 swap                swap     defaults     0 0

# swapoff -v /dev/VolGroup00/LogVol01

swapoff on /dev/VolGroup00/LogVol01
```

With swap now turned off, use the *lvm* command to resize this volume. The *+1024M* tells *lvm* to add 1024M to this volume. Then use the *mkswap* command to format the expanded volume for use as swap and re-enable the partition for use as swap using the *swapon* command.

```
# lvm lvresize /dev/VolGroup00/LogVol01 -L +1024M

  Extending logical volume LogVol01 to 2.00 GB
  Logical volume LogVol01 successfully resized

# mkswap /dev/VolGroup00/LogVol01

Setting up swapspace version 1, size = 2147479 kB

# swapon -va
```

```
swapon on /dev/VolGroup00/LogVol01
```

```
# grep SwapTotal /proc/meminfo
```

```
SwapTotal:     2097144 kB
```

A final check confirms that there is now 2 GB of swap available to the system. If there is not enough free space available, consider reducing the size of a partition, but that can cause problems with the resized partition.

More about resizing partitions will be covered in Chapter 12 on disk management. If there is a small swap partition without enough free space to expand it, consider reinstalling Linux and sizing swap appropriately at the time of installation. This may save headaches down the road.

Disk Requirements

Certain disk space is required to install Oracle database. Like with the memory parameters, these are minimum requirements. Actual disk space needs will depend largely on the data stored in the database and the applications using it.

Oracle recommends that there be at least 400 MB of space available in the */tmp* directory and, depending on the installation type, that there be up to 3.5 GB of space available in the location that is being installed the Oracle software. Check for these requirements using the *df* command.

```
$ df -h /tmp
```

```
Filesystem             Size  Used Avail Use% Mounted on
/dev/mapper/VolGroup00-LogVol00
                       9.7G  2.0G  7.3G  22% /
```

```
$ df -h /u01
```

```
Filesystem             Size  Used Avail Use% Mounted on
/dev/mapper/VolGroup00-LogVol02
                       4.0G  137M  3.7G   4% /u01
```

If there is not sufficient space on either of these partitions, use steps similar to those above for expanding swap. This is covered in detail in Chapter 12 concerning file system management.

Software Requirements

The quick installation guide contains a long list of software requirements that must be met before Oracle is installed. Thankfully, many of these will already be present on most Linux systems.

While each and every prerequisite will not be introduced here, these examples should give a good idea of how to examine the installed software and add what is needed to meet the prerequisites. The requirements vary by Linux distro and version so be sure to look at the right list in the documentation.

Check for packages using the RPM package manager command *rpm*. The *-q* option is used to query for a given package and the name of the package, with version information removed, is passed as an argument.

```
# rpm -q binutils

binutils-2.17.50.0.6-9.el5

# rpm -q compat-libstdc++-33

compat-libstdc++-33-3.2.3-61

# rpm -q elfutils-libelf

elfutils-libelf-0.137-3.el5

# rpm -q elfutils-libelf-devel

package elfutils-libelf-devel is not installed
...
```

The example above shows some packages that were found (*binutils*, *compat-libstdc++-33*, *elfutils-libelf*) and others that were not (*elfutils-libelf-devel*). When a package is found, the version must be confirmed. Typically, a higher version than required is acceptable but if a lower version is found, then pursue a newer version of that package.

It can sometimes be difficult to identify the correct name to query for using *rpm*. An alternate way to check for installed software is to add *a* to the options to list all installed packages, then use the beginning of the package name with the * wildcard to display entries beginning with a certain string. This example shows this method when looking for packages beginning with *compat*.

```
# rpm -qa compat*
```

```
compat-libstdc++-33-3.2.3-61
compat-libgcc-296-2.96-138
compat-libstdc++-296-2.96-138
```

Often, required packages are available on the media that was used to install Linux. If the media is inserted, then *cd* into the /*media* directory and the disk should appear in an *ls* listing. Change directory into the disk and then into the *Server* subdirectory of the disk and a series of *rpm* files will be seen. If the required packages are not available on the install media, they can be found online. The Linux vendor's website is a good place to start.

To install a missing package, use the *rpm* command with the options *-ihv* which will *i*nstall, display a *h*ash to indicate progress, and give *v*erbose output. The following example shows how to add the required package *elfutils-libelf-devel-0.125*. While installed packages can generally be viewed by any user, the DBA needs to be root to install, update or remove packages.

```
# cd /media/Enterprise\ Linux\ dvd\ 20090127/Server
# ls elfutils*

elfutils-0.137-3.el5.i386.rpm                elfutils-libelf-devel-0.137-3.el5.i386.rpm
elfutils-devel-0.137-3.el5.i386.rpm          elfutils-libelf-devel-static-0.137-3.el5.i386.rpm
elfutils-devel-static-0.137-3.el5.i386.rpm   elfutils-libs-0.137-3.el5.i386.rpm
elfutils-libelf-0.137-3.el5.i386.rpm
```

In the *Server* directory of the CD, there are several *rpm* files starting with *elfutils*. Only the file *elfutils-libelf-devel-0.137-3.e15.i386.rpm* matches the package name, and since it is of a later version, this one is installed using *rpm*.

```
# rpm -ihv elfutils-libelf-devel-0.137-3.el5.i386.rpm

warning: elfutils-libelf-devel-0.137-3.el5.i386.rpm: Header V3 DSA signature: NOKEY, key ID 1e5e0159
error: Failed dependencies:
      elfutils-libelf-devel-static-i386 = 0.137-3.el5 is needed by elfutils-libelf-devel-0.137-
3.el5.i386
```

When attempting an installation, *rpm* identifies a missing prerequisite for this package. It would appear that the choice is to install the prerequisite before this package, but an attempt to install the prerequisite fails.

```
# rpm -ihv elfutils-libelf-devel-static-0.137-3.el5.i386.rpm

warning: elfutils-libelf-devel-static-0.137-3.el5.i386.rpm: Header V3 DSA signature: NOKEY, key ID
1e5e0159
error: Failed dependencies:
      elfutils-libelf-devel-i386 = 0.137-3.el5 is needed by elfutils-libelf-devel-static-0.137-
3.el5.i386
```

Since these packages are dependent on each other, they need to be installed at the same time. This can be done by listing them both after the same *rpm* command.

```
# rpm -ihv elfutils-libelf-devel-0.137-3.el5.i386.rpm elfutils-libelf-devel-static-0.137-
3.el5.i386.rpm

warning: elfutils-libelf-devel-0.137-3.el5.i386.rpm: Header V3 DSA signature: NOKEY, key ID 1e5e0159
Preparing...                ######################################### [100%]
   1:elfutils-libelf-devel-s################################### [ 50%]
   2:elfutils-libelf-devel  ######################################### [100%]
```

Both packages are now installed. Dependencies like these are common and can typically be resolved with a little experimentation.

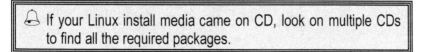

If your Linux install media came on CD, look on multiple CDs to find all the required packages.

If you have an older installation of Linux, you may find that you need to upgrade an installed package. To use *rpm* to update rather than install, download the new package file and use the *U* option instead of *i* when calling *rpm*. If a package needs to be removed for some reason, the *e* option is used.

Systemwide Requirements

Since the Oracle database is so specialized, there are several system settings that must be verified or configured for Oracle to run. Many of these settings adjust how Oracle can use the system's memory or how many processes Oracle can start.

Specific instructions are available in the Quick Install Guide for checking and setting each system parameter, but here some of the most common required changes are shown. These changes must be made as root. The first parameters to check are the semaphore settings. The required values for *semmsl*, *semmns*, *semopm* and *semmni* are listed in the Quick Install Guide as 250, 3200, 100 and 128, respectively. The following command displays the current values:

```
# /sbin/sysctl -a | grep sem

kernel.sem = 250    32000   32      128
```

This reveals that the value for *semopm* is below the required value. To change this setting, edit the */etc/sysctl.conf* file. If there is already a line for *kernel.sem*, edit the values given; otherwise, add a line in the same format as the output above. The line should look like this:

```
kernel.sem = 250 32000 100 128
```

This line can be edited anywhere in the file, but it is best to keep all these changes in one place within the file. Comments can be added by starting a line with a # character.

Continue to review parameters and update the *sysctl.conf* file with the Oracle specific values. When this is done, the result is customizations that look something like this:

```
# Oracle specific changes

kernel.sem = 250 32000 100 128
fs.aile-max = 6815744
net.ipv4.ip_local_port_range = 9000 65000
net.core.rmem_default = 262144
net.core.rmem_max = 4194304
net.core.wmem_default = 262144
```

Restart the system to make these parameters take effect. While there are ways of updating most of these parameters without restarting the system, it is best to restart to make sure the settings correctly persist.

Security Enabled Linux

By default, Linux installs in a mode called Security Enabled Linux or SELinux. This mode invokes a strong set of security restrictions on processes and files, but at the time of this writing it can also prevent Oracle from running! Oracle recognizes this as a bug and offers the following workaround.

To check what mode SELinux is in, run the *getenforce* command as root:

```
# getenforce

Enforcing
```

If the *getenforce* command returns 'Enforcing', it is likely that even though Oracle will install, it will not start properly. If this setting should be changed temporarily to confirm that it is SELinux which is causing the problem, use the *setenforce* command.

```
# setenforce 0
# getenforce
```

```
Permissive
```

If installed properly, Oracle would now start normally, but the change only persists until the next restart. To make this change persist after restart, change the following line in the file */etc/selinux/config:*

```
SELINUX=permissive
```

The default state of SELinux after restart is now permissive, which allows Oracle to function normally. If this change is made, you should also plan to monitor Oracle's progress with this issue and change it back to enforcing if and when the bug is resolved.

> Changing the setting of SELinux to anything but Enforcing disables certain security mechanisms on the system. Extra consideration should be given if this is a production system or if the system contains sensitive information.

Creating the Oracle Software Owner and Group

When you install Oracle software, you install it as the user oracle. This allows you to apply certain security and tuning settings to the software without having to change settings for other users on the system. In this section, the oracle user is created and the dba and oinstall groups which have special permissions on the software are installed.

As root, run the following commands to create the Oracle user and groups:

```
# groupadd dba
# groupadd oinstall
# useradd -m -g oinstall -G dba oracle
```

The oracle user is now set up and belongs to both the oinstall group and the dba group. To set the password for the oracle user, invoke the *passwd* command as root passing the username as an argument.

```
# passwd oracle

Changing password for user oracle.
New UNIX password: password
Retype new UNIX password: password
passwd: all authentication tokens updated successfully.
```

Now that the user and groups are established, just make a handful more of customizations before Oracle can be installed.

Customizing Shell Limits for the Oracle User

Oracle uses much more of the system's resources than most applications. Due to this, there may be a need to alter some of the default limits on how the oracle user can use resources. These changes are outlined in the Quick Install Guide and include adding lines to the */etc/security/limits.conf* and */etc/pam.d/login* files as well as customizing the */etc/profile* file. Each of these changes consists of simply adding lines to the given files using a text editor.

Installing Oracle

With all the requirements out of the way, it is now time to install Oracle! In the installation steps here, Oracle software is installed on a partition located at */u01* and follows Oracle's Optimal Flexible Architecture (OFA) standard for install locations. OFA will be covered more in Chapter 17 on organizing Oracle files.

Since the oracle user should own the installed files, start by connecting as oracle. In addition to the command line session, there is also a GUI available to perform the actual install. See Chapter 4 for setting up and accessing a GUI.

Create Required Directories

The directories that Oracle will be installed into should be created and that they have appropriate permissions. As the root user, use *mkdir*, *chmod* and *chown* to quickly set up the needed directories.

```
$ su -

Password:

# mkdir -p /u01/app/oracle
# chown -R oracle:oinstall /u01/app
# chmod -R 775 /u01/app
# ls -ld /u01/app

drwxrwxr-x 3 oracle oinstall 4096 Oct 19 13:11 /u01/app

# ls -ld /u01/app/oracle
drwxrwxr-x 2 oracle oinstall 4096 Oct 19 13:11 /u01/app/oracle

# exit
```

Since the commands do not give any feedback, they can be confirmed with the *ls* command. The *l* option for *ls* gives the long listing, and *d* causes information about a directory to be listed rather than about the directory's contents.

Download and Unpack Media

Oracle software can be downloaded from www.oracle.com and can be used at no charge for development and testing. For a simple test instance, just download the software, but if a production server is being set up, make sure to be licensed appropriately.

To avoid added permission and ownership issues, you want to be working as the oracle user. You can either download the software to your workstation then transfer it to your server or, since the display needs to be exported anyway, you can launch a web browser directly on the server. To start the Firefox web browser from the command line, just type *firefox &*. The *&* starts Firefox in the background so that the command line session can continue to be used.

To keep things organized, create a folder to hold the install files. Once unpacked, the directory names within the installers rarely give a good indication of the product and version of the software contained within. I have created a folder within the oracle user's home directory called *database_11g* to hold the install files.

Oracle software is distributed in *zip* files. To unpack, simply use the *unzip* command with the file name as an argument.

```
$ unzip linux_11gR1_database_1013.zip
```

Starting the Oracle Installer

To start the Oracle Installer, be positioned in the directory that was unpacked in the step above. From there, start *runInstaller*.

```
$ cd database
$ ./runInstaller

Starting Oracle Universal Installer...

Checking Temp space: must be greater than 80 MB.    Actual 3759 MB    Passed
Checking swap space: must be greater than 150 MB.    Actual 2047 MB    Passed
Checking monitor: must be configured to display at least 256 colors.
Actual 16777216    Passed
Preparing to launch Oracle Universal Installer from /tmp/OraInstall2009-10-
19_01-20-36PM. Please wait ...$
```

If everything was set up properly in the Oracle database, installer GUI should appear on the display. If it does not, your X Windows settings may be incorrect. Remember, xclock can be run to test your X Windows settings.

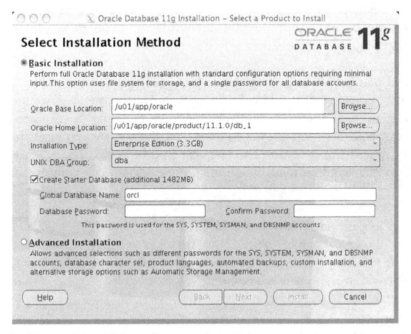

Figure 5.1: *The Oracle Installer GUI*

All the steps of the Oracle install will not be covered completely here as they are well covered in the installation guides. However, some of the settings that are required as they pertain to how the system is set up will be examined.

On the first screen of the Oracle Installer as seen above, the Oracle Base Location and Oracle Home Location can be chosen. These locations determine where things will be installed. You also have the option here to choose the UNIX dba group. This is the dba group that was created earlier. Users in this group have administrative abilities within the database, so it is important to keep this group as restricted as possible. If desired, you can use a different group for the dba group, but you need to add the oracle user to that group before it can be chosen.

If a starter database needs to be created, that is an option here, but databases can also be created later manually. In the next screen, there is a prompt regarding a location for the Oracle inventory. The inventory is where installations and patching activity for this system are tracked. The default location of */u01/app/oraInventory* is fine.

Several product-specific prerequisite checks are performed. Often, one or more of these checks will result in a warning or failure. Any warnings or failures should be investigated. Sometimes they can be ignored, but it is best to always consult the Oracle documentation on any warnings or failures before proceeding.

The installation process typically takes several minutes. Near the end of the installation, there is a prompt to run a couple of scripts as the root user. These scripts make some changes on the system which can only be made by the root user.

One of these scripts prompt for the location of the *local bin* directory. Oracle will install certain scripts, like *oraenv*, explained in the next section, in this location for users to access. The default, */usr/local/bin*, is typically appropriate.

When the installation is complete, exit the Installer GUI. The Oracle software is ready to use, but there are a few customizations that can be made that will make it easier to use.

Customizing the Oracle User's Environment

There are many ways to customize the Oracle user on the system. I strongly recommend making the changes covered in this section. Other less common customizations will be examined in Chapter 8, *Customizing the User Environment.*

To effectively administer the Oracle installation that was just made, it is useful to have several environment variables set whenever a command line session is started. The Oracle provided script *oraenv* is the best way to set these variables automatically. The *oraenv* script is installed in */usr/local/bin* and takes values from the *oratab* file located in */etc*. The *oratab* file typically contains an entry for each database, but in the current configuration, there is no database set up. To use the *oraenv* script, set up a dummy entry in the *oratab* file.

The *oratab* file can be edited by the oracle user using vi or another text editor. Each line in the *oratab* file has three elements separated by colons. The first element is the SID, the second indicates the Oracle Home directory for that SID, and the third indicates if the database should be started and stopped by the *dbstart/dbshut* commands.

Edit the *oratab* file and add the following line:

```
db_11g:/u01/app/oracle/product/11.1.0/db_1:N
```

Though a database does not exist by the name *db_11g*, this entry allows setting up the environment for this home without having to set several variables manually. Make sure the final element is set to N so Oracle does not attempt to start a database that is not there.

With an entry now in the *oratab* file, use the *oraenv* command to set up the environment. To do that, run *.oraenv* which causes the *oraenv* script to be run as part of the current shell rather than as a subprogram.

```
$ . oraenv

ORACLE_SID = [oracle] ? db_11g
The Oracle base for ORACLE_HOME=/u01/app/oracle/product/11.1.0/db_1 is
/u01/app/oracle

$ echo $ORACLE_SID

db_11g
```

```
$ echo $ORACLE_HOME
```

```
/u01/app/oracle/product/11.1.0/db_1
```

```
$ echo $PATH
```

```
/usr/kerberos/bin:/usr/local/bin:/bin:/usr/bin:/home/oracle/bin:/u01/app/ora
cle/product/11.1.0/db_1/bin
```

Among other things, the *oraenv* script sets the *ORACLE_SID* and *ORACLE_HOME* variables. The *PATH* variable is also updated to include the location of the Oracle binaries. Though they could be set manually, the *oraenv* script is the best way to set these variables. Since these variables should be set anytime, log in as oracle and then add the *oraenv* command to the user's profile.

A user's profile, often referred to as the dot-profile, is a hidden file in their home directory that is executed when a user logs in. Since Linux uses the bash shell by default, the profile file is called *.bash_profile*. Using the *-a* option, it can be seen in an *ls* listing.

```
$ pwd
```

```
/home/oracle
```

```
$ ls -a
```

```
.                .bash_logout    database_11g    .gconfd          .mozilla
..               .bash_profile   .emacs          .gnome2          .viminfo
.bash_history    .bashrc         .gconf          .gnome2_private  .Xauthority
```

The profile can be edited with vi or another text editor. To run *oraenv* when the user logs in, add the following lines to the *.bash_profile* file.

```
ORACLE_SID=db_11g
ORAENV_ASK=NO
. oraenv
```

This causes the Oracle variables to be set based on the *oratab* entry for *db_11g* without any prompting. If the variable *ORAENV_ASK* is changed to YES or is not set at all, there is a prompt to enter a SID when logging in.

Conclusion

There are a lot of steps to getting a system ready for Oracle. System requirements, installed software and many settings must all be correct or Oracle will not function properly. As these steps are reviewed, it is a good idea to take notes on what things were set to when they were found and what changes were made to prepare for Oracle. This will make preparing future systems much easier.

The next chapter will start to explore the many things that can be done to further customize and tune the Linux system.

Starting Up, Shutting Down and Runlevels

Though it is likely your Linux system will run happily for months without need for reboot, you will at some point need to shut down, start up, or restart the system. As is with most things in Linux, there are several ways to do each of these operations. In this chapter, we will look at some of the more common ones.

Linux passes through several stages during normal startup and shutdown cycles. It will be shown here how these stages can be controlled and what is run when each stage is entered.

Starting Up

Starting up a Linux system is generally as simple as pressing the power button, but having an understanding of what is going on during the boot process can be very helpful when something goes wrong. Many of these steps are typical for all operating systems but are often hidden from the end user. Some of the information here pertains specifically to x86 platforms, but similar steps happen on all platforms.

The Boot Process

At startup, the Linux system goes through these five main stages, each of which launches the next stage:

1. The BIOS checks the system, then launches the first stage boot loader found in the master boot record of the primary partition.

2. The first stage boot loader launches the second stage boot loader from the /*boot* partition.

3. The second stage boot loader loads the kernel from the /*boot* partition.

4. The kernel starts the *init* program that will complete the boot process.

---

5. The *init* program performs tasks like mounting disks, starting networking and other services and starts processes like X Windows and Oracle if configured.

The first three stages may be different on other hardware platforms, but the idea remains the same. The hardware BIOS checks the system, and then knows enough to look for a small program; in this case, the boot loader. That then loads the kernel into memory, and the kernel launches the *init* process. Now take a look at these steps in a little more detail.

The BIOS

The BIOS (Basic Input/Output System) is the first thing loaded into the system's processor at boot. The BIOS performs a series of tests referred to as the Power-On Self-Test or POST. These tests check for hardware problems within the system.

If a hardware problem is found during POST, the system typically stops running even before an operating system splash screen is displayed. Information about the problem is printed to the screen to help identify the issue. The hardware vendor is the best resource to help diagnose issues which arise during POST.

Once the system passes the self-tests, the BIOS looks in certain locations for an available boot device. Though configurable, the BIOS typically looks for a floppy disk, CD/DVD, ROM, then a hard drive, in that order. The first one of these items found will be used as the boot device.

Once a boot device is found, the BIOS reads the Master Boot Record (MBR) into memory. The MBR is limited to the first 512 bytes of the boot device and contains the first stage boot loader that has instructions on how to proceed with the next stage of starting up the machine.

While the system is running, the BIOS continues to act as an interface between running processes and the hardware, but at this point, the boot loader continues the boot process.

The Boot Loaders

The first stage boot loader must be extremely small due to the 512-byte limitation on the master boot record. Because of this limitation, the first stage boot loader simply mounts the */boot* partition and launches a larger and more powerful second stage boot loader from there.

The second stage boot loader reads a configuration file (*/boot/grub/grub.conf* when using the grub boot loader) to determine what kernel should be started. The kernel is located in */boot* and loaded into memory.

The second stage boot loader's final task is to load a disk image from the */boot* partition into memory. The disk image contains resources needed to boot the system into memory and is also specified in the boot loader configuration file. The kernel decompresses the image and uses it to continue the boot process. At this point, the boot process is handed over to the kernel.

The Kernel

When the kernel first starts up, it initializes all the memory in the system, determines what hardware is attached to the system, and configures interfaces to it using drivers from the disk image loaded by the boot loader. Low-level virtual devices like the Logical Volume Manager are also loaded at this time. Then the kernel releases the disk image containing the drivers from memory to free up that space.

The kernel then mounts the *root* (/) partition and starts the *init* program from */sbin/init* to continue the boot process. The kernel continues to function as the core of the Linux operating system, but the *init* program completes additional startup tasks.

The *init* Program and Runlevels

The *init* program starts all the processes that are needed to interact with the system, connect over the network, run databases and just about everything else that needs to be running on the system. Typically, *init* starts dozens of processes and while these processes may start additional processes, any process on the system can be tracked back through its creators to the *init* process.

The *init* program brings the system up in a certain runlevel. Runlevels define a mode for the system, and in each runlevel, different processes can be started. The default runlevels for Linux are as follows:

Runlevel	Description
0	Halt (shutdown)
1	Single user mode
2	Multi-user mode, without NFS
3	Full multi-user mode
4	Unused
5	Full multi-user mode with X11 (GUI)
6	Reboot

Table 6.1: *The Default Runlevels for Linux*

The runlevel is changed when a command, such as a *shutdown* or *restart* is issued by root, is sent to the *init* process. *init* then executes a series of scripts to change to the new runlevel. A system that is up and running normally is typically at runlevel 5 or 3, depending on if an X11 GUI is desired on the machine's local console.

Most of what *init* does is controlled by the */etc/inittab* file. It contains a short description of each runlevel and several settings that control which scripts get run at each runlevel.

When the kernel first starts up the *init* program, it reads the */etc/inittab* to determine what runlevel the system should be started into. The runlevel is determined by the *initdefault* entry in the *inittab* file.

```
id:5:initdefault:
```

The example above causes *init* to bring the system into runlevel 5. The starting runlevel should never be set to 0 or 6 or the system would not boot. Rarely should levels 1 or 2 be used. They are typically only useful when troubleshooting or upgrading the system.

Each runlevel has a set of scripts associated with it. Those scripts control which processes are run or stopped for the given runlevel. The scripts are organized into directories within /etc called rc0.d, rc1.d, rc2.d and such. Each directory holds the scripts that should be run for the corresponding runlevel.

> 🔔 The *rc#.d* directories are actually symbolic links (shortcuts) to directories in */etc/rc.d/*, but this is purely organizational. When the runlevel is changed, the scripts are run from the */etc/rc#.d* directories.

Within each of these directories are two kinds of scripts. Scripts which begin with *K* are *kill* scripts. These are run first and stop processes that should not be running at a given runlevel. Scripts which begin with *S* are *start* scripts. They are run after all *K* scripts are completed and services started that should be running at the given runlevel. Once the *kill* and *start* scripts are run for the given runlevel, the *init* process initializes some final interfaces, including starting an X server if the runlevel is 5. The system is now fully started.

The *init* process continues to run as long as the system is up. It continues to monitor processes on the system and comes back into play, executing the appropriate *kill* and *start* scripts if the runlevel is changed; for example, when a shutdown or restart is signaled.

Shutting Down and Restarting

The Linux system can be shut down in a variety of ways. If you are in front of the system and it is running a GUI, you should see shutdown and restart buttons. If you log into the GUI, there is a shutdown item in the System menu which will give the option to shut down or restart. Both of these methods work about the way that would be expected, but often you will want to shut the system down from the command line.

Shutting Down

At the command line, use the *shutdown* command to shut down or restart the system. The *shutdown* command must be executed as the root user and requires a time to shut down be specified. The simplest form of shutdown is to specify *now* as the time.

```
# shutdown -h now
```

The *-h* option tells the system to halt, causing the *shutdown* command to signal the *init* process to enter runlevel 0. Processes receive a signal that the system is going down, users in command line sessions are warned and scripts in the */etc/rc0.d* are executed.

> 🔔 The *-h* option may not be necessary to cause a system halt, but it is good practice to use it. If you are working at the console and do not use the *-h* option with shutdown, the system may automatically reboot into single user mode rather than shutting down.

When the system is completely down, a message is received that the system has been halted. If the hardware is capable, it automatically powers off at this point. If not, it is known that it is safe to shut down when the message is received that the system has been halted.

```
Unloading ip6tables modules:                          [  OK  ]
Flushing firewall rules:                              [  OK  ]
Setting chains to policy ACCEPT: filter               [  OK  ]
Unloading iptables modules: Removing netfilter NETLINK layer.
                                                      [  OK  ]
Starting killall:                                     [  OK  ]
Sending all processes the TERM signal...              [  OK  ]
Sending all processes the KILL signal...              [  OK  ]
Saving mixer settings                                 [  OK  ]
Saving random seed:                                   [  OK  ]
Syncing hardware clock to system time type=1111 audit(1256400000.999:16): user
id=3546 uid=0 auid=4294967295 subj=system_u:system_r:hwclock_t:s0 msg='changing
system time: exe="/sbin/hwclock" (hostname=?, addr=?, terminal=console res=succe
ss)'
                                                      [  OK  ]
Turning off swap:                                     [  OK  ]
Turning off quotas:                                   [  OK  ]
Unmounting pipe file systems:                         [  OK  ]
Unmounting file systems:                              [  OK  ]
Halting system...
md: stopping all md devices.
Shutdown: hdb
Shutdown: hda
System halted.
```

Figure 6.1: *The System Completely Halted and Ready to be Shut Down*

Instead of specifying *now* as the time, give a wall clock time in the format of HH:MM (using 24 hour format) or in the format of +*m* with a number of minutes to wait until shutdown. Here are a couple examples:

Shutdown in 20 minutes:

```
# shutdown -h +20
```

Shutdown at 11:30pm:

```
# shutdown -h 23:30
```

Users receive a warning an hour before the system shuts down or when the *shutdown* command is executed if there is less than an hour until shutdown.

Restarting

The *shutdown* command is also used to restart. The same options are available, but the *-r* option is given. In the case of a restart, the *shutdown* command signals *init* to enter runlevel 6. The same options exist for the time.

Restart immediately:

```
# shutdown -r now
```

Restart in 5 minute:

```
# shutdown -r +5
```

Restart at 5:00 pm:

```
# shutdown -r 17:00
```

Again, users receive a warning an hour before reboot or when the shutdown *-r* is executed if less than an hour remains. While there is a *reboot* command, under most circumstances it simply calls shutdown with the *-r* flag, so it is unnecessary.

Canceling a Shutdown or Reboot

If the user or another administrator has issued the *shutdown* command with a delay, the command line session hangs. If *control-c* is typed, the *shutdown* command is cancelled. If that is not possible, a reboot can be cancelled using the *-c* option for the *shutdown* command.

```
# shutdown -c
```

This cancels the *shutdown* command. If a different *shutdown* command should now be sent, it can be.

Setting What Runlevel to Start Into

By default, Linux starts up and enters runlevel 5. That starts a graphical interface on the local console of the system. If the graphical console is not used or it needs to be shut down to reduce memory usage, tell Linux to start into runlevel 3 which suppresses the GUI and presents a command line login at the console.

To set Linux to start into runlevel 3, edit the */etc/inittab* file as root. The file can be edited using vi or another text editor, but be careful. It is important that the file remains valid. It is good practice to make a copy of the file to another file name before it is edited.

Edit the following line in the */etc/inittab* file, changing the 5 to a 3.

```
id:5:initdefault:
```

Now when the system is restarted, it comes up in runlevel 3 and a command line login screen appears. If the system needs to be brought up in single-user mode or another runlevel, change the number to the appropriate runlevel.

 Never set the default runlevel to 0 or 6. This leaves the system unusable until start up is done from another disk and the problem corrected.

Changing Runlevels Without Restarting

Occasionally, switching between runlevels without shutting down or restarting may be the ticket. The *telinit* command allows doing exactly that.

```
# telinit 3
```

The *telinit* command accepts a runlevel number as an argument. *telinit* signals *init* to switch to the given runlevel and all appropriate *K* and *S* scripts in the /etc/rc#.d directory are executed.

 If work is being done on the system, be sure to consider what scripts, especially *kill* scripts, will be run when runlevels are switched.

This method can be useful when something like switching between the command line and GUI at the console (levels 3 and 5) is needed. However, if something like switching to single-user mode for maintenance is desired, a reboot is often a cleaner way to do it.

Booting Directly into Single User Mode

If there is a problem with the system booting or if you need to bring the system into single user mode but want to avoid having to start it up completely in order to change the startup runlevel, you can interrupt the boot loader before the boot process starts and force the system to come up in single user mode.

The following steps bring the system up in single-user mode. These steps assume the GRUB boot loader is being used, but the steps are similar for other boot loaders.

1. Power on the system. When prompted, press any key to enter the boot loader menu. There will only be a few seconds before the boot process continues, so it is important to watch for this message:

```
Press any key to enter the menu

Booting Enterprise Linux (2.6.18-128.el5) in 2 seconds...█
```

Figure 6.2: *Entering Boot Loader Menu*

Now the boot loader menu can be seen. If there is only a single kernel installed, there is just one option. If there are multiple kernels, choose the one to be booted from with the arrow keys. The selection is indicated by the white block on the right.

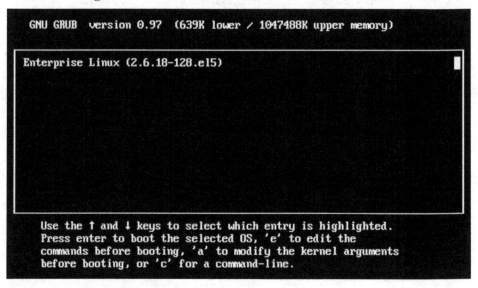

```
GNU GRUB  version 0.97  (639K lower / 1047488K upper memory)

┌──────────────────────────────────────────────────────────────────┐
│ Enterprise Linux (2.6.18-128.el5)                                █ │
│                                                                    │
│                                                                    │
│                                                                    │
│                                                                    │
│                                                                    │
│                                                                    │
│                                                                    │
└──────────────────────────────────────────────────────────────────┘
    Use the ↑ and ↓ keys to select which entry is highlighted.
    Press enter to boot the selected OS, 'e' to edit the
    commands before booting, 'a' to modify the kernel arguments
    before booting, or 'c' for a command-line.
```

Figure 6.3: *Boot Loader Menu*

2. Once the kernel is selected, press *a* to modify the kernel arguments.

3. The kernel arguments are shown on the screen and they can be edited. The only change that should be made is to add a space and the word *single* to the arguments.

Figure 6.4: *Modify Kernel Parameters*

4. Press Enter to accept the change and the boot process is resumed. The system comes up into single-user mode and you are brought directly to a prompt.

5. When the necessary maintenance is done, restart the system or use *telinit* to bring the system into a higher runlevel to resume normal operation.

In single user mode, file systems are mounted but network related services are not started. If there are problems with file systems or the boot files, a boot from install media may be needed as described in the next section.

Booting from a CD or DVD

Sometimes it may be necessary to start your system from the install media to repair disks or recover damaged files. Both Red Hat and Oracle Enterprise Linux install media include a rescue mode that allows you to start from the install disk and get into a limited shell where you can scan for problems and manipulate your system disk.

When it is necessary to start the system in rescue mode, start up with the install disk in the optical drive that was used to perform the install. When the main screen appears, press the F5 key to enter rescue mode.

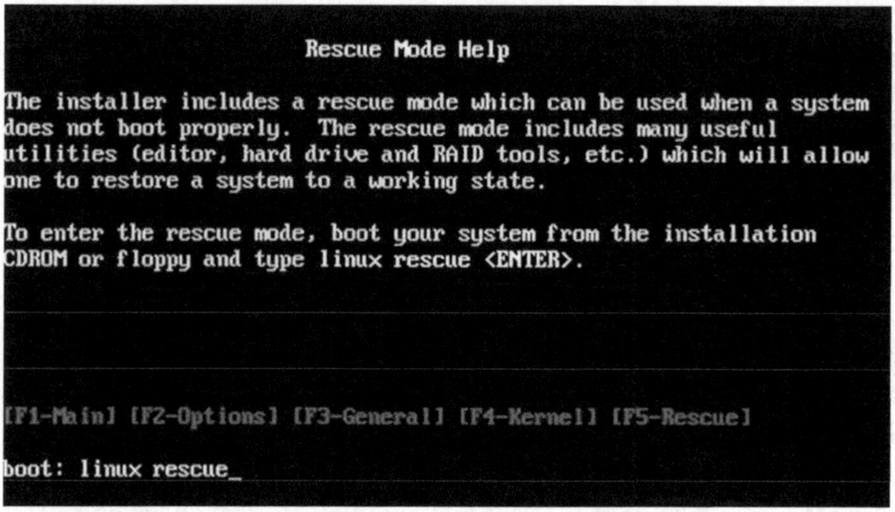

```
                        Rescue Mode Help

The installer includes a rescue mode which can be used when a system
does not boot properly.  The rescue mode includes many useful
utilities (editor, hard drive and RAID tools, etc.) which will allow
one to restore a system to a working state.

To enter the rescue mode, boot your system from the installation
CDROM or floppy and type linux rescue <ENTER>.




[F1-Main] [F2-Options] [F3-General] [F4-Kernel] [F5-Rescue]

boot: linux rescue_
```

Figure 6.5: *The Rescue Mode*

You are brought to the screen above where you must type *linux rescue* to enter
rescue mode. You are then prompted for some information about what will
be needed for resources and then are presented with the rescue mode shell.

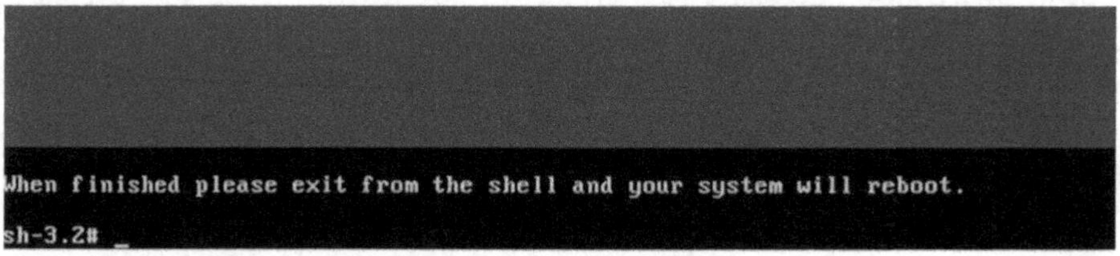

```



When finished please exit from the shell and your system will reboot.

sh-3.2# _
```

Figure 6.6: *The Rescue Mode Shell*

From here, scan for disk errors or manipulate the files on the system. When
this is done, eject the install disk, type *exit* and the system will reboot.

Startup and Shutdown Scripts

As covered in the section on starting up, when Linux enters a given runlevel,
the *init* process executes the scripts found in */etc/rc#.d*. Scripts within this

directory starting with a *K* are *kill* scripts and are run first. They stop processes that should not be running at the given runlevel. Scripts starting with *S* are *start* scripts and start processes that should be running at the given runlevel.

These scripts are automatically passed an argument of *stop* in the case of *K* scripts, or *start* in the case of *S* scripts. Because of this, it is typical for a *start* and *kill* script for a given process to actually be the same script linked to *S* or *K*. The script uses the argument to determine what action to take.

The *S* and *K* scripts in the *rc#.d* directories should always be symbolic links pointing at the original script in the */etc/init.d* directory. This allows one copy to be maintained but referenced at different runlevels. These scripts can be manipulated by manually creating and removing symbolic links but the *chkconfig* command offers a more streamlined method to maintain them.

Automating Oracle Startup and Shutdown

As an example, here is a script that starts the Oracle listener and database at startup. The third line of the script contains information that *chkconfig* will use to determine what symbolic links should be created.

💾 oracle_db script

```
#!/bin/bash
#
# chkconfig: 35 99 10
# description: Starts and stops the Oracle listener and database
#
# Define variables for use in this script
# Set ORA_HOME to the Oracle Home where the lsnrctl and dbstart
# commands can be found
ORA_HOME=/u01/app/oracle/
# Set ORA_OWNER to the owner of the Oracle software
ORA_OWNER=oracle

case "$1" in
    'start')
            # Start the listener:
            su - $ORA_OWNER -c "$ORA_HOME/bin/lsnrctl start"
            # Start the databases:
            su - $ORA_OWNER -c $ORA_HOME/bin/dbstart
    ;;
    'stop')
            # Stop the listener:
            su - $ORA_OWNER -c "$ORA_HOME/bin/lsnrctl stop"
            # Stop the databases:
            su - $ORA_OWNER -c $ORA_HOME/bin/dbshut
```

```
         ;;
esac
```

 The double-semicolon in the script is not an error. It marks the end of an option in a case statement and must be preserved.

When *chkconfig* is called to examine this script, it reads the line *# chkconfig: 35 99 10*. The first number on this line indicates that this service should be running at runlevels 3 and 5. The second number indicates the sequence number that should be associated with the *start* scripts and the third number indicates the sequence number for the *kill* scripts.

To implement this script, copy it to or create it in */etc/init.d* as root. Make sure the *ORA_HOME* and *ORA_OWNER* variables are modified in the script to match your environment. Once the file is in */etc/init.d*, change the permissions on it to allow execution. Typically, the permissions are set to 755 to allow root full privileges but others only read and execute.

```
# chmod 755 oracle_db
```

 Though the *oracle_db* script is intended to be used by root with these permissions, it can be run by other users as well. They just need to remember to provide stop or start as an argument. If it is run by a non-root user, the user is prompted for the Oracle password by each of the *su* operations.

To implement the script, call *chkconfig* with the *--add* option and the script name as an argument. The *--list* option allows what runlevels this service is started in to be confirmed. To view all services configured with *chkconfig*, use the *--list* option but omit the argument.

```
# chkconfig --add oracle_db
# chkconfig --list oracle_db

oracle_db      0:off    1:off    2:off    3:on    4:off    5:on    6:off
```

To see what the *chkconfig* command has done, look at the *rc#.d* directories. Note the start and kill sequence numbers have been implemented, but all scripts link back to the original script.

```
# ls -l /etc/rc3.d/*oracle_db

lrwxrwxrwx 1 root root 19 Oct 27 12:26 /etc/rc3.d/S99oracle_db ->
../init.d/oracle_db

# ls -l /etc/rc5.d/*oracle_db

lrwxrwxrwx 1 root root 19 Oct 27 12:26 /etc/rc5.d/S99oracle_db ->
../init.d/oracle_db

# ls -l /etc/rc6.d/*oracle_db

lrwxrwxrwx 1 root root 19 Oct 27 12:26 /etc/rc6.d/K10oracle_db ->
../init.d/oracle_db

# ls -l /etc/rc0.d/*oracle_db

lrwxrwxrwx 1 root root 19 Oct 27 12:26 /etc/rc0.d/K10oracle_db ->
../init.d/oracle_db
```

To keep a service from being automatically started or stopped during runlevel changes, use the *--del* option for *chkconfig*.

```
# chkconfig --del oracle_db
```

When used with the *--del* option, *chkconfig* removes the symbolic links in the */etc/rc#.d* directories but preserves the original script in the */etc/init.d* directory. Because of this, it is reasonable to use *chkconfig* to disable and enable services temporarily.

Starting and Stopping Other Services

The same methods mentioned previously can be used to maintain services other than Oracle. The *oracle_db* script can be copied and the commands altered to start other programs. The *su* statements should be changed to reflect the appropriate user who the services should be started as unless the service is to be started as the root user, in which case, it can be omitted.

Conclusion

A lot happens when a Linux system starts up. Though it is impossible to cover every detail, there should now be enough information that is needed to start troubleshooting startup problems when they happen.

Since you may not always be around when the system is shut down or started, it is a good practice to have services like Oracle databases controlled automatically. This gives Oracle a chance to close cleanly when the system is being shut down and will start the database when the system is brought back up.

In the next chapter, setting up other accounts on the Linux system and how who can do what can be controlled will be covered.

Users and Groups

Management of users and groups is central to security on Linux. The main concerns are first to assure that a user has rights to access the system and second, to determine what they can do with a given file, process or system resource.

This chapter will be an examination of the overall security model, then how to set up and maintain user security on the system will be covered.

The Linux Security Model

Based on the UNIX model, all files, directories, running processes and system resources on the Linux system are associated with a user and group. The security can be set independently for the user, or owner, and group.

A third set of permissions is maintained for everyone on the system who is neither the owner nor in the group associated with a resource. This is commonly referred to as the permissions for 'other' users. These security levels, *user*, *group* and *other*, each have a set of permissions associated with them. Typical permissions are *read*, *write* and *execute* and depending on the type of resource, these will determine what a given user is allowed to do with the resource.

In this example, the *ls -l* command is used to show the ownership and permissions of the file *status.sh*.

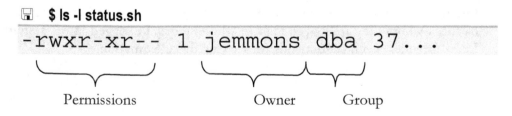

```
$ ls -l status.sh
-rwxr-xr-- 1 jemmons dba 37...
```
Permissions   Owner   Group

The permissions portion of the output breaks down further to indicate the level of access for the owner, group and other users. In this example, the owner has *read*, *write* and *execute*, the group has *read* and *execute* and other has only *read*.

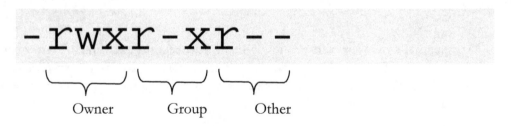

Owner   Group   Other

Managing these permissions will be delved into in Chapter 12 on file management.

Each user on the system is associated with a primary group but can also belong to additional groups, adding to the flexibility of Linux security. A user has access rights granted to his or her primary group as well as any additional groups to which the user belongs.

Though user and group names are used to interact with the system, these identifiers are tracked within the system by ID numbers. The user ID (UID) and group ID (GID) numbers are associated with user and group names through the */etc/passwd* and */etc/group* files, respectively.

With this understanding of why users and groups are so important, now take a look at how to create, modify and remove them.

Determining the Current User, Group and Who is on the System

Often many accounts are worked with on different systems and you will want to check whom they are logged in as or who else may be logged into a system. Linux provides several commands for viewing this information.

Who am I Logged in As?

The *whoami* command is the simplest and easiest command to remember for checking who you are currently logged in as. It requires no options or arguments and returns the current user's login name.

```
$ whoami
oracle
```

If you use *su* or another method to change the current user, as described later in this chapter, *whoami* reports the user you are currently acting as. If you are interested in seeing the user you initially connected as, the *who* command can be used with the argument *am i* to print that information.

```
$ whoami
oracle
$ su - jemmons
Password:
$ whoami
jemmons
$ who am i
oracle     pts/0          2009-11-04 11:40 (192.168.1.112)
```

This unusual command syntax is actually equivalent to entering *who –m*, but most people find it easier to remember. The *who* command is also used to print information about other users connected to the system, but in this special case, it only prints information about the user associated with the current session.

What Groups am I In?

When called with no arguments, the *groups* command prints the groups to which the current user belongs.

```
$ groups
oinstall dba
```

Later in this chapter, the *groups* command used to check the group information for other users will be seen as well.

Who Else is Logged into the System?

When called without any options or arguments, the *who* command returns a list of all the users currently in command-line sessions on this system.

```
$ who

root     tty1        2009-11-04 12:14
oracle   pts/0       2009-11-04 11:40 (192.168.1.112)
jemmons  pts/1       2009-11-04 12:10 (192.168.1.112)
```

The default output includes the username for each user currently connected, the terminal device that they are connected to, the date and time when they logged in and, if appropriate, the system to which they are connected.

Another more detailed view of current user activity is provided by the *w* command.

```
$ w

12:23:18 up 58 min,  3 users,  load average: 0.05, 0.03, 0.00
USER     TTY     FROM            LOGIN@   IDLE   JCPU   PCPU WHAT
root     tty1    -               12:20    2:44   0.03s  0.03s -bash
oracle   pts/0   192.168.1.112   11:40    0.00s  0.18s  0.06s sshd: ora
jemmons  pts/1   192.168.1.112   12:10    1:13   0.15s  0.04s vim hello
```

The first line of the *w* output shows the same info as the *uptime* command, including the load average and the number of users currently on the system. After that, each user is listed with the following columns:

- *User*: The username for the connected user

- *TTY*: The terminal device this user is connected to

- *From*: The machine address the user is connecting from (if a dash appears here, they are connected from the local system)

- *Login@*: The time this session was started

- *Idle*: How long it has been since the last command was executed by this user

- *Jcpu*: The total amount of processor time this session has used

- *Pcpu*: The amount of processor time used by the current process
- *What*: The command currently being executed in this session

 You will be able to see more information in the *what* column if you make the terminal wider.

This information makes it easy to determine who is currently connected to a command line session and what they are up to, but sometimes it can be useful to see who has been logging in.

Who Has Recently Logged into the System?

It is possible to get information on who has been connecting to the system using the *last* command. Without any options, *last* prints all the logins it can find, possibly since Linux was installed. Since you should usually only be interested in recent logins, call *last* with a dash and a number of lines to show as an option.

```
$ last -10
root      tty1                               Wed Nov  4 12:20   still logged in
root      tty1                               Wed Nov  4 12:14 - 12:16  (00:02)
jemmons   pts/1         192.168.1.112        Wed Nov  4 12:10   still logged in
oracle    pts/1         192.168.1.112        Wed Nov  4 11:54 - 12:09  (00:14)
oracle    pts/0         192.168.1.112        Wed Nov  4 11:40   still logged in
root      tty1                               Wed Nov  4 11:34 - 11:37  (00:02)
reboot    system boot   2.6.18-128.el5       Wed Nov  4 11:26          (01:16)
root      tty1                               Sun Nov  1 13:18 - down   (00:00)
roy       pts/3         192.168.1.112        Sun Nov  1 10:27 - down   (02:50)
jemmons   pts/3         192.168.1.112        Sun Nov  1 10:24 - 10:27  (00:02)

wtmp begins Mon May 18 13:47:41 2009
```

The last command has similar information to the *w* command but includes information about log out. Users who are still logged in are indicated as such, but otherwise, users either have a log out time or *down*, indicating they were connected when the system shut down or was restarted.

By providing a username as an argument, it is possible to get information on a specific user's connection history.

```
$ last -5 oracle
oracle    pts/1         192.168.1.112        Wed Nov  4 11:54 - 12:09  (00:14)
oracle    pts/0         192.168.1.112        Wed Nov  4 11:40   still logged in
oracle    pts/2         192.168.1.112        Sun Nov  1 07:18 - 13:17  (05:59)
```

```
oracle    pts/0        192.168.1.112    Sun Nov  1 05:41 - 13:17  (07:36)
oracle    pts/0        192.168.1.100    Tue Oct 27 12:43 - down   (01:08)
```

The *last* command gets its information from the file */var/log/wtmp*. Since information about shutdown, reboot and runlevel change operations are also stored in this file, use *last* to get information about these system events. Reboots always appear in the last output, but to display shutdown and runlevel change events, use the *-x* option:

```
$ last -x -10

runlevel (to lvl 5)   2.6.18-128.el5   Wed Nov  4 12:49 - 12:58  (00:09)
root     tty1                           Wed Nov  4 12:20    still logged in
root     tty1                           Wed Nov  4 12:14 - 12:16  (00:02)
jemmons  pts/1        192.168.1.112     Wed Nov  4 12:10    still logged in
oracle   pts/1        192.168.1.112     Wed Nov  4 11:54 - 12:09  (00:14)
oracle   pts/0        192.168.1.112     Wed Nov  4 11:40    still logged in
root     tty1                           Wed Nov  4 11:34 - 11:37  (00:02)
runlevel (to lvl 3)   2.6.18-128.el5   Wed Nov  4 11:26 - 12:49  (01:22)
reboot   system boot  2.6.18-128.el5   Wed Nov  4 11:26          (01:32)
shutdown system down  2.6.18-128.el5   Sun Nov  1 13:19 - 12:58  (2+23:39)

wtmp begins Mon May 18 13:47:41 2009
```

Shutdown, reboot and runlevel changes can also be filtered by adding the type of event you would like to see as an argument.

```
$ last -x -5 runlevel
runlevel (to lvl 5)   2.6.18-128.el5   Wed Nov  4 12:49 - 13:03  (00:14)
runlevel (to lvl 3)   2.6.18-128.el5   Wed Nov  4 11:26 - 12:49  (01:22)
runlevel (to lvl 0)   2.6.18-128.el5   Sun Nov  1 13:18 - 13:19  (00:00)
runlevel (to lvl 3)   2.6.18-128.el5   Sun Nov  1 05:03 - 13:18  (08:15)
runlevel (to lvl 0)   2.6.18-128.el5   Tue Oct 27 13:52 - 13:52  (00:00)

wtmp begins Mon May 18 13:47:41 2009
```

This information can be very useful when trying to figure out who was connected when an event happened or who may have made a change to the system.

Files Associated with User, Group and Password Management

Linux stores most information about users in the */etc/passwd* file, but some additional information is kept in the */etc/group* and */etc/shadow* files. These files are text files maintained by the commands examined in this chapter. While it is possible to modify these files manually, it is best to maintain them with the commands covered here.

The */etc/passwd* file contains a line for every user on the system. Each line contains a series of fields separated by colons (:). Below is a partial listing of the */etc/passwd* file.

```
root:x:0:0:root:/root:/bin/bash
bin:x:1:1:bin:/bin:/sbin/nologin
daemon:x:2:2:daemon:/sbin:/sbin/nologin
adm:x:3:4:adm:/var/adm:/sbin/nologin
lp:x:4:7:lp:/var/spool/lpd:/sbin/nologin
...
jemmons:x:501:501:Jon Emmons:/home/jemmons:/bin/bash
oracle:x:504:505::/home/oracle:/bin/bash
auser:x:505:506::/home/auser:/bin/bash
```

The fields of the *password* file are as follows: the user ID, password (given as an *x* as passwords are now kept in the */etc/shadow* file), the UID, the user's primary group ID, comment (often used for full name), home directory and login shell.

The */etc/group* file contains a line for each group on the system and again each line has fields separated by colons. Here is a partial listing of the */etc/group* file.

```
jemmons:x:501:oracle
dba:x:504:oracle,jemmons
oinstall:x:505:
```

The following are the fields for the */etc/group* file: group name, password (not typically used, but listed as an *x* because they have been moved to the */etc/gshadow* file), the group ID number, and a comma separated list of users who have the given group as a supplemental group.

The final file to examine here is the */etc/shadow* file. This file contains the encrypted password and information about password expiration. Next is a partial listing of the */etc/shadow* file:

```
jemmons:$1$YiMgqqQz$CocqVnqNzyNB.HHno5iE4.:14503:0:99999:7:::
oracle:$1$HPOlWa8r$Xy9eRhAo36gP5dtMdUqrj0:14535:0:99999:7:::
auser:!!:14549:0:99999:7:::
```

The first field is the username and the second the encrypted password. When a user is created, the password is set to an exclamation point (!) until an initial password is set. The remaining fields have to do with password expiration.

Getting UID and GID Information for a User

Since permissions on Linux are based on user ID (UID) and group ID (GID) numbers, there sometimes is a need to look up these numbers for a given user. While this could be looked up in the files mentioned in the last section, the *id* command gives a faster way to retrieve UID and GID information for a given user.

If called without any argument, *id* prints the user and group information for the current user. More often, *id* should be used to look up information for another user by providing their username as an argument.

```
# id oracle

uid=504(oracle) gid=505(oinstall) groups=505(oinstall),504(dba)
context=user_u:system_r:unconfined_t
```

The *id* command provides the UID for the user and the GID corresponding to their primary group. Supplemental groups are listed with their GID numbers as well.

Managing Users

As DBAs, we need to first manage the oracle user who the Oracle software is installed as, but setting up accounts on the Linux system for other users may be desired. Depending on specific security needs, many DBAs have personal accounts on the system so they do not need to log in as the privileged oracle user each time they connect.

Developers, users, and third party products may need access to the system for various tasks and it is never a good idea to give the Oracle password out to non-DBAs. Instead, create individual users on the system for these purposes that allow for considerably more control over access.

For security reasons, these tasks must be performed by the root user.

Adding a User

The *useradd* command allows you to add users to the system. In its simplest form, *useradd* can be called providing only a username as an argument.

```
# useradd roy
# passwd roy
```

```
Changing password for user roy.
New UNIX password: password
Retype new UNIX password: password
passwd: all authentication tokens updated successfully.
```

When a user is created, initially it is locked. It is unlocked by setting a
password with the *passwd* command. For more on the *passwd* command, see
the section "Managing Passwords".

By using the *useradd* command without options like this, several default settings
will be used. To view the default settings, call *useradd* with the *-D* flag:

```
# useradd -D
```

```
GROUP=100
HOME=/home
INACTIVE=-1
EXPIRE=
SHELL=/bin/bash
SKEL=/etc/skel
CREATE_MAIL_SPOOL=yes
```

Each of these values is used unless the value is specified at the *useradd*
command. The one exception to this is the *group* value. By default, *useradd*
creates a group with the same name as the user created. This is a Linux
specific security enhancement and can be overridden by specifying a group
with the *-g* option or by giving the *-n* option that causes the default group to be
used.

These defaults can be changed by specifying the *-D* option and one or more
option for the value you would like to change. Common options include *-b* for
the home directory location and *-s* for the default shell the user will be given.

This example changes the default location for users' home directories and the
default shell.

```
# useradd -D -b /users -s /bin/ksh
```

Several options are available to modify the *useradd* command. Here are a few
of the more commonly used ones. The text in italics after the option should
be replaced with the desired value for that option.

Option	Action
-d directory	Specify a non-default location for the user's home directory
-c comment	Add a comment for this user. Often used for the full name. (Hint: if the comment contains multiple words, put the entire comment in single or double quotes.
-g group	Set the user's primary group. This overrides the default Linux behavior of creating a group with the same name as the user.
-G group1, group2...	Add the user to one or more supplemental groups. Multiple groups should be separated by commas and there should be no spaces between groups.
-s shell	Specify a non-default shell for this user
-u UID	Create a user with a specific user ID number. (See the section "The importance of consistent user and group IDs.")
-D	Update the default value for the given option(s) used at user creation. (Do not specify a user name with the -D option

Table 7.1: *Commonly Used Options for the useradd Command*

One or more of the options above can be specified. The user name is given after the last option.

```
# useradd -d /home/maurice -c "Maurice Moss" -g users -G dba,staff -u 1005 mmoss
```

In this example, the UID for this user has been specified with the *-u* option. This is explained further later in this chapter. Any of the options can be excluded in favor of the default value.

The groups used for either the primary or supplemental group in the *useradd* command must already exist on the system. If they do not, an error appears from the *useradd* command. To add the groups, see the next section on managing groups.

Modify a User

Often, it is necessary to modify users who have already been created. The *usermod* command gives the ability to change any attribute of a user who has already been created.

The syntax for *usermod* is similar to that for *useradd* but the login given is for an already existing user. Here are some commonly used options for the *usermod* command:

Option	Action
-d directory	Change the user's home directory
-c comment	Update the comment for this user. (Hint: if the comment contains multiple words, put the entire comment in single or double quotes.)
-g group	Change the user's primary group
-a -G group1,group2...	Add the user to one or more supplemental group. Existing supplemental groups are preserved. Multiple groups should be separated by commas but there should be no spaces between groups.
-G group1,group2...	Change the supplemental groups to only this list of groups and remove any other supplemental groups. Multiple groups should be separated by commas and there should be no spaces between groups.
-s shell	Change the default shell for this user
-u UID	Update the user's UID number. This also updates the user's home directory and files within it to the new UID number but files elsewhere must be updated using *chown* (see the section "The importance of consistent user and group IDs.)
-L	Lock this account by disabling the password
-U	Unlock this account, re-enabling its previous password

Table 7.2: *Commonly Used Options for the usermod Command*

Changing Group Information

To change the primary group of a user, use the *-g* option. This makes dba the primary group for the user roy.

```
# usermod -g dba roy
```

Another common operation is to add a user to a supplemental group. The following command adds the user jemmons to the dba group without changing the primary group or any existing supplemental groups.

```
# groups jemmons

jemmons : jemmons staff
# usermod -a -G dba jemmons
# groups jemmons

jemmons : jemmons dba staff
```

The *-a* option is used in conjunction with the *-G* option to assure that any existing supplemental groups are preserved. Without the *-a* option, existing supplemental groups would be replaced by the groups listed here. As with user creation, any groups specified with the *usermod* command must already exist.

Changing a User's Login Shell

The *usermod* command can also be used to change a user's default shell. The full path to the shell must be provided.

```
# usermod -s /bin/ksh jemmons
```

The user now starts in the Korn shell at their next login. Unlike most user attributes, the shell can be changed by the user using the *chsh* command.

```
$ whoami

jemmons

$ chsh
Changing shell for jemmons.
Password: password
New shell [/bin/ksh]: /bin/bash
Shell changed.
```

Changing a User's UID

When it is necessary to change a user's UID, use the *-u* option for *usermod*. Before changing the UID of a user, note the existing UID for cleanup purposes. The *id* command is the easiest way to check the UID.

```
# id roy

uid=506(roy) gid=504(dba) context=user_u:system_r:unconfined_t

# usermod -u 600 roy
# id roy

uid=600(roy) gid=504(dba) context=user_u:system_r:unconfined_t
```

When a user's UID is changed, all files and directories owned by that user should also be updated. The *usermod* command automatically updates the user's home directory and any files or directories within it, but if the user owns any files outside their home directory, they also need to be updated.

The first command below lists any files or directories on the system still associated with the old UID of 506. The second command updates the files to again be owned by the user roy.

```
# find / -uid 506 -exec ls -l {} \;
# find / -uid 506 -exec chown roy {} \;
```

 Use these commands with caution! Be sure that only the ownership of files are changed which should be owned by the user that has just been changed. If what these commands do is not well known, review the find and chown syntax in the chapter on file management.

There should be no need to change the UID of a user very often, but when a user has already been created and used, it is often easier to change the UID than to delete and recreate the user.

Locking and Unlocking an Account

To lock an account, call the *usermod* command with the *-L* option.

```
# usermod -L roy
```

The user is locked by having the character *!* added to the beginning of the password stored in the */etc/shadow* file. This renders the password unusable. To restore the password, the *-U* option is used.

```
# usermod -U roy
```

The user is now able to log in again using their existing password.

Delete a User

Before deleting a user, you should clean up any files owned by them. Consider locking an account for a while to give you time to clean up their files. It is easier to locate and handle a user's file before they are removed than after.

The *userdel* command is used to delete a user. In its most basic form, it can be used providing just a user name as an argument.

```
# userdel mmoss
```

This deletes the user from the system. They will no longer be able to log in, but any files owned by that user will remain on the system showing the deleted user's UID instead of the user name in *ls -l* output.

Often when you want to remove a user from the system, you will also want to remove their home directory. To do that, use the *-r* option for userdel.

 Before using the *-r* option, make sure it is safe to delete the entire contents of the user's home directory. There is no warning and this operation cannot be undone!

```
# userdel -r roy
```

This removes the user roy and the home directory for that user. Files owned by this user but in other directories on the system are not deleted.

Managing Groups

Group management is similar to user management but with fewer attributes, and therefore fewer options.

Adding a Group

The *groupadd* command is used to add groups. The group name is given as an argument.

```
# groupadd staff
```

If a group already exists by the given name, *groupadd* returns an error. Once the given group is created, it can be used with the *useradd* or *usermod* commands to assign it to a user or users.

The group ID number (GID) is used by the system to associate a group with files or processes. To create a group with a specific ID number, use the *-g* option.

```
# groupadd -g 550 dba
```

Modifying a Group

With the *groupmod* command, the name or the group ID of a group can be changed. To change the name, use the *-n* option. The following command changes the name of the group staff to employee.

```
# groupmod -n employee staff
```

Since the associations between a group and both files and users are made through the GID number, changing the name of a group does not affect files or users associated with the group.

To change the group ID number for a group, use the *-g* option. This updates the group ID number but any files associated with the given group, as well as any users with this as their primary group, need to be updated. Before changing a group's GID, note the original group ID for the group. It can be viewed in the */etc/group* file.

```
# groupmod -g 1000 dba
```

The *find* command can be used to search for files associated with the given group as long as the previous group ID of the changed group is known. Like when changing the user ID of files, it is good practice to check which files will be modified by listing them first.

```
# find / -gid 504 -exec ls -l {} \;
# find / -gid 504 -exec chgrp dba {} \;
```

Users who have the modified group as their primary group also need to be updated. That includes any users with the original group ID listed in the fourth field of the */etc/passwd* file.

The Importance of Consistent User and Group IDs

User and group IDs are typically transparent to the end user. Under normal circumstances, these identifiers can be completely arbitrary, but since the UID and GID are the only things associating files with a given user and group, their ID numbers become very important when storage is accessed by more than one system.

When storage is shared, either via a shared disk technology like Networked File Systems (NFS) or by removing a disk from one system and attaching it to another, the UID and GID numbers associated with the files on that storage are maintained. If the UID and GID numbers do not exist or are not the same on all the systems which access that storage, the ownership and permissions will not be properly preserved.

For example, say a file is created on a system where the UID for Oracle is 504. If the file system is viewed on another system, the file appears to be owned by whichever user has the UID of 504. If your UIDs have been kept consistent from system to system, the file still appears to be owned by 'oracle' and all permissions will still apply correctly. If there is no user with UID of 504, the UID number appears instead of a username, or if another user has the UID of 504, they gain the access to that file meant for the oracle user and appear to be the owner.

Even if there is no immediate plan to share storage between systems, it is best to keep UIDs and GIDs consistent. This gives the flexibility to share storage in the future and can ease the transition to using external directories for login information.

Managing Passwords

Most systems use passwords to verify that a given user has access to a system. Passwords can be set to expire over time, forcing the user to change their password. Linux also tries to force users to use difficult-to-guess passwords to increase security.

It is important that passwords are fairly long and hard to guess. Current best practices suggest passwords be at least 15 characters and should contain both uppercase and lowercase letters as well as numbers and special characters. While passwords this long and complex are cumbersome, it is important to maintain the security of the system and databases on it.

Changing Passwords

A user can change their password using the *passwd* command. No arguments are needed, but the *passwd* command prompts for the user's current password before allowing it to be changed.

```
$ passwd

Changing password for user jemmons.
Changing password for jemmons
(current) UNIX password: password
New UNIX password: newpassword
Retype new UNIX password: newpassword
passwd: all authentication tokens updated successfully.
```

When the new password is provided to *passwd*, it is checked to see if it is too short or otherwise may be easily guessed. The *passwd* command uses the Pluggable Authentication Manager (PAM) to perform this check. If the given password fails the check, the user is asked to provide a more complex one.

The root user can use the *passwd* command to update other user's passwords by providing the username as an argument.

```
# passwd jemmons

Changing password for user jemmons.
New UNIX password:
```

```
BAD PASSWORD: it is based on a dictionary word
Retype new UNIX password:
passwd: all authentication tokens updated successfully.
```

The root user is not prompted for the old password. This allows the root user to set an initial password for a new account or to change a password when the current one has been lost.

 While *passwd* warns the root user if the password is not complex enough, it does not prevent root from using an insecure password.

Password Aging

Password aging can be used to force users to change their passwords after a certain period of time. If an intruder has discovered a password, it is only useful until the next change, but it is important to not force users to change their passwords too often or they will be more likely to write them down.

The *chage* command is used to set password aging rules for a given user. Since it modifies the */etc/passwd* file, *chage* must be run as root.

```
# chage jemmons

Changing the aging information for jemmons
Enter the new value, or press ENTER for the default
    Minimum Password Age [0]:
    Maximum Password Age [99999]: 90
    Last Password Change (YYYY-MM-DD) [2009-11-01]:
    Password Expiration Warning [7]:
    Password Inactive [-1]: 30
    Account Expiration Date (YYYY-MM-DD) [1969-12-31]: 2010-03-31
```

The *chage* command prompts for several parameters related to password and account expiry. The current value for each parameter appears in brackets. To accept the current value, simply press Enter. The parameters for *chage* can also be set through command line options. The requested parameters for *chage* with their command line options are as follows.

- Minimum password age: The shortest number of days a user can go between password changes. A value of 0 allows the user to change their password as often as they want. (*-m days*)

- Maximum password age: The longest number of days a user can go before they are prompted to change their password. The default of 99,999 (more than 273 years) will essentially disable the maximum password age. (*-M days*)

- Last password change: Set the date of the last password change. (*-d YYYY-MM-DD*)

- Password expiration warning: Set the number of days before expiry that the user will be warned that their password is expiring. (*-W days*)

- Password inactive: Set the number of days after password expiry an inactive account will be locked. A value of -1 will cause the account to never become locked. (*-I days* or -1)

- Account expiration date: Set a static date upon which the user's account is locked. (*-E YYYY-MM-DD*)

If the command line options for *chage* are used, the specified value is updated and there is no prompt for other values. These values are stored in the */etc/shadow* file beginning after the encrypted password and in the same order listed above. The values, which are entered in a date format, are stored as the number of days since January 1st 1970.

```
# grep jemmons /etc/shadow
jemmons:$1$wXfUmfD1$NWmVbGFEx4t1vUMqU1cP90:14549:0:90:7:30:14699:
```

Acting Like Other Users and Groups

As administrators, it is often necessary to assume another user's identity to perform a user-specific task. This is particularly common when it comes to administrative tasks like managing users and rebooting the system. There are a few ways that a DBA can act like another user and the right solution depends on individual security needs.

Using *su* to Change Users

Possibly the simplest way to assume another user's identity is using the *su* or 'substitute user' command. The *su* command can be called in a few different ways depending on the DBA's needs. If called without any options or arguments, *su* attempts to assume the role of the root user. There is a prompt for the root password to confirm that the DBA has the rights to make this change.

```
$ whoami
oracle
$ su
Password:
$ whoami
root
```

By adding a dash to the *su* command, any login files (*.profile*, *.bash_profile* and the like) will be run when the user substitution is performed. Shell variables are also updated, but this usually manifests itself by changing the prompt.

```
$ su -
Password:
#
```

The *su* command can also be used to assume the identity of other users on the system. To do this, simply provide a username as an argument. Again, a dash can be included to run the user's login files when switching.

```
$ whoami
oracle
$ su - jemmons
Password:
$ whoami
jemmons
```

When you are done working under the other user's credentials, type *exit* to return to the original session.

> 🔔 If there is a problem with a user's login files which is preventing them from logging in, you can connect as a different user and use *su* without a dash to become that user and correct their login files.

The root user has the unique privilege of being able to use *su* without providing the user's password. This can be useful when managing users, but it also highlights the importance of protecting the root account.

Using *su* to Run Commands as Other Users

The *su* command can also be used to run an individual command as another user. This was seen in the startup script for oracle in the last chapter. Below is a partial listing:

💾 oracle_db script

```
case "$1" in
    'start')
            # Start the listener:
            su - $ORA_OWNER -c "$ORA_HOME/bin/lsnrctl start"
            # Start the databases:
            su - $ORA_OWNER -c $ORA_HOME/bin/dbstart
            # Start Management Server
    ;;
```

Here the *su* command is being used with the *-c* option. The command in the argument following the *-c* option is executed with the rights of the specified user, in this case oracle. Since the command contains more than one word, it is put into quotes, but a single-word command could be provided without quotes.

```
$ su - -c 'shutdown -h now'

Password:
```

It is good practice to use the dash to indicate running login files with this method as it assures that the user's PATH and other variables are set up properly.

sudo, a More Secure Alternative to *su*

In environments where the system administration is handled by a different group than the database administration or where security is a large concern, it may be desirable to limit access to the root password. The *sudo* command offers a way to grant partial or full access to the root account without the users needing the root password.

The *sudo* command is highly flexible and access can be restricted as tight as a single command or script, or access can be given to fully assume the root user's role, and therefore assume other user's role if desired. Advanced *sudo* configuration is beyond the scope of this book, but the following examples should get you started.

sudo is configured through the file */etc/sudoers*. Like with most Linux configuration files, any text following a pound sign in the *sudoers* file is a comment. Within the *sudoers* file, sets of commands, groups of users, and associate users or groups with command sets can be configured.

A simple way to configure *sudo* is to allow a user to perform any operation as root. This essentially gives the user root permission without the need for them to know the root password.

 Configuring *sudo* to allow a user to perform any operation is equivalent to giving that user root privileges. Consider carefully if this is appropriate for your security needs.

To set up this broad *sudo* permission, edit the */etc/sudoers* file by adding the line in bold below in the *commands* section:

```
## The commands section may have other options added to it.
##
## Allow root to run any commands anywhere

root    ALL=(ALL)      ALL
oracle  ALL=(root)     ALL
```

In this example, oracle is the user who you will connect as. ALL=(root) indicates that on any host this *sudoers* file is on, permission to run commands as root needs to be given. The *sudoers* file is designed so that one *sudoers* file can be copied to multiple hosts with different rules on each host. The final ALL in this line indicates that any command can be run. The oracle user can now use the *sudo* command to execute any command as root by prefixing the command with *sudo*.

```
$ whoami
oracle
$ sudo /usr/sbin/useradd mark
Password: password
$
```

The first time a *sudo* operation is called by a user, they are prompted to re-enter their password but if they call another *sudo* operation in the same command line session within five minutes, they do not have to enter their password again. The operation is then executed as the root user and any output is printed to the current session. Note that the *useradd* command must be called using its full path as it does not appear in the oracle user's search path.

To start a session as the root user, call the *su* command with *sudo*. Just like when using the *su* command by itself, the dash causes the root user's login files to be run.

```
$ sudo su -
Password: password
# whoami
root
```

Again, you see that the oracle user is prompted to re-enter his or her password, then the session is continued as the root user. When you are done and want to return to the original session, you can type *exit*, just like when using the *su* command without *sudo*.

A slightly more complicated way to configure *sudo* is to configure certain commands that are allowed to be run by certain users. To do this, add lines like the one below to the *sudoers* file.

```
jemmons ALL=(oracle) /u01/app/oracle/product/11.1.0/db_1/bin/dbstart
```

In this case, indicating that the user jemmons can execute the *dbstart* command as oracle occurs. When using *sudo* to assume the role of a user other than root, use the *-u* option and give the user name as an argument, followed by the command that should be executed.

```
$ whoami

jemmons

$ sudo -u oracle /u01/app/oracle/product/11.1.0/db_1/bin/dbstart

Password:
Processing Database instance "TEST": log file /u01/app/oracle...
```

These are just examples of the simplest way *sudo* can be used. It is possible to configure groups of users and sets of commands to simplify *sudo* administration. Even hosts can be grouped to allow similarly configured systems to share a single *sudoers* file.

Conclusion

User and group administration are central to Linux security. By carefully managing users, passwords and group membership, you can help secure your system against intruders.

This chapter also showed how to view what is happening on the system and who has logged in recently. Furthermore, some different ways to assume the role of another user for administrative tasks are now known.

The next chapter will show how to customize a user's environment to suit the needs of the DBA and simplify use of the system.

Customizing the User Environment

A tremendous amount of customization is possible within the command line environment. Some changes will be made to accommodate Oracle; others will make it easier to use the system.

As you customize the shell to suit your needs, it is important to consider all users who will be using a given login. When accounts like Oracle need to be shared, consider if these customizations will help or hinder other users who need to use the account. Another consideration is whether you will become dependent on the customizations and therefore, be seriously handicapped if your customizations are not available for some reason, e.g. on a new system.

Most of these customizations are made on a user-by-user basis in files that are read when a command line session is started. Since the files that are read may depend on what shell a login is using, this chapter will start with how to change a user's login shell.

The Login Shell

The login shell controls much of how you interact with the system. Several shells are available for use, and at first, they all seem very similar. They do, in fact, all provide basically the same functionality, but as you become a more advanced shell user, the differences will quickly become apparent.

The default login shell on Linux is the Bourne-Again Shell (bash) which combines many desirable features while maintaining compatibility with the popular Bourne shell (sh). Most users find bash to have a desirable combination of flexibility, features and compatibility, but if you are more comfortable with another shell or if you have software which requires another shell, Linux allows you to easily change your login shell.

A list of the valid shells on a system is maintained in the */etc/shells* file. The file can be viewed with the *more* command or any text editor.

```
/bin/sh
/bin/bash
/sbin/nologin
/bin/tcsh
/bin/csh
/bin/ksh
```

Some applications, like ftp daemons, will only allow access if a user's login shell is listed in this file. If new shells are added, it is important to list them in this file.

Regardless of which shell you choose as your login shell, I strongly recommend using the same login shell on all your accounts, if possible. This will assure that you have the commands and tools you are comfortable with in each of your accounts.

What Shell Am I Using?

When you start a command line session, the variable *SHELL* is set to the login shell. This variable can be echoed to check the current login shell.

```
$ echo $SHELL
```

```
/bin/bash
```

This variable is only set when a command line session is started, e.g. at initial login, or when *su -* is called to invoke a login shell as another user, so it will not be updated if shells are temporarily switched as described in the next section.

To check what shell is currently being run, regardless of whether it was invoked at login or not or if it was switched into after, check another *shell* variable, 0.

```
$ echo $0
```

This variable returns the name of the current running program. It can be used within *shell* scripts to print the name of the script, but in a shell session, it will return the name of the shell.

Switching Shells Temporarily

Sometimes you may want to run in a different shell temporarily. To accomplish that, just give the command for the shell you want to enter. When you are done, type *exit* to return to your original shell.

```
$ ksh
$ echo $0

ksh

$ exit
$ echo $0

-bash
```

This is useful if a command or script must be run in a certain shell, but do not permanently change the user's login shell.

Changing a User's Login Shell

The login shell for a user is set when the user is created. If one is not specified, Linux will use the default bash shell. The *usermod* command allows the root user to change a user's login shell after user creation.

```
# usermod -s /bin/ksh jemmons
```

 The *usermod* command does not confirm that the given shell is a valid command or in the */etc/shells* file. Make sure to give a valid shell exactly as it appears in the */etc/shells* file.

The *usermod* command changes the */etc/passwd* file to reflect the new shell. This shell will now be used at login for the user jemmons.

Linux provides another method of changing the login shell which does not require root privileges. The *chsh* command can be run by any user to change that user's login shell.

```
$ chsh

Changing shell for jemmons.
Password: password
```

```
New shell [/bin/ksh]: /bin/bash
Shell changed.
```

The *chsh* command uses special *setuid* permissions to update the */etc/passwd* file which normally can only be edited by root. Unlike *usermod*, *chsh* verifies that a shell is in the */etc/shells* file before changing the user's login shell. If a user is not sure what shells are available, the *chsh* command can be called with the *-l* option to view valid shells.

The Nologin Shell

There is an entry in the */etc/shells* file for */sbin/nologin*. This entry is not a shell, but rather, is intended as a place keeper for use with accounts that are disabled. Setting a user's shell to nologin prevents them from being able to start a command line session on the system but preserves the account for other purposes. If an account needs to be completely disabled, it should be locked using the *usermod* command as described in the previous chapter.

A common use of the nologin shell is to assign it to a user who needs only ftp access to a system. The user's account and password remain valid for FTP and possibly other services, but if they try to connect to the system via SSH, they receive a message that "This account is currently not available."

Login and Logout Files

At login or when switching users with *su* -, the shell executes a series of commands from files known as login files. Some shells, bash included, also execute commands at logout. These files typically contain variable definitions that control the user environment, application behavior and command aliases, but they may also contain commands that perform cleanup routines and other tasks on the system.

Next to be covered in detail is the login behavior of the bash shell. Different shells may use different file names, but the overall steps are the same.

Bash Shell Login Behavior

The first file to be read and executed is */etc/profile*. This is the systemwide configuration file and is always read by a login shell if it exists. The */etc/profile*

---

file is typically maintained by the system administrator and should only contain settings and defaults applicable to every user on the system.

Next, bash goes looking for one of the following files in the user's home directory:

- *.bash_profile*
- *.bash_login*
- *.profile*

The bash shell reads and executes the first of these files that it finds, looking in the order listed above. Once it has located and executed one of these startup files from the home directory, all others are ignored. If none of these files are available, the user only has settings from the systemwide */etc/profile* file. If bash goes looking for one of these files and it exists but is not readable, it reports the error.

Since these files begin with a period (.), they are hidden by default. If they need to be viewed in a directory listing, use the *-a* option for the *ls* command. With these startup files, it is important to remember that only the first one found is read. If, for instance, there are both a *.bash_profile* and a *.profile* in the home directory, the *.bash_profile* is read and executed and the *.profile* ignored.

When a user is created on the Linux system, several baseline files are created including *.bash_profile* and *.bash_logout files*. These files are copied from the */etc/skel* directory and provide a baseline for the login and logout files. The copy of these files in a user's home directory can be edited to change the default behaviors.

Any of the login files may call other login files. For example, the default *.bash_profile* has this entry to call the *.bashrc* file. Here is a partial listing of the *.bash_profile* file:

```
# Get the aliases and functions

if [ -f ~/.bashrc ]; then
    . ~/.bashrc
fi
```

This section uses an *if* statement to determine if the file *.bashrc* exists in the user's home directory. If it does, it is executed as part of the current session as indicated by the period before ~/.*bashrc*. This allows parts of the login files with different functions to be separated out into different files.

Modifying Login Files

The login files are simply text files full of shell commands and as such, they are easily edited using vi or another text editor. The most common operations in login files are variables and aliases.

Since the /*etc*/*profile* file affects multiple users, it is owned by and can only be edited by the root user. The /*etc*/*profile* file should only be edited when a permanent change needs to be made to all users.

Most changes for a user are made on the individual's .*bash_profile*. It can be edited by the user who owns it or the root user. Errors in an individual's login files can cause problems when they log in. If a user has problems with their login files, they can *su* from another user's login without using the - , which will prevent login files from being executed, and correct the error.

When editing login files, keep in mind that they are executed in a linear fashion. Something which has been set up in the login files can be edited or unset later in the files. This can be very useful, but can also cause confusion if files are not kept organized.

Login files are typically only read at the start of a command line session. To force a login file to be read during a command line session and, therefore, update settings in the current session without having to log out and back in, execute the file using a period before it.

```
$ . .bash_profile
```

This is not exactly the same as logging out and back in again as it does not unset variables which have been set since login, but it is sufficient under most circumstances to update the variables in the current command line session.

Sharing Login Files

Under certain circumstances, there may be multiple users who need the same settings in their profile. For example, you could set up all the DBAs to have the *oraenv* configuration script run at login. In this situation, add the series of commands to run *oraenv* to each user's *.bash_profile*, or maintain a separate file with these settings which is then called from the *.bash_profile* of each user.

To set up a shared profile, first create a file in a common location that can be read by all the users who will need to execute it. Keep in mind that users will not only need read privileges on the file, but on all the directories in its path. As an example, I have created a file called *oracle_profile* in */u01/app/oracle/admin*.

For the user jemmons to be able to execute the file, I had to add *read* permission for the 'other' class i.e. *chmod o+r*, to the *oracle_profile* file, but also had to grant read and execute for the other class, i.e. *chmod o+rx*, to the admin directory.

Add the desired settings to the shared login file. With the settings there, now simply add one line to the *.bash_profile* for each user who needs these settings.

```
. /u01/app/oracle/admin/oracle_profile
```

This method can simplify management of user's login files when multiple users need the same settings.

Oracle-specific Environment Settings

Oracle provides the *oraenv* script to set up most environment variables necessary for Oracle administration. The *oraenv* script sets the ORACLE_HOME, ORACLE_BASE and LD_LIBRARY_PATH variables and updates the PATH variable with Oracle specific values.

Calling the *oraenv* File

The *oraenv* script should be called from a user's *.bash_profile* to make these configuration changes. It is typically installed in the */usr/local/bin* directory and as long as that is included in the PATH variable, it can be called with the following syntax.

```
. oraenv
```

If the *ORACLE_SID* variable is set before the *oraenv* script is run, the value of *ORACLE_SID* is given as a default when the user is prompted to enter a SID. Additionally, if the *ORAENV_ASK* variable is set to *NO* before *oraenv* is called, then *oraenv* does not prompt for a SID to be entered; instead, the value from *ORACLE_SID* is used. Below is a script showing *oraenv* being called without being prompted to enter a SID.

```
export ORACLE_SID=TEST
export ORAENV_ASK=NO
. oraenv
```

These are both valid methods for calling the *oraenv* script. Which one you choose will depend on if you wish a user to be prompted to give a SID when they log in.

 When setting up accounts which will be accessed from other systems through scripts, avoid having the user prompted to enter a SID.

The *oratab* File

When the *oraenv* script is run, it reads the *oratab* file found in */etc* to determine where the Oracle home for a given database is located. The *oratab* file contains entries in the form of *ORACLE_SID:ORACLE_HOME:Y*, the last character being a *Y* or *N* indicating if the database should be started and stopped with the *dbstart* and *dbstop* commands, respectively. Here is a typical *oratab* entry:

```
TEST:/u01/app/oracle/product/11.1.0/db_1:Y
```

Lines beginning with a pound sign (#) in the *oratab* file are comments. Valid entries are typically found at the end of the *oratab* file.

The *oratab* file can be edited manually using vi or another text editor. This is often necessary if you the *ORACLE_HOME* of a database should be changed.

Never set *ORACLE_HOME* and *ORACLE_BASE* variables manually.

Under certain circumstances, it is useful to add an entry to the *oratab* file that does not refer to a database. This can allow setting the necessary variables for Oracle without having a database associated with the session. To do that, follow the format mentioned above to add an entry, making sure to set the last character to *N* so the *dbstart/stop* commands do not attempt to start a database that is not there. This script shows an *oratab* entry not associated with a database.

```
11g_db1:/u01/app/oracle/product/11.1.0/db_1:N
```

A dummy *oratab* entry like this can be useful on a system that does not yet have a database configured on it or on an Oracle Application Server or a Client install where there may never be a database.

Adding Custom Code to the *oraenv* File

Sometimes it is necessary to have product-specific environment settings for a product associated with a given Oracle database. The end of the *oraenv* script has a special section to accommodate this kind of setting.

Custom settings can be added to the *oraenv* script after the comment reading 'Install any "custom" code here'. The *oraenv* script is a Bourne shell script - most common shell scripting syntax will work. Here is a short example of custom code added to the *oraenv* script:

```
...
#
# Install any "custom" code here
#

TEMP_DIR=/tmp
export TEMP_DIR

case $ORACLE_SID in
    TEST)
            SCRIPT_DIR=/u01/app/laftdba/test
            export SCRIPT_DIR
    ;;
    PROD)
            SCRIPT_DIR=/u01/app/laftdba/prod
            export SCRIPT_DIR
    ;;
```

```
      *)
            unset SCRIPT_DIR;
      ;;
esac
```

In the example above, the first two lines setting and exporting the variable
TEMP_DIR are run for any database. The *case* statement then executes
additional code based on the setting of *ORACLE_SID*. *case* statements will be
explained further in the section on shell scripting.

Variables

The login files define several variables. Variable names are case sensitive, so
the variable *TEST_VARIABLE* would be different from *Test_Variable* and
test_variable. Environment variables affect or describe the behavior of the shell
or other software on the system and conventionally have all uppercase names.

Some variables like *ORACLE_HOME* and *ORACLE_SID* relate only to
Oracle. Others, like *PATH* and *HISTSIZE* affect how the shell will behave.
As described in the previous section, it is best to let the *oraenv* script set the
Oracle related values, but it is not unusual to have to modify other variables.

Variables are set by giving the variable name, an equal sign, and the value the
variable should be set to. A good example of this is the *ORACLE_SID*
variable which is the only Oracle related variable that should be set manually.

```
ORACLE_SID=TEST
export ORACLE_SID
```

Exporting a variable with the *export* command makes that variable available to
subsequent commands. Environment variables must be exported for software
like SQL*Plus in order to be aware of the variable. The *env* command prints
all exported variables and is a good way to check if a variable has been
exported.

In bash and some other shells, a variable can be set and exported in a single
line. The following command is equivalent to the two lines given above.

```
export ORACLE_SID=test
```

The *PATH* Variable

Some variables contain a single value, but others, like the *PATH* variable, are actually a colon-separated list. Be careful when updating these variables as order is important. Several scripts, including *oraenv*, manipulate the *PATH* variable. Each script may add or replace an element in the *PATH* list but if the entire *PATH* is replaced, the shell may not be able to find the commands it needs.

To update the *PATH* to find new software, use its current value, retrieved with *$PATH*, so the contents are not lost. Then add an additional location to search for software in a new variable definition.

```
PATH=$PATH:/usr/local/bin
export PATH
```

Above is a typical update to the *PATH* variable, adding */usr/local/bin* to the end of the binary search path. You could also choose to add a new location to the beginning of the search path by putting the location before the *$PATH* variable in the definition. That can sometimes affect the behavior of running software, so it is best to add new binary locations to the end unless it is necessary to have it earlier in the *PATH*.

Other variables like *LD_LIBRARY_PATH* are updated in a similar manner. Order should be considered whenever a variable contains a list of values.

Aliases

As covered in Chapter 3, aliases allow assigning a nickname to a command. One common alias for folks coming from a DOS background is making an alias for the *ls* command called *dir*.

```
$ alias dir='ls'
$ dir -l

total 16
drwxr-xr-x 2 jemmons jemmons 4096 Sep 16 13:19 Desktop
drwxrwxr-x 2 jemmons jemmons 4096 Sep 20 10:39 notes

$ which dir

alias dir='ls'
    /bin/ls
```

The *which* command can be used to show an alias. An alias is only available in the command line session it is made in, but as with variables, you can add them to the login files, i.e. typically *.bash_profile*, to have the alias set up automatically each time you log in. A line for the alias listed above would look like this:

```
alias dir='ls'
```

Aliases do not need to be exported, but they are not available to subsequent commands either. Several aliases are set up by default in Linux. To view the current aliases, type *alias -p*.

```
$ alias -p
alias l.='ls -d .* --color=tty'
alias ll='ls -l --color=tty'
alias ls='ls --color=tty'
alias vi='vim'
alias which='alias | /usr/bin/which --tty-only --read-alias --show-dot --
show-tilde'
```

If you want to change an alias, simply add another alias command with the new command. If you want to unset an alias that has been set in login files or earlier in a command line session, then use the *unalias* command.

```
$ unalias ls
```

An *unalias* command can even be added to a user's *.bash_profile*, near the end being best, to unset the alias each time someone logs in.

> If the color ls output is hard to read on your screen (or if you are colorblind like I am), you can add *unalias ls* to your *.bash_profile* and even update the other ls aliases to exclude the *--color=tty* option so that output is in black and white.

When creating an alias, use the *which* command to make sure another command does not already exist with that name. If an alias is created with the same name as an existing command, it effectively replaces that command, e.g. with the alias for *ls* which calls *ls --color=tty*.

These example aliases should give a good idea of how aliases can be used. Aliases can be created for a single command or for a series of commands separated by semicolons or connected by pipes. Though shown on multiple lines here, aliases should be defined in a single line.

This alias lists the last 80 lines of the alert log. It needs to be modified with the location of the alert log.

```
alias alert='tail -80
$ORACLE_BASE/admin/$ORACLE_SID/bdump/alert_$ORACLE_SID.log'
```

This alias gives a shortcut to change directory into the Oracle home directory.

```
alias orahome='cd $ORACLE_HOME'
```

This alias displays the current value of the *ORACLE_SID* variable:

```
alias sid='env | grep ORACLE_SID'
```

The following alias sets the *ORACLE_SID* variable and executes *oraenv* to set up the environment. This allows the Oracle variables to be changed with a single command.

```
alias TEST='export ORAENV_ASK=NO; export ORACLE_SID=TEST; . oraenv'
```

These examples are just a starting point. Any time a command is being used frequently or a shorter way to call a long command is needed, consider an alias, but be careful about becoming dependent on the aliases as it will make it more difficult to work on systems where they do not exist.

Customizing the Prompt

The command prompt you get when you connect to a command line session is highly customizable. I have used a simplified prompt of just a dollar sign ($) in the examples in this book, but the default prompt in Linux includes the user name, host name and the current directory.

```
[jemmons@oelinux-test1 u01]$
```

The prompt is set by defining the *PS1* shell variable. If you want the prompt to just contain text, simply define it just like any other variable.

```
$ PS1=:

:PS1=': '
: PS1='Enter a command: '
Enter a command: PS1=$

$PS1='$ '
$
```

Changes to the *PS1* variable are seen immediately in the current session. In the example above, first set the prompt to a colon (:). It is seen on the next line that with just the colon, your prompt is not separated from your command. To make the prompt more obviously separate from the command, set *PS1* to a colon with a space after it. To set a variable to a value with a space in it, enclose the value between single or double quotes. The space makes it a bit more clear where the prompt ends and the command begins.

Next, change the prompt back to the familiar dollar sign but now notice that the default prompt is not just a dollar sign, but rather, a dollar sign followed by a space, so set *PS1* to reflect that. When you get to a prompt you are happy with, put the definition of it in your *.bash_profile* file with other alias definitions. Now every time you log in, your prompt will automatically be set and ready to go.

Special Prompt Characters

Bash allows several special characters to be used in a user's prompt which will then be expanded when the prompt is printed. These characters can be used in combination with text in the prompt, but always begin with a backslash (\). Here are a few of the more useful special characters:

Special Character	Description
\d	The date spelled out in the form of "Weekday Month Date"
\@	The current time in 12 hour format with AM/PM
\u	The username of the current user
\h	The hostname of the system you are on
\w	The current working directory

Table 8.1: *Sample of Special Prompt Characters*

Here are a few examples of how these special characters can be used in a prompt. Note that the prompt following the change represents the results of that change.

```
$ PS1='\d \@ $ '

Thu Oct 12 04:34 PM $ PS1='\u@\h$ '
oracle@ oelinux-test1$ PS1='\w $ '

~ $ cd /usr/local

/usr/local $
```

The change directory (*cd*) command in this example is used to demonstrate that the \w character is showing the user's present working directory. Commands and shell variables can also be used in command prompts.

Variables and Commands in Prompts

Almost anything can be put in your prompt with shell variables and commands. Oracle administrators often want their current *ORACLE_SID* listed in their command prompt. This is easily accomplished:

```
$ PS1='$ORACLE_SID $ '

oss $
```

Be sure to use single quotes when enclosing variables and commands within the prompt. If double quotes are used, any variables or commands are interpreted and substituted when the prompt is set but are not updated if the value changes during the session. By using single quotes, the variables and commands are substituted when the prompt is displayed. If, for instance, the *ORACLE_SID* variable is changed to connect to a different database, the new value for *ORACLE_SID* is reflected in the prompt.

To use commands in the prompt, they must be enclosed between two grave symbols (`), more commonly called backquote or backtick in UNIX circles. Here is an example:

```
$ PS1='`uptime | cut -f 3-5 -d ","`$ '

  load average: 0.03, 0.04, 0.01$
```

Here the *PS1* prompt is set to show the current load average of the system by using the *uptime* and *cut* commands. Everything within the backquotes is evaluated and the result substituted in the prompt. Then *$* is added to make it clear where the prompt ends.

I suggest keeping your prompt simple. Remember, whatever you put in there will be executed over and over while you are on the system. Most of the time, I find username and hostname and perhaps *ORACLE_SID* to be sufficient.

```
$ PS1='\u@\h $ORACLE_SID $ '

oracle@ oelinux-test1 oss $
```

A secondary prompt is used when entering commands on multiple lines. This *PS2* prompt is seen when a backslash (\) is entered to continue a command on the next line. The default is usually good for this since you do not see it much, but if you wish to change it, set the *PS2* environmental variable in the same way you would set *PS1*.

Prompts *PS3* and *PS4* can also be set but these are rarely seen. *PS3* is used only in very specific shell syntax and *PS4* is used when using a special trace option within the shell.

Conclusion

A handful of meaningful customizations can make the Linux environment easier to use and more flexible. Changes to the login shell, variables and binary search path may sometimes be necessary when setting up new software.

It is important to remember that many of these customizations change the way the shell works and can affect how software runs. Changes to the *PATH* variable in particular can have unexpected consequences.

The next chapter will examine the use of the *at* and *cron* utilities when scheduling tasks.

Scheduling Commands with *cron* and *at*

CHAPTER

9

As DBAs, we are often saddled with tasks which must be repeated on a regular schedule and/or must be done off-hours. Tasks like backups, cleanup routines and monitoring are prime examples of these.

Linux provides two very useful utilities for scheduling these tasks, *cron* and *at*. The *cron* utility allows a user on the system to set up repeating tasks to be scheduled on a regular basis at a specified time, day of the week or month, and month. The *at* utility allows a user to specify a one-time execution of a task sometime in the future. While both of these tools have their quirks, they are easily mastered and are very useful.

Using *cron* for Repeating Tasks

Before jumping into how to set up tasks in *cron*, a little background needs to be covered on it.

The Cron Daemon

The cron daemon is the system process that runs scripted jobs on a pre-determined schedule. The *crontab* command is used to tell the cron daemon what jobs the user wants to run and when to run those jobs. The cron daemon is started through startup scripts in the */etc/rc#.d* directories.

Checking and Restarting the Cron Daemon

To check to see if the cron daemon is running, search the running processes with the *ps* command. The cron daemon's command will show up in the output as *crond*.

```
$ ps -ef | grep crond

root      2560      1  0 07:37 ?        00:00:00 crond
```

```
oracle     2953  2714  0 07:53 pts/0     00:00:00 grep crond
```

The entry in this output for *grep crond* can be ignored but the other entry for *crond* can be seen running as root. This shows that the cron daemon is running.

By default, the cron daemon runs at runlevels 2 through 5 inclusive, but it can occasionally fail and needs to be restarted. To start or stop the cron daemon, use the *crond* script in */etc/init.d* by providing an argument of *start* or *stop*. You must be root to start or stop the cron daemon.

```
# /etc/init.d/crond stop

Stopping crond:
                                              [  OK  ]

# ps -ef | grep crond

root       3005  2958  0 08:00 pts/0     00:00:00 grep crond

# /etc/init.d/crond start

Starting crond:
                                              [  OK  ]

# ps -ef | grep crond

root       3013     1  5 08:00 ?          00:00:00 crond
root       3016  2958  0 08:00 pts/0     00:00:00 grep crond
```

Setting Up and Editing a User's *crontab* File

A user's list of scheduled jobs is kept in what is referred to as the *crontab* file. A *crontab* file is kept for each user in the */var/spool/cron* directory, but unlike most other configuration files, the *crontab* should never be edited directly.

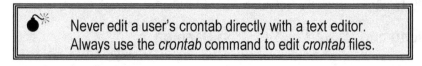

> Never edit a user's crontab directly with a text editor.
> Always use the *crontab* command to edit *crontab* files.

The *crontab* command allows you to view, edit or replace a user's *crontab* file. This table shows the common options for the *crontab* command. Notice that only the root user can change other user's *crontabs*.

Option	Purpose
-e	Edit the current *crontab* file using the text editor specified by the *EDITOR* environment variable or the *VISUAL* environment variable
-l	List the current *crontab* file
-r	Remove the current *crontab* file
-u	Specifies the user's *crontab* to be manipulated. This is usually used by root to manipulate the *crontab* of other users or can be used by you to correctly identify the *crontab* to be manipulated if you have used the *su* command to assume another identity.

Table 9.1: *Common Options for crontab Command*

To list the current user's *crontab*, use the *-l* option for the *crontab* command.

```
$ crontab -l

# Daily full export
00 01 * * *     /u01/app/oracle/admin/test/scripts/full_export.sh
# Weekly full hot backup
00 03 * * 0     /u01/app/oracle/admin/common/scripts/hot_backup.sh oss 0
# Nightly incremental hot backup
00 03 * * 1-6   /u01/app/oracle/admin/common/scripts/hot_backup.sh oss 1
```

Using the *-e* option for the *crontab* command, the current user's *crontab* can be edited. This brings a copy of the *crontab* up in the default editor. Then the *crontab* is edited and when the editor is exited, the *crontab* command puts your changes in place.

crontab also accepts a file name and uses the specified file to create the *crontab* file. Many users prefer to use this option rather than the *crontab -e* command because it provides a master file from which the *crontab* is built, thus providing a backup to the *crontab*. The following example specifies a file called *mycron.tab* to be used as the input for *crontab*.

```
$ crontab mycron.tab
```

To delete the current user's *crontab*, use the *-r* option. This removes all jobs from the *crontab*.

```
$ crontab -r
```

As root, you can view or manipulate another user's *crontab* file using the *-u* option to specify a username.

```
# crontab -u oracle -l
* * * * * touch /tmp/file.txt
# crontab -u oracle -e
```

Alternatively, the root user could use *su* to act as a user then manipulate their *crontab*, but using the *-u* option is often easier.

The Format of the *crontab* File

The *crontab* file consists of a series of entries specifying what command to run and when to run it. It is also possible to document *crontab* entries with comments. Anything on a line after a pound sign (#) is considered a comment and will be ignored. Placing a pound sign in front of a *crontab* entry can temporarily disable it. Blank lines in the *crontab* file are completely ignored.

Crontab Entries

Each *crontab* entry line is comprised of six positional fields specifying the time, date and the command to be run. The format of a *crontab* entry is described in the table below:

Field	Minute	Hour	Day of Month	Month	Day of Week	Command
Valid values	0-59	0-23	1-31	1-12	0-7	Command path/command

Table 9.2: *Format of a crontab Entry*

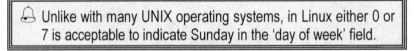
Unlike with many UNIX operating systems, in Linux either 0 or 7 is acceptable to indicate Sunday in the 'day of week' field.

Each of these fields can contain a single number, a range of numbers indicated with a hyphen (such as 2-4), a list of specific values separated by commas (like 2,3,4) or a combination of these designations separated by commas (such as

1,3-5). Any of these fields may also contain an asterisk (*) indicating every possible value of this field. This can all get rather confusing, so take a look at a few examples.

```
# Daily full export
00 01 * * *     /u01/app/oracle/admin/test/scripts/full_export.sh
```

This entry will run the *full_export.sh* script at 0 minutes past 1 am, every day of the month, every month of the year and every day of the week. As with scripts and other configuration files, comments help make the *crontab* file more readable.

```
# Weekly full hot backup
00 03 * * 0     /u01/app/oracle/admin/common/scripts/hot_backup.sh oss 0
```

This entry runs at 3:00 am, but only on Sundays (day 0). While the day of month and month fields have asterisks, this entry will only be run on Sundays since *crontab* entries will only be executed when all the given values are met.

```
# Nightly incremental hot backup
00 03 * * 1-6   /u01/app/oracle/admin/common/scripts/hot_backup.sh oss 1
```

In this entry, it has been specified that the script should be run at 3:00 a.m. Monday through Saturday.

```
00,15,30,45 * * * * /u01/app/oracle/admin/common/scripts/check_disk_space.sh
```

This entry has minutes separated by a comma indicating that it should be run at each of the indicated times. Since all the other fields are wildcards (*), the entry is run on the hour (00), 15 minutes past the hour, 30 minutes past the hour and 45 minutes past the hour for every hour of the day and every day of the year.

```
00 12 * * 1-5 /home/oracle/lunch_time.sh
```

This lunch reminder is set up to run at 12:00 p.m. Monday through Friday only.

The most important thing to remember is that a *crontab* entry will execute every time all of its conditions are met. To take the last entry as an example, any time it is 00 minutes past the hour of 12 on any day of the month and any

---

month of the year and the day of the week is between Monday and Friday inclusive (1-5), this *crontab* will be executed.

Wildcards are used in most *crontab* entries, but be careful where they are used. For instance, if a * is mistakenly placed in the minute position of the last *crontab* example above, the script would end up being run for every minute of the 12:00 hour instead of just once at the beginning of the hour. I do not think anyone needs that many reminders to go to lunch, do they?

Quite a bit of this chapter has been about how to specify the date and time in the *crontab*, but what about the command? Well, most folks will write shell scripts to execute with their crontab entries, but you can actually just execute a command from the *crontab* as well. Either way, be sure the absolute path to the command is placed in the *crontab*.

When a script or command is run from a user's *crontab*, the user's environment files (*.bash_profile* and the like) are not run. If scripts and commands are dependent on environment variables, i.e. SQL*Plus can rely on the *ORACLE_SID* variable, those variables need to be set as part of a script.

If the command or script you call in your *crontab* sends output to the screen, some systems will attempt to email the output to the owner of the *crontab* file. This can be useful, but where is that email going? If you are checking the account regularly or forwarding the email to another account, this may be sufficient; but as will be seen in the shell scripting section, it may be much better to create a custom email within the script and handle any output that way.

Another option is to redirect that output to a log file with the >> symbol so it can be checked later. Be careful with this as the log files may get rather large over time!

Controlling Who Can Use *cron*

By default, every user on the system will be able to schedule *cron* tasks. To restrict a user from using *cron*, add their username to the */etc/cron.deny* file. This file is simply a list of users (one user per line) who are not allowed to call the *crontab* command.

If a user who is listed in the *cron.deny* file tries to edit their *crontab*, they receive an error.

```
$ crontab -e

You (jemmons) are not allowed to use this program (crontab)
```

 Adding a user to the */etc/cron.deny* file only keeps them from editing their *crontab*. Any entries already in their *crontab* continue to be executed on their original schedule.

```
See crontab(1) for more information
```

Another option available to limit the use of *cron* is the *cron.allow* file. The file does not exist by default, but if the file */etc/cron.allow* is created, all users are restricted from using *crontab* unless they are listed in the *cron.allow* file.

Scheduling One-Time Tasks with *at*

It has been seen how *cron* can be used to schedule repeating tasks, but it is not unusual to have a task which needs to be run once but at a time when it should not be run manually. For these tasks, use the *at* command to schedule the job.

The *at* Daemon

Like *cron*, *at* relies on a daemon to run scheduled processes. It should be started automatically but it can be checked and controlled manually if necessary.

Checking and Restarting the At Daemon

The at daemon process shows up in *ps* output as *atd*. Using *grep* to limit the output, the *atd* process can be seen.

```
# ps -ef | grep atd
root      2177     1  0 07:37 ?        00:00:00 rpc.statd
root      2627     1  0 07:37 ?        00:00:00 /usr/sbin/atd
root     24120  2958  0 08:51 pts/0    00:00:00 grep atd
```

There may be other commands running with *atd* as part of their command name, but you should be interested specifically in */usr/sbin/atd*.

The *atd* script from */etc/init.d* can be used to stop and start the at daemon if necessary.

```
# /etc/init.d/atd stop
Stopping atd:                                             [ OK ]

# ps -ef | grep atd
root       2177    1  0 07:37 ?        00:00:00 rpc.statd
root       4220 2958  0 08:54 pts/0    00:00:00 grep atd

# /etc/init.d/atd start
Starting atd:                                             [ OK ]

# ps -ef | grep atd
root       2177    1  0 07:37 ?        00:00:00 rpc.statd
root       4493    1  0 08:54 ?        00:00:00 /usr/sbin/atd
root       4621 2958  0 08:54 pts/0    00:00:00 grep atd
```

Using *at* to Schedule Tasks

The *at* command is used to schedule tasks for execution at a certain date and time. The syntax for *at* is surprisingly simple! The *at* command takes the time you wish to run the command as an argument and allows you to enter a command or series of commands to be executed. If you are running a command later in the same day, you do not have to specify any more than that.

```
$ at 23:30
at> /u01/app/oracle/admin/oss/scripts/full_export.sh
at> ctrl-d <EOT>
job 5 at 2007-01-21 23:30
```

After entering *at* and the desired time of execution, the *at* command allows you to enter the commands or scripts that you wish to run. You can enter one or many commands here and when you are done, type *control-d*. *at* then prints the job number and date which it will be run.

at can also take a date on which to run the command. The date is given in MMDDYY format (two digit month, two digit day, two digit year), but the word *tomorrow* can also be used instead of a numeric date. Here the *-m* option has also been added to send mail to the user upon completion of this *at* job.

```
$ at -m 11:00 tomorrow

at> /u01/app/oracle/admin/oss/scripts/full_export.sh
at> ctrl-d <EOT>
job 6 at 2007-01-22 11:00
```

Just like with *cron*, *at* jobs email any output from the script to the job owner, but it is often better to handle output within the shell script if possible. Of course, once you have scheduled jobs to run with *at*, you may find that you need to check when things are running or cancel a job. The command *atq* gives a simple way to check what is scheduled.

```
$ atq

6          2007-01-22 11:00 a oracle
5          2007-01-21 23:30 a oracle
```

The output of the *atq* command includes the job number, date and time that it is running and the job owner. If you find you need to remove a scheduled job, use the *atrm* command, supplying the job number as an argument.

```
$ atrm 6
```

Using the *at* command to run tasks which must be run during non-business hours can keep you from having to work late or get up early, but care should be taken to make sure the jobs run properly.

Controlling Who Can Use *at*

Just like with *cron*, by default all users can use *at* to schedule commands to run in the future. Users can be added to the file */etc/at.deny* to restrict them from using *at* to schedule jobs. The *at.deny* file is a list of users (one user per line) who cannot schedule tasks with *at*.

A user who is listed in the *at.deny* file will get an error if they try to use *at*.

```
$ at

You do not have permission to use at.
```

Also, like with *cron*, the file */etc/at.allow* can be created to restrict all users from using *at* except those listed in this file.

Conclusion

Effectively scheduling tasks for backups, monitoring, cleanup, and more is essential to automating routine tasks. By automating routine tasks, you can free up your time for higher-level work and avoid some off-hours work.

In the section on shell scripting in Chapter 8, you were shown how to make automated tasks perform complex series of commands, make decisions and send you notifications. By using the techniques from this chapter combined with those methods, you can create very low maintenance systems.

Process and Service Management

When any command is run on the Linux system, a resulting process is created to carry out the requested work for that command. Some commands start and complete so quickly they seem instant, others may start when the system is booted and run until it shuts down.

Services are processes, often started when the system starts up, that run in the background in order to provide some additional functionality. These are often called daemons (pronounced like demon) and provide facilities such as SSH, email and automatic mounting of disks.

Examining Running Processes

The first step to managing processes is being able to identify what processes are running. Even if the system has just been started up and nothing else, there will be dozens of processes running. These are mostly daemons started from the *init* scripts at system startup. Daemons will be covered in further detail later in this chapter.

Several attributes are tracked for each process running on the system. When it is started, each process receives a process number to uniquely identify it on the system. The owner and the process number of the process that starts it (the parent process) are also tracked as well as the start time.

The *ps* command is used to report the processes currently running on the system. If no options are given, *ps* reports minimal information on processes owned by the current user. To get more information, the *-e* and *-f* options may be used. The *-e* option requests every process and the *-f* option is for full information on processes listed. These may be combined as *–ef*, causing all running processes to be reported in a long output format.

```
$ ps -ef
```

```
UID         PID  PPID  C STIME TTY          TIME CMD
root          1     0  0 06:45 ?        00:00:12 init [3]
root          2     1  0 06:45 ?        00:00:00 [migration/0]
root          3     1  0 06:45 ?        00:00:00 [ksoftirqd/0]
...
oracle     2718  2716  0 06:50 ?        00:00:00 sshd: oracle@pts/0
oracle     2719  2718  0 06:50 pts/0    00:00:00 -bash
root       2897  2361  0 07:14 ?        00:00:00 sshd: oracle [priv]
oracle     2899  2897  0 07:14 ?        00:00:00 sshd: oracle@pts/1
oracle     2900  2899  0 07:14 pts/1    00:00:00 -bash
oracle     2967  2900  0 07:20 pts/1    00:00:00 ps -ef
```

All running processes are reported, from the *init* process which is the first process started on the system right up to the *ps* command you are running to report the running processes. There can easily be hundreds or thousands of processes running on a system, so you will typically want to restrict which processes you see.

Each line of the *ps* output represents a currently running process. With the *-f* option, the following attributes are displayed:

Column label	Value
UID	The owner of this process
PID	The unique process ID for this process
PPID	The process ID of the parent to this process (the process that started this process)
C	The percentage of CPU time used by this process since it was started
STIME	The time (and date if before today) that this process was started
TTY	The terminal associated with this process (if any)
TIME	The total time this process has spent being processed
CMD	The command and arguments executed

Table 10.1: *Attributes with the –f option*

There are several options to change the output format of the *ps* command, but for most purposes, the standard *-f* output is sufficient.

Commands and arguments can be viewed by any user on the system, so it is important not to reveal any passwords or other sensitive information in command names or arguments.

One way to restrict the output of the *ps* command is to use the *-u* option which causes *ps* to report on a specific user's processes. It is shown here with the *-f* option to give additional information about each process.

```
$ ps -fu oracle

UID        PID  PPID  C STIME TTY          TIME CMD
oracle    2718  2716  0 06:50 ?        00:00:00 sshd: oracle@pts/0
oracle    2719  2718  0 06:50 pts/0    00:00:00 -bash
oracle    2899  2897  0 07:14 ?        00:00:00 sshd: oracle@pts/1
oracle    2900  2899  0 07:14 pts/1    00:00:00 -bash
oracle    3079  2900  0 07:40 pts/1    00:00:00 -bash
oracle    3122  3079  0 07:40 pts/1    00:00:00 -bash
oracle    3172  3122  0 07:40 pts/1    00:00:00 sqlplus
oracle    3179     1  0 07:41 ?        00:00:00 ora_pmon_TEST
oracle    3181     1  1 07:41 ?        00:00:00 ora_vktm_TEST
oracle    3185     1  0 07:41 ?        00:00:00 ora_diag_TEST
oracle    3187     1  0 07:41 ?        00:00:00 ora_dbrm_TEST
oracle    3189     1  0 07:41 ?        00:00:00 ora_psp0_TEST
oracle    3193     1  0 07:41 ?        00:00:00 ora_dia0_TEST
oracle    3195     1  1 07:41 ?        00:00:00 ora_mman_TEST
oracle    3197     1  0 07:41 ?        00:00:00 ora_dbw0_TEST
oracle    3201     1  0 07:41 ?        00:00:00 ora_lgwr_TEST
oracle    3203     1  0 07:41 ?        00:00:00 ora_ckpt_TEST
oracle    3205     1  1 07:41 ?        00:00:00 ora_smon_TEST
oracle    3207     1  0 07:41 ?        00:00:00 ora_reco_TEST
oracle    3209     1  2 07:41 ?        00:00:00 ora_mmon_TEST
oracle    3211     1  0 07:41 ?        00:00:00 ora_mmnl_TEST
oracle    3213     1  0 07:41 ?        00:00:00 ora_d000_TEST
oracle    3215     1  0 07:41 ?        00:00:00 ora_s000_TEST
oracle    3222  3172 11 07:41 ?        00:00:01 oracleTEST
(DESCRIPTION=(LOCAL=YES)(ADDRESS=(PROTOCOL=beq)))
oracle    3224     1  1 07:41 ?        00:00:00 ora_fbda_TEST
oracle    3226     1  0 07:41 ?        00:00:00 ora_smco_TEST
oracle    3228     1  1 07:41 ?        00:00:00 ora_qmnc_TEST
oracle    3230     1  1 07:41 ?        00:00:00 ora_w000_TEST
oracle    3234  2719  0 07:41 pts/0    00:00:00 ps -fu oracle
```

Another way to restrict *ps* output is using *grep*. By using a pipe to send the output of the *ps* command to the *grep* command *ps*, only lines with certain text in them can be displayed. This example looks for lines that contain *_TEST*.

```
$ ps -ef | grep _TEST

oracle     9975     1  0 08:19 ?        00:00:00 ora_pmon_TEST
oracle     9978     1  0 08:19 ?        00:00:00 ora_vktm_TEST
oracle     9983     1  0 08:19 ?        00:00:00 ora_diag_TEST
oracle     9985     1  0 08:19 ?        00:00:00 ora_dbrm_TEST
oracle     9987     1  0 08:19 ?        00:00:00 ora_psp0_TEST
oracle     9991     1  0 08:19 ?        00:00:00 ora_dia0_TEST
oracle     9993     1  0 08:19 ?        00:00:00 ora_mman_TEST
oracle     9995     1  0 08:19 ?        00:00:00 ora_dbw0_TEST
oracle     9997     1  0 08:19 ?        00:00:00 ora_lgwr_TEST
oracle     9999     1  0 08:19 ?        00:00:00 ora_ckpt_TEST
oracle    10001     1  0 08:19 ?        00:00:00 ora_smon_TEST
oracle    10003     1  0 08:19 ?        00:00:00 ora_reco_TEST
oracle    10005     1  1 08:19 ?        00:00:01 ora_mmon_TEST
oracle    10007     1  0 08:19 ?        00:00:00 ora_mmnl_TEST
oracle    10009     1  0 08:19 ?        00:00:00 ora_d000_TEST
oracle    10011     1  0 08:19 ?        00:00:00 ora_s000_TEST
oracle    10019     1  0 08:19 ?        00:00:00 ora_smco_TEST
oracle    10021     1  0 08:19 ?        00:00:00 ora_fbda_TEST
oracle    10023     1  0 08:19 ?        00:00:00 ora_qmnc_TEST
oracle    10025     1  0 08:19 ?        00:00:00 ora_w000_TEST
oracle    10035     1  0 08:19 ?        00:00:00 ora_q000_TEST
oracle    10039     1  0 08:19 ?        00:00:00 ora_q001_TEST
oracle    10125  2719  0 08:20 pts/0    00:00:00 grep _TEST
```

Notice that the command *grep _TEST* appears in the output since it is also being executed and contains the given string. To further limit the output, send the output to another *grep* command using the *-v* option to exclude lines matching *grep*.

```
$ ps -ef | grep _TEST | grep -v grep

oracle    9975    1    0 08:19 ?        00:00:00 ora_pmon_TEST
oracle    9978    1    0 08:19 ?        00:00:00 ora_vktm_TEST
oracle    9983    1    0 08:19 ?        00:00:00 ora_diag_TEST
oracle    9985    1    0 08:19 ?        00:00:00 ora_dbrm_TEST
oracle    9987    1    0 08:19 ?        00:00:00 ora_psp0_TEST
oracle    9991    1    0 08:19 ?        00:00:00 ora_dia0_TEST
oracle    9993    1    0 08:19 ?        00:00:00 ora_mman_TEST
oracle    9995    1    0 08:19 ?        00:00:00 ora_dbw0_TEST
oracle    9997    1    0 08:19 ?        00:00:00 ora_lgwr_TEST
oracle    9999    1    0 08:19 ?        00:00:00 ora_ckpt_TEST
oracle   10001    1    0 08:19 ?        00:00:00 ora_smon_TEST
oracle   10003    1    0 08:19 ?        00:00:00 ora_reco_TEST
oracle   10005    1    0 08:19 ?        00:00:01 ora_mmon_TEST
oracle   10007    1    0 08:19 ?        00:00:00 ora_mmnl_TEST
oracle   10009    1    0 08:19 ?        00:00:00 ora_d000_TEST
oracle   10011    1    0 08:19 ?        00:00:00 ora_s000_TEST
oracle   10019    1    0 08:19 ?        00:00:00 ora_smco_TEST
oracle   10021    1    0 08:19 ?        00:00:00 ora_fbda_TEST
oracle   10023    1    0 08:19 ?        00:00:00 ora_qmnc_TEST
oracle   10025    1    0 08:19 ?        00:00:00 ora_w000_TEST
oracle   10035    1    0 08:19 ?        00:00:00 ora_q000_TEST
oracle   10039    1    0 08:19 ?        00:00:00 ora_q001_TEST
```

Through the combination of these methods, it is possible to restrict the output to a manageable amount, allowing you to identify the specific processes you are interested in.

Another more specialized way to view running processes is the *top* command. The *top* command also gives information about the overall system, but then lists information about the processes which are currently using the most processors.

```
$ top

top - 08:26:57 up  1:41,  2 users,  load average: 0.01, 0.30, 0.89
Tasks: 106 total,   1 running, 105 sleeping,   0 stopped,   0 zombie
Cpu(s):  0.3%us,  1.0%sy,  0.0%ni, 97.7%id,  0.7%wa,  0.0%hi,  0.3%si,  0.0%st
Mem:   1035244k total,   841624k used,   193620k free,    38960k buffers
Swap:  2097144k total,       96k used,  2097048k free,   657532k cached

  PID USER      PR  NI  VIRT  RES  SHR S %CPU %MEM    TIME+  COMMAND
10005 oracle    15   0  537m  51m  45m S  0.7  5.1   0:01.48 oracle
 2603 root      18   0  1968  676  592 S  0.3  0.1   0:08.97 hald-addon-stor
 9993 oracle    15   0  533m  16m  15m S  0.3  1.6   0:00.48 oracle
10157 oracle    15   0  537m  29m  24m S  0.3  2.9   0:00.83 oracle
10168 oracle    15   0  2196 1000  792 R  0.3  0.1   0:00.05 top
    1 root      15   0  2064  620  532 S  0.0  0.1   0:13.21 init
    2 root      RT  -5     0    0    0 S  0.0  0.0   0:00.00 migration/0
    3 root      34  19     0    0    0 S  0.0  0.0   0:00.04 ksoftirqd/0
    4 root      RT  -5     0    0    0 S  0.0  0.0   0:00.00 watchdog/0
    5 root      10  -5     0    0    0 S  0.0  0.0   0:00.47 events/0
    6 root      10  -5     0    0    0 S  0.0  0.0   0:01.41 khelper
    7 root      11  -5     0    0    0 S  0.0  0.0   0:00.11 kthread
   10 root      10  -5     0    0    0 S  0.0  0.0   0:01.89 kblockd/0
   11 root      20  -5     0    0    0 S  0.0  0.0   0:00.00 kacpid
```

```
48 root      20  -5      0    0    0 S   0.0  0.0   0:00.00 cqueue/0
51 root      10  -5      0    0    0 S   0.0  0.0   0:00.00 khubd
53 root      10  -5      0    0    0 S   0.0  0.0   0:00.00 kseriod
```

The output of the *top* command is somewhat different from *ps*. The following columns are included in the process listing part of the *top* output.

Column Label	Value
PID	The unique process ID for this process
USER	The user who started this process
PR	The priority of this process
NI	The *nice* value of this process
VIRT	The amount of virtual memory used by this process
RES	The resident (real) memory used by this process
SHR	The shared memory used by this process
S	The process status (Typically *Running* or *Sleeping*)
%CPU	The percentage of processor used by this process since the last screen refresh
%MEM	The percentage of physical memory currently used by this process
TIME+	The total amount of time this process has spent executing since the process started
COMMAND	The command executed

Table 10.2: *Columns in Processing List of top Output*

The output of the *top* command is automatically updated every three seconds in order to give the most up-to-date information. If a different delay is desired, start *top* with the *-d* option and give a number of seconds to delay. As an example, to view *top* with a 10-second delay, the command will look like the following:

```
$ top -d 10
```

Each time the output of *top* is updated, it reflects all activity since the last update. *top* also has options to order processes by most used memory instead of processor usage.

Examining Running Processes **191**

Different Ways to Start Processes

Some processes start automatically when the system starts up. The *init* scripts, as described in Chapter 6, control these processes. Each time a command is run, a process is created to carry out that command. Even then, there is some control over how the command will be handled.

Starting and Managing Background Jobs

Normally a command is expected to start, do some work, and then exit gracefully, usually in a short period of time. During that time, typically nothing else can be done with the shell session that command was executed, but there is an alternative.

By following a command with an ampersand (&), that command can be made to run in the background. The shell reports a job number in brackets and the process number for the backgrounded command.

```
$ dbstart &

[1] 11022
Processing Database instance "TEST": log file
/u01/app/oracle/product/11.1.0/db_1/startup.log
```

Things can become very confusing if you have a bunch of background processes writing to your terminal, so it is best to background processes with little or no output or redirect the output to a file or other resource using > or >> and a file name.

Now that you have a process running in the background, you might want to know when it completes. The shell typically reports a Done message with the job number when a process completes, but if you want to check what is going on in the meantime, use the *jobs* command to check the status.

```
$ jobs

[1]+  Running                 dbstart &
```

The *jobs* command reports back the job number, status and command for any processes currently running or stopped in the background. The status is indicated as Running if the process is running in the background, Stopped if the process is waiting for input or has been stopped with the *control-z* command or Done if the process has just finished running.

If a process is started normally without an ampersand and there is a need to either pause the execution or have the process run in the background instead of canceling the process and restarting it with an ampersand, use the *control-z* command to stop the process and manipulate the job from there.

```
$ dbshut
control-z

[1]+  Stopped                 dbshut

$ jobs

[1]+  Stopped                 dbshut

$ bg 1

[1]+ dbshut &

$ jobs

[1]+  Running                 dbshut &
```

Once the job is stopped, it shows up in the job list with a status of Stopped. To start the job executing in the background, use the *bg* command with the job number. As seen above, this changes the status to Running and the job will continue to run as if it were started with an ampersand.

Whether a job is stopped or running in the background, it can be brought back to the foreground with the *fg* command. This allows interacting with the program just as if it were started normally. You get your prompt back when the command completes or you get tired of waiting and background it again with the *control-z* command.

```
$ dbstart &

[1] 2599
Processing Database instance "oss": log file
/u01/app/oracle/product/10.2.0/Db_1/startup.log

$ jobs

[1]+  Running                 dbstart &

$ fg 1

dbstart
```

```
$
```

Here is a table for a quick reference to these job control commands. Job control can allow you to get multiple things running at once, but watch out for commands which might interfere with each other and make sure you can keep track of the output.

Command	Action
&	Append to the end of a command to start it running in the background
jobs	Display all backgrounded jobs whether running or stopped
control-z	Stop the job running in the current shell and background it
bg 1	Start running job 1 in the background
fg 1	Move job 1 to the foreground, moving it into the current shell

Table 10.3: *Job Control Commands*

Keeping Things from Being Interrupted with *nohup*

When a command line session is exited or if the connection is lost for some reason, the system automatically sends all the processes that were running in that session a SIGHUP signal. The SIGHUP signal could also be sent with the *kill* command as described in the next section.

The SIGHUP signal is interpreted by the processes and normally causes them to shut down and die. To prevent this and allow a command to continue running after logout or session failure, add the command *nohup* before the command to be executed.

```
$ nohup vmstat 30 10 &

[1] 4708
Sending output to nohup.out

$ exit
```

In this example, the *vmstat* command is called with arguments that cause it to gather statistics on the use of system resources 10 times, waiting 30 seconds between each execution. Since the *nohup* command was used, the output from the command is automatically redirected to a file called *nohup.out*. The *nohup.out* file is created in the present working directory when the *nohup* command is called, so if the shell session is interrupted, the output can still be picked up.

An ampersand is also used in this execution, so you would immediately get your prompt back to continue working in this shell. Now exit this shell, reconnect with a new command line session and examine the *nohup.out* file for the results.

```
$ more nohup.out

kthr      memory            page                disk          faults      cpu
r b w   swap   free  re  mf pi po  fr de  sr dd dd f0 s1    in   sy   cs us sy id
0 0 0 492872 67664   4  23 15   4   7 4792 8  3  1  0  0   408   94  172  1  3 96
0 0 0 399168 13120   4  28 162  0   0   0  0  2 17  0  0   439   91  199  1  2 97
0 0 0 397760  7192  11  64 88  15  15   0  0  2 10  0  0   428  229  203  1  3 96
0 0 0 399504  7488  70  75 707 36  63   0 16 12  7  0  0   440  190  196  3  4 93
0 0 0 399064  6048   3  17 15  33  41   0  7  3  3  0  0   414   65  178  1  2 98
0 0 0 399848  6728   6  54 66  17  17 248  1  5  2  0  0   416   96  179  1  2 97
0 0 0 399024  5976   2   4  5  16  17   0  0  2  2  0  0   410   83  176  1  2 98
0 0 0 399776  6584  11  63 11  14  16 1208  1  2  1  0  0   408  123  176  1  2 97
0 0 0 399032  5928   2   0  0  16  16   0  0  2  1  0  0   408   59  170  0  1 98
0 0 0 399560  6952  14  78 299 149 183 2088 96 15  1  0  0  433  402  194  9  3 87
```

The *nohup* command is useful when a command is known to take a long time and it is suspected that it might be interrupted for some reason such as auto-logout, network issues, desktop power failure and such.

Stopping Processes

When a command does not respond to normal ways of shutting it down, like a stubborn database process which does not die after the database is shut down, the *kill* command can be used to tell the command to shut down. The *kill* command sends a signal to the given process. The process will try to catch this signal and respond appropriately.

To send a signal to a running process, you first need its process ID. That is usually found using the *ps* command as described above. Once you have the process ID, you should first try sending a SIGTERM to the process. No options are needed to send the SIGTERM, so all you have to do is run the *kill* command with the process ID as an argument:

```
$ kill 2205
```

This command sends a SIGTERM signal to process number 2205. If the process is working properly, it catches the SIGTERM signal, cleans up and releases system resources and shuts down. If things go well, this should not take more than a few seconds, so check for the process again in say, five or ten seconds, and see if it has shut down.

If that does not do the job, send a slightly more urgent SIGINIT signal to the process. To do that, add the *-2* option to the *kill* command.

```
$ kill -2 2205
```

The SIGINIT signal still relies on the process you are signaling, catching the signal, cleaning up, then shutting down. This also should only take a couple of seconds at most, so if you check back and the process is still there, you will need to take stronger actions.

The last resort is to send the SIGKILL signal to the process. SIGKILL cannot be trapped by the process that is being signaled, but instead causes the process to die without performing any cleanup. To send the SIGKILL, use the *-9* option.

```
$ kill -9 2205
```

Since no cleanup is done, the *kill -9* happens almost immediately. Also, since a SIGKILL is not interpreted by the process, there may be system resources such as temp files, allocated memory, and network sockets still allocated by the now deceased process.

Performing a *kill -9* is equivalent to pulling the plug on the system without the benefit of a clean restart to clear memory and system resources. They should be avoided when possible, but will sometimes be the only way to kill a stubborn process.

The *kill* command, along with the *pkill* command that will be covered shortly, can only be used to signal processes owned by the current user. The one exception to this is that the root user has the ability to use these commands against any user's processes.

pgrep and pkill

The *pgrep* and *pkill* commands offer another way to search for and send signals to processes. *pgrep* allows searching for a command using a pattern of characters which are in the command executed or using the *-u* option in the same way it can be used with the *ps* command. The major difference with the *pgrep* command is it reports back only the process ID of processes found suppressing all other information.

```
$ pgrep lsnr

2079
```

Here, *pgrep* has been used to look for any process with the pattern *lsnr* in the command. *pgrep* returns the process ID which could then be used with the *kill* command, but *pkill* offers another option.

The *pkill* command uses the same method of matching processes as the *pgrep* command, but instead of returning the process ID, it automatically sends a signal to the matched process in the same way the *kill* process does. Just like the *kill* command, *pkill* sends a SIGTERM signal if no option is specified.

```
$ pkill lsnr
```

The *-2* and *-9* options for SIGINIT and SIGKILL, respectively, are also valid with *pkill* and have the same affect on processes matched.

 Great caution must be taken when using the *pkill* command! It is very easy to signal the wrong process and you will not be warned or given any feedback by *pkill*! For this reason, I recommend using the *ps* command to identify processes, then using the *kill* command with the appropriate process ID.

The Command Exit Status

Whenever a command is run in UNIX or Linux, it completes with a status of either success or failure. Often the indication of a failure is seen in the form of an error message to the screen. What is typically not seen is the command's exit status.

The exit status of the command is set as the shell variable *?*. If the command is successful, the *?* variable is set to 0. If the command fails, *?* is set to some other integer value.

The value of *?* can be viewed in the same way other shell variables are with the *echo* command.

```
$ ls

database_11g  Desktop  oradiag_oracle

$ echo $?

0
$ ls notes

ls: notes: No such file or directory

$ echo $?

2
```

Any non-zero value is considered some type of failure. While there is no strict set of values to indicate failure types, there is a list of common failure numbers and types in the file */usr/lib/syslinux/com32/include/errno.h*. Here is a partial listing of the *errno.h* file:

```
#define      EPERM         1      /* Operation not permitted */
#define      ENOENT        2      /* No such file or directory */
#define      ESRCH         3      /* No such process */
#define      EINTR         4      /* Interrupted system call */
#define      EIO           5      /* I/O error */
#define      ENXIO         6      /* No such device or address */
#define      E2BIG         7      /* Arg list too long */
#define      ENOEXEC       8      /* Exec format error */
#define      EBADF         9      /* Bad file number */
#define      ECHILD        10     /* No child processes */
#define      EAGAIN        11     /* Try again */
#define      ENOMEM        12     /* Out of memory */
#define      EACCES        13     /* Permission denied */
#define      EFAULT        14     /* Bad address */
#define      ENOTBLK       15     /* Block device required */
#define      EBUSY         16     /* Device or resource busy */
#define      EEXIST        17     /* File exists */
#define      EXDEV         18     /* Cross-device link */
#define      ENODEV        19     /* No such device */
#define      ENOTDIR       20     /* Not a directory */
#define      EISDIR        21     /* Is a directory */
#define      EINVAL        22     /* Invalid argument */
#define      ENFILE        23     /* File table overflow */
#define      EMFILE        24     /* Too many open files */
#define      ENOTTY        25     /* Not a typewriter */
#define      ETXTBSY       26     /* Text file busy */
#define      EFBIG         27     /* File too large */
#define      ENOSPC        28     /* No space left on device */
#define      ESPIPE        29     /* Illegal seek */
#define      EROFS         30     /* Read-only file system */
#define      EMLINK        31     /* Too many links */
#define      EPIPE         32     /* Broken pipe */
...
```

While there are many ways to indicate failure of a command, only an exit status of 0 indicates success. When setting up shell scripts, this is a useful way to determine the success of a command.

Conditional Execution of Processes

Sometimes executing more than one command may be desired, but make subsequent commands' execution conditional on the first command's success or failure. Two different tools, the double-ampersand (&&) and the double-pipe (||), allow for executing a second command based on the success of the first one.

When you want a command to be executed, then a second command to be executed only if the first one was successful, you can separate the commands with the && operation.

```
$ dbshut && exit
```

This set of commands runs the *dbshut* command and, if that command is successful, exits the current command line session. If the *dbshut* command fails, the *exit* command will not be run.

Similarly, separating two commands with || causes the first command to be run, then only if the first command fails, the second command will be run.

```
$ exp USERID=system/manager FULL=y FILE=export.dmp || mail
on@lifeaftercoffee.com -s 'export failure' < /dev/null
```

In this case, the *exp* command is run and, only if there is a failure, the *mail* command will be run. This is a good way to be notified of a process failure.

Much more sophisticated control is possible with shell scripting, but these two methods are sufficient for simple process control.

Timing Processes

Knowing the wall-clock time (the amount of real-world time elapsed) and the amount of processor time a command takes to run can help determine efficiencies and the most efficient way to execute a given command. The *time* command allows you to easily determine these statistics.

Putting the *time* command in front of another command causes the system to examine the amount of time elapsed while the command is running, the amount of time the command spent in user time and the amount of time the command spent in system time.

```
$ time dbstart

Processing Database instance "TEST": log file
/u01/app/oracle/product/11.1.0/db_1/startup.log

real 0m24.594s
user 0m1.004s
sys  0m4.806s
```

The *real* time indicates how much time elapsed between when the script started and when it finished. The real time can vary greatly for a task depending on what else is happening on the system.

The *user* and *sys* times indicate how much time was spent processing during this command. For most purposes, these numbers can be combined to show how much cpu time a process will take. If the combined *user* and *sys* times are lower, that generally indicates a more efficient execution.

Managing Services (Daemons)

Services, also know as daemons on Linux, are typically controlled through *init* scripts and the *chkconfig* command as described in Chapter 6. If you want to start or stop services on-the-fly, use the appropriate *init* script from the */etc/init.d* directory. However, since these services are just running processes, you can manipulate them in that way as well.

Examining Running Services

The *service* command can be used to check the status of configured services using the *--status-all* option. The *service* command should be run as root.

```
# service --status-all

acpid (pid 2320) is running...
anacron is stopped
atd (pid 2528) is running...
auditd (pid 1946) is running...
automount (pid 2295) is running...
...
xfs (pid 2497) is running...
xinetd (pid 2394) is running...
ypbind is stopped
```

```
yum-updatesd (pid 2609) is running...
```

The *service* command produces a lot of output, so it may be best to use *grep* to reduce the output, just like with the *ps* command.

Stopping Running Services

Since these services are just processes running in the background, they can also be seen using the *ps* command. In the following output, the ssh daemon (*/usr/sbin/sshd*) and other ssh processes can be seen in the *ps* output.

```
# ps -ef | grep sshd
root      2361     1  0 06:47 ?        00:00:00 /usr/sbin/sshd
root      2897  2361  0 07:14 ?        00:00:00 sshd: oracle [priv]
oracle    2899  2897  0 07:14 ?        00:00:01 sshd: oracle@pts/1
root     11869  2361  0 11:36 ?        00:00:00 sshd: oracle [priv]
oracle   11871 11869  0 11:36 ?        00:00:00 sshd: oracle@pts/0
root     13236 12564  0 12:18 pts/1    00:00:00 grep sshd
```

 Though any user can see the processes for services, typically only root will be able to manipulate or kill these processes.

While it is best to use the *init* scripts to stop services, it may sometimes be necessary to use the *kill* command as described earlier for other processes.

Forcing a Service to Reread Its Configuration

The *kill* command can also be used to send a request to tell a service to reread its configuration file without restarting. Typically, this is done with the *-sighup* option.

```
# kill -sighup 2361
```

The ability to reread a configuration file with *kill -sighup* is dependent on the specific service. Check the service's man page to confirm that this will not interrupt the service.

Conclusion

Everything that happens on the system is dependent on the processes running on it. Though simple, many of the tools described in this chapter are ones that will end up being used daily to monitor and manage processes.

The next chapter will examine managing the installed software with attention given to the RPM Package Manager.

Managing Linux Software

As DBAs, we frequently need to add or update software on our Linux servers to meet the requirements of Oracle, third party software, and developers.

Linux provides several ways to manage your software, from the fairly automatic RPM Package Manager to the more manual process of compiling software from source code. Which method you use typically depends on how the software you need to install is distributed.

The RPM Package Manager

Formerly known as the Red Hat Package Manager, the RPM Package Manager (RPM) is used to install and manage software distributed in RPM packages. This is the most common way Linux software is distributed, so it is important to become familiar with the RPM.

 The abbreviation RPM can be used to refer to the RPM Package Manager or a file containing software in the RPM format. When referring to software, typically the name of the software is mentioned as well, like 'the RPM for the GCC compiler'.

The RPM Package Manager maintains an inventory of software it has installed on the system. The inventory does not include software installed by other means.

The main command for the RPM Package Manager is *rpm*. The *rpm* command can query the inventory and install, modify or delete software depending on the options and arguments given. Any user can query the RPM inventory, but modifications are typically done by root.

Examining What is Currently Installed

By calling *rpm* with the *-q* option, the database of software installed via RPM can be queried. There are several options that can be used with *-q* to specify what to query. Here are some of the most useful ones.

```
# rpm -qa

busybox-1.2.0-4.el5
cracklib-dicts-2.8.9-3.3
rmt-0.4b41-2.fc6
dump-0.4b41-2.fc6
words-3.0-9.1
gnome-audio-2.0.0-3.1.1
glibc-2.5-34
...
```

The *-qa* options generate a complete list of the software currently installed through RPM. This can be used to get a snapshot of what packages are installed at a certain time. This output can also be used in conjunction with the *sort* and *diff* commands to compare multiple systems.

The output from *rpm -qa* is usually quite long. If you want to look for a specific package, use *-q* and the package name.

```
$ rpm -q gcc

gcc-4.1.2-44.el5
```

This gives more succinct output about the specific package. However, if you are not sure of the exact package name, use a wildcard to fill in the blanks. The *-a* option must be used when using a wildcard.

```
# rpm -qa gcc*

gcc-4.1.2-44.el5
gcc-c++-4.1.2-44.el5
```
Now information about packages starting with *gcc* can be seen. Wildcards can be used to fill in missing characters in the middle of a package name as well.

```
# rpm -qa g*c

glibc-2.5-34
gcc-4.1.2-44.el5
gjdoc-0.7.7-12.el5
```

By default, *rpm* prints the name of the software, its version and its release number separated by dashes. This format can be confusing for packages whose names contain numbers. For this reason, or to display additional data, the output format can be altered using the *--queryformat* option.

```
# rpm -qa --queryformat '%{NAME}\t%{VERSION}\n'

busybox      1.2.0
cracklib-dicts      2.8.9
rmt  0.4b41
dump 0.4b41
words        3.0
gnome-audio 2.0.0
glibc        2.5
...
```

The output format is specified in single-quotes following the *--queryformat* option. This example inserts a tab character, indicated by the \t, between the name and version and a newline, indicated by \n at the end of each entry. If the newline was not included, all the packages would be printed on a single line.

Additional text can be included in the *rpm* output as in this example:

```
# rpm -qa --queryformat '%{NAME}\t%{VERSION}\t%{RELEASE} installed on

%{INSTALLTIME:date}\n'
busybox        1.2.0      4.el5 installed on Mon 18 May 2009 01:30:31 PM EDT
cracklib-dicts 2.8.9      3.3 installed on Mon 18 May 2009 01:30:54 PM EDT
rmt    0.4b41  2.fc6 installed on Mon 18 May 2009 01:30:56 PM EDT
dump   0.4b41  2.fc6 installed on Mon 18 May 2009 01:30:56 PM EDT
words 3.0      9.1 installed on Mon 18 May 2009 01:31:01 PM EDT
gnome-audio    2.0.0      3.1.1 installed on Mon 18 May 2009 01:31:01 PM EDT
glibc 2.5      34 installed on Mon 18 May 2009 01:31:03 PM EDT
...
```

A full list of fields that can be queried for using *rpm* is available by running *rpm* with the *-querytags* option, but it is quite a long list. For most purposes, you should only be interested in the *NAME, VERSION, RELEASE* and *INSTALLTIME:date* tags. To be sure you are looking at exactly the right software package, it is important to consider both the *VERSION* and *RELEASE* tags.

Installing and Updating Software with RPM

The first step to installing an RPM is to acquire one. A lot of common software is included in the Server subdirectory on the Linux install disks.

Other software may be available online from your Linux vendor, from the folks who make the software or from a download site.

RPM packages are distributed as files with names in the format of *software_name-version-release.platform.rpm.* When looking for RPM software packages, it is important that the name, version and release match specified requirements and the platform is correct. The platform should match the output of the command *uname -i.*

Once a package that needs to be installed is acquired, it can be added using the *-i* option for *rpm.* It is additionally common to add the *h* option to provide a hash to indicate progress and the *v* option to give verbose output. Position yourself in the directory that the RPM file is in, execute *rpm -ihv* and give the file name.

rpm -ihv zsh-4.2.6-1.0.1.i386.rpm

```
Preparing...                ########################################### [100%]
   1:zsh                     ########################################### [100%]
```

If the RPM has no dependencies, the software is now installed and ready to use, but often RPM packages are dependent on other RPM packages and display an error if those packages are not already installed. In these cases, track down the dependency before installing this software.

Under some circumstances, two RPM packages can be codependent on one another and need to be installed at the same time. To do that, it is necessary to name both RPM files to be installed in the same command.

```
# rpm -ihv elfutils-libelf-devel-0.137-3.el5.i386.rpm elfutils-libelf-devel-static-0.137-
3.el5.i386.rpm

warning: elfutils-libelf-devel-0.137-3.el5.i386.rpm: Header V3 DSA signature: NOKEY, key ID 1e5e0159
Preparing...                ########################################### [100%]
   1:elfutils-libelf-devel-s########################################### [ 50%]
   2:elfutils-libelf-devel  ########################################### [100%]
```

Both packages are now installed. Dependencies like these are common and can typically be resolved with a little experimentation. If you are trying to update software already installed on the system, use the *U* option instead of *i.* The procedure is exactly the same.

Removing Software with the RPM

To remove software installed using RPM, use the *-e* option. Only the software name needs to be given and no feedback is displayed on screen.

```
# rpm -e zsh
```

The software that has been removed can be confirmed by querying the RPM database.

```
# rpm -q zsh

package zsh is not installed
```

If the software to be removed is needed by other software, *rpm* reports an error such as the following:

```
# rpm -e elfutils-libelf-devel

error: Failed dependencies:
    elfutils-libelf-devel-i386 = 0.137-3.el5 is needed by (installed) elfutils-libelf-devel-static-
0.137-3.el5.i386
```

Like with installation, either remove the dependent software first or remove codependencies together.

Using Update Tools like Yum

Managing RPMs can become cumbersome, especially when managing large numbers of servers. Several update tools are available to help automatically download and update RPM packages more automatically, including satisfying dependencies.

One popular update manager is the Yellowdog Updater Modified (Yum). Yum uses an update repository to look up the latest version of RPM packages and automatically download and update them if necessary. A Yum update repository may be available from your Linux vendor or you can create one yourself.

Configuring Yum and setting up a repository are beyond the scope of this book. Depending on your Linux vendor and license, Yum may already be configured when you register your installation. The following examples of

---

using Yum should give an idea of how it can be used to simplify package management.

Yum can be used to examine installed packages without being configured. The output is somewhat different from the default output of *rpm*. The software name is listed followed by the platform. Version and release information show up in the middle column, then a status indication is given.

```
# yum list installed

Loaded plugins: security
Installed Packages
GConf2.i386                    2.14.0-9.el5          installed
ImageMagick.i386               6.2.8.0-4.el5_1.1     installed
MAKEDEV.i386                   3.23-1.2              installed
NetworkManager.i386            1:0.7.0-3.el5         installed
...
```

Once configured, running *yum update* will cause Yum to automatically update all installed RPMs to the latest version available. The *-y* option can be added to automatically answer Yes to any prompts that come up.

```
# yum -y update
```

 While it is very convenient to be able to do a mass-update with tools like Yum, great care must be taken. An update to a dependency may have unexpected results! Always work on a test system first.

If only specific software needs to be updated, give its name as an argument.

```
# yum update gzip.i386
```

Yum can be used to install an RPM package and will automatically install any required dependencies. The software name and platform are given as a parameter.

```
# yum install firefox.i386
```

Yum can also remove software. The syntax is similar to that used to install.

```
# yum remove firefox.i386
```

Yum both simplifies the syntax and streamlines the installation of RPM packages. If your Linux vendor provides a repository, I highly recommend using it. Creating your own repository probably is not worth it for a small number of systems, but if you have many systems to manage, it may be worth it.

Compiling Software from Source Code

RPM packages are very convenient, simplifying installation into a single command, but not all software is available in RPM packages. Some software is only available as source code that must be downloaded and compiled on the system. It may also be found that though an RPM may be available for a software package, it needs to be compiled it from source code in order to integrate certain customizations for a given purpose.

Most source code comes with directions on how to compile and install it. As with packages, there are prerequisites that need to be installed before software can be compiled. Though the steps will vary, the overall steps are typically as follows:

1. Download and unpack the source code on the server.

2. Configure the software. This may include editing configuration files and/or tuning a *configure* script.

3. Compile the software.

4. Test the software, optional in most installs.

5. Install the compiled software.

One common example is compiling the Apache HTTP server. Source can be downloaded from apache.org, and while RPM packages are available for Apache, it is often necessary to compile it from source in order to customize it.

The source is typically downloaded using a web browser. Once downloaded, it has been moved to */u03/httpd* and unpacked. The actual install location is specified as part of the configuration step and the software could be configured and compiled in any directory.

```
# mv ~/Desktop/httpd-2.2.14.tar.gz  ./
# gunzip httpd-2.2.14.tar.gz
```

```
# tar xf httpd-2.2.14.tar
# cd httpd-2.2.14
```

A text file called *INSTALL* in the extracted directory provides installation
instructions. In this case, the configuration step is simple. A *configure* script is
run with an argument that specifies the location where Apache should be
installed.

```
# ./configure --prefix=/u03/httpd

checking for chosen layout... Apache
checking for working mkdir -p... yes
checking build system type... i686-pc-linux-gnu
checking host system type... i686-pc-linux-gnu
checking target system type... i686-pc-linux-gnu

Configuring Apache Portable Runtime library ...
checking for APR... reconfig
configuring package in srclib/apr now
checking build system type... i686-pc-linux-gnu
checking host system type... i686-pc-linux-gnu
checking target system type... i686-pc-linux-gnu
...
```

As part of the configuration step, prerequisites are checked and information is
gathered about the system. If any prerequisites are not found, the *configure*
script exits with an error. The next step is to compile the source code.

```
# make

Making all in srclib
make[1]: Entering directory `/u03/httpd/httpd-2.2.14/srclib'
Making all in apr
make[2]: Entering directory `/u03/httpd/httpd-2.2.14/srclib/apr'
make[3]: Entering directory `/u03/httpd/httpd-2.2.14/srclib/apr'
/bin/sh /u03/httpd/httpd-2.2.14/srclib/apr/libtool --silent --mode=compile gcc -g -O2 -pthread   -
DHAVE_CONFIG_H -DLINUX=2 -D_REENTRANT -D_GNU_SOURCE -D_LARGEFILE64_SOURCE   -I./include -
I/u03/httpd/httpd-2.2.14/srclib/apr/include/arch/unix -I./include/arch/unix -I/u03/httpd/httpd-
...
```

Some of the output during the compile and install steps may appear to be
errors. An error generally stops the compile process, but the output should be
examined to confirm there were no problems. Finally, the install step moves
the compiled software into its final location.

```
# make install

Making install in srclib
make[1]: Entering directory `/u03/httpd/httpd-2.2.14/srclib'
Making install in apr
make[2]: Entering directory `/u03/httpd/httpd-2.2.14/srclib/apr'
make[3]: Entering directory `/u03/httpd/httpd-2.2.14/srclib/apr'
make[3]: Nothing to be done for `local-all'.
```

```
make[3]: Leaving directory `/u03/httpd/httpd-2.2.14/srclib/apr'
...
```

The software is now in place and ready to test. Note that just because software does not give an error during compilation or installation does not mean it will work as expected. Always test software before releasing it for general use.

Any software received as source code should include installation instructions. Read them. They can vary greatly between different programs and even between different versions of a program.

Conclusion

Software management is a big part of Linux system administration. Some installations and updates have to be done just to install Oracle. Using the RPM Package Manager simplifies software management, and an update manager like Yum can simplify it even further. Sometimes software needs to be compiled manually when RPM packages are not available or the software must be customized during installation.

Chapter 12 deals with file systems and goes into detail regarding working with file systems, storage, viewing and creating them and using Logical Volume Manager (LVM).

Managing Disks and File Systems

As the name suggests, the primary role of file systems in Linux is to hold files. File systems allow you to represent the location of files in different paths using directories.

Linux, like UNIX, uses file systems to represent other objects that the system needs to operate. Processes, I/O devices and storage devices are typically represented on file systems so the system can take advantage of the input, output, and permission mechanisms offered to files.

The next chapter will go into more depth on files and directories. For now, look at the file systems that hold them.

> In many places, the term file system can be found written as filesystem. These two terms are synonymous.

File Systems, Disk Devices and Mount Points

While file systems are often equated to disks, it is important that a distinction is made between the two. A disk is a piece of hardware that is capable of storing data. A file system is a set of methods to access and organize storage. File systems are comprised of some amount of storage from a disk or disks, a logical method to name, organize and secure its contents, and a set of system calls to allow programs, including the operating system, to interact with it.

Disks and Partitions

As mentioned previously, a disk is a physical storage device. Under most circumstances, it cannot be used directly by a user or program; instead, you

---

must use the methods provided by a file system. A disk can be, and often is, divided into partitions. Each partition can then be assigned a different purpose. With the large size of modern disks, this is often the case.

Disk partitions are displayed in the first column of output from the *df* command, as shown below.

```
$ df -h /boot

Filesystem          Size  Used Avail Use% Mounted on
/dev/hda1           99M   12M   83M  13% /boot
```

This entry shows the file representing partition 1 on the first hard drive (hda). Depending on the hardware configuration, hard disks may also appear as sda, sdb, and such or with a higher letter designation, i.e. hde or higher.

Each disk has a partition table which tracks what partitions have been created on it, their type, and where on the disk they start and end. On new disks, the partition table needs to be created before any partitions can be made.

On x86 hardware, you are limited to four primary partitions. Only these four primary partitions are recognized natively by the hardware, but one primary partition can be subdivided into logical partitions. In a modern Linux system there are few differences between primary and logical partitions, but it is highly recommended that the boot partition (*/boot*) be on a primary partition. This will simplify recovery if there is a problem with the disk.

File Systems

When you hear about a file system, it typically refers to an amount of storage, meaning one or more partitions from a storage device, and the methods used to access and organize that storage. An example is the */u01* file system. While this may sometimes be referred to as a partition or even a disk, it is important to remember that a file system like this may actually be made up of several partitions on multiple disks.

Linux supports several different types of file systems. Some of them are specialized while others are nearly interchangeable. Here are a few of the most common file system types that can be seen:

File System Type	Description
ext2	A high-speed, general purpose file system. Generally faster than ext3, but lacks journaling.
ext3	A successor to ext2 which includes journaling
proc, sysfs	Virtual file systems used to interface with the kernel
tmpfs	This file system allows access to memory

Table 12.1: *Common File System Types*

When preparing file systems for general use, use ext3 unless there is some compelling reason to use a different file system type. While ext2 is also acceptable, the addition of journaling, covered next in this chapter, makes ext3 the better choice. The other types mentioned above are generally managed by the system but are included here as they show up in file system listings.

Journaling

File systems which support journaling track changes that are made to the file system in a journal, a small log in a dedicated space on the file system. If the system goes down unexpectedly, say due to a crash, power failure or other unexpected event, the journal is used to determine what changes may have been in process when the system went down. Changes can then be re-applied if necessary.

Since journaling involves the extra step of writing changes to the journal before the change is made, journaling file systems have slightly lower performance than their non-journaling counterparts. In most circumstances the performance impact is minimal compared to the advantages of journaling, so ext3 is typically chosen over ext2.

File System Blocksize

When a file system is created, it is assigned a blocksize, typically 4096 bytes for ext3 file systems. The operating system then reads and writes one or more blocks at a time.

Whenever a file is created on the file system, enough blocks are allocated to hold the file. Since all blocks must be the same size, there is almost always some empty space in the final block for a given file. For example, if a file of exactly 10,000 bytes on a file system is written with the default 4096-byte blocksize, two blocks are filled to capacity. Then the final block contains the last 1,808 bytes of the file and 2,288 bytes remain unused.

As a very general rule of thumb, a large blocksize is more efficient for reading and writing large files and a small blocksize is more efficient for small files. The default ext3 blocksize of 4096 bytes is also the maximum allowed on RHEL 5 and OEL 5. It is appropriate for most Oracle databases. If there is strong justification for a different blocksize, a good alternative may be to use Oracle Clustered File System (OCFS) which replaces the traditional operating system's file system.

Inodes and Files

Each file on a file system is associated with an inode. The inode is kept on the same file system as the file it is associated with and contains information such as the file's last modification time, the last time it was accessed and the file's permissions. When a file system is created, a number of inodes are created to handle files on that file system. Since each file on the file system uses one inode, this limits the total number of files that can be on a file system.

The default is somewhere in the range of 130,000 inodes per gigabyte. While this is sufficient for nearly all purposes, some applications that create a large number of small files may exceed this limit. The only way to change the number of inodes available is to recreate the file system, which will erase its contents.

Later in this chapter the file system creation step will be seen where the number of inodes can be specified. The next chapter will examine how inode information can be viewed or manipulated.

What About Swap?

Linux allocates space on disk called swap that is to be used as memory. Swap may be referred to as a file system, but since it is accessed and organized directly by the kernel, it does not need the structure and rules of a file system. For more information on managing swap, see Chapter 14 on memory and system management.

Logical Volume Manager

Recent versions of Linux have adopted the Logical Volume Manager (LVM) as a method to offer more flexibility in how disk storage is made available to the operating system. LVM is a form of storage virtualization where disk partitions can be combined in several different ways, and then the space from those disks can be presented to the operating system for use. This level of abstraction allows maximum flexibility in the physical layout of the disks while still presenting the operating system with what appears to be traditional partitions.

When LVM partitions are made available to the operating system, they appear under a slightly different path than other disk partitions.

```
$ df -h /u01

Filesystem            Size  Used Avail Use% Mounted on
/dev/mapper/VolGroup00-LogVol02
                      4.0G  3.5G  291M  93% /u01
```

The device name makes it clear that this is a logical volume. The LVM program (there is a GUI and a command line version) is needed to determine where the storage for this device actually resides.

LVM has advantages and disadvantages and depending on your needs and your storage hardware, you may have alternatives to LVM, or you may even use LVM in conjunction with other disk virtualization solutions. There is a section later in this chapter with more detail about LVM.

Mount Points

A mount point represents a location on the system where a file system can be made available. The root file system is mounted at the location /, referred to as slash, and forms the base for all other files, directories and mount points. Other file systems can be mounted at any location on the system where a directory exists.

Unlike Microsoft Windows, which requires file systems to be mounted with specific names, i.e. A:, B:, C:, D:, and such, Linux offers considerably more flexibility in mount points. It is possible to mount a file system under */u01/app/oracle/product* just to hold Oracle software, or as */u03/backup* to store backups. File systems can be mounted below slash or under another file system.

Complex layouts of file systems and mount points can make a system difficult to manage. On the other hand, overly simplistic file system layouts like putting nearly everything under one big root partition can cause performance and reliability issues. Common practice is to keep Oracle software on file systems with a naming scheme like /u01, /u02, /u03, and such. Serious consideration should be given before departing from this convention.

The *fstab* File

When the Linux system starts up, file systems listed in the /etc/fstab file are automatically mounted and made available to the system. Like most configuration files found in Linux, the *fstab* file is plain text and can be viewed or edited with vi or another text editor.

```
/dev/VolGroup00/LogVol00 /                    ext3    defaults        1 1
LABEL=/boot              /boot                ext3    defaults        1 2
tmpfs                    /dev/shm             tmpfs   defaults        0 0
devpts                   /dev/pts             devpts  gid=5,mode=620  0 0
sysfs                    /sys                 sysfs   defaults        0 0
proc                     /proc                proc    defaults        0 0
/dev/VolGroup00/LogVol01 swap                 swap    defaults        0 0
/dev/VolGroup00/LogVol02         /u01         ext3    defaults        1 2
/dev/VolGroup00/LogVol03         /u02         ext3    defaults        1 2
/dev/VolGroup00/LogVol04         /u03         ext3    defaults        1 2
```

Each line in the *fstab* file represents a file system which is mounted during booting. Comments can be added by starting a line with a pound symbol (#). Each line is made up of six fields which can be separated by spaces or tabs. The fields, in order, represent the following:

1. The device to be mounted. Typically in the /dev directory for local drives. May also be in the format of *hostname:/path/to/* directory for remote NFS mounts.

2. The directory where this device should be mounted. The directory must exist for the mount to work successfully.

3. The type of file system to mount

4. Mount options which should be used with this device or defaults to use default options

5. Controls the behavior of the *dump* command in backing up this file system

6. Controls when file systems should be checked by *fsck*. 1 indicates that the file system should be checked in the first pass, 2 indicates that it should be checked in the second pass and 0 indicates that this file system does not need to be checked.

Editing the *fstab* file will be covered later in this chapter. The *fstab* file indicates which devices are mounted at startup, but does not necessarily reflect what is currently available.

Viewing Current File System Information

Since the file system is at the core of the Linux system, there are many things you may want to investigate about it, and many ways to look at them. Here are some of the fundamental ways to investigate what file systems are available and what is their current status. File systems generally need to be mounted and unmounted as root, but other users are able to check the status of mounted file systems.

Viewing Mounted File Systems with the *mount* Command

The *mount* command can be used without any options or arguments to see what file systems are currently mounted.

```
# mount

/dev/mapper/VolGroup00-LogVol00 on / type ext3 (rw)
proc on /proc type proc (rw)
sysfs on /sys type sysfs (rw)
devpts on /dev/pts type devpts (rw,gid=5,mode=620)
/dev/hda1 on /boot type ext3 (rw)
tmpfs on /dev/shm type tmpfs (rw)
/dev/mapper/VolGroup00-LogVol02 on /u01 type ext3 (rw)
/dev/mapper/VolGroup00-LogVol03 on /u02 type ext3 (rw)
/dev/mapper/VolGroup00-LogVol04 on /u03 type ext3 (rw)
none on /proc/sys/fs/binfmt_misc type binfmt_misc (rw)
sunrpc on /var/lib/nfs/rpc_pipefs type rpc_pipefs (rw)
```

The output includes the device mounted, the mount point, the type and the options. In this output, *rw* is usually seen indicating that the device is mounted and available for read and write. Also, *ro* may be seen indicating that it is read only.

Viewing File System Space and Inode Usage

The *df* command allows you to investigate the space usage on file systems in several different ways. Without any options, *df* is the disk usage in 1k blocks for all file systems currently mounted.

```
# df
```

```
Filesystem            1K-blocks      Used Available Use% Mounted on
/dev/mapper/VolGroup00-LogVol00
                        9014656   7606072    943280  89% /
/dev/hda1                101086     11871     83996  13% /boot
tmpfs                    517620         0    517620   0% /dev/shm
/dev/mapper/VolGroup00-LogVol02
                        4128448   3621320    297416  93% /u01
/dev/mapper/VolGroup00-LogVol03
                        3096336   1687792   1251260  58% /u02
/dev/mapper/VolGroup00-LogVol04
                        2031952    147632   1781104   8% /u03
```

The output includes the device mounted, the total amount of space, space used, space free, and a percentage of space currently used. The directory that the device is mounted on is listed last.

To make this information easier to interpret, add the *-h* (human readable) option that instead uses K, M and G in the output to indicate kilobytes, megabytes and gigabytes.

```
# df -h
```

```
Filesystem            Size  Used Avail Use% Mounted on
/dev/mapper/VolGroup00-LogVol00
                      8.6G  7.3G  922M  89% /
/dev/hda1              99M   12M   83M  13% /boot
tmpfs                 506M     0  506M   0% /dev/shm
/dev/mapper/VolGroup00-LogVol02
                      4.0G  3.5G  291M  93% /u01
/dev/mapper/VolGroup00-LogVol03
                      3.0G  1.7G  1.2G  58% /u02
/dev/mapper/VolGroup00-LogVol04
                      2.0G  145M  1.7G   8% /u03
```

To get information on only a specific file system, specify the mount point as an option.

```
# df -h /u01
```

```
Filesystem            Size  Used Avail Use% Mounted on
/dev/mapper/VolGroup00-LogVol02
```

```
                    4.0G  3.5G  291M  93%  /u01
```

This will also work on any sub-directory on the mount point. A sub-directory can be specified or even the current directory '.' used to check for space.

```
# df -h /u01/app

Filesystem              Size  Used Avail Use% Mounted on
/dev/mapper/VolGroup00-LogVol02
                        4.0G  3.5G  291M  93%  /u01

# pwd

/root

# df -h ./

Filesystem              Size  Used Avail Use% Mounted on
/dev/mapper/VolGroup00-LogVol00
                        8.6G  7.3G  922M  89%  /
```

The *df* command can also be used with the *-i* option to examine inode usage.

```
# df -i /u01

Filesystem              Inodes    IUsed   IFree IUse% Mounted on
/dev/mapper/VolGroup00-LogVol02
                        524288    42686  481602    9%  /u01
```

As with space usage, *df* reports total inodes, inodes used, inodes free, and a percentage used for a file system. If inode usage hits 100%, no more new files are able to be created. The symptoms seem just like a full disk, but *df -h* shows space available.

Checking the File System Blocksize

The *stat* command can be used to check the file system blocksize. *stat* can be used on a file system's mount point or any file or directory within that file system.

```
# stat -f /u01

  File: "/u01"
    ID: 0         Namelen: 255      Type: ext2/ext3
Blocksize: 4096        Fundamental blocksize: 4096
Blocks: Total: 1032112    Free: 126782      Available: 74354
Inodes: Total: 524288     Free: 481602
```

220   Linux for the Oracle DBA

Both blocksize and fundamental blocksize should be equal in this output, but for accuracy, blocksize should be used. Like the inode count, blocksize cannot be changed after a file system is created.

Viewing What Files Are in Use

Before unmounting a file system or changing files, it can be useful to first check who is using those files. The *lsof* command allows you to do exactly that. The *lsof* command can be used on a file system, an individual file, or on multiple files using a wildcard.

```
# lsof /u01

COMMAND  PID  USER    FD   TYPE DEVICE    SIZE   NODE NAME
lsnrctl 6253 oracle  txt   REG  253,2   105943 345127 /u01/app/oracle/product/11.1.0/db_1/bin/lsnrctl
lsnrctl 6253 oracle  mem   REG  253,2    45632 247219 /u01/app/oracle/product/11.1.0/db_1/lib/libnque11.so
lsnrctl 6253 oracle  mem   REG  253,2  5839373 247220 /u01/app/oracle/product/11.1.0/db_1/lib/libnnz11.so
lsnrctl 6253 oracle  mem   REG  253,2 35201555 429542 /u01/app/oracle/product/11.1.0/db_1/lib/libclntsh.so.11.1
lsnrctl 6253 oracle   3r   REG  253,2    38400 311373 /u01/app/oracle/product/11.1.0/db_1/rdbms/mesg/diaus.msb

# lsof /u01/app/oracle/product/11.1.0/db_1/rdbms/mesg/diaus.msb

COMMAND PID  USER    FD   TYPE DEVICE SIZE    NODE NAME
tnslsnr 2859 oracle   3r   REG  253,2 38400 311373 /u01/app/oracle/product/11.1.0/db_1/rdbms/mesg/diaus.msb

# lsof /u01/app/oracle/product/11.1.0/db_1/bin/*

COMMAND PID  USER FD   TYPE DEVICE  SIZE    NODE NAME
tnslsnr 2859 oracle txt   REG  253,2 826754 345126 /u01/app/oracle/product/11.1.0/db_1/bin/tnslsnr
```

The output includes the command and process ID that has the file open, the user who the process belongs to, some additional information about the file and finally, the full path to the file in question. Using this information, it is easy to tell who is using what files right at the moment. When unmounting file systems, it is best to check them with *lsof* first to make sure nothing on the file system is in use.

Like most other commands that have been mentioned, the *lsof* command can be run by any user on the system. However, it is located in */usr/sbin*, so it is not typically in the binary search path for users other than root. If users other than root want to use *lsof*, they can either use its full path (*/usr/sbin/lsof*) or add */usr/sbin* to the *PATH* variable.

Creating a New File System

These steps cover how to create a new file system on a Linux system which is using disks directly rather than some kind of storage virtualization. Though the Logical Volume Manager may be used to handle several of these steps, a

---

good understanding of them helps in comprehending what the storage virtualization software is doing for you.

> 💣 There are several steps in creating a new file system where you could unexpectedly erase a disk! It is a good idea to back up critical data and configuration files before attempting to create a file system.

The basic steps for creating a new file system are as follows. These steps must be performed by the root user.

1. Add disk to the system if free space is not available on the current disks.

2. Identify and partition the space to be used.

3. Build the file system.

4. Mount the file system for use.

5. Consult your hardware documentation if you need to add a disk to your system. Each system is different and any details on adding disks should be included in the documentation.

New disks appear in the */dev* directory after startup. They typically have a name starting with *hd* or *sd* followed by another letter, but disks may appear under different names depending on the hardware configuration. In the following example, the disk I added appears as */dev/hdd*.

Identifying and Partitioning Space to be Used

Whether adding a new disk or using space on an existing disk, a partition now needs to be created on the disk to identify what space on the disk should be used. A disk can be partitioned into a single partition or several partitions can be made on that disk. GNU *parted* can be used to create the necessary partitions, but some users prefer to use *fdisk*. While *fdisk* offers some advanced options that *parted* does not, *parted* is easier to use and sufficient for most purposes.

Any of these steps may result in lost data if performed on a disk with existing partitions. A backup of essential data and configuration files should be taken before proceeding.

The *parted* utility expects an argument to be provided to identify the device to be partitioned. In this case, I started *parted* to modify */dev/hdd*:

```
# parted /dev/hdd

GNU Parted 1.8.1
Using /dev/hdd
Welcome to GNU Parted! Type 'help' to view a list of commands.
(parted)
```

At any time, enter *help* at the *parted* prompt for a list of commands with short descriptions. Now you can use the *print* command to show the current partition table, also referred to as a disklabel, before you make any modifications to it.

```
(parted) print

Error: Unable to open /dev/hdd - unrecognised disk label.
```

Since this is a new disk, there is no partition table to read, so an error appears. To create a label on this device, use the *mklabel* command. There are several label types available, but for most purposes, *msdos* is more appropriate.

```
(parted) mklabel msdos
(parted) print

Model: VBOX HARDDISK (ide)
Disk /dev/hdd: 10.7GB
Sector size (logical/physical): 512B/512B
Partition Table: msdos

Number  Start  End  Size  Type  File system  Flags
```

The newly created partition table can now be printed without error. The column headers are shown here, but since no partitions have been created, no rows are shown. One thing that can be done at this point is show unused space by typing *print free* at the *parted* prompt.

```
(parted) print free

Model: VBOX HARDDISK (ide)
Disk /dev/hdd: 10.7GB
Sector size (logical/physical): 512B/512B
```

```
Partition Table: msdos

Number  Start    End      Size     Type  File system  Flags
        0.00kB   10.7GB   10.7GB          Free Space
```

The free space is shown under the *Size* column. The free space should be close to the size of the disk added, but is rarely exactly the same. The *Start* and *End* columns represent where that contiguous space begins and ends on the disk.

When you create partitions, you are prompted to enter start and end values in megabytes, but the default output of the *print* command adjusts to use gigabytes and terabytes on large disks. You can change the display units to megabytes to make the print output consistent with what you need to enter.

```
(parted) unit mb
(parted) print free

Model: VBOX HARDDISK (ide)
Disk /dev/hdd: 10737MB
Sector size (logical/physical): 512B/512B
Partition Table: msdos

Number  Start    End       Size      Type  File system  Flags
        0.00MB   10737MB   10737MB          Free Space
```

Now that an idea of how much space is available on the disk has been illustrated, create a new partition using the *mkpart* command. After entering the *mkpart* command, you are prompted to enter some information about the kind and size of the partition you want to create.

```
(parted) mkpart
Partition type?  primary/extended? primary
File system type?  [ext2]? ext3
Start? 0
End? 5000
```

These values can also be entered as arguments to the *mkpart* command. The following command would do exactly the same as above.

```
(parted) mkpart primary ext3 0 5000
```

The first question is if this partition should be primary or extended. Only four primary partitions can be created on each disk. A larger number of extended partitions can be created, but one primary partition number is used to create the additional extended partitions.

Linux for the Oracle DBA

Next, you are prompted to enter the file system type. Typically, you will want to use ext3 unless you have some specific reason to use another file system type. Finally, the start and end values are entered to indicate where on the disk the new partition should start and end. These values are entered in megabytes. The partition cannot overlap any other partitions.

The *print* command can now be used to show the partition table contents. The free option is used to also show free space available.

```
(parted) print free

Model: VBOX HARDDISK (ide)
Disk /dev/hdd: 10.7GB
Sector size (logical/physical): 512B/512B
Partition Table: msdos

Number  Start    End      Size     Type     File system  Flags
1       0.03MB   5001MB   5001MB   primary
        5001MB   10734MB  5733MB                Free Space
```

When adding additional partitions, care needs to be taken not to overlap existing ones. Taking the example you have so far, you would not want to start a new partition lower than 5001. *parted* is smart enough, however, to give a warning if you request space already allocated to a different partition.

The start and end locations need to be entered for the new partition. If a partition to use the remaining space needs to be created, give the same start and end values currently listed as free space.

```
(parted) mkpart primary ext3 5001 10734
(parted) print free

Model: VBOX HARDDISK (ide)
Disk /dev/hdd: 10737MB
Sector size (logical/physical): 512B/512B
Partition Table: msdos

Number  Start    End      Size     Type     File system  Flags
1       0.03MB   5001MB   5001MB   primary
2       5001MB   10734MB  5733MB   primary

(parted) quit
```

Information: Don't forget to update /etc/fstab, if necessary.

Now that you have used up all free space on this disk, you no longer see an entry for free space. Changes made in *parted* are automatically written to the partition table, so you can simply type *exit* when you are done. *parted* prints a

---

Creating a New File System   **225**

reminder to update the *etc/fstab* file if necessary but before you do that, you need to build the file system on the partition.

After the partitions are created, they automatically show up in */dev* with the drive name (*hdd* in this case) appended with the partition number.

```
# ls /dev/hdd*
```

```
/dev/hdd   /dev/hdd1   /dev/hdd2
```

These device names will be used in the upcoming steps to create the file systems and mount them for use.

Building the File System

Building a file system prepares the given partition for use by the system. Use the *mkfs* command to create the file system. The commands *mke2fs* and *mkfs.ext3* could also be used to create the file systems with the same results.

 Creating a new file system destroys anything previously contained on the given partition. Make sure you have the correct device name and that there is no data needed from the partition before creating a file system.

Use the *-t* option for *mkfs* to specify the file system type and then provide the device name for the appropriate disk and partition.

```
# mkfs -t ext3 /dev/hdd1
```

```
mke2fs 1.39 (29-May-2006)
Filesystem label=
OS type: Linux
Blocksize=4096 (log=2)
Fragment size=4096 (log=2)
611648 inodes, 1220932 blocks
61046 blocks (5.00%) reserved for the super user
First data block=0
Maximum filesystem blocks=1254096896
38 block groups
32768 blocks per group, 32768 fragments per group
16096 inodes per group
Superblock backups stored on blocks:
    32768, 98304, 163840, 229376, 294912, 819200, 884736
```

```
Writing inode tables: done
Creating journal (32768 blocks): done
Writing superblocks and filesystem accounting information: done

This filesystem will be automatically checked every 39 mounts or
180 days, whichever comes first.  Use tune2fs -c or -i to override.
```

File system creation may take a few seconds or several minutes depending on the speed and size of the disk. Quite a bit of information about the new file system is printed to the screen. For the most part, all that is needed here is to check for errors.

A new file system must be created on each new partition before it is used. Once the file systems are created, you are ready to mount them for use.

File System Labels

Each new file system can be assigned a label as a way to refer to that file system without using the device name. An example of this can be seen on the /*boot* file system in the /*etc*/*fstab* file. Labels can act as an alias and may be useful under certain circumstances, but generally it is simpler to refer to a file system by its device name. If disk labels are to be implemented, the *e2label* command is used to manage the device labels.

Mounting and Unmounting File Systems

In this section, how to mount the file systems created in the previous section as well as how to mount CDs and DVDs for use will be seen. Also, how to edit the /*etc*/*fstab* file to automatically mount file systems at system startup will be shown. As with the previous steps, these will need to be run as root.

Mounting a File System

The first steps to mounting a file system are to determine the device name for the file system to be mounted and the mount point where you would like it to appear. Use the file system created in the last section, /*dev*/*hdd1*, as an example and mount it at the location /*u04*.

The mount point where the file system should appear must be a directory. Since it does not exist already, create it.

```
# mkdir /u04
```

While the directory does not need to be empty, it is best if it is, otherwise the contents of the directory become unavailable after the file system is mounted.

Now use the *mount* command to mount a file system at a specific location. The *-t* option is used to indicate the file system type which should match the type specified when the file system was created, then the device name and mount point are given.

```
# mount -t ext3 /dev/hdd1 /u04
```

The *mount* command can now be used without any options to confirm that the file system was mounted.

```
# mount
/dev/mapper/VolGroup00-LogVol00 on / type ext3 (rw)
proc on /proc type proc (rw)
...
/dev/hdd1 on /u04 type ext3 (rw)
```

Also, the space available on the device can be checked using the *df* command.

```
# df -h /u04

Filesystem          Size  Used Avail Use% Mounted on
/dev/hdd1           4.6G  138M  4.3G   4% /u04
```

The device is now available to the system, but with default permissions, can only be written to by root. To make space on this device available to other users, either change the permissions on the device itself or create subdirectories on it and grant permission for others to write to those. Permissions will be examined more in the next chapter.

Unmounting a File System

A file system can be unmounted using the *umount* command. Which file system to unmount using either its mount point or its device name can be specified. This example unmounts the file system previously mounted at */u04* using the mount point:

```
# umount /u04
```

This example unmounts the file system */u01/hdd1* regardless of where it is mounted.

```
# umount /dev/hdd1
```

To be unmounted, the file system must not be in use. If a user or running process is using the file system, an error occurs when unmounting. This is where *lsof* can be useful to determine what process is using the file system.

```
# umount /u04
```

```
umount: /u04: device is busy
umount: /u04: device is busy
```

```
# lsof /u04
```

```
COMMAND  PID USER   FD   TYPE DEVICE SIZE NODE NAME
bash    3298 root   cwd   DIR  22,65 4096    2 /u04
```

Then stopping the process using the file system is somehow needed before it can be unmounted.

Mounting and Unmounting the CD/DVD Drive

Unlike on desktop systems when a CD or DVD is inserted into a Linux server, it typically will not be mounted automatically. Instead, use commands like above to mount and unmount the disk. As with other file systems, the mount point must be a directory that exists before the *mount* command is given.

Here is an example of how a disk can be mounted. The disk should first be inserted into the appropriate drive.

```
# mount /dev/cdrom /mnt
```

```
mount: block device /dev/cdrom is write-protected, mounting read-only
```

```
# df -k
```

```
Filesystem        1K-blocks       Used Available Use% Mounted on
...
/dev/hdc           2850578    2850578         0 100% /mnt
```

The disk is now mounted and its contents available at */mnt*. The directory */mnt* typically exists on Linux systems as a place to mount file systems temporarily, but any preferably empty directory could be used.

To unmount the disk, use *umount* as usual. The *eject* command can also be used to eject the disk through software rather than using the button on the drive, but the *eject* command needs the device name rather than the mount point.

```
# umount /mnt
# eject /dev/cdrom
```

The CD or DVD drive on most systems has several device names. Typically, the drive can be mounted using any of the following device names: */dev/cdrom, dev/dvd* or */dev/hdc*.

Managing File Systems Using the *fstab* File

Unless a file system is only going to be used temporarily, it should be added to the *fstab* file so it will be mounted automatically each time the system starts up. The *fstab* file is described in detail in the section about it earlier in this chapter.

To create an *fstab* entry for the file system created in the previous section, add a line like the following to the *fstab* file.

```
/dev/hdd1          /u04          ext3    defaults        1 2
```

The columns of the *fstab* file can be separated by spaces or tabs. The device name is given first, then the mount point, file system type, options or defaults to use default options, the dump level and *fsck* pass number. With this entered in the *fstab* file, the file system is mounted automatically at system startup. Also, the file system can now be mounted using just the mount point.

```
# mount /u04
```

Specific circumstances may necessitate mount options other than the defaults. One example is the *ro* mount option which mounts file systems for read only. Other options exist to disable or enable special features or restrict access to the file system. A complete list of the options can be found in the man page listing for the *mount* command.

Checking and Repairing File Systems

Errors on the file system are a nightmare for the Linux administrator and the DBA, but regular checking of the file systems can help catch problems before they cause data loss or downtime.

Manually Checking File Systems with *fsck*

The primary tool enabling checking for and repairing file systems is *fsck* (short for *file system check*.) The *fsck* command calls specific utilities based on the type of file system that needs to be checked. If errors are found, *fsck* gives the option to fix them.

Since *fsck* can modify the contents of a file system, it should only be used on a file system when it is not mounted. If you try to run *fsck* on a mounted file system, you get a warning. Instead, you should unmount the file system, check it, and remount it.

```
# fsck /u04

fsck 1.39 (29-May-2006)
e2fsck 1.39 (29-May-2006)
/dev/hdd1 is mounted.

WARNING!!!  Running e2fsck on a mounted filesystem may cause
SEVERE filesystem damage.

Do you really want to continue (y/n)? no

check aborted.
# umount /u04
# fsck /u04

fsck 1.39 (29-May-2006)
e2fsck 1.39 (29-May-2006)
/dev/hdd1: clean, 11/611648 files, 54398/1220932 blocks

# mount /u04
```

The *fsck* command calls *e2fsck* which is used to check ext2 and ext3 file systems. Since this is a journaled file system (ext3), the check can read the journal and apply any changes. This happens very quickly and, unless the file system has been previously marked by the system as needing a further check, *fsck* considers the file system clean and exits. Non-journaled file systems generally take longer to check than journaled ones.

Checking File Systems Without Unmounting Them

It is possible to check file systems without unmounting them by using the *-n* option. When *-n* is specified, *fsck* assumes the file system is mounted and only reports errors, but does not give the option to fix them.

```
# fsck -n /u04
```

```
fsck 1.39 (29-May-2006)
e2fsck 1.39 (29-May-2006)
Warning!  /dev/hdd1 is mounted.
Warning: skipping journal recovery because doing a read-only filesystem
check.
/dev/hdd1: clean, 11/611648 files, 54398/1220932 blocks
```

This allows checking a file system for errors while it is still available to users. If errors are found, the file system should be taken offline and *fsck* rerun without the *-n* option to repair the errors.

Full Checks on Journaled File Systems

Occasionally, a more complete check will be run, even on journaled file systems. When either a time limit or number of mounts since the last full check has been exceeded, *fsck* automatically checks the entire file system. This takes longer than the journal-only check but should be performed occasionally.

```
# umount /u04
# fsck /u04
```

```
fsck 1.39 (29-May-2006)
e2fsck 1.39 (29-May-2006)
/dev/hdd1 has been mounted 41 times without being checked, check forced.
Pass 1: Checking inodes, blocks, and sizes
Pass 2: Checking directory structure
Pass 3: Checking directory connectivity
Pass 4: Checking reference counts
Pass 5: Checking group summary information
/dev/hdd1: 11/611648 files (9.1% non-contiguous), 54398/1220932 blocks
```

```
# mount /u04
```

A full check can also be forced to run on an ext3 file system by using the *e2fsck* command directly. When using *e2fsck*, the device name needs to be given rather than the mount point.

```
# umount /u04
# e2fsck -f /dev/hdd1
```

```
e2fsck 1.39 (29-May-2006)
Pass 1: Checking inodes, blocks, and sizes
Pass 2: Checking directory structure
...
```

Changing When Full Checks are Run

Information about when the last full *fsck* run was done and when the next one should be is kept in the file system's superblock. The superblock of ext2 and ext3 file systems can be read with the *tune2fs* command using the *-l* option and the device name.

```
# tune2fs -l /dev/hdd1

tune2fs 1.39 (29-May-2006)
Filesystem volume name:   <none>
Last mounted on:          <not available>
Filesystem UUID:          1bfe3b00-95e6-4c3b-b97e-9559c375f775
Filesystem magic number:  0xEF53
Filesystem revision #:    1 (dynamic)
Filesystem features:      has_journal resize_inode dir_index filetype
sparse_super large_file
Default mount options:    (none)
Filesystem state:         clean
Errors behavior:          Continue
Filesystem OS type:       Linux
Inode count:              611648
Block count:              1220932
Reserved block count:     61046
Free blocks:              1166534
Free inodes:              611637
First block:              0
Blocksize:                4096
Fragment size:            4096
Reserved GDT blocks:      298
Blocks per group:         32768
Fragments per group:      32768
Inodes per group:         16096
Inode blocks per group:   503
Filesystem created:       Sat Dec 26 11:06:33 2009
Last mount time:          Sun Dec 27 08:51:38 2009
Last write time:          Sun Dec 27 09:03:12 2009
Mount count:              0
Maximum mount count:      39
Last checked:             Sun Dec 27 08:53:40 2009
Check interval:           15552000 (6 months)
Next check after:         Fri Jun 25 09:53:40 2010
Reserved blocks uid:      0 (user root)
Reserved blocks gid:      0 (group root)
First inode:              11
Inode size:           128
Journal inode:            8
Default directory hash:   tea
Directory Hash Seed:      144e3310-0a01-481f-94b3-34fea6898ebd
Journal backup:           inode blocks
```

As can be seen, there is a lot of information about the file system stored in the superblock. The *fsck* command will do a full check on a file system if any of the following conditions are true:

- The filesystem state is listed as something other than clean, or

- The mount count is greater than the maximum mount count, or

- The date is after the next check after date

After a full check is run, the file system state is set to *clean*. Assuming the check and any repair was successful, the mount count is reset to zero, the last checked timestamp is updated to the current date and time, and a new next check after date is calculated based on the check interval. If the *-n* option is specified to scan the file system in read only mode, the superblock is not updated.

The *tune2fs* command can also be used to modify the contents of the superblock. You can change the maximum number of mounts allowed before a full check is forced using the *-c* option, or change the interval between full checks with the *-i* option. The interval can be specified in days, months or weeks by appending a *d*, *m* or *w* to the number.

```
# tune2fs -c 10 /dev/hdd1

tune2fs 1.39 (29-May-2006)
Setting maximal mount count to 10

# tune2fs -i 30d /dev/hdd1

tune2fs 1.39 (29-May-2006)
Setting interval between checks to 2592000 seconds
```

As can be seen in the previous output, the time interval for full checks is converted to seconds. In the superblock, the maximum mount count has been updated and the next check after value has been recalculated.

```
# tune2fs -1 /dev/hdd1

...
Mount count:            0
Maximum mount count:    10
Last checked:           Sun Dec 27 08:53:40 2009
Check interval:         2592000 (1 month)
Next check after:       Tue Jan 26 08:53:40 2010
...
```

Also, *tune2fs* can be used to change the mount count. This allows for forcing a full check the next time *fsck* is run by setting the mount count higher than the maximum mount count.

```
# tune2fs -C 11 /dev/hdd1

tune2fs 1.39 (29-May-2006)
Setting current mount count to 11

# tune2fs -l /dev/hdd1

...
Mount count:            11
Maximum mount count:    10
...

# fsck /dev/hdd1

fsck 1.39 (29-May-2006)
e2fsck 1.39 (29-May-2006)
/dev/hdd1 has been mounted 11 times without being checked, check forced.
Pass 1: Checking inodes, blocks, and sizes
Pass 2: Checking directory structure
...
```

Since *fsck* is also run every time the system starts up, use this method to force a full file system check the next time the system reboots.

fsck Running at Startup

When the system starts up, *fsck* is run from the */etc/rc.d/sysinit* script. This is ideal since most file systems are not yet mounted. The *fsck* command behaves the same way as when a manual check is done using the mount count and check interval to determine if a full check should be run. If a full check should be forced to be run on a file system at the next system startup, use the method described above to increase the mount count to more than the maximum mount count.

Running full file system checks at startup take time and therefore, delay other services starting up. While they are typically unnecessary, it is best to do a full check occasionally. The default interval of six months and maximum of 39 mounts are reasonable for most purposes, but a more frequent check may be desirable.

> 🔔 Full checks can take a long time on very large file systems. This can cause a restart to be extremely slow if several file systems need to be checked during the same restart. To avoid this, it may be a good idea to set the check interval and maximum mount count very high (say, a year or 100 mounts) and force a full check manually during a scheduled maintenance window. This prevents unexpected slow restarts.

Storage Virtualization Concepts

The Logical Volume Manager (LVM) is a form of storage virtualization that allows you to divide a disk for different purposes or combine multiple disks or partitions for flexibility, redundancy or speed. Essentially, the goal of storage virtualization is to give maximum flexibility in how the operating system can use the available disk. LVM will be referred to a lot in this section as it is included with Linux, but the concepts here apply to any storage virtualization technology, though the terminology may vary.

The flexibility provided by LVM and other storage virtualization comes at the price of added complexity. While LVM is fairly straightforward to use, it can make recovery of failed disks more difficult as taking a disk out of one system and having it just work in another can no longer be counted on. As always, frequent backups are the best defense.

Disks and Disk Partitions

LVM identifies space that can be used on unused disks and disk partitions attached to the system. A disk or partition is then associated to a volume group. The volume group is simply an organizational structure.

Once added to the volume group, the space available on disks and partitions becomes available to the virtual devices managed within that volume group. The space can be used to extend existing file systems or create new ones.

Virtual Devices

A volume group, containing one or many partitions or disks, is separated into logical volumes that are made available to the system. The logical volumes appear to the system like real devices with just a slightly different device name. LVM virtual devices typically have names something like */dev/mapper/VolGroup00-LogVol04*. Since LVM is integrated into the Linux kernel, applications on the system do not need to be aware that the device they are accessing may actually be on several disks.

When a logical volume is created, there is a chance to define what kind of virtual device should be created. Below are some of the common options for logical volumes.

Linear Concatenation

In LVM, the default option is to create a linear volume. This creates a logical volume that uses space on one or more physical disks or partitions in order to make a single, apparently contiguous space available for use. When more than one disk or partition is used, this is referred to as concatenation.

The space available on a linear volume is equal to the sum of the space used for that volume on each device. No space is lost to formatting or redundancy. Linear volumes are excellent for combining small disks or partitions to make a larger space available but do not offer any data protection or performance improvement.

Striping

Striping is a way to combine two or more physical devices where data is divided evenly between the disks in such a way that when a piece of data needs to be read, part of that data is read from each physical device. A stripe segment, referred to as granularity in LVM, determines the size of information that is cut up and separated on disks.

As an example, take a logical volume that is created with striping on two disks with a 4k segment size. If a single 4k file is written to this volume, 2k of that is put on the first device and 2k on the second. Since each disk can be written to simultaneously, the write takes roughly half as long to write as it would if it were being written to a single disk. Similarly, the file can be read in roughly half the time it would otherwise take.

Though there is some overhead to dividing and combining data for stripes, striping can offer considerable performance improvements over linear concatenation if space is allocated from separate disks. If separate partitions on the same disk are used, striping becomes a disadvantage as the system still has the overhead of dividing the data and increased seeking is the result. Striping, like concatenation, offers no data protection.

Mirroring

Mirroring is the simplest way to gain data redundancy to safeguard data against disk failure. In mirroring, two or more (minimum of three in LVM) disks or partitions are combined and identical data is written to each device. The space available is only as large as the smallest device in the mirror.

Some implementations of mirroring offer increased read performance, but write performance is typically similar to traditional disk performance. What mirroring does offer is the ability to keep running or recover more quickly as a redundant copy of the data is kept online and up-to-date.

RAID and RAID Levels

Mirroring and striping are both forms of RAID (Redundant Array of Inexpensive Disks) methods which allow more than one physical device to be combined to achieve redundancy and/or performance. Often people talk about RAID levels for disk. Below is a short description of common RAID levels. Many of these are not available through LVM and most, other than levels 0 and 1, are typically implemented in hardware in external storage devices rather than in software solutions like LVM.

RAID Level	Description	Redundancy	Space Available
RAID 0	Striping - Data is divided evenly between two or more devices. Same as described above.	No	Sum of all devices combined
RAID 1	Mirroring - Data is duplicated between two or more devices for redundancy. Same as described above.	Yes	The size of a single device

RAID 4	Not typically used. Data is divided on three or more devices, one of which contains a parity so if any single device fails, its contents can be recreated from the other devices and the parity.	Yes	Sum of all devices minus one (e.g., If four 10g disks are used, 30g will be available for use)
RAID 5	Same as RAID 4, but the parity is distributed evenly among all disks in the group, thereby preventing the single parity disk from becoming a bottleneck.	Yes	Sum of all devices minus one (e.g., If four 10g disks are used, 30g will be available for use)
RAID 6	Though loosely defined, typically RAID 6 is similar to RAID 5 but two parities are kept to protect against up to two simultaneous disk failures. Four or more devices are typically combined.	Yes	Sum of all devices minus two (e.g., If seven 10g disks are used, 50g will be available for use)

Table 12.2: *Common RAID Levels*

The parity used in RAID levels 4 and 5 is a value that indicates if bits from each disk which data is written to add up to odd or even. Since this data is binary, meaning it can only have a value of 1 or 0, use this single parity bit to determine if any missing bit should be a 1 or a 0 by adding all the known bits and comparing it to the parity.

In many modern applications, RAID levels can also be combined. A common disk configuration for Oracle databases may be RAID 10 or RAID 1+0, which is a combination of devices that have been mirrored for redundancy, then striped together for improved performance. Similarly, RAID 0+1 can refer to a configuration in which disks have been striped together, and then data is mirrored between two stripes.

Other RAID levels and combinations exist, but the most common ones have been described here. RAID levels more complicated than mirroring and striping can most efficiently be implemented in hardware. Some server systems include hardware to implement RAID on internal disks and most external enclosures and SAN (Storage Area Network) solutions support it independent of the server.

Using the Logical Volume Manager

There are two ways to manage file systems through LVM: a GUI that provides a visual representation of disks and a command line utility. The concepts are the same in both and this chapter will show how to do some of the more common configurations through each interface.

In these examples, I have unmounted the previously created /*u04* and will recreate it as a 5 GB logical volume as well as add space to the /*u01* volume.

 Any of these steps may result in lost data if performed on a disk with existing partitions. A backup of essential data and configuration files should be taken before proceeding.

 Many of the steps in this section can be done online while the file system is mounted and in use, but there may be a performance impact or even data corruption under certain circumstances. If possible, this maintenance should be done when the system is not in use by other applications.

Starting the Logical Volume Manager GUI

The graphical interface to LVM can be launched from the GNOME desktop from the System menu, Administration, Logical Volume Management, or at

the command line by executing *system-config-lvm*. The LVM GUI should appear
on the screen or in the X Windows server.

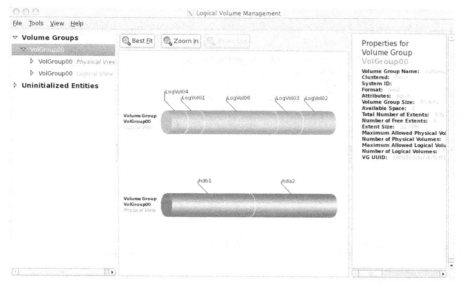

Figure 12.1: *The LVM Interface at Startup*

When it first starts up, examining currently created volume groups and both
the physical and logical volumes that they are made of can now be done. The
physical view of a volume group shows what disks and partitions are being
used in that group while the logical view shows what space from this volume
group is being allocated to which logical volumes.

Adding a Partition or Disk to a Volume Group

A partition or disk can be added to a volume group. If adding a partition, it
must already have been created using *parted* or *fdisk*. Existing partitions can be
found by expanding, i.e. clicking on the triangle to the left of the Uninitialized
Entities item, then expanding the device that contains the partitions.

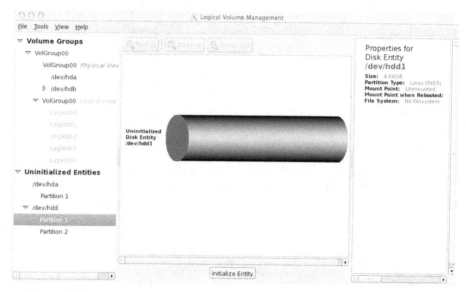

Figure 12.2: *Expanding Uninitialized Entities Section*

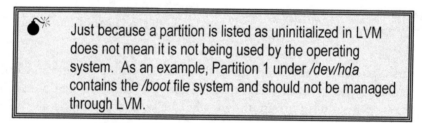

Just because a partition is listed as uninitialized in LVM does not mean it is not being used by the operating system. As an example, Partition 1 under */dev/hda* contains the */boot* file system and should not be managed through LVM.

If adding an entire disk, all partitions should first be removed from the disk using *parted* or *fdisk*. The disk then appears in the same location but does not have partitions listed under it.

Select the partition or disk you wish to add to the LVM disk group and click the Initialize Entity button to initialize the selected partition or disk for use by LVM. You should receive a warning that data on this partition will be lost if you proceed. Once you are sure the data will not be needed, click Yes to proceed.

If a disk is being added to the LVM group, a message is also received asking if a single partition should be created to encompass the entire disk. Creating a partition causes a partition table to be written to the disk, so the space appears to be allocated to other programs and operating systems. Choose Yes and one partition the size of the disk is created and initialized.

The disk partition has now been initialized and should appear on the left under Unallocated Volumes.

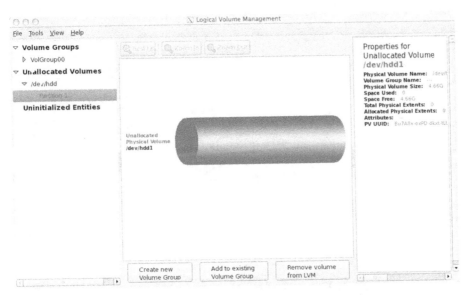

Figure 12.3: *Unallocated Volumes Showing Disk Partition*

With the partition selected under Unallocated Volumes, there is now the option to create a new volume group starting with this partition or to add it to an existing volume group. Choose Add to the existing volume group and a dialog appears to choose which volume group to add it to. Select the appropriate volume group.

The new partition now appears in the Physical View of the volume group it was added to. The space also becomes available for use by the volume group.

Editing or Removing Logical Volumes

With the new space added, existing logical volumes can now be manipulated or new ones added. To edit a volume, expand the Volume Group which it belongs to, then expand the Logical View section to display existing logical volumes.

Logical volumes are listed by their device name. If a device name is selected, additional information including the volume's mount point is given in the right pane of the LVM GUI, and there are buttons at the bottom to remove the volume, create a snapshot or edit the properties.

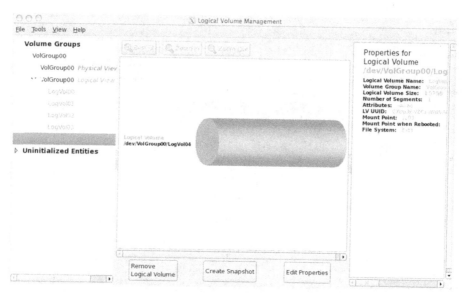

Figure 12.4: *Edit Logical Volume Screen*

Removing a Logical Volume

To remove this logical volume, click Remove Logical Volume. There is a warning that shows up saying that this will erase any data on the device and the device will be removed. If the logical volume was mounted, it is unmounted before it is removed. If it was set up to mount on boot in the */etc/fstab* file, its entry there is also removed. If files on the file system are in use, an error is received and may need to end the processes using those files before removing the volume.

Editing a Logical Volume

To edit the properties of a logical volume, click the Edit Properties button and a dialogue appears giving the option to edit several properties related to the logical volume.

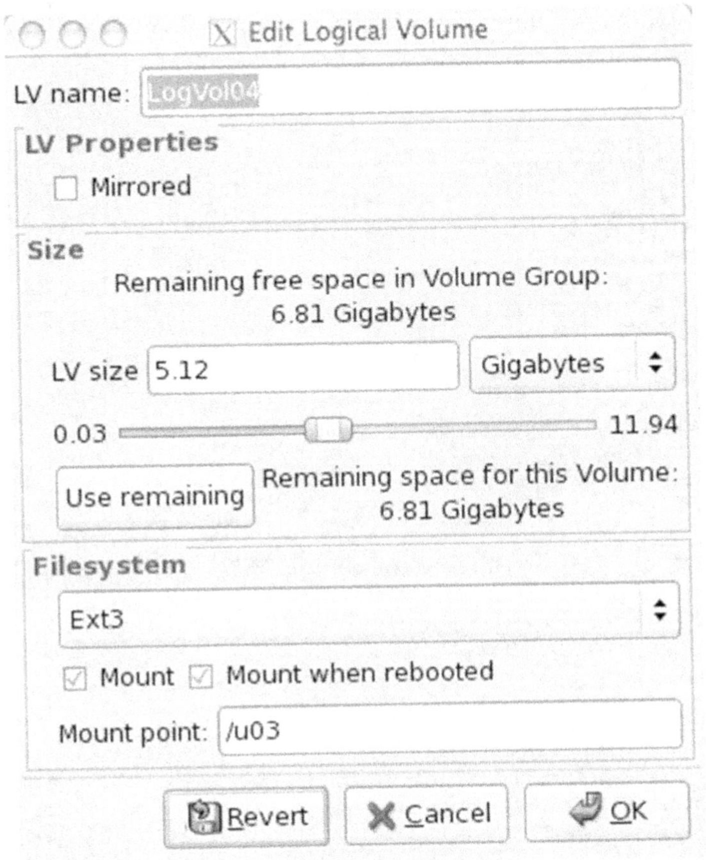

Figure 12.5: *Editing a Logical Volume*

The default unit of measure in this dialogue is extents, but it is typically easier to work with if you change it to megabytes or gigabytes. As long as free space is available, you can adjust the size of the partition by moving the slider in the Size section. You can also click Use Remaining to use all available space in the volume group. When you are done editing the logical volume, click OK and your changes will be applied immediately.

Adding a Logical Volume

Logical volumes can be added by selecting the Logical View item within a volume group, then clicking Create New Logical Volume. The dialogue box for creating logical volumes is almost identical to the edit dialog.

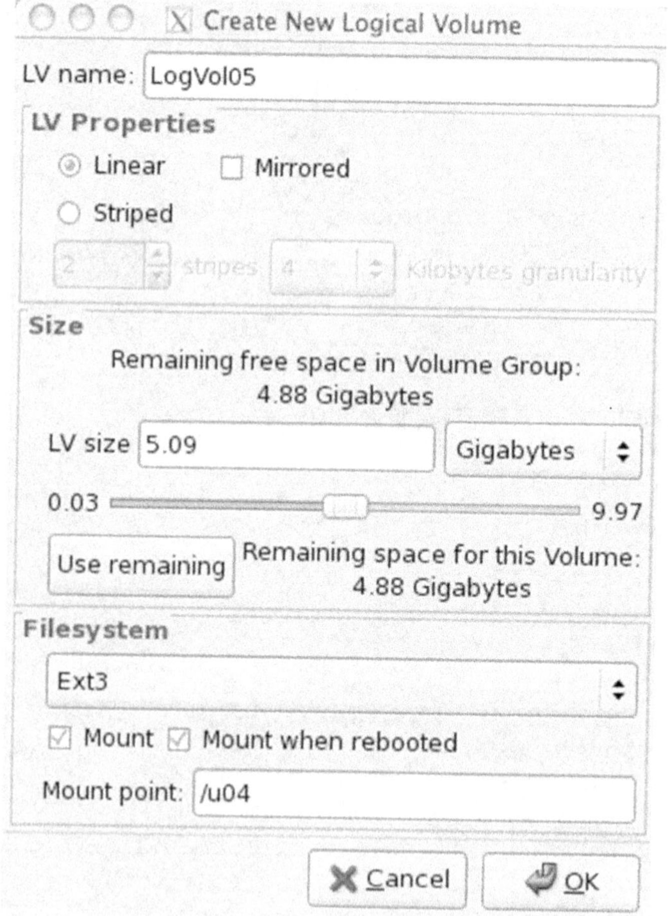

Figure 12.6: *Creating a New Logical Volume*

Enter a name for the logical volume. This becomes its device name in the /dev/mapper directory. While any valid file name can be used, I recommend using a convention like the default one. Even naming devices with their intended purpose can be misleading if the logical volume is repurposed in the future.

In the LV Properties section, a choice is given to make this a mirrored or striped device. LVM checks to see if the requirements for mirroring or striping are available, but it is not always intelligent enough to determine if all requirements are met.

In the Size section, you can set the unit you wish to set the size in and use the slider or enter the desired size. If a size which is not possible since LVM only allows space to be allocated in 32 MB extents is entered, it rounds to the nearest size that is possible.

Finally, choose the file system type and if this logical volume should be made available immediately, check the *mount* option and specify a mount point. If the mount point does not exist, there is a prompt to create it. Also, to automatically add the volume to the /etc/fstab file, check the *mount when rebooted* option.

Click OK and LVM creates and mounts the logical volume. When you are done using the LVM GUI, exit it through the file menu.

Starting the Command Line LVM

To enter the command line version of the Logical Volume Manager, enter the command *lvm*. This leads to the LVM prompt. The LVM commands included in this section actually exist outside of the LVM utility, so they can be called with the same options and arguments directly from root's command prompt. Man pages are also available to describe the behavior and options for each command.

A list of commands can be displayed anytime by typing *help* at the LVM prompt. Information about the existing physical and logical volume setup can be displayed using the commands *pvdisplay* and *lvdisplay*, respectively.

```
# lvm
lvm> pvdisplay
```

```
--- Physical volume ---
PV Name                 /dev/hda2
VG Name                 VolGroup00
PV Size                 9.90 GB / not usable 22.76 MB
Allocatable             yes (but full)
PE Size (KByte)         32768
Total PE                316
Free PE                 0
Allocated PE            316
PV UUID                 5Oewrp-Og2K-sH9i-QyqC-VAHl-U9OJ-Y4Y0DX

--- Physical volume ---
PV Name                 /dev/hdb1
VG Name                 VolGroup00
PV Size                 10.00 GB / not usable 32.00 MB
...
```

lvm> **lvdisplay**

```
--- Logical volume ---
LV Name                 /dev/VolGroup00/LogVol00
VG Name                 VolGroup00
LV UUID                 N9QzXw-4Q3k-eC9t-PHHM-f7F8-BhUJ-p0krLq
LV Write Access         read/write
LV Status               available
# open                  1
LV Size                 8.88 GB
Current LE              284
Segments                1
Allocation              inherit
Read ahead sectors      auto
- currently set to      256
Block device            253:0

--- Logical volume ---
LV Name                 /dev/VolGroup00/LogVol01
VG Name                 VolGroup00
LV UUID                 UHWq2h-0yY7-gi90-OoiN-z6xy-UCgo-GCTBJz
LV Write Access         read/write
LV Status               available
# open                  1
LV Size                 2.00 GB
```

Adding a Partition or Disk to a Volume Group

To add a partition to a disk group, it must first be initialized with the *pvcreate* command. Provide the device name for the partition to the command.

lvm> **pvcreate /dev/hdd1**

```
Physical volume "/dev/hdd1" successfully created
```

If initializing a complete disk, it is best to create a single partition through *parted* or *fdisk* and add that partition to LVM using the step above. This assures there is a partition table on the disk so the space appears allocated to other programs and operating systems. Once the partition is created, the steps are the same as adding any other partition.

With the partition initialized by LVM, add it to the existing volume group using the *vgextend* command, providing the volume group name and the device to add as arguments.

```
lvm> vgextend VolGroup00 /dev/hdd1

  Volume group "VolGroup00" successfully extended
```

The space is now available for use in the volume group specified.

Editing Logical Volumes

With the space available to the volume group, it can now be used to change existing logical volumes. The size of a logical volume can be edited using the *lvextend* command. Either specify the size the volume needs to be or the amount that needs to be added to it.

```
lvm> lvextend -L4G /dev/VolGroup00/LogVol04

  Extending logical volume LogVol04 to 4.00 GB
  Logical volume LogVol04 successfully resized

lvm> lvextend -L+1G /dev/VolGroup00/LogVol04

  Extending logical volume LogVol04 to 5.00 GB
  Logical volume LogVol04 successfully resized
```

While this extends the volume, the file system still appears as its original size until the file system is extended. For ext3 file systems, the *resize2fs* command is used to resize the file system.

```
# df -h /u03

Filesystem              Size  Used Avail Use% Mounted on
/dev/mapper/VolGroup00-LogVol04
                        2.0G  146M  1.6G   7% /u03

# resize2fs /dev/mapper/VolGroup00-LogVol04

resize2fs 1.39 (29-May-2006)
Filesystem at /dev/mapper/VolGroup00-LogVol04 is mounted on /u03; on-line
resizing required
```

```
Performing an on-line resize of /dev/mapper/VolGroup00-LogVol04 to 1310720
(4k) blocks.
The filesystem on /dev/mapper/VolGroup00-LogVol04 is now 1310720 blocks
long.

# df -h /u03

Filesystem             Size  Used Avail Use% Mounted on
/dev/mapper/VolGroup00-LogVol04
                       5.0G  146M  4.6G   4% /u03
```

This example takes advantage of online resizing to make new space available to
a file system without having to unmount it. This is a fairly new feature and
may not be available on the Linux distribution. Check the *resize2fs* man page
for more details.

If a logical volume needs to be shrunk, first use *resize2fs* to shrink the file
system; then the logical volume can be reduced using the *lvreduce* command in
LVM.

Adding a Logical Volume

Logical volumes can be created using the *lvcreate* command. A size is given
with the *-L* option, a name specified after *-n* and the volume group name is
given as a final argument.

```
lvm> lvcreate -L5G -nLogVol05 VolGroup00

  Logical volume "LogVol05" created
```

The logical volume is now available with the device name of
/dev/VolGroup00/LogVol05. Just like with a new disk partition, a file system
must be created on this device and it must be mounted before it can be used.
If it needs to be mounted when the system starts up, it needs to be manually
added to the */etc/fstab* file.

Deleting a Logical Volume

Before a logical volume can be removed, any important data needs to be
copied from it and it should be unmounted. If there is an *fstab* entry for the
volume, it should also be removed or commented out. Once that is done, the
lvremove command is used to remove the logical volume using the device name.

```
lvm> lvremove /dev/VolGroup00/LogVol05
```

```
Do you really want to remove active logical volume "LogVol05"? [y/n]: y

  Logical volume "LogVol05" successfully removed
```

The space previously used by this logical volume is now available in the volume group. When you are done working with the LVM command line utility, type *exit* to leave the program.

File System Performance

Oracle databases often put great demands on file systems. Data must be able to be written and retrieved efficiently in order for the database to run well. File system tuning is a broad subject which could easily be a book of its own, but the content in this section should give an idea how to examine file system performance.

Monitoring I/O with *iostat*

One of the primary tools for examining disk usage and performance is the *iostat* command. This command allows you to see at a device level data written to and read from disks.

```
# iostat

Linux 2.6.18-128.el5 (oelinux-test1.lifeaftercoffee.com)       12/28/2009

avg-cpu:  %user   %nice %system %iowait  %steal   %idle
           1.15    0.02    2.91    0.48    0.00   95.44

Device:           tps   Blk_read/s   Blk_wrtn/s   Blk_read   Blk_wrtn
hda              1.66        28.74        16.03     740939     413228
hda1             0.04         0.22         0.00       5627          4
hda2             1.60        28.47        16.03     733905     413224
...
```

The default output of *iostat* gives information about CPU usage, then information about the disk devices attached to the system. A row is listed for each disk device and each column gives some insight on the activity on the given disk since system startup. Here is a brief description of the columns:

Device	The Device Name
tps	The number of transfers (I/O requests) per second. Each transfer could actually contain multiple commands and may be small or large
Blk_read/s	The number of blocks read per second
Blk_wrtn/s	The number of blocks written per second

Blk_read	Total number of blocks read
Blk_wrtn	Total number of blocks written

Table 12.3: *Device Column Description of iostat*

By default, these statistics are reported from system startup, but by adding a couple of arguments to the *iostat* command, live I/O information can be monitored. To do that, specify an interval and a count as arguments. This causes *iostat* to provide a report, wait the number of seconds indicated by the interval, then provide another report until the count has been reached. The first report shows stats since system startup, but subsequent reports only show activity since the last report was printed to the screen.

```
# iostat 3 10

Linux 2.6.18-128.el5 (oelinux-test1.lifeaftercoffee.com)        12/28/2009

avg-cpu:  %user   %nice %system %iowait  %steal   %idle
           1.12    0.02    2.85    0.46    0.00   95.55

Device:            tps   Blk_read/s   Blk_wrtn/s   Blk_read   Blk_wrtn
hda               1.63        27.82        15.78     740963     420132
hda1              0.04         0.21         0.00       5627          4
hda2              1.57        27.56        15.78     733929     420128
hdb               0.73        10.78         4.16     287174     110790
hdb1              0.73        10.77         4.16     286918     110790
hdd               0.88        13.05        26.57     347495     707687
hdd1              0.05         0.12         3.74       3244      99651
dm-0              2.89        26.09        15.76     694802     419720
dm-1              0.04         0.32         0.00       8536          0
dm-2              1.12         9.32         0.02     248154        584
dm-3              0.04         0.35         0.01       9218        320
dm-4              1.04         0.44         7.86      11730     209304
fd0               0.00         0.00         0.00         32          0

avg-cpu:  %user   %nice %system %iowait  %steal   %idle
           0.33    0.00    1.32    0.00    0.00   98.34

Device:            tps   Blk_read/s   Blk_wrtn/s   Blk_read   Blk_wrtn
hda               0.00         0.00         0.00          0          0
hda1              0.00         0.00         0.00          0          0
hda2              0.00         0.00         0.00          0          0
hdb               0.00         0.00         0.00          0          0
hdb1              0.00         0.00         0.00          0          0
hdd               0.00         0.00         0.00          0          0
hdd1              0.00         0.00         0.00          0          0
dm-0              0.00         0.00         0.00          0          0
dm-1              0.00         0.00         0.00          0          0
dm-2              0.00         0.00         0.00          0          0
dm-3              0.00         0.00         0.00          0          0
dm-4              0.00         0.00         0.00          0          0
fd0               0.00         0.00         0.00          0          0
...
```

In this mode, *iostat* still delivers a lot of information so that viewing only information about a certain device can be specified further. Device names can be added as another argument to the *iostat* command.

```
# iostat 3 10 hdb1
```

```
Linux 2.6.18-128.el5 (oelinux-test1.lifeaftercoffee.com)        12/28/2009

avg-cpu:  %user   %nice %system %iowait  %steal   %idle
           1.13    0.02    2.91    0.59    0.00   95.34

Device:            tps   Blk_read/s   Blk_wrtn/s   Blk_read   Blk_wrtn
hdb1              1.00        21.93         4.84     593742     130974

avg-cpu:  %user   %nice %system %iowait  %steal   %idle
           8.00    0.00   47.00    0.00    0.00   45.00

Device:            tps   Blk_read/s   Blk_wrtn/s   Blk_read   Blk_wrtn
hdb1              0.00         0.00         0.00          0          0

avg-cpu:  %user   %nice %system %iowait  %steal   %idle
          20.33    0.00   47.33    3.33    0.00   29.00

Device:            tps   Blk_read/s   Blk_wrtn/s   Blk_read   Blk_wrtn
hdb1             12.67         2.67       197.33          8        592
...
```

Two other useful options for formatting the output are *-d*, which suppress the CPU utilization, and *–k*, which prints the output in kilobytes instead of blocks.

```
# iostat -dk 3 10 hdb1

Linux 2.6.18-128.el5 (oelinux-test1.lifeaftercoffee.com)        12/28/2009

Device:            tps    kB_read/s    kB_wrtn/s    kB_read    kB_wrtn
hdb1              1.02        10.88         2.67     299099      73295

Device:            tps    kB_read/s    kB_wrtn/s    kB_read    kB_wrtn
hdb1              0.00         0.00         0.00          0          0

Device:            tps    kB_read/s    kB_wrtn/s    kB_read    kB_wrtn
hdb1             13.67         1.33       106.67          4        320
...
```

When you compare numbers over time like this, you can start to see trends in disk usage. Disk usage, especially reads, are usually high when databases are started up and during large operations; but with proper caching and tuning, they should be manageable on most partitions. If high reads and writes are consistently being seen, consider re-examining the database cache parameters or distributing I/O over different disks.

The output that has been reviewed so far deals mostly with the volume of data being read and written to devices. If looking more closely at the number of requests going to a device is desired instead, use the *-x* option for extended output. Again, the interval and count parameters can be used and/or a specific disk device can be given. In this case, a disk device has not been given, so requests can easily be compared to different devices in the output.

```
# iostat -x 5 5

Linux 2.6.18-128.el5 (oelinux-test1.lifeaftercoffee.com)         12/28/2009

avg-cpu:  %user   %nice %system %iowait  %steal   %idle
           1.15    0.02    3.01    0.59    0.00   95.23

Device:        rrqm/s   wrqm/s    r/s    w/s    rsec/s   wsec/s avgrq-sz avgqu-sz   await  svctm  %util
```

File System Performance   **253**

```
hda            0.43    1.20  0.83  0.78    26.82   15.83   26.46    0.04   22.80    3.12    0.50
hda1           0.04    0.00  0.04  0.00     0.20    0.00    5.27    0.00    2.04    1.35    0.01
hda2           0.38    1.20  0.77  0.78    26.57   15.83   27.36    0.04   23.67    3.21    0.50
hdb            0.77    0.60  0.92  0.13    21.64    5.83   26.38    0.01    7.91    3.36    0.35
hdb1           0.77    0.60  0.91  0.13    21.63    5.83   26.40    0.01    7.91    3.36    0.35
hdd            3.73    3.09  0.73  0.12    12.56   25.58   45.00    0.03   37.39    0.74    0.06
hdd1           0.01    0.43  0.03  0.02     0.12    3.60   71.95    0.00   11.37    1.28    0.01
dm-0           0.00    0.00  0.89  1.98    25.15   15.81   14.29    0.14   49.19    1.71    0.49
dm-1           0.00    0.00  0.04  0.00     0.31    0.00    8.00    0.00    2.84    0.51    0.00
dm-2           0.00    0.00  1.15  0.06    13.39    0.47   11.48    0.01    8.37    1.77    0.21
dm-3           0.00    0.00  0.24  0.17     7.17    1.38   20.93    0.00    7.26    3.16    0.13
dm-4           0.00    0.00  0.05  0.95     0.42    7.56    8.00    0.03   25.82    0.16    0.02
fd0            0.00    0.00  0.00  0.00     0.00    0.00    8.00    0.00   30.75   30.75    0.00

avg-cpu:  %user   %nice %system %iowait  %steal   %idle
           5.99    0.00   28.54    0.40    0.00   65.07

Device:       rrqm/s   wrqm/s   r/s   w/s   rsec/s   wsec/s avgrq-sz avgqu-sz   await  svctm  %util
hda            0.00     1.60  0.00  2.20    0.00    30.34   13.82    0.00    1.09    0.64    0.14
hda1           0.00     0.00  0.00  0.00    0.00     0.00    0.00    0.00    0.00    0.00    0.00
hda2           0.00     1.60  0.00  2.20    0.00    30.34   13.82    0.00    1.09    0.64    0.14
hdb            0.00    11.38  0.00 10.38    0.00   174.05   16.77    0.01    0.79    0.75    0.78
hdb1           0.00    11.38  0.00 10.38    0.00   174.05   16.77    0.01    0.79    0.75    0.78
hdd            0.00     0.00  0.00  0.00    0.00     0.00    0.00    0.00    0.00    0.00    0.00
hdd1           0.00     0.00  0.00  0.00    0.00     0.00    0.00    0.00    0.00    0.00    0.00
dm-0           0.00     0.00  0.00  3.79    0.00    30.34    8.00    0.00    1.05    0.37    0.14
dm-1           0.00     0.00  0.00  0.00    0.00     0.00    0.00    0.00    0.00    0.00    0.00
dm-2           0.00     0.00  0.00  0.80    0.00     6.39    8.00    0.00    0.75    0.25    0.02
dm-3           0.00     0.00  0.00 20.96    0.00   167.66    8.00    0.02    0.78    0.37    0.78
dm-4           0.00     0.00  0.00  0.00    0.00     0.00    0.00    0.00    0.00    0.00    0.00
fd0            0.00     0.00  0.00  0.00    0.00     0.00    0.00    0.00    0.00    0.00    0.00
...
```

The columns in this output are different from the standard *iostat* output. These columns are defined as follows:

Device	The Device Name
rrqm/s	Read requests merged per second. The kernel merges requests whenever possible for more efficient disk operation.
wrqm/s	Write requests merged per second
r/s	Read requests per second
w/s	Write requests per second
rsec/s	Sectors read per second
wsec/s	Sectors written per second
avgrq-sz	Average size of requests to this device
avgqu-sz	Average queue length of requests to this device
await	Average wait time (in milliseconds) for requests to this device
svctm	Average service time (in milliseconds) for requests to this device
%util	Percentage of CPU time which IO requests were issued to this device

Table 12.4: *Device Columns Using –x Option*

Now there is much more information to digest, but instead of looking at summary volume of I/O to devices, number of requests are being viewed.

High numbers of read and write requests indicate that a lot of activity is happening on a given device. A high number of requests alone is not necessarily a reason for concern, but if it is accompanied by high wait times and user complaints, then there may be an issue.

If the average wait and service times are low, that indicates that requests are being received and fulfilled in a fairly timely manner and that the disk is keeping up. High wait times may indicate too much disparate activity on a file system or that a device is running slowly for some reason.

I hope that this has given an idea of the type of information that can be extracted from *iostat* reports. It is important to remember that *iostat* reports are on disk devices, not on logical volumes, so if LVM or another storage virtualization tool is being used, there is a need to combine this information with knowledge of the disk layout to properly interpret *iostat* reports.

Conclusion

This chapter was all about file systems, but we have barely even touched on files! The next chapter will be all about those and how to organize them, manipulate them and keep them safe.

File and Directory Management

By now, you may have started noticing the theme that files are at the heart of the Linux operating system. Files are used to hold data and programs, of course, but they are also used to hold configuration information for the system and services.

Like its UNIX ancestors, Linux also uses files to represent devices attached to the system. This was already revealed while configuring file systems when a reference was made to devices like */dev/hdd1*. Virtual devices with paths like */dev/mapper/VolGroup00-LogVol0* which were created by LVM were also present.

Many other physical devices can be seen in the */dev* directory, including audio and serial devices, but not all the files there represent physical devices. Other entries like */dev/random* and */dev/null* represent special files which give access to structures provided by the system. */dev/random* can be read from to generate random data. Similarly, */dev/null* can be read from to generate an empty file or written to in order to discard data.

These are just a few examples of the non-traditional files available in Linux. While these appear in directory listings, they actually represent interfaces to devices, structures in memory, or programs. Since reads, writes and access are all handled in the same manner as other files, no special programming tools or libraries are necessary to use these devices. They are easily used from the command line, shell scripts and programs.

Files, File Types and Directories

While data within a file can take several forms, there are only a handful of file types recognized by the Linux operating system. You will mainly only create and change the first three types listed here, but you will encounter the other

---

types. The file type of a given file is indicated by the first character in *ls -l* output.

Regular Files

The first and most common type of file in Linux is the regular file. Regular files can contain any type of data or be completely empty. Regular files appear with a dash (-) in the first character of *ls -l* output.

```
$ ls -l chapter1.txt

-rw-rw-r-- 1 jemmons jemmons 1027 Nov  8 07:12 chapter1.txt
```

Data files, configuration files, and executable programs are all examples of regular files.

Directories

The first of the special file types to be reviewed is the directory. Directories are indicated by a *d* in the first character of *ls -l* output.

```
$ ls -l
total 24
drwxr-xr-x 2 jemmons jemmons 4096 Sep 16 13:19 Desktop
drwxrwxr-x 2 jemmons jemmons 4096 Nov  8 07:12 notes
drwxrwxr-x 2 jemmons jemmons 4096 Nov  8 08:37 scripts
```

If an individual directory needs to be looked at with *ls -l*, then add the *d* option; otherwise, information on its contents are given rather than information on the directory itself.

```
$ ls -ld notes/

drwxrwxr-x 2 jemmons jemmons 4096 Nov  8 07:12 notes/
```

Typically, directories can contain files of any of the other types, but this may vary between file systems. The contents of a directory do not affect the directory object itself.

Symbolic Links

A symbolic link, often referred to as a symlink, is a reference to another file. It may reference a regular file or a special file. Symbolic links are identified by an *l* (lower-case L) in the first column of *ls -l* output as seen with the entry for *oracle_home_1* in the output below.

```
$ ls -l
total 28
drwxr-xr-x 3 oracle oinstall 4096 Dec  6 07:51 database_11g
drwxr-xr-x 2 oracle oinstall 4096 May 19  2009 Desktop
lrwxrwxrwx 1 oracle oinstall   35 Jan  9 06:27 oracle_home_1 ->
/u01/app/oracle/product/11.1.0/db_1
drwxr-xr-x 3 oracle oinstall 4096 Oct 27 12:37 oradiag_oracle
```

Symbolic links behave much like the file they are linked to. In fact, if just the symbolic link is listed, the system redirects the *ls* command and displays information on the file or directory it is referencing.

```
$ ls -ld oracle_home_1/
drwxr-xr-x 62 oracle oinstall 4096 Oct 24 13:29 oracle_home_1/
```

The difference in file permissions between the *ls* outputs above is evident. Symbolic links are typically represented with full read, write and execute permissions, but this does not apply to the object they reference. In the example above, the permissions on the directory */u01/app/oracle/product/11.1.0/db_1* are the ones that determine access, not the permissions on the symbolic link.

Symbolic links can be used to make files or directories appear in a different location than they reside. This offers great flexibility on disk use, but symbolic links should be used judiciously. If, for example, there is a lot of space on a newly created */u04*, some large data files from */u02* to can be moved to */u04*, then a symbolic link created to make them appear to still be on */u02*. To someone unfamiliar with this workaround, the files on */u04* may appear unused and they may delete them, thinking they are unneeded. A better permanent solution would be to move the files, then make Oracle aware of their new location.

Block Devices

In Linux, things like hard disks and disk partitions are represented by special files called block devices. These files can be written to and read from randomly in order to read and manipulate the contents of the disk. Block devices are indicated by a *b* in the first character of the *ls -l* listing.

```
$ ls -l /dev/hd*

brw-r----- 1 root disk  3,  0 Jan  9 05:04 /dev/hda
brw-r----- 1 root disk  3,  1 Jan  9 05:05 /dev/hda1
brw-r----- 1 root disk  3,  2 Jan  9 05:04 /dev/hda2
brw-r----- 1 root disk  3, 64 Jan  9 05:04 /dev/hdb
brw-r----- 1 root disk  3, 65 Jan  9 05:04 /dev/hdb1
brw-rw---- 1 root disk 22,  0 Jan  9 05:05 /dev/hdc
brw-r----- 1 root disk 22, 64 Jan  9 05:04 /dev/hdd
brw-r----- 1 root disk 22, 65 Jan  9 05:04 /dev/hdd1
```

System memory and removable media are also represented as block devices. Block devices often need to be referred to when configuring disks and file systems, but the devices typically are created and used by the system.

Character Devices

Special files called character devices represent another kind of I/O device. Like block devices, these devices can be read and manipulated, but in the case of character devices, they must be read and written to sequentially rather than randomly. Character devices are denoted by a *c* in the first column of *ls -l* output.

```
$ ls -l /dev/null

crw-rw-rw- 1 root root 1, 3 Jan  9 05:04 /dev/null

$ ls -l /dev/random

crw-rw-rw- 1 root root 1, 8 Jan  9 05:04 /dev/random
```

These are two typical examples of character devices. The */dev/null* device can be read from in order to create or simulate an empty file and data written to this device will be deleted. The */dev/random* device can be read to generate random data to use for encryption or other purposes.

Files, File Types and Directories

In some instances, character devices are used to allow random access to devices without buffering. This can allow a lower level of access to a device by bypassing the system buffer. In some cases, reading or writing directly from these files is preferred, but more often, scripts and programs will use them.

Named Pipes

Among the more rarely used file types is the named pipe. The named pipe allows you to facilitate communication between processes similar to how the pipe character (|) does, but with more flexibility. Named pipes are indicated by a *p* as the first letter of *ls -l* output. One example of this is the *initctl* pipe which is created at system startup as an interface to the *init* process.

```
$ ls -l /dev/initctl

prw------- 1 root root 0 Jan  9 05:05 /dev/initctl
```

A few named pipes are created by the system, but administrators rarely have to create or manipulate them.

Sockets

A socket is another special file type that allows for inter-process communication, but unlike named pipes, they offer additional functionality to handle other files. Sockets are represented with an *s* in the first colum of *ls -l* output. As an example, a socket is created in */tmp* when an X Windows session is started.

```
$ ls -l /tmp/.X11-unix/X0

srwxrwxrwx 1 root root 0 Jan  9 07:38 /tmp/.X11-unix/X0
```

Again, administrators generally do not need to manipulate sockets manually; instead, programs or the system typically manage them.

Inodes and Hard Links

When any kind of file is created on a file system, an inode is created to track information about that file. The inode contains information on ownership and permissions as well as access and modification times. Inodes are associated

---

with files through an inode number which can be viewed by adding the *-i* option to *ls*.

```
$ ls -i

524534 hello.sh  524532 status.sh  524584 test.sh

$ ls -li

total 24
524534 -rwxrwxr--+ 1 jemmons jemmons  30 Sep 29 13:28 hello.sh
524532 -rwxr-xr--  1 jemmons dba     370 Sep 29 13:43 status.sh
524584 -rwxr-xr-x  1 jemmons jemmons  20 Nov  8 08:37 test.sh
```

Each inode number is unique to the file system it was created on. From the inode, the system can determine the permissions on a file as well as where the file resides on the physical disk. Most of the time, there is no need to worry about the inode number of a file. The system does everything needed to manage the file-inode connection, but you have the ability to manipulate that and create hard links to files.

Hard links are somewhat similar to symbolic links mentioned previously in that they allow a second pointer to be created in another location for a given file. The difference is this: a symbolic link points from one location on the system to a real file or directory because directories are just a special type of file, but a hard link points from a location on a file system to an inode number which can be used to access that file.

In reality, every time a file is created, the file is being created on disk, an inode that contains metadata about that file (ownership, permissions, and more) and a hard link in the directory structure that users and programs can use to interface with that file. Thus, every file that is used has at least one hard link. The number of links a file has can be seen in the second column of *ls -l* output.

```
$ ls -l

total 24
-rwxrwxr--+ 1 jemmons jemmons  30 Sep 29 13:28 hello.sh
-rwxr-xr--  1 jemmons dba     370 Sep 29 13:43 status.sh
-rwxr-xr-x  1 jemmons jemmons  20 Nov  8 08:37 test.sh
```

Each file in this directory has one hard link, but in some cases files can be found with multiple hard links. One example of this is the *gzip* command.

```
# ls -l /bin/gzip

-rwxr-xr-x 3 root root 62104 Apr 21  2008 /bin/gzip
```

It can be told by the *ls* output that there are three hard links to this file. To find them, list the inode and then search for other file names with that inode. This method will be examined further later in this chapter.

```
# ls -i /bin/gzip

983087 /bin/gzip

# find / -inum 983087

/bin/zcat
/bin/gunzip
/bin/gzip
```

The *find* command turns up three file names using the inode number given. This means all three of these commands refer to the exact same file on disk. Often, a command name needs to be present for certain usages or to maintain compatibility even though its functionality is identical to, or at least supported by, another command. One option would be to create a copy of the command binary, but that would take up more space. Instead, hard links are created to the command names, so each of these refers to the exact same file and only one copy needs to be maintained of the file on disk.

Hard links can be used on any normal file, but since the inode is specific to the file system, a hard link cannot be created on one file system that refers to a file on another file system. With hard links, there is also no original or source and destination file. Each file name contains the inode number and that describes where to find the file's contents on disk, so if one of the file names is moved, changed or even deleted, the other linked files are not affected. Only when all the file names for a given inode are deleted will the space that file occupied be relinquished and reused for other purposes.

Creating Files and Directories

You are probably already familiar with how to create files and directories, but there are a few options here that may be unfamiliar to you.

Create an Empty File

Occasionally you may need to create an empty file as a place keeper. The *touch* command allows you to do exactly that.

```
$ ls

database_11g  Desktop  oradiag_oracle

$ touch testfile
$ ls

database_11g  Desktop  oradiag_oracle  testfile

$ ls -l

total 28
drwxr-xr-x 3 oracle oinstall 4096 Dec  6 07:51 database_11g
drwxr-xr-x 2 oracle oinstall 4096 May 19  2009 Desktop
drwxr-xr-x 3 oracle oinstall 4096 Oct 27 12:37 oradiag_oracle
-rw-rw-r-- 1 oracle oinstall    0 Jan  9 10:55 testfile
```

The *ls* output above shows that the new file is indeed empty, i.e. 0 bytes in size. If a file already exists, the *touch* command simply updates the file's access and modification timestamps but does not alter its contents.

Creating Directories

Directories can be created with the *mkdir* command. Directories are created in the current working directory unless another location is specified preceding the directory name.

```
$ mkdir scripts
$ ls -l

total 32
drwxr-xr-x 3 oracle oinstall 4096 Dec  6 07:51 database_11g
drwxr-xr-x 2 oracle oinstall 4096 May 19  2009 Desktop
drwxr-xr-x 3 oracle oinstall 4096 Oct 27 12:37 oradiag_oracle
drwxrwxr-x 2 oracle oinstall 4096 Jan  9 11:01 scripts
```

Multiple directories can be named after the *mkdir* command, separated by spaces, and each can be created. If directories need to be created within one another, the *-p* option can be used.

```
$ mkdir -p book/notes/chapter1
```

This option may save time, especially when a directory structure must be created on multiple systems.

Managing Ownership and Permissions

Linux security relies heavily on file ownership and permissions to determine who can do what. Proper permissions and both user and group ownership must be maintained to set up and assure that a system continues running properly.

How permissions and ownership of files can be viewed with the *ls -l* command has already been covered. Now it is time to look at how to change the owner, group, and permissions of files.

Managing the Owner and Group of a File

The *chown* and *chgrp* commands are used to manipulate the owner and group of a file, respectively. To maintain security, most changes to file ownership must be done as root.

chown expects two arguments. First, list the username of the user the ownership should be changed to, then the file name.

```
# ls -l accounts.txt

-rwxrwxrwx   1 oracle    oinstall     2069 Oct 29 12:36 accounts.txt

# chown jemmons accounts.txt
# ls -l accounts.txt

-rwxrwxrwx   1 jemmons   oinstall     2069 Oct 29 12:36 accounts.txt
```

chgrp works very similarly to *chown* but, of course, you supply a group name instead of a user name as the first argument. To change the group of a file, you must have write permissions on the file and be a member of the group where you wish the file to go.

```
$ groups

oinstall dba

$ ls -l nohup.out

-rw-------   1 oracle    oinstall     1655 Oct 31 15:26 nohup.out
```

```
$ chgrp dba nohup.out
$ ls -l nohup.out
```

```
-rw-------   1 oracle    dba         1655 Oct 31 15:26 nohup.out
```

The root user is needed if the group of a file needs to be changed to a group in which the owner does not belong.

There is a shortcut for changing both owner and group with the same command. The *chown* command can be used and a username and group supplied separated by a colon followed by a file name to change both simultaneously.

```
# ls -l nohup.out
```

```
-rw-------   1 oracle    dba         1655 Oct 31 15:26 nohup.out
```

```
# chown jemmons:other nohup.out
# ls -l nohup.out
```

```
-rw-------   1 jemmons   other       1655 Oct 31 15:26 nohup.out
```

This also usually requires root privileges since the ownership of the file is being changed.

Managing File Permissions

Different permissions, mainly read, write, and execute, can be granted to different levels of users (user, group, and other) to control access to files and directories. The user permissions apply to the owner of the file, the group applies to anyone in the group associated with the file, and other applies to users who are neither the owner nor in the group associated with the file.

The *chmod* command is used to modify permissions on files and there are several methods for using *chmod*. In the most straightforward method, give *chmod* two arguments: first a string of characters that indicate the permission change, and then the file or directory in which to apply the change.

```
$ ls -l test_script.sh
```

```
-rwxr-xr-x  1 oracle dba 102 Oct 22 14:53 test_script.sh
```

```
$ chmod o-x test_script.sh
$ ls -l test_script.sh
```

```
-rwxr-xr--  1 oracle dba 102 Oct 22 14:53 test_script.sh
```

```
$ chmod g+w test_script.sh
$ ls -l test_script.sh

-rwxrwxr--  1 oracle dba 102 Oct 22 14:53 test_script.sh

$ chmod o=rx test_script.sh
$ ls -l test_script.sh

-rwxrwxr-x  1 oracle dba 102 Oct 22 14:53 test_script.sh
```

Here the first *chmod* command uses the minus symbol (-) to remove the execute permissions from other users who are not the owner or part of the group this file belongs to. The second uses a plus (+) to grant the write privilege to users in the group this file belongs to. The third *chmod* command uses an equal sign (=) to set the permissions for others to read and execute, effectively removing the write permission if it had been granted.

Here are the common symbols used for defining permissions with the *chmod* command:

Privilege group indicator	Meaning	Change indicator	Meaning	Privilege indicator	Meaning
u	User	+	add permission	r	read
g	Group	-	remove	w	write
o	Other	=	update to this permission	x	execute

Table 13.1: *Character Symbols for Permission Modification*

To the left of the change indicator (+, - or =), multiple permission levels to be affected can be given, e.g. *go+w* would grant write to the group and other users. To the right of the change indicator, more than one privilege can be provided to affect as was shown in the example above. If desired, more than one set of changes can be combined in the same command by separating them with a comma like in the following example:

```
$ chmod u=rwx,g=rx,o= test_script.sh
$ ls -l test_script.sh

-rwxr-x---  1 oracle dba 102 Oct 22 14:53 test_script.sh
```

Permissions can also be specified using a number designation. When using this method, three numbers are typically given which stand for, in order, the user, group and other permissions. The numbers range from 0 to 7 and have the following meaning:

Number	Affective Permission
0	---
1	--x (not typically used)
2	-w- (not typically used)
3	-wx (not typically used)
4	r--
5	r-x
6	rw-
7	Rwx

Table 13.2: *chmod Numeric Designations*

Each of these numbers is derived from the sum of the three permissions where read is represented by 4, write by 2 and execute by 1. For instance, read and write without execute would be calculated by 4 (read) + 2 (write) = 6. As mentioned above, these numbers are used in groups of three to represent user, group and other permissions.

```
$ chmod 754 test_script.sh
$ ls -l test_script.sh

-rwxr-xr--  1 oracle dba 102 Oct 22 14:53 test_script.sh
```

This usage of *chmod* allows all three permissions to be set simultaneously and absolutely, so although the numbers are more difficult to remember, they are commonly used.

Controlling Default Permissions with Umask

Each user has a file creation mask, called an umask, which controls what permissions are given to a file when it is created. The umask setting can be examined using the *umask* command.

```
$ umask

0022
```

By default, the umask setting is displayed in a format that is subtracted from a systemwide default permission, typically 666 for files and 777 for directories, but an easier way to view these permissions is to add the *-S* option. This shows how the permissions are applied to files using the symbols rather than numbers.

```
$ umask -S

u=rwx,g=rx,o=rx
```

The umask can be set using the *umask* command as well and the new file creation mask takes effect immediately.

```
$ umask -S u=rwx,g=rwx,o=rx

u=rwx,g=rwx,o=rx

$ umask -S

u=rwx,g=rwx,o=rx
```

The new umask setting remains in place for the remainder of the command line session. If the umask needs to be persistent between sessions, the *umask* command can be added to the user's *.bash_profile* or another appropriate login file.

How Permissions Affect Directories

Directory permissions are changed in the same method as file permissions, but the results can be rather surprising and sometimes confusing. To examine the permissions on a directory, use the *-ld* option for the *ls* command. This shows the properties of the directory rather than listing its contents. Here are the typical directory permissions:

```
$ ls -ld example/

drwxr-xr-x  2 oracle dba 4096 Oct 29 22:38 example/
```

On directories, the read permission controls the ability to list the contents of a directory. By removing the read permission from your example, you see that you no longer can list the contents of the directory:

```
$ chmod u-r example/
$ ls example/
```

```
ls: example/: Permission denied

$ cd example/
$ pwd

/home/oracle/example
$ ls
ls: .: Permission denied
```

Even after changing the directory into *example*, the contents cannot be listed; however, it is significant that *cd*ing into the directory can be done.

The write permission on a directory controls whether a user, group or other users can create or delete a file or subdirectory of a directory. However, the execute permission has the unexpected behavior of controlling if a user can *cd* into a directory. To demonstrate, replace the read permission and remove execute on the example directory.

```
$ cd ../
$ chmod u+r example
$ chmod u-x example
$ ls example/

anotherfile.txt  log2.log  myfile.txt  sample.txt       types_of_unix.txt
log1.log         log3.log  output.txt  test_script.sh

$ cd example/

-bash: cd: example/: Permission denied
```

This shows that after removing the execute privilege, listing the contents of the directory can be done, but the DBA cannot *cd* into it. If a directory needs to be made viewable to other users, it is best to share both the read and execute privileges so users can both list and *cd* into the directory.

Additional Permissions Settings

There are three advanced options for permissions: the *setuid*, *setgid* and *sticky bit* options. The *sticky bit* is not really used much, but on shared directories, it affectively locks files within the directory from being modified by users other than the file creator.

This is how the */tmp* directory is typically maintained since multiple users require access to it. The *sticky bit* is indicated in *ls - l* output by a *t* in the last position of the permissions field.

```
$ ls -ld /tmp
```

```
drwxrwxrwt 9 root root 4096 Jan  9 08:22 /tmp
```

The setuid and setgid permissions allow controlling the user ID or group ID; a command is run regardless of who executes it. One example of this is the *ping* command. Since this command needs to interface with the network controller in a way only root is allowed to, the *setuid* bit is set. It can be seen in the same position where execute is normally indicated.

```
# ls -l /bin/ping
```

```
-rwsr-xr-x 1 root root 35864 Oct 31  2008 /bin/ping
```

When the *ping* command is executed by another user, it assumes the permissions of the root user before executing, but output is sent to the original user's session. Setuid and setgid can be very useful, but due to security concerns, both have been restricted on most modern operating systems including Linux.

Securing Important Files

On a multi-user system, as most Linux systems are, there will be times when access to certain files should be restricted. Often, shell scripts may have passwords in them or there may be documents or directories that other users should not see. The best way to secure these files and directories while still maintaining access to them is to use the *chmod* command to remove all permissions from group and other users.

```
$ ls -l test_script.sh
```

```
-rwxr-xr-x  1 oracle dba 102 Oct 22 14:53 test_script.sh
```

```
$ chmod go-rwx test_script.sh
$ ls -l test_script.sh
```

```
-rwx------  1 oracle dba 102 Oct 22 14:53 test_script.sh
```

This modification assures that this file cannot be viewed, modified or executed by any other user on the system. Assuming others do not have the specific username and password, this makes it safe to keep secure data like passwords on the system. This is necessary for some scripts that require passwords.

> Do not change the permissions on installed software unless you really know what you are doing. A few improper permission changes on files in the ORACLE_HOME directory could quickly render Oracle unusable.

Setting Permissions Beyond the Owner and Group

While the security model used in Linux offers quite a bit of flexibility, there are times when simply managing permissions on an owner/group/other basis is insufficient. To offer more flexibility, Linux offers access control lists, also referred to as ACLs.

ACLs offer the ability to name, individually, a user or group and grant them specific access to a given file. The primary commands for using ACLs are *setfacl*, which sets ACLs for a given file and *getfacl*, which display a file's ACL. When a file has an ACL set, a plus (+) appears after the permission portion of the *ls -l* output.

🖫 -m user:oracle:rwx hello.sh

```
$ setfacl -m user:oracle:rwx hello.sh
$ ls -l

total 24
-rwxrwxr--+ 1 jemmons jemmons  30 Sep 29 13:28 hello.sh
-rwxr-xr--  1 jemmons dba     370 Sep 29 13:43 status.sh
-rwxr-xr-x  1 jemmons jemmons  20 Nov  8 08:37 test.sh

$ getfacl hello.sh
# file: hello.sh
# owner: jemmons
# group: jemmons

user::rwx
user:oracle:rwx
group::rw-
mask::rwx
other::r--
```

To set an ACL on a file, the *-m* option is used with an ACL entry. The ACL entry is typically made up of the word *user* or *group* indicating what permissions should be added for, the name of the user or group and the permissions they should be granted on this file. The example above shows a typical ACL setting.

Permissions for multiple users or groups can be added through ACLs. Permissions for a given user or group can be replaced using the *-m* option in the same way they were added. When you want to remove a user or group from the ACL list, the *-x* option is used with *setfacl*.

```
$ setfacl -x user:oracle hello.sh
```

Since all permissions added through the ACL will be removed, there is no need to specify *r*, *w* or *x*.

Getting More Information on Files

The *ls* command has been covered several times now and it will probably be found to be the most useful command for viewing file information. This section will cover some of the less common but still useful options for the *ls* command as well as some other commands which can help in viewing file information.

Helpful *ls* Options

Beyond the long output (*-l* option) for *ls*, there are several other options that can give additional information. Here are some of the ones I find most useful.

Option	Usage
-l	Show long listing including file type, permission, links, ownership, size and modification date
-h	Used with *-l* shows file size in human-readable format (using K, M and G)
-i	Show the inode number before each file
-a	Show hidden files (files which begin with .)
-Q	Quote names with double quotes. This can be helpful in identifying names with spaces in them.
-t	Sort output by modification time
-r	Reverse sort order
-1	List only one file per line, regardless of how many may fit

Table 13.3: *ls Options*

These options can be combined into almost infinite combinations, but one specific combination particularly useful is to use the options *l*, *t* and *r* together to list the output in a long format with the newest files at the end.

```
$ ls -ltr

total 72
-rw-r--r-- 1 oracle oinstall  8385 Sep 11  1998 init.ora
-rw-r--r-- 1 oracle oinstall 12920 May  3  2001 initdw.ora
-rw-rw---- 1 oracle oinstall  1544 Oct 24 09:11 hc_TEST.dat
-rw-r----- 1 oracle oinstall    24 Oct 24 09:13 lkTEST
-rw-r----- 1 oracle oinstall  1536 Oct 24 09:18 orapwTEST
-rw-r----- 1 oracle oinstall     0 Jan  9 07:38 lkinstTEST
-rw-r----- 1 oracle oinstall  2560 Jan  9 11:27 spfileTEST.ora
```

This can help to quickly identify files which have been recently modified, even in directories with a large number of entries.

Viewing File Info with *stat*

The *stat* command allows you to view most of the information you would want to know about a file from a single command. Information shown includes size, ownership, permissions, last access and modification times and even the inode number and number of links.

```
$ stat test.sh

  File: `test.sh'
  Size: 20          Blocks: 16         IO Block: 4096    regular file
Device: fd00h/64768d    Inode: 524584      Links: 1
Access: (0755/-rwxr-xr-x)  Uid: (  501/ jemmons)   Gid: (  501/ jemmons)
Access: 2009-11-08 08:37:44.000000000 -0500
Modify: 2009-11-08 08:37:37.000000000 -0500
Change: 2009-11-08 08:37:43.000000000 -0500
```

One particular advantage of *stat* output over *ls* output is that *stat* clearly labels each piece of information. Though more verbose, this format is easier to understand.

Identifying File Contents

The *ls* and *stat* commands can be used to look at information about files, but say nothing about the contents of a file unless it is a special file type like a symlink or a directory. To learn more about the contents of a file, try to view it with *cat* or *more*, but that will only produce useful output if the file is a text file.

The *file* command applies a series of tests to a file in order to determine the type of information it contains. If the file is an executable binary, it prints information about what it was compiled for as seen in the output below for */bin/ls*.

```
$ file /bin/ls
```

```
/bin/ls: ELF 32-bit LSB executable, Intel 80386, version 1 (SYSV), for
GNU/Linux 2.6.9, dynamically linked (uses shared libs), for GNU/Linux 2.6.9,
stripped
```

```
$ file database
```

```
database: directory
```

```
$ file linux_11gR1_database_1013.zip
```

```
linux_11gR1_database_1013.zip: Zip archive data, at least v1.0 to extract
```

```
$ file /etc/hosts
```

```
/etc/hosts: ASCII English text
```

```
$ file /u02/oradata/TEST/system01.dbf
```

```
/u02/oradata/TEST/system01.dbf: data
```

The amount of information printed depends on the file type. Special files are identified by their file system file type, but other files like text and zip files are identified by matching the format of their contents. If a file's type cannot be identified, the *file* command simply labels it data.

Identifying Who is Using a File

The *lsof* command can be used to identify if someone is using a file, and if they are, who. In the previous chapter, *lsof* was used on a file system to identify who is using any files on that file system. The output is very similar for individual files.

The *lsof* command is found at */usr/sbin/lsof*, so only root has it in its binary search path by default, but other users can use it by giving the full path to the command. The output identifies the owner and process information for processes using the file.

```
$ /usr/sbin/lsof control01.ctl

COMMAND  PID   USER    FD    TYPE DEVICE    SIZE  NODE NAME
oracle  2904 oracle   18u    REG  253,3 9748480 81927 control01.ctl
oracle  2906 oracle   18u    REG  253,3 9748480 81927 control01.ctl
oracle  2908 oracle   18uW   REG  253,3 9748480 81927 control01.ctl
oracle  2914 oracle   20u    REG  253,3 9748480 81927 control01.ctl
```

The *lsof* command offers a good way to check to see if a file is in use before editing, moving or removing it. If the file is in use, you can shut down the program using it, ask the user to stop using it, or even kill the processes using it if there is no other alternative.

Copying, Moving, Renaming and Removing

Moving files and directories around the system is an essential administration skill. Here are some of the primary tools to use for moving things around.

 In most cases with these commands, the system allows for overwriting or removing existing files without warning! There is no easy way to undo this, so always check for existing files before using these commands.

Copying Files and Directories

The *cp* command enables the copying of files from one location to another. It can be used either with relative paths or full paths.

```
$ cp notes/chapter4.txt ./
$ ls

chapter4.txt  Desktop  notes  scripts

$ cp /u01/app/oracle/product/11.1.0/db_1/dbs/init.ora ./
$ ls

chapter4.txt  Desktop  init.ora  notes  scripts
```

As with most Linux commands, the *cp* command accepts arguments for the source, then the destination. Multiple sources may be specified, but the last

---

argument is always the destination. As an example of this, the two *cp* commands above could be rewritten into a single command like the following.

```
$ cp notes/chapter4.txt /u01/app/oracle/product/11.1.0/db_1/dbs/init.ora ./
$ ls

chapter4.txt  Desktop  init.ora  notes  scripts
```

Whenever the destination given is a directory, the files are copied into that directory and given their original names. If a file needs to be copied to a new name, give it as part of the destination.

```
$ cp /u01/app/oracle/product/11.1.0/db_1/dbs/init.ora ./example_init.ora
$ ls

chapter4.txt  Desktop  example_init.ora  init.ora  notes  scripts
```

To copy directories with their contents, use the *-r* (recursive) option for *cp*.

```
$ cp -r notes /tmp
$ ls /tmp

file.txt      keyring-sYbHqZ   mapping-oracle  notes
gconfd-root   mapping-jemmons  mapping-root
```

A directory can also be copied to a new name by specifying a destination name that does not already exist.

```
$ cp -r notes /tmp/original_notes
$ ls /tmp

file.txt      keyring-sYbHqZ   mapping-oracle  notes
gconfd-root   mapping-jemmons  mapping-root    original_notes
```

When copying files, the new file is typically created with the ownership of the user who copied it as well as permissions determined by their umask. Sometimes preserving permissions and ownership is desired and to do that, add the *-p* option to the *cp* command. As this often involves ownership from multiple users, this option is typically used by the root user.

```
# cp -rp /u01/app/oracle/product/11.1.0/db_1/dbs /tmp/backup_dbs
# ls -ld /tmp/backup_dbs

drwxr-xr-x 2 oracle oinstall 4096 Jan  9 07:38 /tmp/backup_dbs

# ls -l /tmp/backup_dbs/

total 72
```

```
-rw-rw----  1 oracle oinstall  1544 Oct 24 09:11 hc_TEST.dat
-rw-r--r--  1 oracle oinstall 12920 May  3  2001 initdw.ora
-rw-r--r--  1 oracle oinstall  8385 Sep 11  1998 init.ora
-rw-r-----  1 oracle oinstall     0 Jan  9 07:38 lkinstTEST
-rw-r-----  1 oracle oinstall    24 Oct 24 09:13 lkTEST
-rw-r-----  1 oracle oinstall  1536 Oct 24 09:18 orapwTEST
-rw-r-----  1 oracle oinstall  2560 Jan  9 11:27 spfileTEST.ora
```

As can be seen in the output above, the permissions and ownership of both the directory and its contents are preserved.

Moving and Renaming Files and Directories

The *mv* command allows for moving or renaming files and directories. In Linux, renaming can be considered a move to a new file name, either in the current directory or in a different destination if one is specified.

The syntax for *mv* is almost exactly the same as for *cp*. A source is given, then a destination. If the destination is a directory, the file's name is preserved.

```
$ ls

chapter4.txt  Desktop  init.ora  notes  scripts

$ mv init.ora example_init.ora
$ ls

chapter4.txt  Desktop  example_init.ora  notes  scripts

$ mv example_init.ora /tmp
$ ls /tmp

backup_dbs        file.txt      keyring-sYbHqZ   mapping-oracle  notes
example_init.ora  gconfd-root   mapping-jemmons  mapping-root    original_notes
```

Unlike when copying, directories can be moved or renamed without any additional options. Permissions and ownership are also preserved with *mv*.

```
$ ls

chapter4.txt  Desktop  notes  scripts

$ mv notes book_notes
$ ls

book_notes  chapter4.txt  Desktop  scripts
```

When a file or directory is moved from one place on a file system to another place on the same file system, the data on the disk stays in the same location

---

and the file retains the same inode; hence, the permissions and ownership are preserved. This can be seen by using the *-i* option to view inodes.

```
$ ls -di book_notes/

524496 book_notes/

$ mv book_notes notes
$ ls -di notes/

524496 notes/
```

Because only the file's directory entry needs to be changed, the move can happen almost instantly, but this is not the case when files or directories are moved between file systems. When that is the case, the system actually performs a copy to the new location, and then removes the original. The results are essentially the same, but a new inode number is assigned and the *mv* operation takes longer, especially with large files.

Removing (Deleting) Files and Directories

Files and directories can be removed with the *rm* command and the *rmdir* commands, respectively.

 The *rm* command is particularly destructive and fast, especially when used with the *-r* and *-f* options shown below. Think twice before using this command!

```
$ mkdir empty_dir
$ ls

chapter4.txt  Desktop  empty_dir  notes  scripts

$ rm chapter4.txt
$ rmdir empty_dir/
$ ls

Desktop  notes  scripts
```

The *rmdir* command can only be used to remove empty directories. If a directory and its contents need to be removed, use the *rm* command with the *-r* option.

```
$ cp -r notes old_notes
```

```
$ ls
```
```
Desktop   notes   old_notes   scripts
```
```
$ rm old_notes
```
```
rm: cannot remove `old_notes': Is a directory
```
```
$ rm -r old_notes
$ ls
```
```
Desktop   notes   scripts
```

In some cases, an attempt may be made to remove files or directories where there is no permission to modify. In that case, assuming there is permission to modify the directory the file in question exists in, there is a prompt to confirm that removing a write-protected file is wanted. The prompt can be answered with *y* to confirm that the file should be removed, or to avoid being prompted, use the *-f* option for *rm*.

```
$ rm chapter1.txt
```
```
rm: remove write-protected regular file `chapter1.txt'? y
```

Or:

```
$ rm -f chapter1.txt
```

The *-f* option is useful when there are a large number of files without write permissions, but it should be used with caution.

Some Linux administrators and users use the *-i* option for *rm* that causes the user to be prompted before any files are removed. While this may seem like a good failsafe to protect against accidentally deleting a file that was not meant to be deleted, it also results in a false sense of security and the tedium of confirming every file to be removed will quickly grow old. Instead, I recommend thinking twice before running any remove command and being very careful when using wildcards with *rm*.

Managing Hard and Symbolic Links

Hard links and symbolic links give a greater flexibility on where files and directories are stored and how they are accessed. They are used in different ways, but both can be thought of as a way to make a file or directory appear in more than one place.

Symbolic links are more commonly used due to their greater flexibility and clarity in *ls -l* output. The following chart shows the primary differences between hard and symbolic links:

Hard Links	Symbolic Links
Each hard link acts as an original. If a hard link is removed, any other hard link to the same file continues to work properly.	Symbolic links act as pointers to the original file or directory and if the original is removed, the symbolic link stops working as well.
Used for files	Used for files or directories
Must be linked to a location on the same file system	Can link to a location anywhere on the system
Same permissions applied to each file and are properly displayed in the *ls -l* listing	Permissions show as full *rwx* for each level, but permissions from the original are applied when the object is accessed.
In the *ls -l* listing, the link count (second column) shows the total number of hard links for a given file.	In the last column of the *ls -l* listing, the link name appears, followed by an arrow and the location of the original object.

Table 13.4: *A Comparison of Symbolic Links and Hard Links*

Of these differences, the first one is probably the most important. As mentioned earlier in this chapter, one hard link is created when a file is created, but when additional hard links are created, they also act as the original file. There is no differentiating between two hard links to the same file.

Symbolic links (symlinks), on the other hand, are merely pointers to an original file. While you can move the pointer, if you move or remove the original, the symlink ceases to work.

The same command, *ln*, is used to create both symbolic and hard links. By default, the *ln* command creates hard links, but the *-s* option can be added to create symbolic links.

```
$ ln -s /u01/app/oracle/product/11.1.0/db_1 oracle_home_1
```

```
$ ls -l
...
lrwxrwxrwx 1 oracle oinstall   35 Jan 17 08:12 oracle_home_1 ->
/u01/app/oracle/product/11.1.0/db_1
...
```

The symbolic link shows up in the directory listing with the indication of
where the original object is located. When a command or program tries to
access the link, it is redirected to the original object.

The original object for a symbolic link can be given as either an absolute path
starting with / or as a path relative to its location. Symlinks created with
relative paths may break if they are moved, so in general, I recommend using
an absolute path unless there is a good reason to use relative.

Hard links are created in the same way, but keep in mind these two restrictions
on hard links: hard links can only be created on the same file system as the
original, and hard links are not allowed on directories.
Both kinds of links can be removed using the *rm* command, but caution
should be taken to make sure the last hard link is not removed, as this will
result in the file being deleted.

Searching for Files and Directories

The *find* command allows searching part or all of the system for files and
directories based on a number of criteria. Start off by looking for files based
on their name, but also how searching on other attributes and automatically
performing commands on the files can be done is seen. Many of these
methods can be combined into a single command to perform very powerful
and specific searches.

Searching by Name

If you know the name of a file but not where it is on the system, you can use
the *find* command with the *-name* option to locate it. The *find* command expects
an argument indicating where to look for files followed by one or more
options that may have additional arguments. In this example, search the whole
system by specifying the location /.

```
$ find / -name tnsnames.ora
```

```
...
find: /home/areader: Permission denied
find: /u01/lost+found: Permission denied
/u01/app/oracle/product/11.1.0/db_1/network/admin/samples/tnsnames.ora
/u01/app/oracle/product/11.1.0/db_1/owb/network/admin/tnsnames.ora
find: /dev/VolGroup00: Permission denied
...
```

The *find* command prints out each location where a file by the given name is found. Every time *find* encounters a location that the user does not have permissions to read, a 'Permission denied' error is printed. Unless you are logged in as root, you can expect to get a whole lot of these when searching the entire system.

There are two ways to avoid permission errors when searching with *find*. The first is to limit the scope of the search to areas where there is read access.

```
$ find /u01/app/oracle -name tnsnames.ora
```

```
/u01/app/oracle/product/11.1.0/db_1/network/admin/samples/tnsnames.ora
/u01/app/oracle/product/11.1.0/db_1/owb/network/admin/tnsnames.ora
```

You should do this whenever possible as it will result in faster searches, but if you find you need to search the whole system, or at least everywhere you have read access to on the system, there is another method. Typically, output and errors are both printed to the console and appear intermixed. You can manipulate that and send errors to a file. You can choose to use a file in any directory where you can write to, or you can use the special file */dev/null* which causes the output to disappear.

The error output is redirected by indicating *2>/dev/null* after the command. The error output is identified as 2, and this essentially takes its output and deletes it. The final command would look something like this.

```
$ find / -name tnsnames.ora 2>/dev/null
```

```
/u01/app/oracle/product/11.1.0/db_1/network/admin/samples/tnsnames.ora
/u01/app/oracle/product/11.1.0/db_1/owb/network/admin/tnsnames.ora
```

It may be tempting to use this kind of redirection often, but be careful. This causes all errors for the given command to be omitted from the results, so it is best to use it only when it is known what is going to be ignored.

> 🔔 Typically, a directory called lost+found is seen on each partition. If files are recovered as part of a file system check, they are put in this directory. Only root has access to this directory, so it often gives a permission error when searching with *find*.

The method above works very efficiently if the entire name of a file is known, but sometimes only part of the name may be known or searching for files matching a certain pattern may be desired. This can be accomplished with wildcards. While there are other wildcards, the * is most frequently used and matches any string, including a blank string, in its place.

```
$ find /u02 -name "*.dbf"

find: /u02/lost+found: Permission denied
/u02/oradata/TEST/temp01.dbf
/u02/oradata/TEST/example01.dbf
/u02/oradata/TEST/sysaux01.dbf
/u02/oradata/TEST/users01.dbf
/u02/oradata/TEST/undotbs01.dbf
/u02/oradata/TEST/system01.dbf
```

When searching using wildcards, the search string must be put in quotes - single or double will work. This allows the wildcard to be passed in as part of the parameter to be interpreted by the *find* command rather than it being interpreted by the shell.

Searching by Other Attributes

The *search* command supports searching by practically any of the file attributes that have been covered so far in this chapter. Here are some common examples.

Searching for Recently Modified Files

The *find* option *-mtime* allows looking for files that have been modified less than or greater than a given number of days ago. The number of days is given after the *-mtime* option and '-' is specified to search for files modified less than the given number of days ago, or '+' to search for files modified more than the number of days ago. This example finds files modified within the past day.

```
$ find /u01 -mtime -1
```

```
find: /u01/lost+found: Permission denied
/u01/app/oracle/diag/tnslsnr/oelinux-test1/listener/trace/listener.log
/u01/app/oracle/diag/tnslsnr/oelinux-test1/listener/alert/log.xml
/u01/app/oracle/diag/rdbms/test/TEST/trace
. . .
```

As another example, specifying *-mtime +7* will return a list of files with modification dates more than seven days ago.

Searching for Files Owned by a Specific User

Using the *-user* option, all files in a location owned by a specific user can be quickly identified. To be sure of the accuracy of the results, a command like this should be run as root.

```
# find /home -user jemmons

/home/jemmons
/home/jemmons/.metacity
/home/jemmons/.metacity/sessions
. . .
```

Searching by File Size

The *-size* option of *find* allows searching for files larger or smaller than a specific size. After the *-size* option, the size can be specified in kilobytes (k), megabytes (M) or gigabytes (G) amongst other measures. It is possible to search for a file of an exact size, but more likely a + needs to be used to indicate files larger than a given size or - to indicate files smaller.

```
$ find /u02 -size +500M

find: /u02/lost+found: Permission denied
/u02/oradata/TEST/sysaux01.dbf
/u02/oradata/TEST/system01.dbf
```

This example searches for files larger than 500 MB.

Finding a Specific Type of File

The *find* command can search for specific file types using the *-type* option. Types are defined in the same way they are indicated in the first column of the *ls -l* output with the addition of *f* indicating regular files. This example finds all the symbolic links in the */u01* directory.

```
$ find /u01 -type 1
```

```
find: /u01/lost+found: Permission denied
/u01/app/oracle/product/11.1.0/db_1/bin/lbuilder
/u01/app/oracle/product/11.1.0/db_1/precomp/public/SQLCA.H
/u01/app/oracle/product/11.1.0/db_1/precomp/public/ORACA.FOR
/u01/app/oracle/product/11.1.0/db_1/precomp/public/ORACA.COB
...
```

The *-type* option is not overly useful by itself but can be a good way to specify only certain file types when using other options.

Searching by Inode and Identifying Hard Links

When multiple hard links exist for the same file, it is indicated in the second column of the *ls -l* output, but there is no indication where the links can be found. The *find* command offers a couple of ways to search for multiple links to the same file.

If the inode number of a file is viewed using *ls -i*, then use the *find* command with the *-inum* option to search for other locations where the inode number is in use.

```
# ls -i gunzip
```

```
983087 gunzip
```

```
# find / -inum 983087
```

```
/bin/zcat
/bin/gunzip
/bin/gzip
```

It is important to examine this output to make sure items from other file systems are not listed since they would not represent the same file. A simpler way to locate hard links to a given file is using the *-samefile* option. Rather than taking an inode number, this option takes a file name as an argument and identifies all file names hard linked to this file.

```
# find / -samefile ./gzip
```

```
/bin/zcat
/bin/gunzip
/bin/gzip
```

Performing Commands on Search Results

The default behavior of the *find* command is to print out a list of files found matching the given criteria. You can override this default and perform a specific operation on a file using the *-exec* option. The syntax is a little tricky, so start with an example.

```
$ find /u01/app/oracle/diag/rdbms/test/TEST/trace -mtime +30 -exec rm {} \;
```

This command searches in the trace location for files with a modification time of greater than 30 days ago and removes them. The *rm* command is given as an argument after the *-exec* option. Each time a file is found matching the search criteria, the name of the found file is substituted into the command in place of the '{}' curly braces and the command is executed. The escaped semicolon '\;' indicates the end of the *-exec* command.

A command like this can be powerful but also very dangerous. Great care must be taken to make sure *find* does not execute its command on files it was not intended for. One way to test this type of command is to use *ls -l* as the command after the *-exec* to view the results and make sure the correct files are being found before using more destructive commands like *rm* with *find*.

Combining Search Criteria

Any of the search criteria listed above can be combined to make more specific searches possible. The order of the options is not important as long as each option is accompanied by its own arguments. Here is a more specific example of the *find* command shown above. This goes further in specifying a pattern for the file name and the file type.

```
$ find /u01/app/oracle/diag/rdbms/test/TEST/trace -name "*.trm" -type f -
mtime +30 -exec rm {} \;
```

The more specific the DBA can be with a *find* command the better, especially when a command is reused or run automatically through *cron* or *at*.

Comparing Files and Directories

Being able to compare files or directories can enable you to quickly determine differences between things without having to manually examine file or directory contents. In some cases, you may want to display the differences, in others you may just need to know that things are different.

Comparing File and Directory Contents with *diff*

The *diff* command allows comparing two files and displaying lines that differ. Lines that show up in one file but not in another are also displayed.

```
$ diff init.ora initTEST.ora
78c78
< db_name=DEFAULT
---
> db_name=TEST
92c92
< shared_pool_size = 3500000                              # SMALL
---
> shared_pool_size = 10000000                             # SMALL
98c98
< processes = 50                                          # SMALL
---
> processes = 300                                         # SMALL
```

The *diff* command indicates the line numbers on which the differences were found and displays the lines with a < indicating the line contents from the first file given and a > indicating the corresponding contents of the second file.

If you just want to see if two files differ, ignoring their contents, use the *-q* option for *diff*.

```
$ diff -q init.ora initTEST.ora

Files init.ora and initTEST.ora differ
```

When comparing configuration files where white space, i.e. spaces and tabs, is ignored, it can be handy to use the *-w* option to cause *diff* to also ignore white space.

The *diff* command can also be used with the *-r* option to examine directories and their contents to see how they differ. Any file found in one directory but not another is noted as such. Files found in both directories are compared and their differences printed as seen when *diff* is used on files.

```
$ diff -r notes old_notes

Only in notes: chapter13.txt
diff -r notes/chapter5.txt old_notes/chapter5.txt
2,5d1
<
```

```
< We will investigate individual tools in more depth in the upcoming
chapters
< but for now we will first gain a familiarity with basic command line
< navigation.
```

Using Checksums to Compare Files

A checksum is a short string of characters created by applying an algorithm to a file. It acts as a fingerprint of the contents of the file. Two identical copies of a file always have the same checksum. Conversely, two different files almost never have the same checksum. It is possible for two different files to have the same checksum, but it is very, very unlikely.

Checksums can be used to compare files on the same system or different systems. Software download sites often provide a checksum so the checksum of your download can be compared to their sum to confirm they are identical. As long as the checksums match, it is almost certain the file has not been modified or corrupted.

Several methods are available to generate a checksum of a file, but the MD5 checksum generated by the command *md5sum* has become the most broadly accepted. The *md5sum* command accepts a file name as an argument.

```
$ md5sum chapter1.txt

08152aa6547e578d3d737b18c4bae5f4  chapter1.txt
```

If a file's contents change, the checksum does as well. In this example, I added a line to the file and regenerated the checksum. Note that it is not only part of the checksum that has changed, but rather the whole thing.

```
$ md5sum chapter1.txt

08152aa6547e578d3d737b18c4bae5f4  chapter1.txt

$ echo 'The flexibility of linux has been key to its success.' >>
chapter1.txt
$ md5sum chapter1.txt

d5ce4e2e681653fc0d2876c823480892  chapter1.txt
```

The *md5sum* command generates the same checksum for identical files regardless of the location, system or platform. It can be used to compare one file to another, or a checksum of a file can be saved and the checksum of that file can be compared to it at a later date. Some security software even uses MD5 checksums to identify if software has been changed by an intruder.

Backing Up, Archiving and Compressing

Several methods are available for backing up, archiving and compressing files on the Linux system. Which method is used depends on which file or files are being backed up and if they should be compressed.

In this section, backing up specific data on the system will be shown. These methods only create an additional copy of your files on the system but if there is a system failure, you would still lose them. For long-term backup, these files should be copied to another system or removable media and preferably stored in a different physical location. How you back up your entire system depends on your backup hardware and software and is beyond the scope of this book.

Here is a brief list of pros and cons of archiving and compression methods. This should give a good start to deciding what method to use.

Method	Pros	Cons
tar	Universally available, maintains permissions and other file information, handles multiple files very well	Does not compress files
cpio	Good compatibility between systems	No compression, clumsy syntax
zip	Format readable on nearly all platforms, good space saving on compression	More space can be saved with other compression methods
gzip	Very good space saving on compression, broadly adopted	*gzip* utilities may not be available for some platforms

Table 13.5: *Pros and Cons of Common Archiving and Compression Methods*

Using *tar*, the Tape Archiver

Originally written to manipulate magnetic tape devices, the *tar* command, short for tape archiver, can be used to create or read tar archives. Tar archives, sometimes called tarballs, typically can be identified by the *.tar* file extension, though this is not a requirement.

The *-cvf* options are typically used to create *tar* files. The *-c* indicates that you are creating an archive, *-v* tells *tar* that you would like verbose output, e.g. each file name and location will be printed as it is added to the archive, and the *-f* option tells tar that you are working with a file rather than a magnetic tape drive.

When creating archives, the *tar* command requires at least two arguments. The first argument is the archive file with which to work. The second argument is the file or directory to add to the archive. Additional arguments can also be given to indicate more files to add to the archive.

```
$ tar -cvf notes.tar notes

notes/
notes/chapter3.txt
notes/chapter5.txt
notes/chapter2.txt
notes/chapter4.txt
notes/required_packages.txt
notes/chapter13.txt
notes/chapter1.txt
notes/chapter10.txt
```

To create a tar archive from a file or directory, it is best to *cd* to the directory the source resides in. It is possible to specify the source directory with an absolute path, but that causes the files to be extracted to that path regardless of where the file is extracted from.

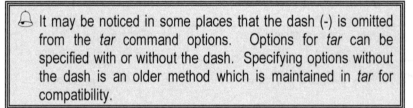

It may be noticed in some places that the dash (-) is omitted from the *tar* command options. Options for *tar* can be specified with or without the dash. Specifying options without the dash is an older method which is maintained in *tar* for compatibility.

To extract files from a tar archive, the *-x* option is used instead of *-c*. Files are extracted based on the current working directory as long as an absolute path was not used during archive creation. Only one argument is needed to indicate where the tar archive can be found.

```
$ cd /tmp
$ tar -xvf /home/jemmons/notes.tar

notes/
notes/chapter3.txt
notes/chapter5.txt
notes/chapter2.txt
notes/chapter4.txt
notes/required_packages.txt
notes/chapter13.txt
notes/chapter1.txt
notes/chapter10.txt
```

Tar archives can be compressed using *zip* or *gzip* to save space. If the archive is already created, it can be compressed using the method described in the part of this section on *gzip*, but if an archive needs to be created in a compressed format, add the *-z* option to the *tar* command.

```
$ tar -cvzf notes.tar.gz notes

notes/
notes/chapter3.txt
...
```

When using *tar*, the file names are arbitrary. It is best to follow the common convention of *.tar* for tar archives and *.tar.gz* or *.tgz* for compressed tar archives. If, for some reason, you are unsure of the contents of a file, use the *file* command to check it.

```
$ file notes.tar.gz

notes.tar.gz: gzip compressed data, from Unix, last modified: Sun Jan 17
13:07:47 2010
```

```
$ file notes.tar

notes.tar: POSIX tar archive
```

Using *cpio*

While I do not recommend *cpio* for creating backups or moving files between systems, it may be found that software that has been downloaded is delivered in *.cpio* files. For quite some time Oracle delivered their software in this format, so it is important to be able to extract these files.

Unlike many other utilities, *cpio* reads data from standard input. To extract data from a *.cpio* file, redirect the file contents into the *cpio* command using the

---

< character. The flags *idmv* tell *cpio* to extract data, create directories if they do not exist, preserve file and directory modification times, and print verbose output.

```
$ cpio -idmv < disk1.cpio
```

Using *zip* and *unzip* to Compress and Uncompress Files

Software is frequently delivered in *zip* files since extraction utilities are available on just about every modern operating system. *Zip* files can be easily extracted using the *unzip* command, providing only a file name as an argument.

```
$ unzip 10201_database_linux32.zip

Archive:  10201_database_linux32.zip
   creating: database/
   creating: database/doc/
   creating: database/doc/dcommon/
   creating: database/doc/dcommon/css/
  inflating: database/doc/dcommon/css/blafdoc.css
  inflating: database/doc/dcommon/css/darbbook.css
  inflating: database/doc/dcommon/css/darbbook.css~
  inflating: database/doc/dcommon/css/doccd.css
   creating: database/doc/dcommon/gifs/
  inflating: database/doc/dcommon/gifs/bookbig.gif
  inflating: database/doc/dcommon/gifs/bookicon.gif
. . .
```

The *unzip* command prints a list of directories created and files extracted from the source file.

Creating a *zip* file is similar to creating a *tar* file, but no options are needed. A destination file name is given as the first argument, then the files to be added to the *zip* file can be given in one or more additional arguments.

```
$ zip oracle_profile.zip oracle_profile

  adding: oracle_profile (deflated 15%)

$ ls

devl  emrep  oracle_profile  oracle_profile.zip  orcl  TEST
```

Note that unlike on Windows, the original file is not deleted when a *zip* file is created. If space needs to be saved, go back and delete the original.

To create a *zip* file with the contents of a directory, use the *-r* (recursive) option.

```
$ zip -r dev1_admin_dir.zip dev1

  adding: dev1/ (stored 0%)
  adding: dev1/dpdump/ (stored 0%)
  adding: dev1/dpdump/dp.log (deflated 16%)
  adding: dev1/pfile/ (stored 0%)
  adding: dev1/pfile/init.ora.22201013228 (deflated 71%)
  adding: dev1/adump/ (stored 0%)
...
```

When this *zip* file is extracted, the directory structure and files are recreated.

Using *gzip* and *gunzip* to Compress and Uncompress Files

The *gzip* compression format has become one of the most broadly accepted formats thanks to its very good compression algorithm and fast performance. To compress a file, use *gzip* with the file name as an argument.

```
$ gzip notes_chapter1.txt
$ ls -l

total 48
drwxr-xr-x 2 jemmons jemmons 4096 Sep 16 13:19 Desktop
drwxrwxr-x 2 jemmons jemmons 4096 Jan 17 13:17 notes
-rw-rw-rw- 1 jemmons jemmons  589 Jan 17 07:46 notes_chapter1.txt.gz
-rw-rw-r-- 1 jemmons jemmons 1525 Jan 17 13:07 notes.tar.gz
drwxrwxr-x 2 jemmons jemmons 4096 Jan 17 11:18 old_notes
drwxr-xr-x 2 jemmons jemmons 4096 Nov  8 08:37 scripts
```

Unlike *tar*, *gzip* removes the original file after creating the compressed version. The *.gz* file name extension is also automatically added to the file name. To uncompress a *gzip* file, the *gunzip* command is used with the file name as an argument.

```
$ gunzip notes_chapter1.txt.gz
$ ls -l

total 48
drwxr-xr-x 2 jemmons jemmons 4096 Sep 16 13:19 Desktop
drwxrwxr-x 2 jemmons jemmons 4096 Jan 17 13:17 notes
-rw-rw-rw- 1 jemmons jemmons 1027 Jan 17 07:46 notes_chapter1.txt
-rw-rw-r-- 1 jemmons jemmons 1525 Jan 17 13:07 notes.tar.gz
drwxrwxr-x 2 jemmons jemmons 4096 Jan 17 11:18 old_notes
drwxr-xr-x 2 jemmons jemmons 4096 Nov  8 08:37 scripts
```

Again, the compressed version of the file is removed after it is uncompressed.

Getting Rid of the Wrong New Line Characters

If you have worked with other UNIX platforms or older versions of Linux, you have probably seen files where each new line was accompanied by the characters ^M. These come from the file being created or transferred to a Windows or older Macintosh system where the new line characters are represented differently. RHEL5 and some of its UNIX contemporaries now display or at least hide these characters properly, but they are still there and may occasionally give some trouble with applications that are not prepared to handle them.

For that reason, there is a utility to convert files from the Windows format to what UNIX expects. Since RHEL5 displays files correctly regardless of the file format, use the *file* command to identify the Windows formatted files. If the *file* command returns a format 'with CRLF line terminators', there are Windows-style new lines. In that case, use the *dos2unix* command to convert them.

```
$ file hosts.txt

hosts.txt: ASCII English text, with CRLF line terminators

$ dos2unix hosts.txt

dos2unix: converting file hosts.txt to UNIX format ...

$ file hosts.txt

hosts.txt: ASCII English text
```

Similarly, when copying files from a Linux system to a Windows system, it may be found that everything displays on a single line in some editors, especially Notepad. To avoid this, use a similar utility called *unix2dos*. This accomplishes the opposite result, adding the new line characters Windows will expect.

Splitting and Combining Large Files

When working with large files like Oracle data files, it is sometimes necessary to split them up, either to transfer them over the network in smaller chunks or to fit them onto backup media. Linux offers the *split* command to split up large files and the *cat* (short for concatenate) command can be used to recombine them.

The *-b* option for the *split* command allows for specifying how many bytes are wanted in each piece a file is split up into. Rather than specifying in bytes, *k* or *m* can also be used after the number to specify it in kilobytes or megabytes, respectively. The *split* command also takes the file name to be split up and the base name that should be used for the pieces of the file. The base name has *aa, ab, ac,* and such appended to it in order to give the file pieces unique names.

The following example shows the *md5sum* command being used to take a checksum of the file *system01.dbf,* and then the *split* command is used to split it into pieces. Finally, the *cat* command is used to combine the file. The *cat* command normally prints the contents of each file to the display, but in this example, the output is redirected to the file *system01.dbf.* Finally, the *md5sum* command is used to generate a checksum on the recreated file.

```
$ md5sum system01.dbf

14ec97e010fa9568abcda44b58bb7624  system01.dbf

$ ls

system01.dbf

$ split -b 100m system01.dbf system01.
$ ls -l

total 1414584
-rw-r--r-- 1 oracle oinstall 104857600 Jan 18 15:19 system01.aa
-rw-r--r-- 1 oracle oinstall 104857600 Jan 18 15:19 system01.ab
-rw-r--r-- 1 oracle oinstall 104857600 Jan 18 15:19 system01.ac
-rw-r--r-- 1 oracle oinstall 104857600 Jan 18 15:19 system01.ad
-rw-r--r-- 1 oracle oinstall 104857600 Jan 18 15:19 system01.ae
-rw-r--r-- 1 oracle oinstall 104857600 Jan 18 15:19 system01.af
-rw-r--r-- 1 oracle oinstall  94380032 Jan 18 15:19 system01.ag
-rw-r----- 1 oracle oinstall 723525632 Jan 18 15:16 system01.dbf

$ rm system01.dbf
$ cat system01.* > system01.dbf
$ ls -l

total 1414584
-rw-r--r-- 1 oracle oinstall 104857600 Jan 18 15:19 system01.aa
-rw-r--r-- 1 oracle oinstall 104857600 Jan 18 15:19 system01.ab
-rw-r--r-- 1 oracle oinstall 104857600 Jan 18 15:19 system01.ac
-rw-r--r-- 1 oracle oinstall 104857600 Jan 18 15:19 system01.ad
-rw-r--r-- 1 oracle oinstall 104857600 Jan 18 15:19 system01.ae
-rw-r--r-- 1 oracle oinstall 104857600 Jan 18 15:19 system01.af
-rw-r--r-- 1 oracle oinstall  94380032 Jan 18 15:19 system01.ag
-rw-r--r-- 1 oracle oinstall 723525632 Jan 18 15:22 system01.dbf

$ md5sum system01.dbf

14ec97e010fa9568abcda44b58bb7624  system01.dbf
```

You can see by this point with the *md5* checksums match that the recreated *system01.dbf* is almost definitely identical to the original. Since the *split* and *cat* utilities work the same way on any UNIX or UNIX-like operating system, you can be confident that a file you split on one system can be put back together on another.

Conclusion

Mastery of file manipulation is one of the core competencies of Linux administration and the foundation of database administration. Knowledge of ownership and permissions management methods helps someone be a more efficient DBA and helps in communicating better with system administrators.

Almost every area of Linux and database administration will involve some level of file administration. Do not feel like all the topics in this chapter need to memorized, but plan to return to this chapter often for reference.

Memory and System Settings

When running Oracle on a Linux system, there are some system-level settings that need to be tuned to allow Oracle to make the best of the resources available. Most of these relate to memory but a few other system settings are important as well.

Understanding Memory

Computer memory is probably a familiar topic, but to cover all the bases, take a quick look at memory and how it compares to the other storage methods used on the Linux system.

Types of Memory

Random access memory, or RAM (referred to as physical memory or just memory), is the system's primary working space. This is in contrast to disk storage, which is more like a long-term storage space. Like most other modern operating systems, Linux also has the ability to use some disk space as virtual memory, referred to as swap.

Since it resides on disk, swap is much slower to read and write than RAM, but it has the overall effect of making the system appear to have more memory than it does and, therefore, more programs or larger programs can be run at a given time. To use swap more efficiently, the system tries to determine what areas of memory are not being used frequently and moves those to swap, keeping the most frequently or, at least, most recently used information in memory.

The process of moving data between physical memory and swap space is referred to as swapping. When data is moved from memory to disk, it is said to be swapped out, while moving data from disk to memory is referred to as swapping in. Programs, including Oracle, running on the system have no

---

power over the use of swap. They are at the mercy of the system to determine what should be kept in RAM and what can be moved to swap.

The processor or processors in the system have dedicated memory referred to as processor cache. This specialized segment of very fast memory, typically measured in megabytes, is used to improve processor performance. As with RAM, more processor cache is better and it is likely that a larger processor cache is found on higher-end machines. But unlike RAM, processor cache cannot be upgraded without replacing the processors. The processor cache is managed at a hardware level, so it will not be examined much further.

This quick list should summarize memory on the Linux system:

- The fastest memory on the system is processor cache, but it is very small and there is very little control over it.

- RAM is the next fastest and is where most of your process memory will hopefully reside.

- Swap is slower than RAM as it resides on disk, but it allows the system to appear to have more memory than it has. The system will try to keep information most often used in RAM and move the least recently used information to swap.

How Memory is Used

Linux allocates memory for use in three different ways. The first, kernel memory, is memory used specifically for the operating system. The second, private memory, is memory that is allocated for use by a single program. Finally, shared memory can be accessed by more than one program simultaneously.

While many single-user programs rely exclusively on private memory, Oracle makes extensive use of shared memory for the SGA, which includes the database buffer cache, the shared pool and the redo log buffer. Holding these resources in shared memory allows Oracle to manipulate them with multiple processes and, therefore, service many requests at once without requiring a separate cache for each resource. Since this is different from how many programs use memory, parameters often have to be adjusted to allow such a large segment of shared memory.

Memory Limits

There is a lot of confusion around the memory limitations on Linux. The fundamental argument is that due to hardware limitations, a 32-bit operating system is only capable of addressing 4 GB of memory. While this is true from a purely hardware standpoint, 32-bit Linux has the capability of supporting 16 GB memory with the standard SMP kernel included with Red Hat and Oracle Enterprise Linux distributions. Additionally, a per-process limit of 4 GB affects how a program can use memory.

A hugemem kernel is available for Versions 3 and 4 of RHEL and OEL which can support up to 64 GB RAM. Changing to the hugemem kernel involves applying a series of packages to the system and possibly changing some boot settings and restarting the system. Consult Linux documentation for the exact steps. Some workarounds since RHEL and OEL Version 5 no longer support the hugemem kernel, limiting these to 16 GB RAM. While it is unclear why hugemem is not supported, it is likely due to the proliferation of 64-bit hardware.

64-bit hardware is capable of natively handling a much larger memory address than its 32-bit counterpart. As a result, recent 64-bit Linux distributions are certified for use with up to 256 GB of RAM and can address up to 1 TB. If your hardware is capable of 64-bit operation, 64-bit Linux should be installed unless there is some compelling reason to stay with 32-bit.

File Caching

Linux tries to make the most out of the available memory. As such, it is often found that there is very little free memory, even on a relatively idle system. This is because Linux tries to cache information from the disk for future use.

When information is needed from disk, the kernel reads it into memory so programs can display or manipulate it. When a program is done with data, the kernel writes out changes to disk if necessary, but it keeps the copy of the file in memory until another process needs that segment of RAM. If another program needs to access the file before the copy in RAM is overwritten, it can be opened very quickly as it has already been loaded from disk to RAM. While all of this happens automatically (controlled by the kernel), it is important to

---

understand that this is why the system may report very little free memory even when there is not much running.

Oracle Required Settings

Many Oracle products require that certain memory settings be in place before they are installed. These requirements vary somewhat by product and platform and can be found in the platform-specific installation guides. This section should take the mystery out of what some of these settings do.

Swap Space

The amount of swap space available to the system helps to increase both the number of processes and the amount of memory they can acquire without exhausting the system's RAM. Remember that although swap is slower than RAM, the system is intelligent enough to move data which is less likely to be needed to swap, thus freeing up more RAM for data in higher demand. In this way, adding swap, a slower resource, can increase performance.

If you find your current swap allocation is lower than the Oracle recommendation, you need to increase the size of the swap partition or create a new partition on a different disk. This is covered in detail in Chapter 5.

Semaphores

Semaphores act as flags for shared memory. Semaphores are either set on or off. When an Oracle process accesses the SGA in shared memory, it checks for a semaphore for that portion of memory. If it finds a semaphore set on for that portion of memory, indicating another process is already using that portion, the process will sleep and check again later. If there is no semaphore set on for that portion of memory, it sets one on and proceeds with its operation. When it is done, it switches that semaphore back to off.

Oracle specifies *semaphore* values for *semmsl*, *semmns*, *semopm* and *semmni* as 250, 3200, 100 and 128, respectively. These can be found in the output of the *sysctl* command in this same order.

```
# /sbin/sysctl -a | grep sem
kernel.sem = 250    32000   32      128
```

The values for the semaphores represent the following:

- *semmsl*: The number of semaphores per set

- *semmns*: The total number of semaphores available

- *semopm*: The number of operations which can be made per semaphore call

- *semmni*: The maximum number of shared memory segments available in the system

The Oracle recommended values is a good starting point for these parameters, but when running multiple Oracle databases on a system, *semmsl* and *semmns* may need to be increased to accommodate the additional instances.

To change this setting, edit the */etc/sysctl.conf* file. If there is already a line for *kernel.sem*, edit the values given; otherwise, add a line in the same format as the output above. The line should look like this:

```
kernel.sem = 250 32000 100 128
```

This line can be added anywhere in the file, but it is best to keep all the changes in one place within the file. Comments can be added by starting a line with a # character.

Shared Memory Settings

The parameters *shmall*, *shmmax* and *shmmni* determine how much shared memory is available for Oracle to use. These parameters are set in memory pages, not in bytes, so the usable sizes are the value multiplied by the page size, typically 4096 bytes. To confirm the page size, use the command *getconf -a | grep PAGE_SIZE*.

- *shmall*: The total amount of shared memory (in pages) which can be allocated on the system

- *shmmax*: The maximum size of a shared memory segment (in pages)

- *shmmni*: The maximum number of shared memory segments available on the system

Given that the SGA for a database must be kept in shared memory, the value of *shmmax* needs to be as big as the largest SGA. The value for *shmall* needs to be bigger than the sum of all your databases. The value for *shmmni* needs to be at least as high as the number of databases that are intended to be put on the system, but in practice is generally much higher (Oracle recommends 4096.)

The quick install guide includes directions on checking these parameters. If they need to be modified, they can be set in the */etc/sysctl.conf* file with entries like the following:

```
kernel.shmall = 2097152
kernel.shmmax = 2147483648
kernel.shmmni = 4096
```

Keep in mind that *shmall* and *shmmax* are set in 4 KB pages, not in bytes.

Other System Settings

A few additional settings are needed for Oracle. These are not directly related to the system memory, but are included in this section for completeness.

- *fs.file-max*: Controls the total number of files which can be opened at once
- *ip_local_port_range*: This controls the number of network connections which can be allocated at once. These are unrelated to the network ports on which incoming connections are made.
- *rmem_default* and *rmem_max*: Represent the default and maximum size of the network receive buffer
- *wmem_default* and *wmem_max*: Represent the default and maximum size of the network send buffer

Under most circumstances, the Oracle recommended values should be used for these parameters. These can be set in the */etc/sysctl.conf* file.

```
fs.file-max = 6815744
net.ipv4.ip_local_port_range = 9000 65500
net.core.rmem_default = 262144
net.core.rmem_max = 4194304
net.core.wmem_default = 262144
net.core.wmem_max = 1048576
```

While many of these settings can be changed dynamically, it is best to set them in the */etc/sysctl.conf* file and restart. After restart, confirm that the settings are working.

Monitoring Memory Usage

There are several tools available on Linux to allow monitoring the memory, but the most important part is being able to interpret the output of these tools. The following will give a good start, but with experience, memory statistics can be interpreted more easily.

Monitoring Memory Usage Using *top*

One place to get information on memory usage is the familiar *top* command. As seen in the output below, the fourth line gives information on the physical memory (RAM) and the fifth line provides information on swap usage.

```
$ top

top - 09:54:41 up  4:52,  2 users,  load average: 0.54, 0.13, 0.04
Tasks: 105 total,   2 running, 103 sleeping,   0 stopped,   0 zombie
Cpu(s):  0.2%us,  1.8%sy,  1.3%ni, 95.1%id,  0.9%wa,  0.1%hi,  0.6%si,  0.0%st
Mem:   1035244k total,   896300k used,   138944k free,    50916k buffers
Swap:  2097144k total,        0k used,  2097144k free,   712016k cached

  PID USER      PR  NI  VIRT  RES  SHR S %CPU %MEM    TIME+  COMMAND
 9555 oracle    17   0  533m  35m  33m R  5.9  3.5   0:00.36 oracle
 9571 oracle    16   0  534m  39m  36m D  3.9  3.9   0:00.75 oracle
    1 root      15   0  2064  620  532 S  0.0  0.1   0:06.46 init
    2 root      RT  -5     0    0    0 S  0.0  0.0   0:00.00 migration/0
    3 root      34  19     0    0    0 S  0.0  0.0   0:00.07 ksoftirqd/0
    4 root      RT  -5     0    0    0 S  0.0  0.0   0:00.01 watchdog/0
    5 root      10  -5     0    0    0 S  0.0  0.0   0:00.70 events/0
    6 root      10  -5     0    0    0 S  0.0  0.0   0:00.32 khelper
    7 root      10  -5     0    0    0 S  0.0  0.0   0:00.09 kthread
   10 root      10  -5     0    0    0 S  0.0  0.0   0:00.41 kblockd/0
   11 root      20  -5     0    0    0 S  0.0  0.0   0:00.00 kacpid
   48 root      20  -5     0    0    0 S  0.0  0.0   0:00.00 cqueue/0
   51 root      10  -5     0    0    0 S  0.0  0.0   0:00.00 khubd
   53 root      11  -5     0    0    0 S  0.0  0.0   0:00.00 kseriod
  112 root      16   0     0    0    0 S  0.0  0.0   0:00.00 pdflush
  113 root      15   0     0    0    0 S  0.0  0.0   0:00.10 pdflush
  114 root      11  -5     0    0    0 S  0.0  0.0   0:00.00 kswapd0
```

Additionally, it can be seen that *top* provides memory usage information for each of the top processes listed. First the summary information will be examined, then the process information.

In the fourth line of the *top* output, information can be seen on RAM. The first value indicates the total amount of physical memory available on this system. The next value shows how much of that memory is currently in use. Keep in mind that Linux will cache data in memory if the memory is not being used for anything else, so even though *top* reports only 35 MB free, it can be seen by the last value of the following line that over 800 MB is being used as cache. This memory could be freed up for other processes if needed.

The third value on the fourth line indicates the amount of memory currently unallocated and not being used for cache. This memory is available for immediate use. Finally, the *buffers* value indicates how much RAM is being used to track disk block information.

On the next line, the total amount of swap is indicated followed by the amount of swap currently in use and the amount of swap free. This example shows 0 K used, but a system which has been running longer will likely be using swap.

On the lower part of the *top* output, the information on each process can be seen. Specifically the *VIRT*, *RES*, *SHR* and *%MEM* columns are of interest for memory usage. Here is what these values represent:

- *VIRT*: The total amount of memory the process is using, including RAM, swap and any shared memory being accessed

- *RES*: The amount of resident memory, or real RAM being used by this process

- *SHR*: The amount of shared memory being accessed by this process

- *%MEM*: The percentage of physical (resident) memory used by this process

When investigating memory usage, it may be useful to sort processes by one of these columns. In *top*, you can change the sort order by pressing 'F', then choosing from a list of sort columns. The output listed below is sorted by the *VIRT* column.

```
top - 10:37:36 up  5:35,  2 users,  load average: 0.00, 0.00, 0.00
Tasks: 106 total,    2 running, 104 sleeping,   0 stopped,   0 zombie
Cpu(s):  0.1%us,  0.3%sy,  0.0%ni, 97.8%id,  0.3%wa,  0.1%hi,  1.3%si,  0.0%st
Mem:   1035244k total,  1005404k used,    29840k free,    47772k buffers
Swap:  2097144k total,        0k used,  2097144k free,   811668k cached

  PID USER      PR  NI  VIRT  SHR S %CPU %MEM    TIME+  COMMAND
10038 oracle    15   0  548m  32m S  0.0  3.4  0:00.24 oracle
10046 oracle    15   0  537m  44m S  0.0  5.0  0:01.11 oracle
10176 oracle    15   0  537m  23m S  0.0  2.9  0:00.45 oracle
10042 oracle    15   0  535m  78m S  0.0  8.0  0:00.65 oracle
10036 oracle    15   0  535m  13m S  0.1  1.6  0:00.18 oracle
10063 oracle    18   0  534m  19m S  0.0  2.1  0:00.17 oracle
10018 oracle    15   0  533m  13m S  0.0  1.4  0:00.24 oracle
10050 oracle    18   0  533m  10m S  0.0  1.2  0:00.09 oracle
10052 oracle    18   0  533m  10m S  0.0  1.2  0:00.07 oracle
10032 oracle    18   0  533m  13m S  0.0  1.4  0:00.22 oracle
10044 oracle    15   0  533m  17m S  0.0  1.9  0:00.14 oracle
10079 oracle    15   0  533m  14m S  0.1  1.5  0:00.11 oracle
10020 oracle    -2   0  533m  11m S  0.1  1.2  0:01.07 oracle
10024 oracle    18   0  533m  11m S  0.0  1.2  0:00.14 oracle
10026 oracle    15   0  533m  16m S  0.1  1.8  0:00.16 oracle
10028 oracle    15   0  533m  11m S  0.0  1.2  0:00.32 oracle
10034 oracle    15   0  533m  14m S  0.0  1.6  0:00.21 oracle
```

This output shows that several processes report the shared memory occupied by the SGA. This makes the *VIRT* column only minimally useful when examining Oracle processes. Instead, the *RES*, *SHR* and *%MEM* columns are better indicators.

The */proc/meminfo* file

Much of the summary information displayed in *top* actually comes from the *meminfo* file in the */proc* directory. This file is updated constantly to reflect the current state of the system.

```
$ cat /proc/meminfo

MemTotal:      1035244 kB
MemFree:         29096 kB
Buffers:         48216 kB
Cached:         811836 kB
...
```

Around 30 values appear in the *meminfo* file. Here are the meanings for some of the more useful ones:

- *MemTotal*: The total amount of physical memory available

- *MemFree*: The amount of memory currently free on the system. Keep in mind that memory may be used for disk cache, as indicated by Cached, but this memory can be quickly freed up for other uses if needed.

- *Buffers*: The amount of memory used for buffering disk information

- *Cached*: The amount of information used to cache filesystem contents including files and executables

- *Active*: The amount of memory being actively used. This is a good indicator of the current memory demands.

- *Inactive*: Memory which has been allocated but is not currently being used

- *SwapTotal*: The total amount of swap available to the system

- *SwapFree*: The amount of swap currently unused

- *SwapCached*: The amount of data already written out to swap (on disk) but still cached in memory

- *Dirty*: Data which has been modified in memory but not yet written to disk

- *Writeback*: Dirty data currently being written to disk

Of these values, the most useful may be *active*. It indicates how much memory is being actively used as opposed to memory which has been allocated but is not currently in use. If the value for *active* is close to the amount of memory in your system, you may be exhausting the available memory and should reduce the memory demands by moving services off this system or adding more physical memory to the system.

Using *vmstat* to Monitor Memory Usage

Another popular memory-monitoring tool is *vmstat*. It can be used to see summary information about the system, or a parameter can be given causing *vmstat* to gather new statistics every few seconds to get point-in-time information.

To get summary information from the last time the system started, call *vmstat* with no arguments. Alternately, *vmstat* can be called with one or two arguments. The first argument indicates how many seconds *vmstat* should wait before gathering new memory statistics. The second argument, if included, specifies how many samples *vmstat* should gather.

```
$ vmstat 2 10

procs -----------memory---------- ---swap-- -----io---- --system-- -----cpu------
 r  b   swpd   free   buff  cache   si   so    bi    bo   in    cs us sy id wa st
 0  0      0 392920  47844 497032    0    0    26    10 1008    76  1  3 95  1  0
 2  0      0 392304  47844 497032    0    0     0     0 1003   107  6 32 63  0  0
 2  0      0 383584  47852 502692    0    0     0    72 1013   186 15 82  2  1  0
 3  0      0 187416  47860 683068    0    0     2    70 1026   147 18 73 10  0  0
 0  0      0  53984  47860 805960    0    0     0     0 1027   205 12 51 38  0  0
 0  0      0  53240  47868 805960    0    0    42   128 1028   177  4 10 83  4  0
 1  0      0  46916  47880 811832    0    0     4   918 1092   304  8 28 61  4  0
 2  0      0  37244  47892 811888    0    0    24   398 1077   311 28 71  0  1  0
 3  0      0  28068  47900 811920    0    0     6   124 1022   203 32 68  0  0  0
 2  0      0  25960  47916 811916    0    0     0    30 1014   147 36 64  0  0  0
```

The output above is an example of *vmstat* gathering memory information 10 times, waiting two seconds between each sample. The information provided on each line represents the total activity since the last line executed. The output of *vmstat* includes the following columns:

- *procs*

- *r*: The run queue. How many processes are currently waiting to be run

- *b*: Processes blocked waiting for a resource like disk I/O

- *memory*

- *swpd*: Swap usage in kb
- *free*: The amount of free memory on the system
- *buff*: The amount of buffers used in kb
- *cache*: The amount of memory being used for file system cache in kb
- *swap*
- *si*: The total kb swapped from disk to memory during the sample period
- *so*: The total kb swapped from memory to disk during the sample period
- *io*
- *bi*: Blocks read from a block device (disk) during the sample
- *bo*: Blocks written to a block device (disk) during the sample period
- *system*
- *in*: The number of interrupts per second during the sample period
- *cs*: The number of context switches per second during the sample period
- *cpu*
- *us*: The percentage of time spent running user processes (anything other than the kernel)
- *sy*: The percentage of time spent running kernel code
- *id*: The percentage of idle time
- *wa*: The percentage of time spent waiting for I/O
- *st*: The percentage of time stolen by a virtual machine (guest OS)

Many of these values may seem cryptic, but as you examine how they change over time, you can learn quite a bit about the state of the system. It can also be very valuable to have some statistics to compare with from when the system is running well. This helps identify what is different when the system is running poorly.

Here are some examples of conclusions you may be able to draw from *vmstat* output. These are just examples, and you should consider all factors and possible solutions before making a change to your system.

If the run queue is very high for a long period of time, too much is happening at once. Try to spread out large or processor-intensive tasks. If the number of blocked processes is high and/or the CPU wait percentage is high, there is contention for disk I/O. Consider tuning disk cache wherever possible, spreading out I/O or moving to faster disks.

If the amount of memory free and used for cache are both quite low, the system may be exhausting available memory. This may be accompanied by high swap-in and swap-out numbers. Consider moving some services to other systems to reduce memory usage or adding more RAM to the system.

If I/O numbers are very high but the amount of memory free and/or used as cache are comparatively high, the available memory is probably not being used efficiently. In the case of Oracle databases, consider increasing the SGA size.

Like memory usage, a high CPU usage may not indicate an overloaded system. Other factors like the run queue and blocked processes need to be considered.

Managing the System Clock

The Linux system clock is used as a time reference for many different things on the system. It is used to mark the timestamp on files as they are accessed or modified, used to trigger jobs scheduled with *cron* and *at*, as well as used by applications for marking the time in log files and within Oracle as a reference for the *sysdate* value. The system clock needs to be accurate so that dates and times set on the systems can be trusted.

To view the current date and time, use the *date* command with no options.

```
# date

Tue Aug 24 18:13:39 EDT 2010
```

The date, time, time zone and year are all reported. A format can be specified in quotes after the *date* command to restrict or add to the date information.

```
# date '+%A %B %d, %Y'

Tuesday August 24, 2010
```

Formatting symbols for the *date* command can be found in the command's man page.

Setting the System Clock

The date and time can be set by the root user using the *date* command with the -*s* option.

```
# date
Tue Aug 24 18:36:28 EDT 2010
# date -s "24 AUG 2010 22:38:00"
Tue Aug 24 22:38:00 EDT 2010
# date
Tue Aug 24 22:38:01 EDT 2010
```

The date here is specified in the format of DD MON YYYY HH:MI:SS, but the date can be set in other formats as long as the format is specified using the formatting symbols as shown above for displaying the time. The system clock and time zone can also be set graphically using the *system-config-date* command. An X Windows session needs to be available to use this method.

Setting the Time Zone

The time zone for the system is maintained in the file */etc/sysconfig/clock.*

```
# more /etc/sysconfig/clock
# The ZONE parameter is only evaluated by system-config-date.
# The timezone of the system is defined by the contents of /etc/localtime.

ZONE="America/New_York"
UTC=true
ARC=false
```

There are two easy ways to modify the time zone: the *system-config-date* command as mentioned above or the *timeconfig* command. The *system-config-date* command works best when an X Windows session is available. If it is not, it behaves like *timeconfig* and allows the time zone to be chosen through a text menu.

Conclusion

With a strong understanding of how Linux uses memory, both the system and Oracle should be able to be coaxed into using memory more efficiently.

Additionally, when things go wrong, it helps in determining if more memory is needed.

Though often overlooked, it is important to keep the system clock accurate on all systems. This assures the accuracy of times within applications as well as timestamps set by the system. It also assures scheduled jobs happen on time.

The next chapter will delve into networking in Linux.

Networking

As database administrators, we are dependent on the network to serve out the data we store. The basics of networking can be easily understood, but you must constantly be thinking about network security and reliability as well. This chapter will illustrate each of these topics in detail as they are managed on the Linux system.

Networking Fundamentals

Two computers can be interconnected in many different ways. They may both be plugged into the same networking device that facilitates their communication, or information may pass through dozens of networking devices to connect the systems. Regardless of the path taken, most information is communicated using the Internet Protocol Suite, also referred to as TCP/IP.

Basic Layers of Networking

TCP/IP is the standard protocol for communicating information over a network, be it a small local network or over the Internet to a different part of the world. Without getting into too much detail, TCP/IP is implemented in four layers, each one encapsulating the previous layer to meet a different need.

Application Layer	Contains data to be communicated between applications. The data is formatted for the specific application in protocols. Protocols include SSH, FTP, Net8 (Oracle) and HTTP (web.).
Transport Layer	Packages data from the application layer to allow for error correction and to ensure the data is delivered to the correct host and port on the receiving end. Small communications may be sent in a single packet, but larger ones will be broken up and sent as a series of packets.

Networking Fundamentals   **311**

Internet Layer	Handles the routing and delivery of packets to the desired destination
Link Layer	The physical transmission of signals from one point in the network to the next

Table 15.1: *Layers of TCP/IP*

When sending data, each of these layers does its job and then passes its product on to the next layer. On the receiving end, all the same layers are involved, but they work in the reverse order and undo the work done on the sending end.

Take a simplified example of displaying a web page. At the application layer, for example, say a web server has received a request for a web page. The application goes to work putting together the information in a format (http) that the web browser on the receiving end will understand. Once the information is formatted, it is handed off to the transport layer. The transport layer creates one or more packets to hold the information. Error correction information is added and the packets are labeled for delivery.

The Internet layer now receives the packet and attempts to determine the best place to send the packet next to get it closer to its ultimate destination. Once the next step is determined, it passes the packets to the link layer with delivery information to get it to that next step.

The link layer transmits the data to the next network device in the chain, at which point the internet layer on that device will again determine where to send the packet next to get it closer to its destination and pass it to the link layer with information to get it to the next step again.

This series of steps can be repeated a number of times until the packet is delivered to its final destination; in this example, the system with the web browser on it. At that system, the other layers again come into play.

The link layer on the destination host receives each packet and passes them to the Internet layer. The Internet layer removes the routing information, which is no longer needed and passes the information to the transport layer which checks for errors and removes the packaging that was added at the transport layer on the sending end. This is also where larger pieces of data that were sent in multiple packets are reassembled.

The transport layer then sends the assembled data to the application layer. The application layer reads the data and interprets the application-specific formatting within it to display the web page for the user who requested it.

The major advantage of the layered structure of TCP/IP is the independence afforded to each layer. For example, the sending application does not need to know where the receiving application is or how many network hops it will take to get there. Similarly, the transport layer does not need to be aware of what kind of connection the link layer will use to transmit the information. The resulting flexibility allows using the same network for different protocols and different types of systems.

IP Addresses and Hostnames

The routing and delivery examined above is highly dependent on IP addresses. These are the numbers that are assigned to systems so they can be found on the network. Currently, there are two versions of IP addresses in widespread use: the older IPv4 address, e.g. 208.80.152.2 and the newer IPv6 address, e.g. 2001:0DB8:AC10:FE01 that were introduced to replace IPv4 due to concerns about exhausting the addresses available to it.

Any time communication happens between systems, it is done using IP addresses, but thankfully for us as humans using these systems, we can use a system's hostname instead of its IP address. The system always has to know a system's IP address before it can try to communicate with it.

There are several ways a system can look up a hostname, like www.google.com, to get an IP address, but the most common way is to check a local *hosts* file or use the Internet DNS service. The file */etc/nsswitch.conf* contains a line such as the following which determines what methods will be used for hostname lookup and in what order.

```
hosts:      files dns
```

The first method listed is *files,* which refers to looking up host names/IP addresses using the */etc/hosts* file. Hosts listed in this file can be looked up very quickly, but the file must be manually updated whenever a change is made.

The second method listed is *dns* which stands for Domain Name System (DNS) in which a system can call an Internet service on a DNS server to look up a host's IP address. The DNS server checks with the authority on a given domain to get the IP address for a system and return it to the requesting system. Most of the time, rely on DNS to look up IP addresses.

DNS, the Domain Name System

The use of DNS allows the administrators who maintain systems to also maintain their own lookup table for looking up IP addresses for host names within their own domain. For example, administrators at Google maintain the host/IP address lookup information for all hosts ending in google.com. This means that rather than adding all hosts to the *hosts* file which there should be a connection to, instead use a DNS service to look up most of them.

Just like other Internet services are expected to enter their host information in DNS for lookup, you need to provide host/IP address lookup information for systems you want accessible to others. For each domain name, one or more systems are considered authoritative and can provide lookup information for that domain. If you set up a system and expect it to be accessible by name, you have to find out who controls the authoritative DNS server and have them add an entry for your system.

In some circumstances, like in Oracle RAC configurations, it is desirable to look up host names in the */etc/hosts* file instead of using DNS as these are faster and more reliable. Similarly, it may be desirable to configure application servers to look up the database server's IP address in the */etc/hosts* file to assure connections are not interrupted if DNS becomes unavailable for some reason. Since address lookups are performed in the *hosts* file first, then in DNS only if they are not found in the *hosts* file, this can be accomplished by simply adding an entry for a given host to the */etc/hosts* file.

The Loopback Interface

A special network device is configured on Linux called the loopback or localhost interface. It is configured automatically and provides a means by which the system can access resources on the local system without traveling through any network devices.

The loopback interface can be configured as the network device *lo* and it can be accessed by the address 127.0.0.1 or the hostname *localhost*. No matter what system the DBA is on, these should always refer to the local system.

Netmasks

TCP/IP networks are organized into subnets. A subnet may include only a few machines or it might contain hundreds or even thousands of systems. A subnet is used to logically organize systems that should appear local to one another.

When a system is configured to connect to a network, a netmask needs to be provided which is used to calculate the network's subnet. A typical IPv4 netmask is 255.255.255.0, which tells the system that any addresses where the first three segments of the address are the same as the system's address should be considered local, meaning they are found on the same network.

Gateways and Routing

A gateway address is also provided when configuring a system on a network. The gateway provides a point where information can be sent in order to be forwarded on to other networks either elsewhere within an organization or over the Internet.

Your network administrator should provide both the netmask and gateway values. These values are used to determine where traffic should be routed. Specifically, when the link layer of the TCP/IP protocol starts, the routing table is used to determine the first step the data should take to get closer to its destination.

Non-routable Private Networks

Systems that must be accessed by others on the Internet typically use an IP address that is unique to that machine. This allows other systems on the Internet to route traffic to the system by its IP address. Some systems, however, may not need to be publicly addressable; instead, they can exist in a non-routable private network.

Private networks are typical in home and office networking, thereby allowing multiple systems to be connected to the Internet without each needing its own public IP address. The result is a system that can request and receive information from the Internet only through a properly configured gateway, but which cannot be directly accessed from outside the private network.

Private networks are becoming more popular for databases and even web servers as the inability to route traffic directly to them offers a considerable security advantage. Special routes must be set up to allow traffic to theses servers from the Internet, and security is still increased as only specified services will be forwarded.

Managing Network Connections

When setting up a system, many network configuration steps are automatically performed; however, if the network configuration needs to be managed after the system is set up, some networking commands need to be known.

Determining the Current Hostname and IP Address

To determine the hostname of a system, use the *hostname* command. The hostname is set at startup with a value from the */etc/sysconfig/*network.

```
# hostname
```

```
oelinux-test1.lifeaftercoffee.com
```

The hostname may be the fully qualified domain name like oelinux-test1.lifeaftercoffee.com or may be just the short name like oelinux-test1, depending on how it was specified when the system was set up. Most configurations use the fully qualified domain name.

The current network interface configuration can be viewed using the *ifconfig* command. This prints information on the configuration, current state and activity since startup for each network interface.

```
# ifconfig
```

```
eth0      Link encap:Ethernet  HWaddr 08:00:27:AA:75:F0
          inet addr:192.168.1.20  Bcast:192.168.1.255  Mask:255.255.255.0
          inet6 addr: fe80::a00:27ff:feaa:75f0/64 Scope:Link
          UP BROADCAST RUNNING MULTICAST  MTU:1500  Metric:1
          RX packets:2033 errors:0 dropped:0 overruns:0 frame:0
```

```
          TX packets:1045 errors:0 dropped:0 overruns:0 carrier:0
          collisions:0 txqueuelen:1000
          RX bytes:183588 (179.2 KiB)  TX bytes:146538 (143.1 KiB)
          Interrupt:10 Base address:0xd020

lo        Link encap:Local Loopback
          inet addr:127.0.0.1  Mask:255.0.0.0
          inet6 addr: ::1/128 Scope:Host
          UP LOOPBACK RUNNING  MTU:16436  Metric:1
          RX packets:8 errors:0 dropped:0 overruns:0 frame:0
          TX packets:8 errors:0 dropped:0 overruns:0 carrier:0
          collisions:0 txqueuelen:0
          RX bytes:560 (560.0 b)  TX bytes:560 (560.0 b)
```

The *eth0* interface in the output above is the primary network configuration, but also the loopback device indicated as *lo* is seen. Each interface has an address associated with it marked as *inet addr*.

Changing the Hostname

There are several things that need to be considered when changing a system's hostname. The configuration file that sets it at system startup needs to be changed, but also the *hosts* file and DNS entries may need to be updated for the system.

> Changing the hostname on a system may have unexpected effects on running network services. It is best to shut down services like Oracle and web services before changing the hostname, or better yet, make the change to the appropriate configuration files, then reboot for the change to take effect.

When the system starts, it checks the file */etc/sysconfig/network* to determine the hostname.

```
# cd /etc/sysconfig
# cat network

networking=yes
networking_ipv6=no
hostname=oelinux-test1.lifeaftercoffee.com
```

While this file can be modified using a text editor, the correct way to manage the hostname is using the *system-config-network* command. This command launches a GUI if there is an X Windows session available; otherwise, it starts a menu-based command line utility.

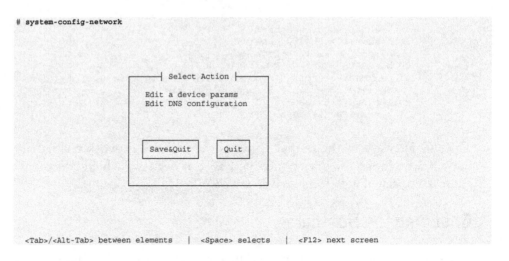

The menus in this utility can be navigated using the arrow keys and the tab key moves between the menus and buttons. Enter can be used to choose a menu item or button.

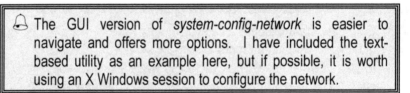

To change the host name, choose *Edit DNS configuration.*

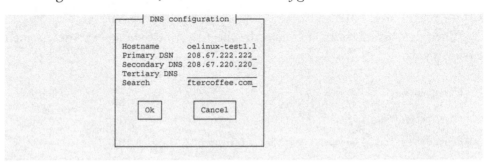

The first line contains the hostname. DNS servers and the search domain can also be edited here. After changing the hostname, use Tab to choose OK, and then Save & Quit. The new hostname is updated immediately and can be used next time the system reboots.

There is typically a corresponding entry in the */etc/hosts* file showing the IP address for this host name. If there is, this also needs to be updated to reflect the new hostname for the system.

```
# grep oelinux-test1 /etc/hosts

192.168.1.20        oelinux-test1.lifeaftercoffee.com oelinux-test1
```

The first column of the *hosts* file is always the IP address. After that, one or more host name aliases can be listed. The entry above is pretty typical showing the fully qualified domain name followed by the short host name. Spaces or tabs should separate the IP address and names. This is a requirement for many Oracle products, but if it is not already there, it can be added.

When changing a hostname, a system's DNS entry should also be updated. Whoever is managing your authoritative DNS server should be able to make this change for you.

 When a DNS record is created, a value referred to as *time to live* is set. This indicates to other DNS servers on the Internet how long they can cache and reuse this record before it should be checked again. A typical *time to live* value is 24 hours and if a hostname or IP address is changed on the authoritative DNS server, it may take up to 24 hours for the change to propagate to other servers. During that time, the system may appear unavailable to some.

Changing the IP Address

Just like with the host name, when changing the IP address of a system, consider the configuration file used to set it at startup, the *hosts* file and any DNS entries associated with this address. The system's IP address is set at system startup based on a configuration file in the */etc/sysconfig/network-scripts* directory. In this directory, there is a file for each active network interface.

```
# cd /etc/sysconfig/network-scripts
# ls

ifcfg-eth0       ifdown-ipv6      ifup-bnep      ifup-ppp
ifcfg-eth0:1     ifdown-isdn      ifup-eth       ifup-routes
ifcfg-eth0:2     ifdown-post      ifup-ippp      ifup-sit
ifcfg-eth0.bak   ifdown-ppp       ifup-ipsec     ifup-sl
ifcfg-lo         ifdown-routes    ifup-ipv6      ifup-tunnel
ifdown           ifdown-sit       ifup-ipx       ifup-wireless
ifdown-bnep      ifdown-sl        ifup-isdn      init.ipv6-global
ifdown-eth       ifdown-tunnel    ifup-plip      net.hotplug
ifdown-ippp      ifup             ifup-plusb     network-functions
ifdown-ipsec     ifup-aliases     ifup-post      network-functions-ipv6

# cat ifcfg-eth0
# Advanced Micro Devices [AMD] 79c970 [PCnet32 LANCE]

DEVICE=eth0
BOOTPROTO=none
ONBOOT=yes
HWADDR=08:00:27:aa:75:f0
NETMASK=255.255.255.0
IPADDR=192.168.1.20
GATEWAY=192.168.1.1
TYPE=Ethernet
USERCTL=no
IPV6INIT=no
PEERDNS=yes
```

This file contains information about the IP address, netmask, gateway and other settings associated with this device and the network it connects to. Again, this file could be changed using a text editor, but it is better to use the utility *system-config-network* to change the IP address and settings associated with the interface.

Start *system-config-network* and choose "Edit a device params". A list of available devices is presented. Choose the primary device; in this example, it is *eth0*.

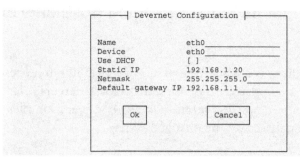

```
                  ┤ Devernet Configuration ├

         Name              eth0_____
         Device            eth0_____
         Use DHCP          [ ]
         Static IP         192.168.1.20_____
         Netmask           255.255.255.0_____
         Default gateway IP 192.168.1.1_____

             ┌──────────┐           ┌──────────┐
             │    Ok    │           │  Cancel  │
             └──────────┘           └──────────┘
```

In this screen, you want to avoid editing the *Name* and *Device* fields, but you can edit the *Static IP* to the new address and update the netmask and gateway, if necessary. When done editing, select Ok, Save, and then Save & Quit. The configuration files are updated and network devices are restarted. The new IP address becomes active immediately and will be used at system startup.

 If you are connected to a host over the network, you lose your connection when the network devices restart and have to reconnect to the new address.

It can now be confirmed that the system has picked up the new IP address using the *ifconfig* command. You will also want to change any entries in the */etc/hosts* file on the system and make your DNS administrator aware of the change.

 The same warning given earlier for changing a hostname regarding DNS and *time to live* applies when changing an IP address.

Application Considerations When Changing Hostname or IP Address

When a hostname or IP address is changed, keep in mind that all references to the changed value need to be updated. For Oracle database servers, plan to review the listener configuration, *tnsnames.ora* file and any configuration files on systems which connect to databases on the changed system.

Oracle Application Server and many other applications are more sensitive to the change of IP address or hostname. OAS specifically comes with a script that can be run to change the hostname or IP address. Some other applications may even need to be reinstalled after a change like this.

Managing Multiple Network Interfaces

Many servers are capable of connecting to more than one network through multiple network interfaces. In those cases, multiple configuration files are found in the */etc/sysconfig/networking* directory, each corresponding to a different interface. If these do not exist, use the *system-config-network* command to create them. Just know the device name of the additional device.

The steps are the same as those given for changing an IP address, but select <New Device> instead of an existing one, then select Ethernet. Then the connection information for the new device can be filled out. For consistency, it is best to keep the *Name* and *Device* values the same. After exiting, if the network service is not automatically restarted, issue the command *service network restart* to restart it.

A typical use of multiple interfaces is to allow backups to run over one dedicated adapter while application traffic travels over another adapter. This helps reduce the impact of backups on application performance.

Multihoming a Single Interface

Another useful technique referred to as multihoming allows one network interface to listen for traffic on two different IP addresses. This can be useful when consolidating or migrating services as it offers the flexibility of moving one IP address around while keeping the system running and responding to another.

Multihoming can be set up using the *system-config-network* command to add an additional network device, but specify a virtual interface. Virtual interfaces have the same name as an existing network interface with a colon and number following them. Our example will be *eth0:1* which is a virtual interface on the device *eth0*.

After starting *system-config-network*, choose *Edit a device params*, then <New Device> and Ethernet. In the configuration window, enter *eth0:1* for both the *Name* and *Device* fields, and then enter the IP address, netmask and gateway information.

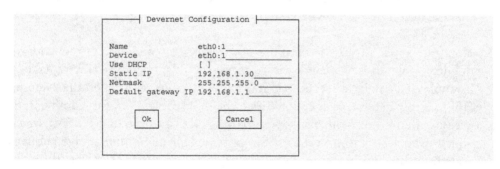

```
                    ┤ Devernet Configuration ├


      Name                eth0:1_____
      Device              eth0:1_____
      Use DHCP            [ ]
      Static IP           192.168.1.30_____
      Netmask             255.255.255.0_____
      Default gateway IP  192.168.1.1_____


          ┌──────┐          ┌────────┐
          │  Ok  │          │ Cancel │
          └──────┘          └────────┘
```

Again select OK, Save, then Save & Close. After exiting, if the network service is not automatically restarted, issue the command *service network restart* to restart it. The system will now respond to both 192.168.1.20 and 192.168.1.30.

 At the time of this writing, there is a bug that causes virtual devices not to display properly in the text-based *system-config-network* utility. While the device will be created properly, it may not display properly if edited. If editing a virtual device, it may be best to use the X Windows based interface.

Network Security

No system can be considered completely secure. It is important not only to pay close attention to security when configuring a system, but also to keep up with operating system and application patches as they become available. Security needs to be considered an ongoing responsibility, not a one-time task.

The Principle of Least Privilege

Whether at the network, application or database level, it is best to follow the principle of least privilege which dictates that every program, user or system is given access to only the resources necessary to carry out normal operations. The idea is to start with everything restricted, then remove only the restrictions that are necessary for a given system.

You can apply this to networking by closing all network ports, and then opening only those needed for services on this system. If you take the example of a database server, you may close all ports, then open the Net8 port (1521) for database connections and the SSH port (22) for administration access. Better yet, you may open up the Net8 port to only a few systems which need access to it and the SSH port to only an administrative subnet of systems. By limiting your exposure to only necessary services through a combination of firewall rules and service restrictions, you can reduce the risk of an intruder gaining access to your systems or data.

Network Firewalls

One of the primary means of restricting access to a system is via a network firewall. Network firewalls are hardware devices that sit between two networks, typically a server network and the Internet, to restrict incoming and sometimes outgoing access. They can be configured to restrict access to certain systems (by IP address) or applications (by port number). Access can even be controlled based on the requestor's IP address.

While configuring hardware firewalls is beyond the scope of this book, it is something that you are likely to encounter. A typical configuration would be to allow access to the applications that end users need through the firewall. That may include only port 1521 or maybe a web port to an application server. SSH access may be allowed through the firewall for administrative access.

While SSH is generally considered secure, it is still best if even SSH access can be restricted to only systems where administrators are likely to connect from.

The Linux Firewall

While a network firewall should be considered the first line of defense, Linux also has a built-in firewall for further protection. Though it can be disabled, it is usually kept on to block connections to insecure or unused protocols.

The Linux firewall simply blocks traffic to all ports on the system except ones that are enabled. To set or change which ports are disabled, use the *system-config-securitylevel* command to launch either a text-based menu system or an X Windows GUI. In this case, the X Windows GUI is far more complete and easier to use than the text-based one.

Figure 15.1: *X Windows GUI of Firewall Options*

In this utility, the entire firewall can be enabled or disabled or what services are allowed through it can be changed. Remember, any services not allowed here will be blocked.

For database hosts, there is a need to allow SQL traffic through the firewall to allow applications to connect to the database. To do this, add an entry for your listener port (typically 1521) by expanding the Other ports section of the configuration window, then clicking Add. Enter the port number 1521 and make sure the protocol is set to TCP and click OK, then click Apply in the main window. The change takes effect immediately after clicking Apply. Clients should now be able to make Oracle connections.

 Any services marked as trusted in the Linux firewall configuration will become available to use. If non-encrypted services (like HTTP or Oracle Net8) are enabled, traffic over them could be intercepted by a third party. Whenever possible, these unencrypted protocols should be protected behind a network firewall.

If a higher level of granularity and flexibility is needed at the operating system level, a more advanced form of traffic filtering is available throuh *iptables*. Configuring *iptables* is beyond the scope of this book, but it will allow a series of rules to be applied to network traffic based upon any number of criteria including the source and type of traffic. More information on *iptables* can be found from the operating system vendor.

Disabling Unused Services

Another level of security can be attained by disabling services that are unused. You can check which services are enabled at a given runlevel using the command *chkconfig --list*. If a service you do not expect to use is listed as ON at a runlevel you commonly use (3 or 5), you can disable it.

One example is the *hidd* service that is used to manage Bluetooth keyboards and mice. If Bluetooth devices are not going to be used, this can be disabled.

```
# chkconfig --list hidd
hidd       0:off    1:off    2:on     3:on     4:on     5:on     6:off
```

```
# chkconfig hidd off
# chkconfig --list hidd

hidd          0:off    1:off    2:off    3:off    4:off    5:off    6:off
```

Care should be taken in choosing which services can be disabled, but if needed in the future, services can be re-enabled.

Setting Up Passwordless SSH

SSH, as well as SCP and SFTP, support multiple ways of authenticating. While traditionally an interactive authentication where users are prompted to enter their password is used, another possible option is to use key authentication where a private key is kept on the system to be connected from and a corresponding public key is placed on the system in which to be connected. This can allow SSH and associated tools to be used without entering a password.

To use RSA key authentication, you should have the following three lines in your SSH configuration file *(/etc/ssh/sshd_config)* on the machine you wish to connect to:

```
RSAAuthentication yes
PubkeyAuthentication yes
AuthorizedKeysFile  .ssh/authorized_keys
```

These will allow SSH to check for SSH keys and use them for authentication. These settings are enabled by default, so the SSH configuration file should not need to be edited.

To set up a user for key authentication, generate a key on the system you wish to connect from. A key may have already been generated and if it is being used, you do not want to overwrite it. If a key exists, the file *~/.ssh/id_rsa* is already there and you can skip this step. If it is a UNIX or Linux machine, all you need to do is run the command like the following example.

```
$ ssh-keygen -t rsa

Generating public/private rsa key pair.
Enter file in which to save the key (/Users/jemmons/.ssh/id_rsa):
Enter passphrase (empty for no passphrase): <enter>
Enter same passphrase again: <enter>
Your identification has been saved in /Users/jemmons/.ssh/id_rsa.
Your public key has been saved in /Users/jemmons/.ssh/id_rsa.pub.
...
```

When prompted for a passphrase, just press Enter. This generates a public and private key pair. The public key is copied to the host you wish to connect to, but the private key is left on the host you wish to connect from. The keys are saved in your home directory in the hidden *.ssh* directory.

If connecting is being done from a Windows machine, determine if your SSH utility supports key authentication and if so, how. The popular utility *PuTTY*, for example, supports keys generated using *PuTTYgen*, but the keys must be loaded into the *Pageant* utility. Both *PuTTYgen* and *Pageant* can be downloaded for free from the *PuTTY* download site. When creating a key pair, *PuTTYgen* gives you the option of where the public and private keys should be stored.

The next step is to copy the public key to the server account you want to connect to.

```
$ cd .ssh
$ cat id_rsa.pub

ssh-rsa
AAAAB3NzaC1yc2EAAAABIwAAAQEA6KnwSyxv8qHV/UUEmCScEX0QU9MohkDZqzq7tFF0YWde4dp0
KhBLfRunM+IabLRiEpnUKTp1xvm2fNVRZRZiJZqwp4/YgiYbOudcAdc48sZRFij/UpoluRdcOXWN
0t8VU2UrJdt/RjYuwtuR7fX0CPEepdOzuqc83AEv+c3oPbby4GGXwa5h+3n0or8mbDVhjyFgf3pS
bU6h6k9W3eaSBGPPbK+9GXkstCCiygBdgUyJMyykw11RbqNDqodW79AWsI10rnvP4nohsdfG5UB/
0FtQTiNv8ths7FfZC2WM6MLQtpI525sMxVDgwvMcYecEDB3g44hefjZfTxab1SYVYw==
jemmons@Satellite-of-Love.local
```

The key wraps over several lines but is really only a single line. It can be copied and pasted using the clipboard or the file itself can be copied to the server. If copying using the clipboard, be sure that the resulting text is all on a single line, not separated by line breaks.

The key should be copied into the *authorized_keys* file within the *.ssh* directory of the user to be connected to. Be careful not to disturb any existing lines and if copying using the clipboard, make sure the resulting text is all on a single line, not separated by line breaks.

> 🔔 For security reasons, both the *.ssh* directory and the *authorized_keys* files cannot be writable by the group or other security classes. If it is writable by anyone other than the file owner, SSH will not use it for authentication.

With the public key added to the *authorized_keys* file, SSH between these users should now work without a password. SCP and SFTP should also work without passwords. If someone tries to connect as this user from a system that does not have the corresponding private key, they will be prompted for the password as usual.

```
$ ssh jemmons@oelinux-test1.lifeaftercoffee.com

Last login: Mon Feb  1 08:12:48 2010 from 192.168.1.109

$ hostname

oelinux-test1.lifeaftercoffee.com
```

When scheduling tasks to copy files between systems or connect to multiple systems for other purposes, SSH key authentication is preferred to storing passwords in scripts.

 Key authentication for SSH is a convenient and secure way to authenticate users, but it should be used with care! Keep in mind that if someone gains access to an account with a private key in it, they will also have access to every account accessible from that account.

Moving Things Between Servers

DBAs often need to securely move data from one server to another. There are several options for this, but the most secure methods are the *scp* and *sftp* commands available as part of the SSH suite of tools. Unlike their predecessors *rcp* and *ftp*, these commands encrypt information before it is sent.

scp and sftp

The *scp* command works almost exactly like the *cp* command except it can connect to other systems. A source and destination file is given, either or both of which may contain a remote hostname or username in addition to the file location. Here is an example:

```
$ scp notes_chapter1.txt jemmons@oelinux-test1.lifeaftercoffee.com:/tmp/
```

```
jemmons@oelinux-test1.lifeaftercoffee.com's password:
notes_chapter1.txt                    100% 1027    1.0KB/s   00:00
```

The first argument given in the example above is simply the file name, just like with the *cp* command, but the second one contains both a username and hostname. When using *scp*, the remote host specification is always in the format of *username@hostname:/path/to/file/ or/directory*. The *username@* is optional and if not specified, the current username is used.

Either the source or destination for *scp* can be a remote system. Both can even be specified as remote hosts, but that is not efficient for large files as all the information passes through the host that the current session is on. Like *cp*, the *scp* command can be used with the *-r* option to transfer multiple files and/or the *-p* option to preserve modification times and permissions.

Another alternative for moving files is the *sftp* command. This works just like traditional *ftp*, allowing navigation and browsing through the directory structure. Then the *get* and *put* commands are used to retrieve or send files, respectively.

```
$ sftp jemmons@oelinux-test1.lifeaftercoffee.com

Connecting to oelinux-test1.lifeaftercoffee.com...
jemmons@oelinux-test1.lifeaftercoffee.com's password:
sftp> cd notes
sftp> ls
chapter1.txt            chapter10.txt            chapter13.txt
chapter2.txt            chapter3.txt             chapter4.txt
chapter5.txt            required_packages.txt
sftp> get chapter2.txt
Fetching /home/jemmons/notes/chapter2.txt to chapter2.txt
/home/jemmons/notes/chapter2.txt              100%  216     0.2KB/s   00:00
sftp> put notes_chapter1.txt
Uploading notes_chapter1.txt to /home/jemmons/notes/notes_chapter1.txt
notes_chapter1.txt                            100% 1027    1.0KB/s   00:00
sftp> quit
```

For quick reference, the *help* command in *sftp* prints a list of command options.

Synchronizing Directories with *rsync*

While *scp* can be used to copy entire directories from one system to another, if you are dealing with large directories, it will often be more efficient to copy only what has changed. The *rsync* command lets you do exactly that and takes advantage of SSH to ensure the copy is done securely.

There is a long list of options to *rsync* which allow control of how files get copied and updated. Here is a basic use of *rsync* to copy the contents of the */u01/app/oracle/admin/common* directory from the local system to the same location on the system redhat-test1.lifeaftercoffee.com. Like *scp*, *rsync* expects two arguments specifying the source and destination. Either can contain a username followed by an at symbol (@) or a hostname followed by a colon (:).

```
$ rsync -a --exclude logs --delete /u01/app/oracle/admin/common \
redhat-test1.lifeaftercoffee.com:/u01/app/oracle/admin/common
```

This example shows some of the most common arguments for *rsync*. The *-a* (archive mode) argument actually has several effects on *rsync* including causing it to work recursively, i.e. copying subdirectories and their contents and copying permissions, ownership, modification times and even symlinks from the source to the destination.

The *-exclude* option tells *rsync* to exclude the *logs* directory from the synchronization, but this option could also be used to exclude an individual file as well. The *-delete* option forces *rsync* to delete files from the destination if they do not exist in the source.

Just like the *scp* command, *rsync* prompts for a password unless key authentication has been set up. Dozens of other options are available for *rsync*. Some of the more useful are *-z* which will cause *rsync* to compress data before sending it, *-v* which will give verbose output on what *rsync* is doing, and *-n* which will run *rsync* in a simulation mode. With the *-n* option, no copies are performed; instead, *rsync* shows what it thinks should be copied based on the command entered. Since the syntax for *rsync* is tricky, I recommend running it with the *-n* and *-v* options first in order to confirm that it does what is expected of it, then remove the *-n* option and confirm that the proper changes are made.

By allowing only files which have changed to be copied, *rsync* can save a considerable amount of network bandwidth and time, but there is a tradeoff. *rsync* takes some time to figure out exactly what needs to be copied and on large, complex directory structures, this can take many minutes or even hours before *rsync* starts copying files. This is not typically a problem on directories with less than a thousand files but should be a consideration on larger directories.

Conclusion

The network exists as the entry and exit point for nearly all information on your systems. Configuring it with the right settings and permissions is essential to the security and reliability of your systems. Virtual interfaces allow you the additional flexibility of responding on more than one IP address at a time.

Tools like *scp*, *sftp* and *rsync* offer secure alternatives to older tools, and along with *ssh*, can be configured to authenticate using a public key/private key pair. These tools will be used in a scripted fashion when shell scripting is examined.

Shell Scripting

16

Shell scripting is a nearly essential skill for Oracle DBAs. Using shell scripts, you can automate complex or repetitive tasks, monitor aspects of the system and simplify administration. Shell scripts allow you to run databases automatically at system startup and tasks like synchronizing directories on different servers can be carried out without user intervention.

Introduction

This chapter will barely scratch the surface of what can be done with shell scripts. The examples provided with this book are designed to be simple and flexible enough to be easily adapted for other purposes. For more information on shell scripting, see my book, *Oracle Shell Scripting: Linux and UNIX Programming for Oracle*, 2007, Rampant TechPress.

 The scripts provided with this book, as well as anything you produce on your own, should always be tested in a non-production, non-critical environment! Even the most basic commands can have unexpected results and the only way to be sure that a script is safe to run is to read it, understand it, and test it thoroughly.

The instructions in this chapter as well as the scripts included in the code depot with this book are written in the bash (Bourne again) shell. It is one of the most popular shells and the default in Linux, but there are several other options and each has its advantages and disadvantages. For example, the C shell is a favorite amongst C programmers because its syntax is largely derived from the C language.

When to Use Shell Scripts

It is possible to put just about any command line commands into a shell script. The best candidates for shell scripting are tasks that are overly complicated involving long or hard-to-remember commands and repeated tasks that are done the same over and over. By automating and simplifying administration, the potential for human error can be reduced in routine tasks.

Shell scripting should be considered just like any other modification to the environment and should be done with caution. Scripts can have unexpected results, and though you may like using scripts to do certain tasks, you should also consider others who work in your environment.

It is also important to follow conventions when developing shell scripts. Script locations, names and formatting should be kept consistent between scripts to make them easier to locate and diagnose.

Getting Started

To get started, look at a couple of very simple examples of shell scripting. Though simple in concept, this type of script can be used to perform a long series of commands in order.

Shell scripts can be written in any text editor that will write plain-text files. I find that I often use vi (which links to vim on Linux) for editing scripts on Linux, but if I am doing more major writing, I tend to use a desktop editor and then move the files to the Linux system. On Microsoft Windows, Notepad or Wordpad will do a nice job, but the editor EditPlus (editplus.com) offers some advanced features like syntax highlighting and SFTP functionality. On Mac OS X, I often use vi from the command line, but TextWrangler (barebones.com) offers many desirable advanced features.

Your First Shell Script

Like with any programming language, it is a good idea to start with a proof-of-concept for shell scripting. Start off with a simple Hello style example, then build upon it to make it into a script that can be used to quickly check some of the vital statistics of the system.

Connect to your system and change to a directory where you can work on your shell scripts. I recommend working in a subdirectory of your home directory called scripts. Keeping scripts separate from other files on your system will reduce the possibility that a mistake in a script could destroy or delete something important.

Using vi or your text editor of choice, create a file named *hello.sh* with the following contents:

```
#!/bin/bash

echo "Hello World!"
```

The first line of this script is special. Known as the shebang or hashbang, this line tells the operating system what program should be used to interpret the contents of this script. In this case, the bash shell has been specified as executable which, on my system, is found at the path */bin/bash*.

Before this shell script can be executed, make the file executable with the *chmod* command. For now, just grant the execute permission to the user who owns this script.

```
$ chmod u+x hello.sh
$ ls -l hello.sh

-rwxr--r--  1 oracle dba 30 Nov 13 17:29 hello.sh
```

Now the script is ready to be run. Since you are in the same directory as the script, you can use the relative path ./ to run the script.

```
$ ./hello.sh

Hello World!
```

If the script gives the output seen above, then this is a good start! If not, check the permissions and review the script for typos.

It is important to always set the shell interpreter on the first line with the shebang and to make your scripts executable. You need to do this with every script you write for them to run properly.

Basic Scripts

The most basic shell scripts are comprised of a list of commands within a file. Commands listed within a file are executed sequentially just as if they were entered on the command line. This provides a good way to automate multi-step processes so they can be run in a single command.

Here is an example of how commands can be combined into a script. This script includes some output using the *echo* command to describe what is being displayed and runs a series of commands to examine the system.

💾 status.sh

```
#!/bin/bash

echo "Hello $USER!"
echo "Welcome to `hostname`"
echo "--- Current Disk Usage ---"
df -h
echo "--- Current uptime, users and load averages ---"
uptime
echo "--- Load average numbers represent the 1, 5 and 15 minute load
averages ---"
echo "--- Lower numbers are better for load averages ---"
```

When the new *status.sh* script is run, not only the output of the *echo* commands is seen, but also the output of the *df* and *uptime* commands executed within the shell script. When run, you see the output from the *echo* commands right in line with the output from the *df* and *uptime* commands.

```
$ ./status.sh
Hello oracle!
Welcome to glonk
--- Current Disk Usage ---
Filesystem            Size  Used Avail Use% Mounted on
/dev/mapper/VolGroup00-LogVol00
                       72G  6.5G   61G  10% /
/dev/hda1              99M  9.8M   84M  11% /boot
/dev/shm             252M     0  252M   0% /dev/shm
--- Current uptime, users and load averages ---
 19:17:41 up 10 days,  6:02,  2 users,  load average: 0.00, 0.02, 0.00
--- Load average numbers represent the 1, 5 and 15 minute load averages ---
--- Lower numbers are better for load averages ---
```

There are three dashes here to make a clear visual separation between the command output and your echoed comments. This is a good way to annotate the output of your shell scripts, with or without the dashes. Any number of commands can be combined in this way. As each command completes, the following command will be executed.

Commenting Your Scripts

In a shell script, a number sign (#) begins a comment. The number sign and anything following it on the same line is ignored when a script is executed. I strongly recommend using comments to help others understand what you have done and to make notes for your own future reference. Here some useful comments have been added to the *status.sh* script you just viewed.

💾 comments added to status.sh

```
#!/bin/sh
#
# status.sh script by Jon Emmons
# Published in Linux for the Oracle DBA, Rampant TechPress, 2010
#
# A simple script to provide some information about the system
# Show the user and host name
#

echo "Hello $USER!"
echo "Welcome to `hostname`"
echo "--- Current Disk Usage ---"
df -h

# On some systems the -h (human readable) option will not work with df
# In that case you can use the -k option to display output in kilobytes

echo "--- Current uptime, users and load averages ---"
uptime
echo "--- Load average numbers represent the 1, 5 and 15 minute load averages ---"
echo "--- Lower numbers are better for load averages ---"

# These are the first two things I check when I think there is a problem
# with a system, but I'm sure you can think of some other things to add here
```

Near the top of this file, some indication of where the script came from and what it does has been given. A line with just a number sign gives a good visual separator to make the comments more readable. Additional comments provide more information on the commands used in the script.

I know what you are thinking. You now have more lines of comments than commands! That is OK. The comments make your script a bit bigger, but even with all these comments, the script is still less than one kilobyte. The small increase in file size is more than made up for by the improved readability and possible benefits for troubleshooting and further development of the script.

Variables

Variables allow you to store values for retrieval within your scripts or elsewhere on the system. As DBAs, the variables *ORACLE_SID* and *ORACLE_HOME* are frequently used. You can use these environment variables in your scripts or define local variables that are for use only within your scripts.

Variables are set using the equal sign (=) with the variable name on the left of the sign and the desired value on the right.

```
$ var1=8
$ text_var='Some text in a variable'
```

Unlike many other languages, in Bourne and bash there is no need to declare the type of data is put in a variable. Numbers and text can both be put into shell variables. Text containing spaces or special characters can be enclosed in quotes to assign the variable.

To retrieve the contents of a variable, reference the variable name prefixed with a dollar sign (*$*).

```
$ echo $var1

8

$ echo $text_var
Some text in a variable
```

The *echo* command is a convenient way to view the contents of a variable. You can also add a description to the output.

```
$ echo "Variable var1=$var1"

Variable var1=8
```

Here the variable has been interpreted by the shell and the contents of the variable output. The use of single quotes prevents variables from being interpreted, so it is important to use double quotes when working with variables.

A variable can be set to the output of a command by enclosing the command in backtics (`).

```
$ start_time=`date`
$ echo $start_time
```

Sun Nov 19 17:34:49 EST 2006

This provides an easy way to capture the output of a command for further manipulation or future reference.

A variable can be unassigned using the *unset* command. This is not often necessary since variables are automatically unassigned when the shell script or shell session is completed.

```
$ unset var1
$ echo $var1
```

You can also see here that you do not get an error from referencing a variable which is not set. Instead, the shell just interprets it as blank.

Occasionally, variable names wrapped in braces like *echo ${var1}* may be seen. This is used to signal to the shell where the variable name begins and ends. It is not usually necessary, but when a variable is being called within strings of text, it is sometimes needed.

When you declare a variable, the variable becomes available from anywhere in the script or session you have declared it in. The variable and any changes to it will remain in effect until it is cleared using the *unset* command or the script or session ends.

By using the *export* command, you can make a variable available to sessions and scripts started by the current session. This allows you to retrieve the value of the variable from subsequent sessions; however, if the value of the variable is changed in a subsequent session, the change is reflected in the original shell.

Input and Arguments

It is very easy to accept arguments into your shell script in the same way arguments are given to other commands. The shell provides a series of variables, *$1, $2, $3* and so on, that refer to the options, in order, that are given to your script. Another variable, *$@*, represents the complete string of arguments with which the script was called.

The variable $* also contains the complete list of arguments passed to a script.

To show these variables in action, consider the following script where the first two arguments are displayed and use the *expr* command to find and print their sum:

```
#!/bin/bash

echo "$1+$2=`expr $1 + $2`"
```

Now in a shell session, put this shell script to work:

```
$ ./add.sh 5 8

5+8=13
```

Arguments can be numbers or character strings. In more complicated scripts, transfer the arguments to variables with more meaningful names, but for now, this example is enough to show how arguments work. Another variable, *$#*, contains the number of arguments passed to a script. This can be useful when checking to see that an expected number of arguments were given.

Another way to assign values into variables is by prompting for input from the user. By taking information interactively, scripts which require input can be written, but the user does not need to know ahead of time what arguments are required. There may even be a script which asks for different information based on other conditions in the system.

By using the *read* command, a single line of input can be read from the standard input, typically a user at a keyboard. The content of that line is then put in the variable specified.

```
#!/bin/bash

echo "Enter your name"
read name
echo "Hi $name.  I hope you like this script"
```

In this script, use *echo* to tell the user what you expect them to enter and then *read* to put the input into the variable *name*.

```
$ ./welcome.sh
```

```
Enter your name
Jon
Hi Jon.  I hope you like this script
```

The *read* command can also be used to grab multiple values into separate variables or even to read a single line from a text file. In some scripts, you will even see how you can use *read* to prompt for input only if arguments are not supplied.

Script Output

There are a few ways you can get output from your script. The most common way is to use *echo* to print text and variables to the terminal session, but if you are writing scripts to be run automatically by *cron* or some other kind of scheduler, there will be no terminal session in which to print the information out.

If output is generated by a script that is run by *cron*, it is automatically emailed to the user it is running under. If this is used to get the output of scripts, check the email on the server frequently, or alternatively, set up *a .forward* file for the user to forward it on to an account that is checked frequently; otherwise, the mail just keeps piling up.

There are a few alternatives that give more flexibility to getting output from scripts. One alternative is to write output to a log file for later review, another is to send a formatted email using the *mail* command which will be covered later in this chapter.

Sending Output to a Log

Two types of output are typically sent to your terminal session, standard output and standard error output. By default, both of these are printed to the screen; however, you can redirect the output from either or both to files.

For simplicity, use the *ls* command for this example. Normally, *ls* prints the contents of the directory to the screen. If you want to make a file with the directory listing, you can easily redirect the output of *ls* with the greater-than symbol (>).

```
$ ls
```

```
log1.log  log3.log  myfile.txt  sample.txt      types_of_unix.txt
log2.log  marx.txt  output.txt  test_script.sh
```

```
$ ls > listing.txt
$ more listing.txt
```

```
listing.txt
log1.log
log2.log
log3.log
marx.txt
myfile.txt
output.txt
sample.txt
test_script.sh
types_of_unix.txt
```

This simple method redirects the standard output to the file *listing.txt*. If the file *listing.txt* already exists, it is overwritten! If output to the same file needs to be appended instead of overwriting the current contents, use two greater-than symbols in place of the one (>>). This has the affect of creating an ongoing log with the newest additions always at the bottom.

But what about standard error? When redirecting standard output with either the > or the >> symbols, errors will still be printed to the screen as can be seen at the beginning of the example below. This is often useful, but if you want to redirect errors to the same file that standard output is going to, you can do that, too.

```
$ ls notthere.txt > listing.txt
```

```
ls: notthere.txt: No such file or directory
```

```
$ ls notthere.txt > listing.txt 2> error.txt
$ more error.txt
```

```
ls: notthere.txt: No such file or directory
```

It can be seen in this example that the *ls* command has failed because it was asked to list a file that does not exist. The error is printed to the screen even though the standard output has been redirected to a file. Then take and redirect standard error, represented by the number *2*, to the file *error.txt*. You now see nothing printed to the screen; however, when you examine the *error.txt* file, you can see the text of your error there.

As shown above, the standard error output is represented by the number *2*. That is its file descriptor, which is the number the system is using to access the file. Standard input and standard output also have numeric file descriptors: standard input is known to the system as *0* and standard output as *1*.

If you want to redirect both output and errors to the same file, you can add the redirect of *2>&1* which redirects standard error to standard output so all the output will be sent to standard output.

```
$ ls notthere.txt > output.txt 2>&1
$ more output.txt

ls: notthere.txt: No such file or directory
```

Alternate Input Methods

Beyond taking input from arguments or from the command line, you can also read input from files or have input inline within your scripts. These methods involve redirecting standard input to be read either from the contents of your script or from a file.

Redirecting Input From a File

Standard input can be redirected to read from a file using the less-than sign (<) between the command and a filename. Note that the command should come first when redirecting input. In this example, I have created the text file *marx.txt* with vi. Then I used the less-than sign to redirect the file to the standard input of *sort*.

```
$ more marx.txt

Groucho
Harpo
Chico
Zeppo

$ sort < marx.txt

Chico
Groucho
Harpo
Zeppo
```

In this example, *sort* would commonly be used on text; however, it can also be used with binary files and commands which can handle them.

Inline Input Redirection

It is also possible to redirect input from the command line (or more likely a script) to a command. To redirect input from the command line, a double less-than sign is used followed by a file marker.

```
$ sort << EOF
> Groucho
> Harpo
> Chico
> Zeppo
> EOF

Chico
Groucho
Harpo
Zeppo
```

In this case, the file marker *EOF* is used, but any contiguous string of characters not broken by whitespace could be used. The shell reads input from the command line or script until it encounters a line that contains only the file marker. After the end file marker is found, all of the input is sent to the command just as if it were coming from a file. This method can be seen being used with several commands, especially *sqlplus*. This enables having the functionality achieved by having an input file without needing to maintain a second file in order for your script to work.

Multiple file markers can be used within a single script; however, they should all be unique. When using multiple file markers, it is common to use *EOA*, *EOB*, *EOC* or *EOF1*, *EOF2*, *EOF3* and so on. Using a file marker which is in all capital letters makes it easy to spot the file markers in a script, but is not necessary.

It is possible to redirect both input and output simultaneously. You This is often seen this with *sqlplus* when taking input from a script and sending the output to a file.

⊟ audit_locked_accounts.sh (partial script shown)

```
sqlplus -S "/ as sysdba" << EOF > /tmp/audit_locked_accounts_oss.txt

    set pagesize

    select 'The following accounts were found to be unlocked and should not
be'
    from dual;
```

```
    define exit_status = 0

    column xs new_value exit_status

    select username, account_status, 1 as xs from dba_users
    where account_status != 'LOCKED'
    and username in ('HR', 'SCOTT', 'OUTLN', 'MDSYS', 'CTXSYS');

    exit &exit_status

EOF
```

In this example, *sqlplus* is called and the input is taken from the script until the file marker *EOF* is reached. Output is also redirected to a file in the */tmp* directory. Redirects like this can cause a lot of confusion but are easily understood if it is simply viewed as two separate redirects. One is << *EOF*, which causes input to be read from the script until the marker *EOF* is reached, and another is > */tmp/audit_locked_accounts_oss.txt* which redirects the output to the appropriate file. Each redirect acts exactly as it would if the other were not there.

Making Decisions

The power of shell scripts really becomes apparent when you start using values to make decisions. You can examine variables, command statuses or even check for files on the system and execute code if certain conditions are met.

In your scripts, use conditional expressions to decide whether to execute a block of code or not. Conditional expressions always evaluate to true or false which is represented by 0 and 1, respectively. Every command in Linux returns a result code called an exit condition that represents the success or failure of that command. The exit condition can be found by examining the variable *$?* immediately after a command is run. Since there are several reasons a command may fail but really only one way it can succeed, interpret the result code of zero to be success and anything else to represent failure.

Everything makes more sense with examples, so here is an example of how conditional expressions can be used as part of an *if* statement at the command line.

```
$ age=29
$ if [ $age -lt 30 ]
> then
```

```
> echo "You're still under 30"
> fi
```

```
You're still under 30
```

More detail will be given on the *if* statement in the next section. For now, focus on the conditional expression. In most applications, enclosing the conditional expression in brackets as seen above is preferable. This example compares the contents of the variable *$age* (which has been set to 29) with the number 30. *-lt* indicates that the shell should check to see if *$age* is less than 30. Similarly, *-gt* would be greater than and *-eq* would be equal. There are several more comparisons which can be done within an expression. Some of the most commonly used ones are listed in the tables below.

Everything between the brackets must evaluate to true or false. Once evaluated, if true the shell executes the text between the *then* and the *fi* keywords. If the expression evaluates to false, the shell skips the code after the *then* keyword and continue with the next command after the *fi*.

Comparing Numbers

The following expressions can be used when writing conditional expressions for numbers.

Comparator	Mathematic Equivalent	Evaluates to true if
-eq or =	=	the values on each side of the comparator are equal
-ne or !=	≠	the two values are not equal
-gt	>	the first value is greater than the second
-ge	≥	the first value is greater than or equal to the second
-lt	<	the first value is less than the second
-le	≤	the first value is less than or equal to the second

Table 16.1: *Mathematical Comparators*

Any of these comparators can be used to compare two numbers, whether expressed as integers or the contents of variables. If you try to compare text with these comparators, you receive an error with the exception of = and !=, which will be seen next. The shell provides you with an often useless error.

Comparing Text

Numbers are not all that can be compared. You might want to know if one string matches another or if there is any information in a string. When comparing strings, you can either use variables that contain strings of text or use strings of text in either single or double quotes.

```
$ if [ $ORACLE_SID = "TEST" ]
> then
> echo "Using the sid for the test database"
> fi

Using the sid for the Oracle Shell Scripting database
```

Here it has been checked to see if the contents of the *ORACLE_SID* environmental variable match the string *"TEST"*. Since it does, the code in the *then* section of the statement is executed. Here are some of the other things that can be checked for with strings.

Comparator	Evaluates to true if
=	the string on each side of the comparator are identical
!=	the string on each side of the comparator are not identical
string	the length of the string is not zero

Table 16.2: *String Comparators*

The comparator *string* is listed here to represent a variable name. If the variable is set to something other than a null string, the condition is evaluated to true. Here is a common example to see if the *$ORACLE_SID* variable is set.

```
$ if [ $ORACLE_SID ]
> then
> echo "ORACLE_SID variable is set to $ORACLE_SID"
> fi

ORACLE_SID variable is set to TEST
```

Checking Files

There are also several things you can check about files. You can check to see if a file exists, compare the last time the files were modified or check the permissions on a file.

Comparator	Evaluates to true if
-nt	the file listed before is newer than the file listed after the comparator
-ot	the file listed before is older than the file listed after the comparator
-e	the file exists
-d	the file is a directory
-h	the file is a symbolic link
-s	the file is not empty (has a size greater than zero)
-r	the file is readable
-w	the file is writable

Table 16.3: *File Comparators*

The first two comparators listed above are used to compare two files to each other. All the other file comparators in this list simply check a specific condition of the file and only expect a file to be listed after the comparator. Here is an example of how you might check for the existence of a file.

```
$ if [ -e $ORACLE_HOME/dbs/init$ORACLE_SID.ora ]
> then
> echo "An init file exists for the database $ORACLE_SID"
> fi

An init file exists for the database oss
```

Since many of your shell scripts are dependent on other files for both input and output, it is often be prudent to check that the necessary files exist and are readable or writeable as you start your script. This gives you the opportunity to abort the script if the required files are not available as well as the chance to give meaningful feedback to the user.

Combining Comparisons

Multiple comparisons can be combined into a single expression in order to perform more complicated checks. The ultimate result of a complex expression is still either true or false, but by combining expressions, several things can be checked for at once.

```
$ if [ -e $ORACLE_HOME/dbs/init$ORACLE_SID.ora -a -e \
> $ORACLE_HOME/dbs/spfile$ORACLE_SID.ora ]
$ then
$ echo "We seem to have both an spfile and an init file"
$ fi
```

```
We seem to have both an spfile and an init file
```

The *-a* comparator in the statement above acts as a logical *and*, causing the entire condition to evaluate to *true* if, and only if, the expression on each side of the *-a* evaluates to *true*. Similarly, *-o* could be used as an *or*, causing the expression to evaluate to true if either the first condition, the second condition, or both evaluate to true.

One final option for modifying comparators is the exclamation mark (!) which can be used to negate any expression. This allows you to check if a condition is false.

```
$ if [ ! -e $ORACLE_HOME/dbs/orapw$ORACLE_SID ]
> then
> echo "There's no password file in the default location for this database"
> fi
```

```
There's no password file in the default location for this database
```

This negation can be used in combination with *and* and *or* to form some fairly sophisticated logic.

Comparator	Evaluates to true if
-a	the expressions on each side of the comparator are both true
-o	one or both of the expressions are true
!	The following expression is false

Table 16.4: *Comparator Modifiers*

Making Simple Decisions with *if* and *else*

Conditional expressions allow you to ask a question about variables, files, or your environment. Once you have the answer to a question, the *if* statement is the simplest way you can go about acting on it.

In the last section, several *if* statements were used to demonstrate some simple conditional expressions. This is the simplest form of the *if* statement where "*If* this condition is true, *then* execute this code" is stated. The end of an *if* statement is indicated by the *fi* keyword, simply *if* spelled backwards.

```
$ age=29
$ if [ $age -lt 30 ]
> then
> echo "You're still under 30"
> fi
```

In order to make more clear where the *if* statement begins and ends, indent everything between the *if* and the *fi*. Further indent the commands between the *then* and the next keyword to show where the execution of that specific part of the *if* completes. While unnecessary, these two conventions become invaluable when dealing with complex scripts.

Within the context of a script, the example above should look like this:

```
#!/bin/bash
age=29
if [ $age -lt 30 ]
    then
            echo "You're still under 30"
fi
```

If the condition given is found to be true, based on the rules detailed in the last section, the code after the *then* keyword is executed until it comes upon either a *fi*, indicating the end of the *if* statement, an *else* keyword which will be introduced next, or an *elif* which will be covered later in this section. When the *if* statement has hit one of these keywords, the rest of the shell script is executed starting directly after the *fi*.

Quite often, one task will need to be performed if a condition is true, but a different task if it is false. Within an *if* statement, commands following the keyword *else* are executed when the conditional statement is evaluated to false.

```
#!/bin/bash
age=29
if [ $age -lt 30 ]
    then
            echo "You're still under 30"
    else
            echo "You're 30 or over"
fi
```

This code now executes the first *echo* command if the variable age is less than 30, but if that turns out to be false, the second *echo* command is executed. Each *if* statement must have a *then* clause, and the *else* is optional. Upon the execution of the *if* statement, either the *then* or *else* (if present) code is executed, but never both.

Another option within an *if* statement is an *elif* or *else-if* clause. If the initial condition of the *if* statement is evaluated to be false, a second condition can be tested with an *elif*. A conditional expression following an *elif* is evaluated in the same way as with an *if*, but it is important to remember that it will only be evaluated if the *if* statement fails.

```
#!/bin/bash
age=39
if [ $age -lt 30 ]
    then
            echo "You're still under 30"
    elif [ $age -ge 30 -a $age -le 40 ]
            then
                    echo "You're in your 30s"
    else
            echo "You're 40 or over"
fi
```

In this example, the *age* variable has been set to 39. Upon execution, the condition after the *if* statement is found to be false, so the code after the *then* is not executed. It proceeds to evaluate the expression after the first *elif* statement which evaluates to true; therefore, the code after the *then* following the first *elif* is executed. After that, the shell continues after the *fi* statement.
Within an *if* statement, there may be multiple *elif* statements, each with their own conditional expression. The shell executes each one in order until the first one succeeds. After the first one succeeds, it exits the *if* statement and continues executing after the *fi*. If neither the *if* nor any *elif* conditional statements evaluate to true, the code following the *else* is executed (if present).

Choosing From a List with *case*

The *case* offers a way to decide between several options more simply than a series of *if then elseif else* statements. While the *case* statement is limited to comparing strings, it can be very powerful for that.

```
#!/bin/bash
case $ORACLE_SID
in
    TEST)
            echo "Using the sid for the test database"
            ;;
    db1)
            echo "Using the default Oracle database"
            ;;
    *)
            echo "I don't have a description for this database"
            ;;
esac
```

This script shows the use of a *case* statement to carry out a specific action if the *ORACLE_SID* variable matches the value *test* or *db1* and then has a separate action for any other value for *ORACLE_SID*.

A *case* statement is followed by the variable that should be compared followed by the *in* keyword. Then one possible pattern is provided, in quotes if it contains whitespace characters, followed by a close parenthesis. The code to be executed is given, and the option is terminated by two semicolons. The final option above is an optional catchall which is executed if no other pattern is matched.

A * is not the only expression which can be used here. In most implementations, *case* takes most of the regular expression syntax. When executed, the patterns are compared in order and only the commands following the first matching statement are executed. Because of this, be careful what order the options are in and put the broader catchall ones, especially *, toward the end of the list. If you want to be a little less specific on your *ORACLE_SID* case above, use a simple regular expression to accept any number in a SID that starts with *db*.

```
#!/bin/bash
case $ORACLE_SID
in
    oss)
            echo "Using the sid for the Oracle Shell Scripting database"
```

```
             ;;
     db[0-9])
             echo "Using something like the default Oracle database"
             ;;
     *)
             echo "I don't have a description for this database"
             ;;
esac
```

This simple modification avoids having a separate case for *db1*, *db2*, *db3* and so on. Using regular expressions like this help keep your code succinct and readable.

Loops

Loops allow repeating a section of code a number of times based on a condition or variable. There are a handful of different loops available. Which one you choose will depend on how to evaluate when the loop should end.

The *while* Loop

The *while* loop behaves like the simple *if* statement in that it checks a condition and executes some commands if the condition is true. Unlike the *if* command, when it is done executing, the code it is given then checks the condition again. If the condition is still true, it executes the same code again.

The *while* loop continues executing the code between the *do* and *done* keywords until the given condition is found to be false, then it skips the given code and the script is continued after the *done* keyword.

```
#!/bin/bash
i=1
while [ $i -le 10 ]
do
    echo "The current value of i is $i"
    i=`expr $i + 1`
done
```

This simple example shows the variable *i* being set initially to 1. The *while* loop checks the conditional statement and notices that *i* is, in fact, less than or equal to 10, so it executes the code between the *do* and *done* keywords. The second line sets *i* to the result of *i + 1* using the *expr* command. This is a typical way to increment the loop counter within a loop.

It is important to make sure that something is modifying the loop counter and that it will eventually cause the while condition to fail. Otherwise, you end up in an infinite loop!

After the first execution of the *while* loop, the variable *i* now contains 2. The conditional statement is evaluated again, and since it is still true, the commands are executed again. This goes on until *i* is equal to 11. At that point, the conditional expression fails, the commands are not executed and the script continues on after the *done* keyword.

When executed, the output of the script above looks like this:

```
$ ./while.sh

The current value of i is 1
The current value of i is 2
The current value of i is 3
The current value of i is 4
The current value of i is 5
The current value of i is 6
The current value of i is 7
The current value of i is 8
The current value of i is 9
The current value of i is 10
```

Keep in mind that any of the conditions examined earlier can be used in *while* loops. You can compare numbers and text or even check to see if a file exists or is writable. This allows scripts to react to changes on the system.

The *for* Loop

The *for* loop offers the ability to repeat the same commands a certain number of times based on a list of values. The commands between the *do* and *done* keywords after a *for* statement are repeated once for each item in a list of values. The *for* loop even places the list item it is currently processing in a variable to use within the loop.

```
#!/bin/bash
count=0
for i in 2 4 6
do
    echo "i is $i"
    count=`expr $count + 1`
done
echo "The loop was executed $count times"
```

In this example, *2 4 6* have been provided as separate values to the *for* loop. The loop is executed once for each of these values and sets the value of *i* to the value for which it is currently executing so the *i* variable can be used within the loop. Within this, a secondary *count* variable also added was used to count and report the number of times this loop executes.

```
$ ./for.sh

i is 2
i is 4
i is 6
The loop was executed 3 times
```

The *for* loops are not just for numbers. They can be used with a list of *ORACLE_SIDs* to perform the same action on several databases. You can even provide a variable that contains a list of values.

```
#!/bin/sh
files=`ls`
count=0
for i in $files
do
    count=`expr $count + 1`
done
echo "There are $count files in the current directory"
```

Here a listing of the current directory has been taken and a *for* loop used to parse over each file in it. Nothing is being done with the files here; instead, 1 is being added to *count* for each file. This shows how a list can easily be parsed over within a variable.

Breaking Out of Loops

Sometimes in a loop, you need to deal with the unexpected and get out of a loop before another evaluation is completed. To do that, you can use a *break* statement. The *break* causes the shell to stop executing the current loop and continues on after the end of that loop.

```
#!/bin/bash
files=`ls`
count=0
for i in $files
do
    count=`expr $count + 1`
    if [ $count -gt 100 ]
    then
            echo "There are more than 100 files in the current directory"
```

```
        break
   fi
done
```

The *break* statement can be called anywhere between the *do* and *done* of a loop. It might be desirable to break if a certain keyword is read or if a value exceeds a threshold. Above, break out of the *for* loop if the variable *count* exceeds 100. After the *break* keyword, the shell skips forward and continues after the *done* of the *for* loop.

Loops are an important method of accomplishing additional work with scripts. Loops can even contain other loops, but this should be done cautiously as it gets confusing quickly.

Checking Results and Sending Notifications

When working with databases and systems, you are constantly concerned with the results of your work. If a command has a syntax error, you want to know about it eventually, but if a backup fails, you want to know about it soon, and if a database is down, you probably want to know about it immediately!

The Exit Status: The Unseen Result

Whenever a command is run in UNIX or Linux, it completes with a status of either success or failure. Often the indication of a failure is seen in the form of an error message to the screen. What is typically not seen is the command's exit status.

The exit status of the command is set as the shell variable *?*. If the command is successful, the *?* variable is set to 0. If the command fails, *?* is set to some other integer value, often 1.

The value of *?* can be viewed in the same way other shell variables are with the *echo* command.

```
$ ls

error.txt     log1.log    log3.log   myfile.txt    sample.txt
types_of_unix.txt
listing.txt   log2.log    marx.txt   output.txt    test_script.sh

$ echo $?
```

```
0
$ ls *.dmp

ls: *.dmp: No such file or directory

$ echo $?

1

$
```

Though 1 is often used to indicate failure, a command may set the value of *?* to something other than 1 to indicate a specific type of failure; for instance, 127 is often used to indicate a 'command not found' error. This can be very useful for error reporting and debugging but is specific to each command. Refer to the man page for a specific command to learn more about its possible exit statuses.

Despite there being several possible values to indicate failure, the point that there is only one to indicate success makes it very easy to programmatically determine and respond to a command's success or failure with an *if* statement.

In this script, *tail* is used to look at the last 42 lines of the alert log for the current instance. If the command fails for some reason, some feedback on why it may have failed can be given, so an *if* statement has been used here to echo some output if the exit status of the command is not zero.

```
#!/bin/sh
#
# Script to show the last 48 lines of the alert log for the
# current Oracle SID.
# Requires ORACLE_BASE and ORACLE_SID be set
# Assumes OFA file layout
#
tail -42 $ORACLE_BASE/admin/$ORACLE_SID/bdump/alert_$ORACLE_SID.log
if
 [ $? != 0 ]
then
        echo "Something went wrong.  Look for errors in this output and"
        echo "check that the TAIL command is in your path, that the alert"
        echo "log is in the appropriate OFA location and that the
ORACLE_BASE"
        echo "and ORACLE_SID variables are set"
fi
```

Sometimes you recognize a failure and report it, others you perform a different action or even exit the script when a command fails.

Scanning Logs for Output

If you are the database administrator, you already know that it is important to check certain log files on a regular basis. This may be one of the most useful things you can put in a shell script.

Typically, you will want to know almost immediately when there is an *ORA-* error in any of your production databases. You can easily use the *grep* command to check your logs and notify you if the pattern *ORA-* is found.

```
#!/bin/sh
#
# Script to check the alert log for ORA- errors
# Requires ORACLE_BASE and ORACLE_SID be set
# Assumes OFA file layout
#
alert_log=$ORACLE_BASE/admin/$ORACLE_SID/bdump/alert_$ORACLE_SID.log
grep -q ORA- $alert_log
if [ $? = 0 ]
then
        echo "The following ORA- errors were found in $alert_log"
        grep ORA- $alert_log
fi
```

This script checks the alert log for the string *ORA-* with the *grep* command. The *-q* option prevents the lines from being printed at this time. Instead, use the exit status of the *grep* command to determine if lines were found. If no matching lines are found, *grep* sets the exit status to 1, indicating a failure. If one or more matches are found, *grep* exits with a status of 0 indicating success.

Then examine the value of *$?* with an *if* statement. If it is zero, then it shows that *grep* found *ORA-* errors in the log. At that point, print a custom message indicating that errors were found and then re-execute the *grep* command, this time allowing the results to be printed to the standard output. Similar scripts can be used to check other logs on the system.

Checking the Output of Commands

Sometimes the exit status of a command does not tell enough. It is fairly easy to manipulate commands with simple output, but complicated output requires more processing.

Command output is often manipulated with a combination of *grep, sed, awk, cut* and other text manipulation commands. Those who do a lot of text manipulation may find that they can accomplish complex text manipulation with only tools like *sed* and *awk*. For the casual scripter, it is often easier to combine several tools, each of which performs a small portion of the processing.

```
up=`uptime`

# Parse out the current load averages from the uptime command

load_1=`echo $up | awk -F "load average: " '{ print $2 }' | cut -d, -f1 |
cut -d. -f1`

load_5=`echo $up | awk -F "load average: " '{ print $2 }' | cut -d, -f2 |
cut -d. -f1`

load_15=`echo $up | awk -F "load average: " '{ print $2 }' | cut -d, -f3 |
cut -d. -f1`
```

The code segment above first takes the results of the *uptime* command and puts them into the variable *up*. This is what the output looks like before processing:

```
$ uptime
 18:08:52 up 24 days,  9:10,  4 users,  load average: 3.87, 37.95, 31.29
```

The *uptime* output is parsed in several steps and the result is stored in a variable. To get the one-minute load average (the first one listed), the *echo* command is used to print the *uptime* output to the standard output. *awk* is then used to print the second column while treating the string *load average:* as a field separator. This is an effective way to print everything that follows a certain string.

After this initial processing, what is left is the following output:

```
3.87, 37.95, 31.29
```

From here, the *cut* command is used to hone in on the exact load average you are looking for. The *-d* option allows you to specify using a comma as a separator and the *-f* option lets you specify which field you want to retrieve. Here, the *cut* command is used to perform a function very similar to what was

---

done with *awk*. Note that *cut* can only be used with a single character delimiter, but *awk* can use a multi-character string.

After the *cut -d -f1*, the output has been cut down to just the number 3.87. Another *cut* command is used to eliminate the decimal point and everything after it. This leaves just the number 3 which is then placed in the variable *load_1*.

All this processing allows taking a mixed text/number ouput and carving it down to a single integer so it can be processed within the shell. If how this fits into the entire script needs to be seen, take a look at the *monitor_load_average.sh* script available in the downloadable code depot with this book.

Emailing From Scripts

There are several ways to send email from a script. The one you choose depends on what tools you have on your system and how the script needs to notify you.

Emailing System Users and Using a *.forward* File

It is possible to send email to a user on the local system. If, for instance, email is sent to the user oracle, that user is notified that they have a message upon their next login and they can then view the message with a mail reader present on the system.

```
$ mail oracle

Subject: Hello
Just a simple little note to say hello.
.
Cc:
```

Above shows the *mail* command being used interactively to send a short message to the oracle user. Since a user is being emailed on the same system the *mail* command is executed on, there is no need to have the *@hostname.com* portion of the email address.

Emails that are sent to local addresses in this manner go into the user's mail file and can be retrieved from the local system. That means unless a *.forward* file is configured, someone has to regularly log into this system and check for emails.

A better approach is to configure the *.forward* file in the user's home directory. If a *.forward* file is present, rather than sending the email to the user's local mail file, the system forwards the email on to each address listed in the *.forward* file. This eliminates the need to regularly check for mail in system users' accounts, but it is important that the mail administrator is worked with to assure these messages are accepted by the specific email server.

Emails from *cron* and *at* Jobs

If a command or script run in *cron* produces some output, the system places that output in an email and sends it to the owner of the script. Say this script is called from the oracle user's *crontab* file:

```
#!/bin/bash
df -h
```

Since there is output to the standard output from this script, an email is produced with the output in the body. The subject of the email typically contains information about the user and system, but very little else.

If there is a *.forward* file present, the output is sent on to the addresses listed. This may be the simplest way to produce an email from a shell script. It is often useful to set up scripts like this as a temporary measure until more sophisticated monitoring can be configured.

Any text sent to the error output is also emailed to the job owner. Even if you do not intend for your scripts to have any output to the standard output, it is useful to have a *.forward* file or check the accounts regularly for errors from scheduled jobs.

Jobs scheduled using the *at* command also send emails with any output from the commands run. If there is no output from commands, a request can be made that an email still be sent by adding the *-m* option to the *at* command when scheduling the job.

The *mail* Command

While the automated emails from *cron* and *at* jobs offer a simple way to send emails, you can get a bit more sophisticated by using the *mail* command. Using it, you can control the subject, carbon copy other users and more.

```
#!/bin/bash
mail -s "Alert log from $ORACLE_SID `hostname`" oracle <
/u01/app/oracle/admin/$ORACLE_SID/bdump/alert_$ORACLE_SID.log
```

By using a redirect, you have specified a file to be used as the body for this email. In this case, use a log file, but this could also be a file to which you have redirected other output. This also shows how variables and commands can be used in the subject line.

For short messages or when you want to include variables in the message body, the *mail* command can also be used with file markers. Sometimes all you need to know is that a script has finished.

```
#!/bin/bash
mail -s "Script complete" oracle <<EOF

Script has completed
EOF
```

A typical method for sending email from a script is to compose the body of the message within a text file by redirecting output of specified commands into the file. The file is then easily redirected into the *mail* command and the subject added with the *-s* option.

It is often useful to put specifics in the subject line including host name, Oracle SID and success or failure status messages. This can make it easier to automatically filter mail.

Conclusion

Shell scripting is an important tool for automating complex and repetitive tasks. A few well-written shell scripts can help you monitor the system and databases as well as perform routine duties to free up your time for other tasks.

There is a lot more to shell scripting than can be covered here, but this chapter should give you the confidence to write some simple scripts and alter existing scripts to suit your needs. If you want to get into more depth with shell scripting, check out my book, *Oracle Shell Scripting*.

Organizing Oracle Files

Any Oracle installation is made up of a long list of files. There are datafiles, of course, then there are control files, configuration files, and log files. The database management system itself has a long list of binary files, configuration files, installation logs and inventory files.

It can be tempting to choose arbitrary locations for files at install time, but it is important to choose and follow a set of standards. By applying standards, you make things easier for yourself and others who access your systems.

Oracle's Optimal Flexible Architecture

Originally drafted in 1990, Oracle's Optimal Flexible Architecture (OFA) is a set of guidelines for installing and running Oracle systems. These guidelines were developed to offer increased flexibility, reliability, scalability, and performance as well as reduced maintenance on Oracle implementations both large and small.

OFA standards have evolved over time to fit new database requirements and usage trends, but over twenty years from its original inception, it still stands as a best practice for how Oracle should be installed. Though there is some flexibility built into the standard, database administrators familiar with OFA in one environment will quickly be able to identify and take advantage of it in another.

OFA Recommendations

The following are the OFA recommendations and how they typically manifest themselves on Linux systems. When possible, changes and additions to OFA between Oracle versions are noted. The full OFA whitepaper can be found online, but the synopsis below should be sufficient for most purposes.

The typical application for each recommendation represents how the standard is commonly applied. Using these settings yields a setup that any experienced DBA should be comfortable with.

Recommendation 1: Mount Point Naming

- Typical application: File system mount points should be named */u01, /u02, /u03*, and so on.

All mount points for file systems should be named in a format to include a standard identifier string and a fixed-length value which can be incremented for each additional mount point. In OFA, whitepaper mount points of */u01, /u02, /u03*, and all are given as examples.

Any string can be used in place of *u* as long as it does not end up misrepresenting the contents of the file system. Similarly, any value can replace the incremented numbers as long as it is fixed length, e.g. 01, 02, and such instead of 1, 2, so an *ls* listing lists the mount points in order and can be clearly incremented. Identifiers like *data01* or *app01* should be avoided if the file systems may contain a mix of data and application files.

File systems are typically mounted with the recommended mount points of */u01, /u02, /u03*, and such. Some may start with */u00* or prefer to use a three-digit number, e.g. u001, both of which are acceptable. The key factor is that the name of the mount point makes it acceptable for use for either data or applications.

Recommendation 2: Software and Owner Home Directory

- Typical application: */u01/app/oracle* is the typical *ORACLE_BASE* location for software installation, but the home directory for the Oracle user is usually */home/oracle*.

The Oracle software can be installed on any of the mount points mentioned in rule 1. In instances with multiple homes, which will be examined later, it is not unusual to have homes on different mount points. The *app* level of this directory (short for application) may be changed to some other name, but should indicate the directory's contents.

The *oracle* level of this directory is intended to indicate the owner of the software installed there, but can also be used to indicate the vendor who provides the software. This can lend a logical organizational structure when multiple applications from multiple vendors are installed on a system.

Recommendation 3: Explicit and Variable Path Names

- Typical application: Whenever possible, use variables to locate files within the Oracle home directory, users' home directories and more.

Using variables like *ORACLE_HOME* and *ORACLE_BASE* that are set dynamically based on the configuration can shorten command syntax and allow the flexibility of using commands and scripts against other Oracle home directories. Similarly, using shortcuts like ~oracle to refer to the Oracle user's home directory allows the contents to be found even if the directory is moved.

Recommendation 4: Oracle Software Install Location

- Typical application: Oracle software should be installed within the *ORACLE_BASE* identified in recommendation 2 with the path *$ORACLE_BASE/product/11.1.0/db_1*. The version number should be substituted in place of *11.1.0*.

The subdirectory *product* identifies the contents of this directory as software rather than data files, configuration files or logs and the version number portion helps administrators quickly find or identify the software they want to work with. The version number can be less specific if desired, e.g. *11.1* instead of *11.1.0*, but should not be too specific. If, for example, a home of *11.1.0.6/db_1* was used, then the *11.1.0.7* upgrade was applied to this home, the version number in the directory name would now misrepresent the version of the home.

The final segment of this path has an identifier for the software installation type and a number that can be incremented if necessary. If another home of this version is set up, it can be created as *db_2* so the homes can coexist. Alternately, an Oracle Application Server home may be created as *oas_1* or, more specifically, with the application server installation type like *soa_1* for a SOA Suite installation. Before version 10g, this level was excluded from the path, so administrators may be found who still install the Oracle home directly under the version number.

Recommendation 5: Administration Files and Logs

- Typical application for Oracle 10g: Administration files and logs are kept within the *ORACLE_BASE* directory defined in recommendation 2 in a subdirectory structure of *admin/$ORACLE_SID/*. Directories in this location include the background and core dump directories and things like the alert log.

- Typical application for Oracle 11g: Oracle 11g has introduced a new directory within the *ORACLE_BASE* directory called *diag*. Logs and diagnostic files for a database would typically be in a directory like */u01/app/oracle/diag/rdbms/test/TEST* where *test* is the database name and *TEST* is the instance name.

Within that directory, logs and diagnostic files are kept under a structure of *diag/product_type/product_id/instance_name*. The *product_type* for the database is *rdbms*. The *product_id* indicates the database name and the *instance_name* is the instance name for the given database. This becomes important in RAC configurations where multiple instances with unique names are employed to serve data for a specific database.

In 11g configurations, log files for the listener can also be found under the product type of *tnslsnr* as well as many other directories depending on what products are installed.

Recommendation 6: Database File Naming Conventions

- Typical application: Within the */u01*, */u02*, and such mount points, Oracle database files are kept within a directory structure of */u01/oradata/$DATABASE_NAME*. The primary file types are named as follows:

  - Control files: *controlnn.ctl* where *nn* is a fixed length indicator that can be incremented. An example would be *control01.ctl*.

  - Data files: *TS_NAMEnn.dbf* where *TS_NAME* indicates the tablespace name the datafile belongs to and *nn* is a fixed length indicator that can be incremented. An example would be *users01.dbf*.

  - Online redo logs: *redonnA.log* where *nn* is a fixed length indicator that can be incremented and *A* indicates the redo log group for multilexed logs. An example would be *redo01a.log*.

Some administrators choose to include the database name in these file names. I do not recommend this practice as it can complicate database cloning and is redundant if the files are already kept in a directory with the database name.

Recommendation 7: Separate Data into Tablespaces by Usage

- Typical application: Keep data separated into tablespaces by application, usage patterns and data type. Even for a single application, it can be useful to separate out indexes and specialized objects like LOBs into different tablespaces. This allows further customization to be done to tablespaces based on their contents.

One important aspect of this recommendation is that application data should never be kept in the system or sysaux tablespaces. Those tablespaces are reserved for system objects and if they are inadvertently filled with application data, some features of the database may become unusable or the database may crash.

Recommendation 8: Tablespace Naming

The original OFA recommendation suggested naming tablespaces with names that are eight or fewer characters. This is no longer necessary, but tablespace names should still be kept reasonably short. It is more important that tablespace names accurately indicate their contents.

With these recommendations in mind, a typical 11g Oracle installation would look like this:

Mount points	/u01, /u02, /u03, etc.
ORACLE_BASE	/u01/app/oracle
ORACLE_HOME	$ORACLE_BASE/product/11.1.0/db_1
Diagnostic files (10g)	$ORACLE_BASE/admin
Diagnostic files (11g)	$ORACLE_BASE/diag
Database file location	/u01/oradata/$DATABASE_NAME, /u02/oradata/$DATABASE_NAME, etc.
Control file names	control01.ctl, control02.ctl, control03.ctl, etc.
Data file names	system01.dbf, sysaux01.dbf, users01.dbf, etc.
Online redo logs	redo01a.log, redo01b, redo02a.log, redo02b.log, etc.

Table 17.1: *A Typical 11g Oracle Installation*

These are all just recommendations and Oracle offers the flexibility to install and move files with very few restrictions, but adhering to standards makes managing the system much easier.

I strongly recommend avoiding path and file names with spaces and other special characters in them when working with Oracle. While there are ways to make Oracle recognize these paths, it will often complicate configuration.

Maintaining Oracle Logs and Diagnostic Files

Prior to version 11g, Oracle databases stored most log and diagnostic information in the *$ORACLE_BASE/admin directory*. Now in 11g, there is a new directory at *$ORACLE_BASE/diag* with a different organizational structure. In either version, it is important to understand what to find in these directories and how to maintain them.

The Admin Directory

In Oracle 10g and earlier, logs and diagnostic information can typically be found in the directory *$ORACLE_BASE/admin*, but sometimes this admin directory is found in *$ORACLE_HOME* or is set to another specific location chosen by the administrator. The admin directory typically contains a folder for each database on a system. Within this folder there are the *bdump*, *cdump* and *udump* directories, among other things.

These directories are populated with diagnostic information by the database. Most of the contents are unique files created by database events, but some files like the alert log are written to on an ongoing basis and will continue to grow if left alone. In either case, these files should occasionally be cleaned up to prevent them from taking up too much disk space.

Checking the Alert Log

The *check_alert_log.sh* script shown below checks for any *ORA-* errors in the alert log of a given database. It will take a SID as an argument, or if no SID is specified, it will use the current one if set. In large environments, it may be more desirable to set up a GRID Controller and use that to monitor multiple databases. However, if only a handful of instances need to be monitored, it can be much easier to just set up monitoring scripts like this one.

In order to avoid reporting the same error twice, this script copies the contents out of the alert log, checks for errors and then saves them in a log file by the same name, but with *.1* appended to it.

check_alert_log.sh

```
#!/bin/bash

# Add /usr/local/bin to the PATH variable so the oraenv command can be found
PATH=$PATH:/usr/local/bin; export PATH

# If a SID is provided as an argument it will be set and oraenv run
# otherwise we will use the current SID.  If no SID is set or provided
# an error message is displayed and the script exits with a status of 1
if [ $1 ]
then
    ORACLE_SID=$1
    ORAENV_ASK=NO
    . oraenv
else
    if [ ! $ORACLE_SID ]
    then
            echo "Error: No ORACLE_SID set or provided as an argument"
            exit 1
    fi
fi

# Set the ORACLE_BASE variable
ORACLE_BASE=/u01/app/oracle; export ORACLE_BASE

cd $ORACLE_BASE/admin/$ORACLE_SID/bdump

# Copy the current alert log into a temporary file and empty the original
cp alert_$ORACLE_SID.log alert_$ORACLE_SID.log.temp
cp /dev/null alert_$ORACLE_SID.log

# Check the copy in the temporary file for ORA- errors
grep 'ORA-' alert_$ORACLE_SID.log.temp > /dev/null
# If found, email the Oracle user with the contents of the alert log
if [ $? = 0 ]
then
    mail -s "$ORACLE_SID database alert log error" oracle < \
            alert_$ORACLE_SID.log.temp
fi

# Move the contents of the temp file onto the permanent copy of the log
# and remove the temp file.
cat alert_$ORACLE_SID.log.temp >> alert_$ORACLE_SID.log.1
rm alert_$ORACLE_SID.log.temp
```

The block of code which starts with the first *if* statement is one that will be seen in many of the scripts in this book. If a SID is provided, the *$1* variable exists and the *oraenv* command is executed. If not, the second *if* statement within the ELSE clause checks to see if a SID has already been set. If it has not, an error message is printed and the script exited with a result code of 1, indicating failure. If this script fails when executed from a *crontab*, the error message is automatically emailed to the *crontab* owner.

Since this will likely be run from a *crontab* entry, you typically provide a SID as an argument. The following *crontab* entry causes this script to be run every 15 minutes.

```
00,15,30,45 * * * * /u01/app/oracle/admin/common/check_alert_log.sh oss
```

Rotating the Alert Log

This script should be considered a companion to the previous one. It takes the alert log created by the *check_alert_log.sh* script, which has a *.1* appended on it, and rotates it out to a tertiary alert log. The previous tertiary alert log is moved to a fourth alert log and so on. The desired number of alert logs to keep can be set in the script by changing the value of the variable keep. The default of seven should be fine for most databases.

rotate_alert_log.sh

```bash
#!/bin/bash

# The keep variable controls how many old alert logs should be kept
keep=7

# Add /usr/local/bin to the PATH variable so the oraenv command can be found
PATH=$PATH:/usr/local/bin; export PATH

# If a SID is provided as an argument it will be set and oraenv run
# otherwise we will use the current SID.  If no SID is set or provided
# an error message is displayed and the script exits with a status of 1
if [ $1 ]
then
    ORACLE_SID=$1
    ORAENV_ASK=NO
    . oraenv
else
    if [ ! $ORACLE_SID ]
    then
        echo "Error: No ORACLE_SID set or provided as an argument"
        exit 1
    fi
fi

# Set the ORACLE_BASE variable
ORACLE_BASE=/u01/app/oracle; export ORACLE_BASE

cd $ORACLE_BASE/admin/$ORACLE_SID/bdump
```

```
# Set the loop variable i to the keep value then rename each alert log
# to one number up from its current value.  Stop after moving log 2
i=$keep
while [ $i -gt 2 ]
do
    if [ -e alert_$ORACLE_SID.log.`expr $i - 1` ]
    then
            mv alert_$ORACLE_SID.log.`expr $i - 1` \
              alert_$ORACLE_SID.log.$i
    fi
    i=`expr $i - 1`
done

# This handles the move of log 1.  If there is no log 1 an error will be
# displayed and the script will exit with a status of 1.
if [ -e alert_$ORACLE_SID.log.1 ]
then
    mv alert_$ORACLE_SID.log.1 alert_$ORACLE_SID.log.2
    touch alert_$ORACLE_SID.log.1
else
    echo "File alert_$ORACLE_SID.log.1 not found"
    echo "Make sure you are using the check_alert_log.sh script"
    exit 1
fi
```

This script uses a *while* loop to work through a number of files without needing to repeat commands. The last file, i.e. the alert log ending with *.1*, is handled separately to allow an error to be raised if the file does not exist.

This script could be run at any interval. I would recommend running this script daily for active databases in order to keep the alert logs from growing too large. Weekly may be acceptable for databases which see less use. The *crontab* entry below shows how this script could be run daily. Note that it has been configured to run at five minutes after the hour in order to run at a time when the *check_alert_log.sh* script is most likely not running.

```
05 00 * * * /u01/app/oracle/admin/common/rotate_alert_log.sh oss
```

Finding and Removing Old Dump Files

Over time, the files created in an instance's dump directories can consume quite a lot of space. Furthermore, since these typically grow slowly, it is easy to forget to check them until they are large enough to cause a space problem. These reasons make this an ideal function for a shell script.

The *clean_dump_dirs.sh* shell script checks the *adump*, *bdump*, *cdump* and *udump* directories for a given database and removes any files older than 30 days. If files in these directories should be kept for more or less time, change the value of the *days_back* variable to the desired number of days.

💾 clean_dump_dirs.sh

```
#!/bin/bash

# days_back should be set to how many days dump files should be kept
days_back=30

# Add /usr/local/bin to the PATH variable so the oraenv command can be found
PATH=$PATH:/usr/local/bin; export PATH

# If a SID is provided as an argument it will be set and oraenv run
# otherwise we will use the current SID.  If no SID is set or provided
# an error message is displayed and the script exits with a status of 1
if [ $1 ]
then
    ORACLE_SID=$1
    ORAENV_ASK=NO
    . oraenv
else
    if [ ! $ORACLE_SID ]
    then
            echo "Error: No ORACLE_SID set or provided as an argument"
            exit 1
    fi
fi

# Set the ORACLE_BASE variable
ORACLE_BASE=/u01/app/oracle; export ORACLE_BASE

# Clean the files matching both the name and modified time criteria
# out of each directory with a find command with an execute clause
find $ORACLE_BASE/admin/$ORACLE_SID/adump/ -name "*.aud" -mtime +$days_back \
    -exec rm {} \;

find $ORACLE_BASE/admin/$ORACLE_SID/bdump/ -name "*.trc" -mtime +$days_back \
    -exec rm {} \;

find $ORACLE_BASE/admin/$ORACLE_SID/cdump/ -name "*.trc" -mtime +$days_back \
    -exec rm {} \;

find $ORACLE_BASE/admin/$ORACLE_SID/udump/ -name "*.trc" -mtime +$days_back \
    -exec rm {} \;
```

Like the other scripts in this book, this script can be used with the current *ORACLE_SID* if it is set, or a SID can be provided as an argument. This script makes excellent use of the *find* command by checking for files which

---

match both a name criteria and have a modification time of more than a certain number of days ago.

This script could be run daily, but weekly is probably sufficient. The following *crontab* entry will execute this script every Sunday morning at 1:00 am.

```
00 01 * * 0 /u01/app/oracle/admin/common/clean_dump_dirs.sh oss
```

The ADR Directory

Much of what was stored in the admin directory in Oracle 10g and earlier has now been moved to the Automatic Diagnostic Repository, or ADR directory, in Oracle 11g. The ADR directory is created in *$ORACLE_BASE/diag* and contains a subdirectory for each different Oracle installation type on the system and may also contain some empty directories for products which are not installed. Within the database, the ADR location is defined by the *diagnostic_dest* initialization parameter, and the *background_dump_dest*, *user_dump_dest* and similar parameters have been deprecated.

The structure of ADR allows for the storage of items like listener logs and diagnostic files to be stored in a format which is not specific to a particular instance or even Oracle home on the system. Similarly, other aspects of Oracle like ASM have specific log locations within the ADR.

Diagnostic files for a specific database on the system are stored within the ADR under *$ORACLE_BASE/diag/database_name/instance_name*. In non-RAC implementations, the database and instance names are typically the same, but this format affords the flexibility needed in a RAC environment where the instance name varies from the database name.

In 11g, two versions of the alert log are maintained in the ADR directory. One, an XML file named *log.xml*, can be found in the ADR directory for that instance under the *alert* subdirectory. An XML reader or web browser should allow viewing the XML version of the log. Another text-only version of the alert log named with the traditional *alert_ORACLE_SID.log* is kept in the *trace* subdirectory and can be viewed with a standard text editor.

Managing the ADR

Along with the new ADR structure, Oracle has introduced a tool called adrci to manage the ADR. Through adrci, the amount of time can be set to retain certain information and purge information older than this time.

The *adrci* command is found in the *$ORACLE_HOME/bin directory*, so if *oraenv* has been run, it will be part of the path. Once launched, issue the *show homes* command to show ADR repositories which can be managed, then use the *set homepath* command to select one.

```
$ adrci

ADR base = "/u01/app/oracle"

adrci> show homes

ADR Homes:
diag/rdbms/test/TEST

adrci> set homepath diag/rdbms/test/TEST
```

With the homepath set, examine the retention period with the *show control* option. The retention period is indicated by the *shortp_policy* and *longp_policy* values and in 11g, is set in hours.

```
adrci> show control

ADR Home = /u01/app/oracle/diag/rdbms/test/TEST:
*********************************************************************
ADRID                 SHORTP_POLICY          LONGP_POLICY
-------------------   --------------------   -------------
4124447422            720                    8760
1 rows fetched
```

The output may wrap over several lines, but it is the second and third values that should be of interest. These values for *shortp_policy* and *longp_policy* are set in hours. Certain information like incidents and problems are retained based on the *longp_policy* while other information like dump files, which can be significantly larger, are deleted based on the *shortp_policy*.

The retention periods for these policies can be set using the *set control* command. To apply the current retention policy to remove diagnostic information which is older than the policy, run the *purge* command.

Maintaining Oracle Logs and Diagnostic Files

```
adrci> set control (shortp_policy = 128)
adrci> set control (longp_policy = 720)
adrci> show control

ADR Home = /u01/app/oracle/diag/rdbms/test/TEST:
**********************************************************************
ADRID                   SHORTP_POLICY         LONGP_POLICY
--------------------    --------------------  --------------------
4124447422              128                   720

adrci> purge
```

The following shell script can be used to routinely apply the ADR retention policies to clean up the diagnostic files. The SID and ADR home of the instance to be purged should be given as arguments to the script.

💾 adr_purge.sh

```
#!/bin/bash

# Check to see if two arguments are given for the script
# if not echo usage
if [ $# -ne 2 ]
then
    ehco "usage: adr_purge oracle_sid adr_home"
    exit 1
fi

# Add /usr/local/bin to the PATH variable so the oraenv command can be found
PATH=$PATH:/usr/local/bin; export PATH

ORACLE_SID=$1
ORAENV_ASK=NO
. oraenv

# Define the adr_home variable for the instance to be purged
adr_home=$2

# Add /usr/local/bin to the PATH variable so the oraenv command can be found
PATH=$PATH:/usr/local/bin; export PATH

adrci << EOF > /tmp/adr_purge.log
set homepath $adr_home
purge
exit
EOF
```

A *crontab* entry to call this script daily would look like the following:

```
10 0 * * * /home/oracle/bin/adr_purge.sh TEST diag/rdbms/test/TEST
```

Managing Multiple Oracle Homes

There are several reasons why you may want to have more than one Oracle installation on a system: you may need to have different versions of RDBMS software on a system for different products, you may be using multiple Oracle homes as part of an upgrade strategy, or you may have different Oracle products installed on the system. Regardless of the reason, managing multiple homes is simple if you use the *oraenv* script and *oratab* file provided by Oracle.

When creating or deleting Oracle homes, it is preferrable to use the Oracle installer so the Oracle inventory is kept up-to-date. Oracle provides instructions on how to copy or clone many types of Oracle homes, but if it is decided to go this route, it is important to follow their instructions closely to assure the inventory gets properly updated.

Managing *oratab* Entries

When the *oraenv* script to set environmental variables for Oracle is run, it reads the */etc/oratab* file to determine the Oracle home for that instance. The *oratab* file should contain one line for each instance on the system. Each line contains the instance name, Oracle home location and a Y or N to indicate if the *dbstart* command should start the given instance when it is run.

Because you can indicate not to start a given instance with *dbstart*, you can insert your own lines into the *oratab* file where the first value is not a valid instance name. Below are two *oratab* entries. The first one is a place keeper entry which can be used to set environment variables for the 11g Oracle home without setting a specific database, the second is the entry for the *TEST* instance.

```
11g_db1:/u01/app/oracle/product/11.1.0/db_1:N
TEST:/u01/app/oracle/product/11.1.0/db_1:Y
```

By indicating N in the final field of the *11g_db1* line, *dbstart* skips this line when starting databases. However, as long as the Oracle home value is valid, this entry can still be used with the *oraenv* command. This is a better method than altering $ORACLE\_HOME$, $PATH$ and other environment variables manually as it properly replaces values in the $PATH$ rather than just adding to it. This

---

method can even be used with Oracle Application Server homes where no database instances are present.

Upgrading with Multiple Oracle Homes

When taking a database from one version to another, e.g. 10g to 11g or even 10.1 to 10.2, you often have to install the Oracle software in a new Oracle home. Even when doing minor upgrades like 11.1.0.6 to 11.1.0.7, employing multiple homes is possible to reduce the amount of downtime required during the upgrade.

Below are the basic steps to perform an upgrade where a database is being moved from one home to another.

1. Install the new version of the software in a new Oracle home

2. Shut down and back up the database

3. Edit the *oratab* file to reflect the new home

4. Run *.oraenv* and select the same SID to correctly set the environment variables with the new home. If you have multiple command line sessions on the system, make sure you run this in each session.

5. Startup the database

6. Run the post-upgrade steps identified in the Oracle upgrade documents

When performing upgrades using this method, it is important to also consider upgrading the listener. It can typically be done anytime during the migration process, but the upgrade documentation should have additional details on that.

The Oracle Inventory

The Oracle installer maintains an inventory of Oracle products installed on the system. The inventory can be reviewed by running the installer and clicking the Installed Products... button.

While managing the contents of the inventory manually is not needed, make sure it is backed up with the Oracle home and that it is not inadvertently overwritten or moved. The inventory location, typically */u01/app/oraInventory*, is set when the first Oracle installation is performed on a system and is stored in the file */etc/oraInst.loc*.

```
$ more /etc/oraInst.loc
```

```
inventory_loc=/u01/app/oraInventory
inst_group=oinstall
```

Moving Oracle Files

You occasionally need to move Oracle files from one location on the system to another. Oracle homes and the Oracle inventory cannot be easily moved. If it is necessary to move one of these items, the safest thing to do is to reinstall, though you may be able to move the software and create a symlink to make it appear at its original location.

Database files, on the other hand, can be moved easily. Just make sure that you do things in the right order so Oracle is aware of the move and not using the files at the time they are moved. The following examples will outline how all the necessary files associated with the TEST database can be moved from */u02/oradata/TEST* to */u03/oradata/TEST*. Where possible, I have shown how these steps can be done with the database running, though it may be desirable to do these with the database either mounted or in a restricted session to avoid applications or users trying to access data while files are being moved.

 Before attempting to move data files, first be sure you have a good current backup of the database. Many of these steps could render a datafile or an entire database useless if they are not done correctly. A backup should also be taken after file locations are changed to ensure the recoverability of the database.

Moving Control Files

Since they are critical to database functionality, control files can only be moved when the database is shut down or in *nomount* state. First determine the current location of the control files and shut down the database.

```
$ sqlplus "/ as sysdba"
```

```
...
SQL>
show
 parameter control_files

NAME                    TYPE      VALUE
------------------      --------  -----------------------------
control_files           string    /u02/oradata/TEST/control01.ct
                                  l, /u02/oradata/TEST/control02
                                  .ctl, /u02/oradata/TEST/contro
                                  l03.ctl

SQL>
shutdown
 immediate;

Database closed.
Database dismounted.
ORACLE instance shut down.
SQL>
exit
```

With the database shut down, you can create the destination folder and move the files themselves. Since this database follows the location and naming standards for control files, use the single statement to move all three.

```
$ mkdir /u03/oradata/TEST
$ mv /u02/oradata/TEST/control*.ctl /u03/oradata/TEST
```

With the files moved, now update the *init* or *spfile* to indicate the new location. If using an *init* file, use a text editor to update the line containing the *control_files* parameter. The *init* file should be in the *$ORACLE_HOME/dbs* directory.

If using a spfile, you need to bring the database into the *nomount* state to change the *control_files* parameter. The parameter is changed using the *alter system* command and the instance must then be shut down and restarted for the new value to be loaded.

```
$ sqlplus "/ as sysdba"

...
Connected to an idle instance.
...

SQL>
startup
 nomount;

ORACLE instance started.
...
```

```
SQL>
alter
system set control_files='/u03/oradata/TEST/control01.ctl',
'/u03/oradata/TEST/control02.ctl', '/u03/oradata/TEST/control03.ctl'
scope=SPFILE;

System altered.

SQL>
shutdown
 immediate;
...
SQL>
startup
 nomount

ORACLE instance started.
...

SQL>
show
 parameter control_files

NAME                   TYPE     VALUE
-------------------    -------  -----------------------------
control_files          string   /u03/oradata/TEST/control01.ct
                                 1, /u03/oradata/TEST/control02
                                 .ctl, /u03/oradata/TEST/contro
                                 l03.ctl

SQL>
alter
 database mount;

Database altered.

SQL>
alter
 database open;

Database altered.
```

> 🔔 The value for *control_files* is displayed as one long string, but
> it is important to put the location of each control file in single
> quotes when setting the parameter.

You can review the value for the *control_files* parameter and if it looks good,
mount the control files. If this step succeeds, you should be able to open the
database for use; if not, double-check the setting of the *control_files* parameter
and the location of the files on disk.

Moving Datafiles

To move a datafile, either take the tablespace it belongs to offline, or shut down the database and bring it back up into a mounted state. The system tablespace, temporary tablespaces and tablespaces used for rollback will require the database be in *mount* state. When possible, it is preferred to move datafiles with the database in a mounted state. To locate datafiles associated with a database, query the *dba_data_files* table.

```
SQL>
select
 tablespace_name, file_name from dba_data_files;

TABLESPACE_NAME    FILE_NAME
-----------------------------------------------------------------
USERS              /u02/oradata/TEST/users01.dbf

UNDOTBS1           /u02/oradata/TEST/undotbs01.dbf

SYSTEM             /u02/oradata/TEST/system01.dbf
...
```

Moving Normal Data Files

To move the datafile associated with the USERS tablespace, first take the tablespace offline and move the file at the OS level. Next, use the *alter tablespace* command to rename the file in the database to reflect the new location. Finally, the tablespace is brought back online.

```
SQL>
alter
 tablespace USERS offline;

Tablespace altered.

SQL>
!
$ mv /u02/oradata/TEST/users01.dbf /u03/oradata/TEST/
$ exit

exit

SQL>
alter
 tablespace USERS rename datafile '/u02/oradata/TEST/users01.dbf' to
'/u03/oradata/TEST/users01.dbf';

Tablespace altered.

SQL>
```

```
alter
 tablespace USERS online;
```

```
Tablespace altered.
```

> When in SQL*Plus, you can enter the character ! to
> temporarily exit to the command line. When you are ready to
> return to SQL*Plus, type exit at the command line.

Data in this tablespace is not available when it is offline.

Moving System, Temporary or Rollback Tablespaces

To move system, temporary or rollback tablespaces, the database should be
shut down and brought back up into a *mount* state. This allows the control file
to be updated while the datafiles are not in use.

```
SQL>
shutdown
 immediate;
```

```
Database closed.
Database dismounted.
ORACLE instance shut down.
```

```
SQL>
startup
 mount;
```

```
ORACLE instance started.
. . .
```

```
SQL>
 !
$ mv /u02/oradata/TEST/system01.dbf /u03/oradata/TEST/
$ exit
```

```
SQL>
alter
 database rename file '/u02/oradata/TEST/system01.dbf' to
'/u03/oradata/TEST/system01.dbf';
```

```
Database altered.
```

```
SQL>
alter
 database open;
```

```
Database altered.
```

The *mv* and *alter database rename file* steps above can be repeated for other files which need to be moved, then the database can be opened.

Moving Redo Logs

Redo logs are moved in the same way the system tablespace is moved. The database is shut down and the files are moved, then the database is brought up into a *mount* state and the *alter database rename file* command is called to tell Oracle where the files have been moved. Finally, the database can be brought back into an *open* state.

```
SQL>
shutdown
 immediate;

Database closed.
Database dismounted.
ORACLE instance shut down.

SQL>
 !
$ mv /u02/oradata/TEST/redo*.log /u03/oradata/TEST
$ exit

exit

SQL>
startup
 mount;

ORACLE instance started.
...

SQL>
alter
 database rename file '/u02/oradata/TEST/redo01.log' to
'/u03/oradata/TEST/redo01.log';

Database altered.

SQL>
alter
 database rename file '/u02/oradata/TEST/redo02.log' to
'/u03/oradata/TEST/redo02.log';

Database altered.

SQL>
alter
 database rename file '/u02/oradata/TEST/redo03.log' to
'/u03/oradata/TEST/redo03.log';

Database altered.
```

```
SQL>
alter
 database open;
```

```
Database altered.
```

There is an alternative method for moving online redo logs without having to shut down the database. If a redo log is inactive, it can be dropped from the database and then recreated in the new location. By switching the active log file, another log file can be made inactive once it is switched and archived, then dropped and recreated. Care should be taken when using this method, especially with very active databases.

Conclusion

It is important that standards are followed. This will not only assure that you can find things in consistent, predictable locations, but also that another DBA will have a good chance of being able to learn your environment quickly. This becomes increasingly important in installations with multiple databases or Oracle home installations.

Regardless of the version, Oracle produces a large amount of diagnostic data. If left alone, this data will continue to grow over time and can become a concern for disk use.

Oracle files can be moved around with relative ease as long as you have the correct syntax handy. This should be done with care, and only when necessary, but it is possible to move any of the files associated with a database.

Managing Oracle Processes

Like other Linux tasks, there are several ways you can manage Oracle processes. There are also several things you have to be concerned with for both security and stability. In this way, some of the tools available from Oracle and Linux will be shown as well as how you can use them to manage Oracle processes.

Using the *dbstart* and *dbshut* Scripts

Oracle provides you with the scripts *dbstart* and *dbshut* to start and stop multiple databases on the system. As mentioned in earlier chapters, these scripts rely on the */etc/oratab* file to determine what databases should be started.

```
11g_db1:/u01/app/oracle/product/11.1.0/db_1:N
TEST:/u01/app/oracle/product/11.1.0/db_1:Y
```

Entries where the third field is *Y* are started when *dbstart* is run; entries with an *N* in this field are ignored by *dbstart*. Note that there is no way to pick and choose which scripts should be started and stopped with these scripts other than indicating it in the *oratab* file. If you want to start or stop an individual database, you need to do it through *sqlplus* by connecting as sysdba and issuing the *startup* command.

The *dbstart* and *dbshut* commands are intended for use at system startup and shutdown in a script like the *oracle_db* script provided in the code depot for this book. It is possible to run these commands directly from the command line as the oracle user, but keep in mind that they will affect all databases indicated with *Y* in the *oratab* file.

The root user can also use the *service* command in the format *service oracle_db start* or *service oracle_db stop* command to start or stop all Oracle services just as they would be at startup or shutdown. This is preferred to running the *dbstart* and *dbshut* commands since it invokes the script from */etc/init.d* and manages the lock file in */var/lock/subsys* which is used to track the status of the service.

In Oracle 10gR2, it is possible to use *dbstart* to start a listener along with the databases. The *dbstart* command must be modified so the line defining the variable *ORACLE_HOME_LISTENER* points to the Oracle home containing the listener you would like to manage.

```
# Set this to bring up Oracle Net Listener
ORACLE_HOME_LISTENER=/u01/app/oracle/product/10.2.0/db_1
```

In 10gR2, the *dbshut* command does not contain logic to stop the listener. It can be stopped using the *lsnrctl* command. For consistency, it may be more desirable to start and stop the listener using the *lsnrctl* command in 10g.

In Oracle 11g, both the *dbstart* and *dbshut* commands can now be used to start and stop an Oracle listener. No modification of the scripts is required; instead, the Oracle home for the listener you want to start is passed as an argument to the *dbstart* or *dbshut* commands. The resulting *startup* command would look like this:

```
$ dbstart /u01/app/oracle/product/11.1.0/db_1
```

This can be included in the *oracle_db* script called at system startup instead of running the *lsnrctl* command.

As of 11g, the *dbstart* and *dbshut* commands also have some additional logging. There is now a *startup.log, shutdown.log* and *listener.log* all contained within the Oracle home directory. These contain the output of the corresponding commands and can help with troubleshooting startup and shutdown issues. The alert logs for each database will also have information on startup and shutdown activities.

Managing the Listener

The listener can be started and stopped with the *lsnrctl* command by using the *start* or *stop* arguments.

```
$ lsnrctl start
```

```
Starting /u01/app/oracle/product/11.1.0/db_1/bin/tnslsnr: please wait...
```

```
...
Listening Endpoints Summary...
  (DESCRIPTION=(ADDRESS=(PROTOCOL=tcp)(HOST=oelinux-
test1.lifeaftercoffee.com)(PORT=1521)))
The listener supports no services
The command completed successfully
```

```
$ lsnrctl stop
```

```
Connecting to (ADDRESS=(PROTOCOL=tcp)(HOST=)(PORT=1521))
The command completed successfully
```

The listener must be aware of each database for which it listens for requests. There are two ways a listener can know about a database: it can have an entry in the $ORACLE_HOME/*network*/*admin*/*listener.ora* file or the instance can register itself with the listener when it starts up. If you want to explicitly define a database rather than having it register itself on listener startup, you will need to create the *listener.ora* file. You can start with the one in the samples subdirectory of *$ORACLE_HOME*/*network*/*admin* and modify it to your needs. This method can be useful for more complex configurations such as having one listener respond to requests for multiple Oracle homes.

Alternately, if a configuration is not set up in the *listener.ora* file, try to assure that the listener will be started before any databases are. When a database starts up, it automatically registers itself with the listener, and the listener starts responding to requests for the database.

To examine what services the listener is listening for, the *lsnrctl services* or *lsnrctl status* command can be called. The following example shows the output of this command before and after a database has registered with the listener.

```
$ lsnrctl services
```

```
Connecting to (ADDRESS=(PROTOCOL=tcp)(HOST=)(PORT=1521))
The listener supports no services
The command completed successfully
```

```
$ lsnrctl services
```

```
Connecting to (ADDRESS=(PROTOCOL=tcp)(HOST=)(PORT=1521))
Services Summary...
Service "TEST" has 1 instance(s).
  Instance "TEST", status READY, has 1 handler(s) for this service...
    Handler(s):
      "DEDICATED" established:0 refused:0 state:ready
         LOCAL SERVER
...
The command completed successfully
```

If the listener is started or restarted when databases are running, it will lose track of instances which have registered with the listener. Databases will re-register themselves with the listener, but this can cause databases to temporarily become unavailable.

Managing Unresponsive Processes

Sometimes, you may find that the listener or a database fails to shut down properly. In that case, you may need to clean up some running processes using the *ps* and *kill* commands.

 This should be done only as a last resort after *shutdown immediate* and *shutdown abort database* commands have failed. Be sure to give these commands several minutes to complete before resorting to killing processes.

The listener is typically running with a command name *tnslsnr*. You can use *grep* to find this in the *ps* output.

```
$ ps -ef | grep lsnr

oracle    18832     1  0 09:06 ?        00:00:00
/u01/app/oracle/product/11.1.0/db_1/bin/tnslsnr LISTENER -inherit
```

If *lsnrctl stop* fails to stop the listener process, use the *kill* command, as described in Chapter 10, with the process ID to kill this process. Oracle server processes for a given database typically have the SID in the process name.

```
$ ps -ef | grep TEST
oracle    2926     1  0 06:16 ?        00:00:09 ora_pmon_TEST
oracle    2928     1  0 06:16 ?        00:01:15 ora_vktm_TEST
oracle    2932     1  0 06:16 ?        00:00:06 ora_diag_TEST
oracle    2934     1  0 06:16 ?        00:00:05 ora_dbrm_TEST
oracle    2936     1  0 06:16 ?        00:00:05 ora_psp0_TEST
...
```

You should first attempt to shut down a database using *shutdown immediate* which disconnects all running sessions and rolls back any uncommitted changes. If, after several minutes, the command is unresponsive, then try *shutdown abort*. This does not rollback or cleanup any data, but instead brings all processes down as quickly as possible.

Even a *shutdown abort* may take several minutes to respond. As a last resort, if *shutdown abort* is unable to shut down all Oracle processes, use the *kill* command to kill the remaining server processes identified by grepping for the SID.

When either *shutdown abort* is used or Oracle processes are killed using *kill*, there is a good chance some data cleanup is needed. Oracle tries to resolve this the next time the database is started up. If you are taking a database down for a cold backup and have to resort to either of these methods, you should then startup the database, in restricted mode if desired, and shut it down cleanly by using *shutdown immediate* before taking your backup. That assures that the database is in a consistent state when the backup is taken.

Managing Oracle User Processes

The processes managed by starting and stopping databases and listeners are considered server processes, but it is likely you will also have users connecting to your system. When initiated on the server, user processes like SQL*Plus and RMAN deserve special consideration.

Tracking Down User Processes

When you need to track down a user process associated with a certain Oracle session, look up some key information about the user in the *v$session* table. You can query based on any number of factors including *username* (which is the database username,) *osuser* (the username at the operating system that started this session,) or *machine* (which indicates what system the connection was made from.)

Regardless of the query criteria, information about a session can be quickly found including the process ID, which is kept in the *process* field.

```
SQL>
select
 username, process, machine from v$session where username='JEMMONS';

USERNAME      PROCESS     MACHINE
-------------------------------------------------------
JEMMONS        20384       oelinux-test1.lifeaftercoffee.com
```

With the process ID, use *ps* to examine this process further as was seen in Chapter 10.

```
$ ps -ef | grep 20384

oracle   20384 20353  0 09:48 pts/0   00:00:00 sqlplus
oracle   20385 20384  0 09:48 ?       00:00:00 oracleTEST
(DESCRIPTION=(LOCAL=YES)(ADDRESS=(PROTOCOL=beq)))
```

If you need to kill a session, it is best to first try to disconnect it through Oracle using the *alter system kill session* command with the SID and *SERIAL#* values from the *v$session* table.

```
SQL>
select
 SID,SERIAL# from v$session where username='JEMMONS';

      SID    SERIAL#
---------- ----------
      125    57
SQL>
alter
 system kill session '125,57';

System altered.
```

In some cases, this syntax may not work and you may have to kill the operating system processes to completely kill a session.

Hiding Passwords in Process Listings

In Chapter 10, how to examine commands running on the system using the *ps* command was seen. Since any user on the system can run the *ps* command and view processes running as other users, it is important that no secure information be included when calling commands.

This becomes important when setting processes up to run automatically. It can be tempting to have syntax like the following in a shell script:

```
sqlplus system/manager <<EOF
@/u01/app/oracle/admin/scripts/check_for_locks.sql
EOF
```

When run in this format, the resulting command may appear with the password in *ps* output. This could reveal your system password to anyone with command-line access to the system!

Managing Oracle User Processes   **391**

```
$ ps -ef | grep sqlplus

oracle   19741 19737  0 09:32 pts/0  00:00:00 sqlplus system/manager
```

Instead, an easy workaround to this is to start *sqlplus* with the *nolog* option, then connect to the database after entering *sqlplus*. The commands above could be rewritten like this:

```
sqlplus /nolog <<EOF
connect system/manager
@/u01/app/oracle/admin/scripts/check_for_locks.sql
EOF
```

When scripts are run as a user in the dba group, you can also *sqlplus "/ as sysdba"* to make a sysdba connection to the database, but this should only be used when sysdba privileges are required for an operation. Other possible workarounds suggest using variables, but still risk exposing the password in *ps* output.

> Command arguments may not show up in *ps* output under certain circumstances, but it is still best practice to exclude them from the command line.

Conclusion

Oracle provides tools which should be used for managing startup and shutdown whenever possible. Logs are created for each of these to aid troubleshooting. When the Oracle tools fail to work properly, you can employ some operating system tools to manage processes, but care must be taken or it is possible to corrupt your database or interrupt important work.

Next to be examined is the Oracle scheduler and how and when to use it.

The Oracle Scheduler

Like the Linux operating system has *cron* for scheduling tasks, each Oracle database also has a scheduler that allows commands to be executed at a specific time and repeated if desired. The syntax for the Oracle scheduler can seem more tedious than *cron*, but it also offers several advantages.

When to Use the Oracle Scheduler

Since newer versions of the Oracle scheduler have the ability to execute commands and shell scripts at the Linux level, it is possible to move tasks from *cron* into the Oracle scheduler, but be careful when choosing jobs to move. You need to consider that jobs in the Oracle scheduler will not be run if the database is down. Furthermore, it may be confusing to have jobs run in the scheduler from one database connect to another.

Another consideration when using the Oracle scheduler is that jobs created in a database will be copied if the database is duplicated using RMAN, datapump or manual datafile backups. This can be both an advantage and a disadvantage.

With these factors in mind, consider using the Oracle scheduler for tasks that affect only the database they are created in and that do not have to be run if the database is down. A good example would be a job that removes old entries from log tables in a database. If the database is down, there would not be any need to empty old entries.

Alternatively, consider a job that checks for available disk space on a system. This is a case where it is not specifically tied to an individual database and, additionally, you would want this job to be running even if the databases were down. This would be best implemented in *cron*.

These are meant only as guidelines and as the Oracle scheduler evolves, it offers more and more features that make it a compelling alternative to *cron*.

The Legacy *dbms_job* Scheduler

Oracle versions 7 through 9i used the package *dbms_job* to schedule tasks in the database. Starting in 10g, a new package, *dbms_scheduler*, was introduced to replace *dbms_job*. The *dbms_job* package is still available in later versions of the database but has been deprecated. I am including information on the legacy *dbms_job* scheduler for those running older database versions or those who may need to move *dbms_job* tasks into the new scheduler. New jobs should be created using the *dbms_scheduler*.

How Jobs are Run

Jobs submitted using the *dbms_job* package have three main portions: a PL/SQL block of code to be executed, the date and time of the first run, and a formula that is used to determine the date and time of future executions. A job number is also generated when the job is submitted. At the date and time of the first run, the job executes. When it is complete, the scheduler evaluates the formula given for future executions to determine the next time the job should be executed and update the date of the next execution.

Examining the Scheduler Setup and Jobs

For jobs submitted through the *dbms_job* package to run, the database parameter *job_queue_processes* must be set to something other than 0. This value controls how many jobs can be run at once in this database. Acceptable values are from 1 to 1,000.

```
SQL>
show
 parameter job_queue_processes

NAME                             TYPE       VALUE
-------------------------------- ---------- ------------------
job_queue_processes              integer    1000
```

To check for jobs which have been submitted using *dbms_job*, you can look at the *dba_jobs* dictionary view. Each user also has a *user_jobs* view for jobs that they have submitted. Here are the most useful fields within the *dba_jobs* and *user_jobs* views:

Field	Description
job	The job number of a given job
log_user	The user who created this job
priv_user	The user who this job will be run as
last_date	Last successful execution date and time
this_date	If the job is currently running, the date and time it started (null if not running)
next_date	The next date and time this job will be executed
interval	The formula evaluated to determine the *next_date*
failures	Number of job failures since the last successful run of this job
broken	Indicates the job has failed too many times since its last successful run. This can also be set manually to suspend a job.
what	Code to be executed when this job is run

Table 19.1: *Popular Fields Within dba_jobs and user_jobs Views*

The *log_user* and *priv_user* are typically the same, but privileged users can create jobs to run under other users' permissions. If they differ, just remember that *log_user* is the user who created the job, but it runs with the permissions of *priv_user*.

An additional view, *dba_jobs_running*, offers additional information on jobs that are currently running. From there, you can query for the SID and instance that a job is running that may be needed in a RAC environment.

Submitting a Job

The procedure *dbms_job.submit* is called to submit a new job to the queue. The procedure is called in the following format:

```
begin
dbms_job.submit(job => :jobnumber
what => 'code to execute',
next_date => first_execution_date,
interval => next_execution_date);
commit;
end;
/
```

Here is an example which calls the *dbms_stats* package:

```
variable jobnumber number
begin
dbms_job.submit(job => :jobnumber,
what => 'dbms_stats.gather_database_stats(options => ''gather auto'');',
next_date => to_date('01:30 02/28/10','hh24:mi mm/dd/yy'),
interval => 'sysdate + 1');
commit;
end;
/
print jobnumber

JOBNUMBER
----------
21
```

Note that the *jobnumber* variable is populated when a job is submitted, not supplied as a parameter. Use the *print* command to print the value that was assigned when the job was scheduled. You could also look this up from the *dba_jobs* or *user_jobs* views.

The *next_date* value can be any valid Oracle date. Here I have specified an explicit date and time, but a value like *sysdate+1/24* to specify that it should start an hour from now would also be acceptable. The *interval* value should be a formula that always evaluates to a future date and time. The example above simply adds a day to the current date and time, but more complicated formulae are possible. For instance, you may use the following to indicate 3:00 AM the following morning:

```
interval => 'trunc(sysdate) + 27/24');
```

In this example, *sysdate* is truncated to midnight and 27 hours (27/24ths of a day) are added to advance the date to 3:00 AM the following day. Any formula which evaluates to a valid Oracle date can be used.

While it is possible to specify complicated PL/SQL in the *what* portion of a job submission, the syntax is often less complicated if you create a PL/SQL package or procedure instead with the code to be executed and call it when creating jobs.

Running a Job Manually

Occasionally, you may find that you need to run a job manually. To do this, call the *run* procedure. This forces a job to run, even if it has previously been marked as broken. If the job runs successfully, it is updated to indicate it is no longer broken and goes back to running on its schedule.

```
begin
dbms_job.run(job => 21);
end;
/
```

 If you use *dbms_job.run* to manually execute a job, the value for *next_date* will be updated based upon using the interval based on the current date and time. This becomes important if you have a job running, for example, at 11:00 pm with an interval of sysdate + 1, but then if you run it manually at 3:45 pm, the *next_date* will be recalculated at that time and it will now be run at 3:45pm each day.

Suspending a Job

If you want to tell Oracle to temporarily suspend the running of a job, manually mark it as broken by executing the following:

```
begin
dbms_job.broken(job => 21, broken => true);
end;
/
```

The job will remain broken and will not be run until you either force it to run or mark it as not broken. When marking it as not broken. you must also specify the next date for the job to run.

Changing a Job

You can update a job with the *dbms_job.change* procedure. This procedure requires that you specify *job number*, *what*, *next date* and *interval*, in that order, as arguments, but any value you do not want to change can be specified as NULL.

With that in mind, the command to change just the *interval* would look something like this:

```
begin
dbms_job.change(job => 21, what => null, next_date => null, interval =>
'sysdate + 7');
end;
/
```

This would change job number 21 to execute every 7 days.

Removing a Job

To remove a job from the job queue, you need the job number. If you are not sure what it is, you should be able to find it by querying one of the views listed above. Once you have the job number, use the *dbms_job.remove* procedure to remove the job.

```
begin
dbms_job.remove(job => 21);
end;
/
```

This removes the job and it is not executed again. You can only remove jobs that you own. If this is run while the job is executing, it will not be interrupted but will not be run again.

Using *dbms_scheduler*

The new *dbms_scheduler* package was introduced in Oracle 10g as a replacement for the *dbms_jobs* package. It has been improved and expanded with each major Oracle version since then and has considerably greater flexibility and capabilities than *dbms_jobs*.

The features available in the *dbms_scheduler* are too numerous to cover in this short chapter; instead, this will cover some basic examples and a few of the advanced features that tie specifically into the operating system. Some of these features are version dependent and will be noted as such where possible. For a full list of available features in your database version, consult the Oracle documentation.

An Overview of the Scheduler

The 10g and later job scheduler expands on the functionality of the previous *dbms_job* scheduler and introduces several new concepts. Each plays a role in making the *dbms_scheduler* more powerful and flexible. Here are some of the key concepts in the new scheduler:

- Job: Scheduled jobs that carry out a defined task

- Job type: Jobs can be defined as one of several different types including *plsql_block* that can contain any PL/SQL code, *stored_procedure* that would execute the contents of a stored procedure, or *executable* that can execute a command or script at the operating system level.

- Program: The commands to be executed by a job can be defined independent of their schedule in a program. This allows a set of commands to be run on multiple schedules while maintaining only one copy of the commands.

- Schedule: A schedule for job execution can be set up independently from the job's commands. Once set up, a schedule can be used on multiple jobs.

- Event: An event can be raised by the scheduler or an external application. Once raised, the scheduler consumes the event and initiates a specified job.

- Chain: A chain is a series of events and rules which control which events should be executed under certain conditions. A chain may simply execute a series of jobs in order, or subsequent jobs may depend on the success or failure of previous ones.

The job coordinator process starts up when there is a job scheduled to run. It spawns job slave processes which perform the actual job execution. Rather than the cumbersome *interval* definition in the *dbms_job* package, the *dbms_scheduler* package allows an interval like daily or weekly to be specified.

Viewing Job Information

A set of dictionary views allows you to view information about jobs scheduled with the *dbms_scheduler* package. The *dba_scheduler_jobs* table is one of the most comprehensive views. Some of the key fields are as follows:

Field	Description
owner	Owner of the job
job_name	Name of the job given at job creation
program	If this job runs a predefined program, it will be named here
job_type	Type of job (e.g. *plsql_block* or *executable*)
job_action	The command(s) to be executed by this job if not defined as a program
schedule_owner and schedule_name	If a predefined schedule is being used, the owner and name for the schedule
start_date	The first date and time that this job should be run
repeat_interval	The interval at which this job should be run
enabled	If this job is currently enabled to run
failure_count	How many times this job has failed
max_failures	The maximum number of failures before the job will be marked as broken
state	The current state of the job. Common values are *scheduled, running, disabled,* or *broken*.

Table 19.2: *Main Fields of dba_scheduler_jobs Table*

Many other job attributes such as end dates, priorities and run counts can be queried from this table, but the ones listed above should be enough to get started with the scheduler. A different view, *dba_scheduler_running_jobs*, allows you to view additional information about running jobs including the OS process ID of the slave process running the job (*slave_os_process_id*) and the instance it is being executed in (*running_instance*), which is useful for RAC environments. This view also shows how long the job has been running (*elapsed_time*) and the amount of CPU time it has consumed (*cpu_used*).

Submitting a Job

The *dbms_scheduler.create_job* procedure is used to create scheduler jobs. Here is an example of it being used to call a stored procedure:

```
begin
dbms_scheduler.create_job (
     job_name          =>   'run_load_sales',
     job_type          =>   'STORED_PROCEDURE',
     job_action        =>   'system.load_sales',
     start_date        =>   '01-MAR-2010 03:00:00 AM',
     repeat_interval   =>   'FREQ=DAILY',
     enabled           =>   TRUE);
END;
/
```

This creates the job named *run_load_sales* which executes the stored procedure *system.load_sales*. The start date is configured as 3:00 AM on March 1 and the frequency is set to daily. Normally, jobs are disabled when they are created,

> 🔔 Scheduled jobs are now treated like other database objects and need to have unique names within a schema. For example, you cannot create a job named *load_sales* if you already have a procedure by that name.

but the line beginning *enabled* automatically enables this job at creation.
Each time this job is executed, the scheduler evaluates the *repeat_interval* to determine the next time this job should be run. In this case, at 3:00 AM on March 1st it evaluates *freq=daily* and determines that the job should be run daily and, with no other criteria, schedules the next running of the job at 3:00 AM on March 2nd.

There are a large number of expressions that can be used to define the repeat interval for a job. Here are a few examples:

repeat_interval	Description
freq=hourly	Run every hour
freq=daily; byhour=3	Run at 3 am every day
freq=daily; byhour=8,20	Run at 8 am and 8 pm every day
freq=monthly; bymonthday=1	Run on the first day of every month
freq=monthly; bymonthday=-1	Run on the last day of every month
freq=yearly; bymonth=sep;	Run yearly on September 20th

bymonthday=20;	

Table 19.3: *repeat_interval Expressions*

There are almost unlimited permutations possible for the *repeat_interval* value. These are only a few possibilities but should get you started.

Creating a Job That Calls an Executable

The job type *executable* allows you to create jobs which execute a command or script at the operating system level. The syntax is similar to creating other jobs, but the job type is set to *executable* and the job action should include the full path to the command or script to be executed.

```
begin
dbms_scheduler.create_job (
    job_name          =>  'migrate_files',
    job_type          =>  'executable',
    job_action        =>  '/home/oracle/bin/migrate_files.sh',
    start_date        =>  '01-mar-2010 07:00:00 am',
    repeat_interval   =>  'freq=daily',
    enabled           =>  true);
end;
/
```

When the date comes up to execute this job, Oracle executes the *migrate_files.sh* script as the user who the database is running under (typically oracle.) That user must already have *execute* privileges on the script or command to be run in order for the job to succeed.

Changing a Job

You can change anything about a scheduled job, except its name, using the *dbms_scheduler.set_attribute* procedure. The job name is given, followed by the attribute that you wish to change, and finally, the new value for that attribute.

```
begin
dbms_scheduler.set_attribute (
name           =>  'run_load_sales',
attribute      =>  'repeat_interval',
value          =>  'freq=daily; byhour=3');
end;
/
```

A job can be changed while it is running, but the changes will not take effect until the next run of the job.

Running a Job Manually

If you want to run a job immediately, call the *dbms_scheduler.run_job* procedure.

```
begin
dbms_scheduler.run_job (job_name => 'run_load_sales');
end;
/
```

This causes the named job to be run immediately.

Stopping Running Jobs

Running jobs can be stopped using the *dbms_scheduler.stop_job* proceure.

```
begin
dbms_scheduler.stop_job (job_name => 'run_load_sales');
end;
/
```

This only stops the running job and does not affect future running of this job.

Disabling and Enabling Jobs

The *dbms_scheduler* package includes the procedures *disable* and *enable* to disable and enable jobs. When a job is disabled, it will not be run.

```
begin
dbms_scheduler.disable (job_name => 'run_load_sales');
end;
/
```

If the job is running when the *disable* procedure is called, you get an error. You can stop the running job as shown in the last example, or you can add *force =>* true to the disable statement.

To re-enable a job which has been disabled, use the *enable* procedure.

```
begin
dbms_scheduler.enable (job_name => 'run_load_sales');
end;
/
```

The job will now be run based on its original schedule. Multiple jobs can be disabled or enabled at the same time by separating their names with a comma.

Dropping Jobs

To permanently drop a job, call the procedure *dbms_scheduler.drop_job*. As with disabling and enabling jobs, multiple jobs can be specified by separating them with commas.

```
begin
dbms_scheduler.drop_job ('run_load_sales');
end;
/
```

If a job is running when you try to drop it, you get an error. You can stop the job, then drop it or set the *force* parameter to *true*. Setting *force* to *true* causes the running job to be stopped, and then the job is dropped from the scheduler.

File Watchers

In Oracle 11gR2, a new feature has been added to the *dbms_scheduler* package called the File Watcher. File watchers can be created to watch in a specific location on the system for files to arrive. When a file is detected, an event is kicked off which can start a job or jobs. The event created by the file watcher process contains some metadata to allow the subsequent jobs to manipulate the file if desired.

By default, file watchers check for files every 10 minutes, but the frequency of checks can be changed. File watchers can even be set up to detect files on a remote system through a scheduler agent.

Setup of a file watcher is complicated, requiring many of the aspects of the *dbms_scheduler* package to be set up and working. The following example shows the steps required to set up a file watcher. More details are available in the Oracle documentation.

Setting Up a File Watcher

To use a file watcher, you need to create OS credentials, create the file watcher itself, create a program to run when files are detected, define a *metadata* argument to allow file metadata to be read by the program, then create an event-based job to be triggered by the file watcher.

1. Create a credential

This are the credentials used to log into the host operating system to check for and access files.

```
begin
dbms_scheduler.create_credential(
credential_name    => 'watch_dataload',
username           => 'oracle',
password           => 'password');
end;
/
```

2. Create the file watcher

This is the object that checks for files as they arrive. The directory to watch is given as well as a pattern for matching incoming files. Only files which match this pattern cause this file watcher to trigger an event, but note that several file watchers can be watching a single directory for files matching different patterns.

```
begin
dbms_scheduler.create_file_watcher(
file_watcher_name => 'dataload_file_watcher',
directory_path    => '/u01/dataload',
file_name         => '*_sales.txt',
credential_name   => 'watch_dataload',
destination       => null,
enabled           => false);
end;
/
```

The credentials created in the previous step are specified, so this watcher connects as the Oracle user to look for these files.

3. Create the program to be triggered by the event

This is a *dbms_scheduler* program, not a scheduled job. It is triggered by the event-based job created later.

```
begin
dbms_scheduler.create_program(
program_name        => 'load_sales_files',
program_type        => 'stored_procedure',
program_action      => 'system.load_sales',
number_of_arguments => 1,
enabled             => false);
end;
```

Keep in mind that jobs define what should be done, independent of when it should be executed.

4. Create a *metadata* argument

The *metadata* argument accompanies the program in order to allow metadata related to the event, like file name and size, to be read by the program that is triggered.

```
begin
dbms_scheduler.define_metadata_argument(
program_name       => 'load_sales_files',
metadata_attribute => 'event_message',
argument_position  => 1);
end;
/
```

5. Create an event-based job

When the file watcher detects a file and creates an event, this is what consumes the event and triggers the program to do some work. The job name needs to be unique in the schema, but the program name should refer to the program created to carry out the work.

```
begin
dbms_scheduler.create_job(
job_name        => 'load_sales_job',
program_name    => 'load_sales_files',
event_condition => null,
queue_spec      => 'dataload_file_watcher',
auto_drop       => false,
enabled         => false);
end;
/
```

The queue spec specifies what should trigger this event; in this case, you want to use the file watcher you created. By default, a second job will not be started if any previous events are still being processed. To override this and assure that the job will be run for each file that arrives, set it to run in parallel.

```
begin
dbms_scheduler.set_attribute('load_sales_job','parallel_instances',true);
end;
/
```

6. Enable the watcher, program and job

The elements needed for the file watcher are created in a disabled state, so you must now enable them.

```
begin
dbms_scheduler.enable('dataload_file_watcher,load_sales_files,load_sales_job
');
end;
/
```

The file watcher now scans the */u01/dataload* directory every 10 minutes (by default) for files matching the pattern **_sales.txt*. If a file is found, it generates an event that kicks off the *load_sales_files* program.

While the file watcher is still a fairly new feature, it has many applications and many attributes about file watchers, including the frequency at which they check for files, that can be adjusted to fit your needs.

Conclusion

While the Oracle schedulers are not a direct replacement for Linux *cron*, they provide a useful utility for scheduling tasks for execution within the database. The older *dbms_job* scheduler allows basic scheduling using a formula to determine the next run date of a job. In recent Oracle versions, it has been deprecated in favor of the *dbms_scheduler* package that accepts a more friendly syntax for scheduling tasks.

Each recent version of Oracle has brought enhancements to the *dbms_scheduler* package, one recent enhancement being the file watcher. File watchers allow the database to check for files in a specific location at the operating system. If files are found, an event is raised which can trigger a job.

These features enhance how you can manage data within the database but also have the ability to impact how you move data between databases and manage the system.

The next chapter is an introduction to Oracle Enterprise Manager (OEM) and Grid Control.

Oracle Enterprise Manager and Grid Control

Oracle Enterprise Manager (OEM) and Grid Control offer a graphical interface for managing Oracle systems. While early versions had limited functionality, OEM and Grid Control have grown to offer comprehensive administration features and some advanced monitoring features for both Oracle products and the operating system.

When you install Oracle Database software, the components for Oracle Enterprise Manager are installed as well. When databases are created, you have the option to create an OEM instance, which consists of a small web server and a schema within the database.

Grid Control, also referred to as Oracle Enterprise Manager Grid Control, is separate from a database installation. It expands on the functionality of OEM by allowing multiple Oracle installations on different servers to be monitored from one location. It also offers some advanced features for monitoring the operating system.

Working with OEM

Oracle Enterprise Manager will be the focus for the database here, but the steps for managing OEM for other Oracle installation types are similar.

Examining the OEM Setup

If you are not sure if OEM is running or even if it has been set up, you can use the *emctl* command to check its status.

```
$ emctl status dbconsole

https://oelinux-test1.lifeaftercoffee.com:5501/em/console/aboutApplication
Oracle Enterprise Manager 11g is running.
----------------------------------------------------------------
```

```
Logs are generated in directory /u01/app/oracle/product/11.1.0/db_1/oelinux-
test1.lifeaftercoffee.com_TEST/sysman/log
```

This command also prints the URL for an About page. You can figure out the
OEM URL by removing the text after *em* from this URL. If you get a message
saying that files for OEM are not found, it is likely that OEM is not yet
configured for this database, but you can follow the steps in the next section
to create it.

Files related to a given OEM configuration are kept in the Oracle home
directory in a subdirectory with the system name and database instance in it.
The files for this example would be in $*ORACLE_HOME*/*oelinux-
test1.lifeaftercoffee.com_TEST*. Within this directory, the *sysman*/*log* directory
contains logs that may be helpful when troubleshooting issues with OEM.
Some of these logs may also get large over time and need to be cleaned up to
free up disk space.

Creating OEM

If you have chosen not to create OEM when you created your database, it can
be created later using the *emca* command with the syntax below. You are
prompted to enter some information about your database and the
configuration agent runs through some setup steps.

```
$ emca -config dbcontrol db

started emca at mar 7, 2010 7:26:17 am

Enter the following information:
Database SID: TEST
Listener port number: 1521
Password for SYS user: password
Password for DBSNMP user: password
Password for SYSMAN user: password
Email address for notifications (optional):
Outgoing Mail (SMTP) server for notifications (optional):
-----------------------------------------------------------------
...
INFO: >>>>>>>>>>> The Database Control URL is https://oelinux-
test1.lifeaftercoffee.com:5501/em <<<<<<<<<<<
...
```

The OEM setup typically takes a few minutes to complete and prints some
status information to the command line. Near the end of the output, there is a

---

line that has the Database Console URL. This is the URL you use to access the console. Take note of this for future use.

> Some older Oracle installations may set up OEM to use non-secure HTTP by default. Additional steps may be necessary to secure it over HTTPS.

Once OEM is set up, you should be able to access it from the system it is on. You can do that by either tunneling X Windows through SSH or by working directly from the system's console. If you want to allow access from another system, you need to allow the port OEM is running on through the Linux firewall and possibly other network firewalls.

Starting and Stopping OEM

OEM can be started and stopped using the *emctl* command. If possible, you should manually stop OEM before shutting down the system, or better yet, set it up as a service. These steps can sometimes be slow, so be patient.

Starting OEM:

```
$ emctl start dbconsole

...
Starting Oracle Enterprise Manager 11g Database Control .............
started.
...
```

Stopping OEM:

```
$ emctl stop dbconsole

...
Stopping Oracle Enterprise Manager 11g Database Control ...
 ...  Stopped.
```

If you are unsure of the status of your OEM instance, you can check it using the steps described earlier.

Accessing OEM

OEM can be accessed through the URL given when it was created or from the status or start commands listed above. Keep in mind whatever system you are accessing OEM from will need to be able to connect to the server it is running on through the OEM web port.

When you first connect to OEM, you get a certificate warning. This is because when it is created, OEM sets up a self-signed certificate for use with HTTPS. Depending on your browser setup, you may just need to accept the certificate or you may need to make further configuration changes to access OEM.

Once you connect through, you receive a login screen. You can log into OEM as the SYSTEM or SYS user. Other users can be granted access to OEM as well, but these two work by default. The home screen shows an overview of the current state of the system and database. Right away, you can see information on the Linux system's CPU as well as further information about the database.

Figure 20.1: *The OEM Database Control Home Screen*

More information can be found in other tabs. The Performance tab shows a graph of the system's load average. It is shown directly over a graph of active sessions. This set of graphs can help correlate high load periods with user activity.

OEM also allows for the setup and maintenance of backups through the Availability tab. The Server tab lets you view and manage information about the physical setup of the database including file layout and memory usage. It also includes a more user-friendly interface to the Oracle scheduler. Additional pages in OEM allow you to control just about everything about the database. Grid Control adds some operating system monitoring on top of these features and allows you to manage multiple databases through a single interface.

Oracle Enterprise Manager Grid Control

As mentioned earlier, Oracle Enterprise Manager Grid Control, now sometimes referred to as just Oracle Enterprise Manager or OEM, is a separate installation from an Oracle database or application server installation. It can be, and often is, installed on a separate host from production databases and can be used to monitor multiple databases, application servers and even systems.

Grid Control is not only capable of monitoring and managing databases, but it can be used to monitor and manage Linux as well. Adding users, monitoring disk space and managing runlevels are just a few things that can be accomplished with Grid Control.

The Anatomy of Grid Control

Installation of Grid Control is beyond the scope of this book. It currently consists of some prerequisites, several upgrades and some patching. It is well documented in Oracle documentation, but you should step carefully through the instructions, making sure to meet prerequisites as you go. It also recommended to refer to another Rampant book, *Oracle Enterprise Manager Grid Control, Advanced OEM Techniques for the Real World* by Porus Homi Havewala.

A Grid Control installation consists of a repository database, i.e. this can be in an existing database, but be sure it is of a supported version and a minimal

OAS installation. Both are installed at once, and both need to be running for Grid Control to work.

Once installed, Grid Control can be used to manage and monitor multiple databases and systems. Multiple users can be configured within the Grid Control console to give different administrators access to different levels of management.

Monitoring and Managing Linux from Grid Control

Within the Targets tab of Grid Control, you can view system information under the Hosts sub-tab. Alerts and some general information about the system can be viewed on the Home page.

The performance page shows historical information about system performance in the form of a set of graphs. CPU, disk and memory information is shown at the top, and additional *top* style information can be found further down the page.

Figure 20.2: *The Grid Control Host Performance Page*

Beyond this summary page, more detailed views of CPU, memory, disk and resource utilization are also available.

The Administration page within Hosts allows you to manage services, the default system runlevel and many other system settings. It even provides an interface for managing users and groups. Note that you may have to install additional software for the Administration tab to work properly.

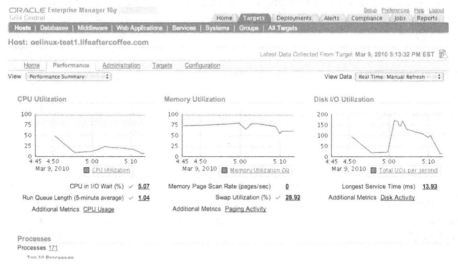

Figure 20.3: *The Grid Control Host Administration Page*

Just like when making system changes from the command line, it is important to know what you are doing within Grid Control! The web interface may make it easy to change something like a user ID number or the default runlevel, but if you do not understand what may result, you could easily cause some pretty big problems or even render the system virtually useless.

Within the Preferences section of Grid Control, it is possible to set up alerts to notify you via email when a certain condition is found on the system. Examples include monitoring disk usage, CPU usage and run queue length (load average.) Monitoring can be set up for all hosts which Grid Control has access to or for only specific hosts.

Conclusion

Oracle Enterprise Manager is included with Oracle Database installations and provides an interface for managing the database and some insight on the activity on the Linux system. Though it is somewhat limited, it is easy to set up and use.

Grid Control offers a much deeper ability to monitor and manage Linux, not only on the host it is installed on, but on all your Linux hosts. A Grid Control installation includes a small database for the repository and a limited Oracle Application Server installation to host the web interface.

Grid Control's main advantages are its ability to manage and monitor several systems from a single interface. In large environments, its advantages far outweigh the extra overhead of its footprint.

The final chapter in this book will briefly touch upon performance tuning with regards to performance issues that occur in the operating system.

Performance Tuning

Performance tuning is the topic of many lengthy books, but this chapter will delve into where the Oracle database tuning intersects with the operating system. By examining statistics and trends within the operating system, you can more effectively tune the Oracle database to take full advantage of the capabilities of the Linux system.

From an operating system point of view, performance issues are most commonly caused by one of the following:

- Processor usage: The application or database is requiring more processor than the system has.

- Memory usage: The application or database is trying to use more memory than is available on the system, or a database is not taking advantage of available memory.

- Disk throughput: Disks cannot keep up with the necessary reads and writes needed either due to high volume or contention for the same resource.

- Network throughput: Data is being delayed in transit over the network due to either high volume or devices not being properly configured.

Now take a brief look at how to examine each of these using tools provided with Linux, then the tools Oracle provides to monitor the system will be reviewed.

Monitoring Processor Usage

There are several key indicators for processor usage. The primary two are the CPU usage percentage and the load average.

Examining CPU Usage

The usage percentage indicates what percentage of time the CPU has been busy. CPU usage is broken down to indicate the amount of time the CPU spends in different states. The most common way to view CPU usage is with the *top* command.

```
top - 07:27:36 up 9 min,  2 users,  load average: 1.59, 2.54, 1.58
Tasks: 131 total,   2 running, 129 sleeping,   0 stopped,   0 zombie
Cpu(s):  7.9%us, 38.6%sy,  0.0%ni,  1.7%id, 49.2%wa,  2.3%hi,  0.3%si,  0.0%st
Mem:   1035244k total,   892864k used,   142380k free,     5584k buffers
Swap:  2097144k total,      108k used,  2097036k free,   465092k cached

PID USER      PR  NI  VIRT  RES  SHR S %CPU %MEM   TIME+   COMMAND
5506 oracle    17   0  533m  52m  51m R 37.8  5.2  0:02.33 oracle
5511 oracle    15   0  2196 1024  792 R  3.2  0.1  0:00.13 top
3295 oracle    16   0  351m  64m  18m S  1.0  6.3  0:12.42 emagent
2545 oracle    15   0  372m  56m  25m S  0.6  5.6  0:06.63 java
2548 oracle    15   0  313m  44m  16m S  0.6  4.4  0:06.18 java
2546 oracle    15   0  297m  42m  14m S  0.3  4.2  0:06.66 java
2549 oracle    18   0 1278m 192m  94m S  0.3 19.0  0:28.38 java
3127 oracle    15   0 54836 9880 4376 S  0.3  1.0  0:00.28 httpd
   1 root      15   0  2064  624  532 S  0.0  0.1  0:13.40 init
   2 root      RT  -5     0    0    0 S  0.0  0.0  0:00.00 migration/0
   3 root      34  19     0    0    0 S  0.0  0.0  0:00.02 ksoftirqd/0
   4 root      RT  -5     0    0    0 S  0.0  0.0  0:00.00 watchdog/0
   5 root      10  -5     0    0    0 S  0.0  0.0  0:00.14 events/0
   6 root      10  -5     0    0    0 S  0.0  0.0  0:00.49 khelper
   7 root      10  -5     0    0    0 S  0.0  0.0  0:00.11 kthread
  10 root      10  -5     0    0    0 S  0.0  0.0  0:01.02 kblockd/0
  11 root      20  -5     0    0    0 S  0.0  0.0  0:00.00 kacpid
```

The third row of *top* output, as shown above, shows the usage of CPU based on the CPU state. These CPU statistics reflect usage only since the last refresh of *top*, so they can be considered nearly real time.

Here is a breakdown of the CPU states. The first state name is the one seen in *top*. The second will be seen in the output of the *mpstat* command which will be covered next.

State	Definition
%us, %user	The percentage of CPU utilization spent executing user application code
%sy, %sys	The percentage of CPU utilization spent running system (kernel) operations
%ni, %nice	Indicates time spent running user processes that had priority set using nice
%id, %idle	The percentage of time spent idle but not waiting for disk I/O
%wa, %iowait	The percentage of time spent idle while waiting for a disk I/O request to be fulfilled
%hi, %irq	The percentage of time spent servicing hardware interrupts

	(IRQs)
%si, %soft	The percentage of time spent servicing soft interrupts (softirqs)
%st, %steal	The percentage of time spent using the processor for things like virtualization

Table 21.1: *List of CPU States*

While *top* shows CPU usage for the time period since the last refresh, the *mpstat* command will give CPU usage statistics since system startup.

```
$ mpstat

Linux 2.6.18-128.el5 (oelinux-test1.lifeaftercoffee.com)        03/18/2010

07:31:11 AM  CPU   %user   %nice   %sys %iowait    %irq   %soft %steal   %idle    intr/s
07:31:11 AM  all   10.81    0.02  24.29   30.07    1.26    1.54   0.00   32.01   1052.76
```

You can also use arguments to force *mpstat* to repeat at a given interval. When you ask *mpstat* to repeat the statistics, what is reported will reflect only the time since the last output. Two arguments are typically given, the first indicates how many seconds *mpstat* should wait between reporting stats, and the second indicates how many times it should repeat. If you want *mpstat* to repeat until cancelled, omit the second parameter.

```
$ mpstat 1 5

Linux 2.6.18-128.el5 (oelinux-test1.lifeaftercoffee.com)        03/18/2010

08:00:10 AM  CPU   %user   %nice   %sys %iowait    %irq   %soft %steal   %idle    intr/s
08:00:11 AM  all    1.98    0.00   1.98    0.00    0.00    0.00   0.00   96.04   1000.00
08:00:12 AM  all    9.18    0.00  22.45   43.88    2.04    0.00   0.00   22.45   1139.80
08:00:13 AM  all    6.86    0.00  16.67   41.18    1.96    0.98   0.00   32.35   1071.57
08:00:14 AM  all    4.00    0.00   6.00    2.00    1.00    3.00   0.00   84.00   1008.00
08:00:15 AM  all    3.00    0.00   3.00    0.00    0.00    3.00   0.00   91.00    978.00
Average:     all    4.99    0.00   9.98   17.37    1.00    1.40   0.00   65.27   1039.12
```

CPU usage is a good indication of how busy your processors are, but it is important to remember that a busy processor is not necessarily a bad thing! Here are some things to consider when looking at specific CPU statistics.

- A high amount of idle time indicates unused processor. This is a good thing if you are concerned about the system being ready to take on more work, but a low amount of idle time does not necessarily indicate the system is overloaded.

- A persistently high amount of system or interrupt utilization may indicate a hardware or operating system issue and warrant additional investigation.

- If the user percentage is high, you can examine the processes using the most CPU within the output of *top*. From there, you should be able to determine top CPU users and identify runaway processes and CPU hogs.

- A high amount of *iowait* indicates that the disk is not servicing requests as quickly as processes are requesting them. While *iowait* is typically high when large amounts of data are read (like when starting databases), persistently high *iowait* percentages should be investigated.

Sometimes you may find CPU statistics point you right at a problem, such as a runaway process. More often, they will simply give you some direction for further investigation.

Examining the Load Average

Another important metric available via *top* output is the load average. It can also be viewed with the *uptime* command.

```
$ top

top - 08:36:25 up  1:18,  3 users,  load average: 1.95, 2.05, 1.36
Tasks: 163 total,   4 running, 159 sleeping,   0 stopped,   0 zombie
Cpu(s):  4.4%us, 13.0%sy,  1.6%ni, 64.4%id, 14.9%wa,  0.6%hi,  1.0%si,  0.0%st
Mem:   1035244k total,  1018360k used,    16884k free,    11268k buffers
Swap:  2097144k total,   110212k used,  1986932k free,   475652k cached

  PID USER      PR  NI  VIRT  RES  SHR S %CPU %MEM    TIME+  COMMAND
13655 root      39  19  4600 1304  980 R 11.8  0.1   0:21.95 makewhatis
  113 root      15   0     0    0    0 S  2.0  0.0   0:01.98 pdflush
  ...

$ uptime

 08:36:29 up  1:18,  3 users,  load average: 1.95, 2.05, 1.36
```

The load average of a system indicates the average number of processes being run, or waiting to run over a given time period on the system. The load average does not take the number of processors or cores into consideration, so it is important to evaluate it with that in mind.

Three load average numbers are reported which indicate the one, five and 15-minute averages, respectively. This allows you to extrapolate some trend information. If, for instance, the 15-minute load average is very high, but the one-minute average is fairly low, you know the system was busy but is currently less busy.

There is no magic number for determining a good or bad load average, but these guidelines should help you when examining load averages.

- Load averages lower than the number of processors or cores generally indicate there is little or no backup of processes waiting for CPU.

- If the load average is one to two times the number of processors or cores, it is likely the system is starting to slow down. You may want to start examining running processes and consider eliminating them or moving some to other systems.

- If the load average is more than twice the number of processors or cores, it is likely things are starting to slow down and database and application performance are probably being affected. Look to reduce the load by shutting down non-essential processes and/or moving them to other systems.

- Remember to consider all three load averages and how they can indicate trends. If the one-minute load average is higher than the five and 15, then the system is getting more active. If the 15-minute load average is high, but the one and five are lower, the system is becoming less active.

Like with CPU and many other operating statistics you look at, you often need to combine information from several sources to determine the exact cause of a performance issue. These guidelines should help move you in the right direction.

If you have identified the processor as a bottleneck, the first thing to do, if possible, is to tune the database or application to use less processor. This may mean rewriting code, adding pre-calculated fields and join indexes or spreading out tasks that use a lot of processor. If you have done all possible tuning, you may need to either move high CPU usage tasks to a different system, or upgrade to a system with faster or more processors.

Memory Usage

One of the biggest performance issues you can face on a Linux system is to exhaust the available physical memory. When the system is out of memory, it starts to write portions of memory to disk to free up space for active processes. If the system has to write your database's memory contents to disk, things will slow just about to a halt.

It is important to remember that Linux takes advantage of unused memory for caching files from the file system. This can make it appear that there is very little free memory, but if additional memory is needed, the file system cache data can be purged to free it up.

Examining Memory Usage

The *top* command provides a good overview of memory usage. Specifically, the fourth and fifth lines contain information on overall memory usage.

```
$ top

top - 08:36:25 up  1:18,  3 users,  load average: 1.95, 2.05, 1.36
Tasks: 163 total,   4 running, 159 sleeping,   0 stopped,   0 zombie
Cpu(s):  4.4%us, 13.0%sy,  1.6%ni, 64.4%id, 14.9%wa,  0.6%hi,  1.0%si,  0.0%st
Mem:   1035244k total,  1018360k used,    16884k free,    11268k buffers
Swap:  2097144k total,   110212k used,  1986932k free,   475652k cached

  PID USER      PR  NI  VIRT  RES  SHR S %CPU %MEM    TIME+  COMMAND
13655 root      39  19  4600 1304  980 R 11.8  0.1  0:21.95 makewhatis
  113 root      15   0     0    0    0 S  2.0  0.0  0:01.98 pdflush
 2548 oracle    15   0  311m  45m  14m S  2.0  4.5  0:18.71 java
 2549 oracle    18   0 1288m 183m  82m S  2.0 18.2  0:46.00 java
 3295 oracle    16   0  351m  67m  16m S  2.0  6.7  0:59.19 emagent
...
```

The *top* command also shows per-process memory usage for the top processes. These values are covered in detail in Chapter 14 in the section on monitoring memory usage. Another good source of information on memory usage is the *meminfo* file. This file represents the current state of the system.

```
$ cat /proc/meminfo

MemTotal:      1035244 kB
MemFree:         29096 kB
Buffers:         48216 kB
Cached:         811836 kB
...
```

To monitor real-time processor usage, use *vmstat*. It allows for continual monitoring of memory usage while the system is running.

```
$ vmstat 2 10

procs -----------memory---------- ---swap-- -----io---- --system-- -----cpu------
 r  b   swpd   free   buff  cache   si   so    bi    bo   in   cs us sy id wa st
 0  0      0 392920  47844 497032    0    0    26    10 1008   76  1  3 95  1  0
 2  0      0 392304  47844 497032    0    0     0     0 1003  107  6 32 63  0  0
 2  0      0 383584  47852 502692    0    0     0    72 1013  186 15 82  2  1  0
 3  0      0 187416  47860 683068    0    0     2    70 1026  147 18 73 10  0  0
 0  0      0  53984  47860 805960    0    0     0     0 1027  205 12 51 38  0  0
 0  0      0  53240  47868 805960    0    0    42     0 1028  177  4 10 83  4  0
 1  0      0  46916  47880 811832    0    0     4   918 1092  304  8 28 61  4  0
 2  0      0  37244  47892 811888    0    0    24   398 1077  311 28 71  0  1  0
 3  0      0  28068  47900 811920    0    0     6   124 1022  203 32 68  0  0  0
```

```
   2  0     0 25960 47916 811916    0    0    0    30 1014  147 36 64  0  0  0
```

Information about CPU utilization is also shown in *vmstat* output, making it a very useful resource for monitoring the system. More information on these tools, as well as suggestions for how they can be used for tuning, can be found in Chapter 14.

Monitoring Disk Throughput

Disk throughput is the measure of how much data can be written to or read from (or both) a file system during a given period. This topic is complicated somewhat by today's storage virtualization options, i.e. SAN and NAS solutions which allow a large amount of storage, typically made up of multiple hard drives and a very large cache to be shared amongst several systems.

Even without a storage virtualization solution, it is possible that you have a few large disks on your system that are partitioned and serve several file systems. Again, this can complicate disk tuning and limit possible solutions.

Both virtualization and partitioning result in a situation where data may appear on separate file systems, but the data is actually served from the same physical disks. When you are examining disk throughput, it is important to consider activity that is happening on all file systems being served from a given disk (or disks) and through a given interface.

Examining Disk Throughput

Disk throughput can be viewed and monitored using the *iostat* command. By default, *iostat* gives information on throughput for all attached devices since the system was started.

```
# iostat

Linux 2.6.18-128.el5 (oelinux-test1.lifeaftercoffee.com)       12/28/2009

avg-cpu:  %user   %nice %system %iowait  %steal   %idle
           1.15    0.02    2.91    0.48    0.00   95.44

Device:            tps   Blk_read/s   Blk_wrtn/s   Blk_read   Blk_wrtn
hda               1.66        28.74        16.03     740939     413228
hda1              0.04         0.22         0.00       5627          4
hda2              1.60        28.47        16.03     733905     413224
...
```

More current information can be found by adding arguments for a delay (in seconds) and a number of repetitions. The output from *iostat* is repeated and then only reflects activity since the last report. You can also narrow the output by specifying the device. More information about *iostat* as well as suggestions on interpreting *iostat* output can be found in Chapter 12 in the section on file system performance.

Like *iowait*, high disk throughput is not unusual during operations like database startup, but if it is consistently high, that may be an indication that the database or applications are performing more reads and/or writes than necessary. For Oracle databases, full table scans on large tables are particularly read-intensive and should be avoided if possible. A few carefully thought out indexes can make a big difference. Smaller tables that are needed frequently can be pinned into memory by implementing a keep pool. Even just increasing the SGA size of a database can considerably reduce disk throughput needs by allowing more data to be kept in the cache at once, but be careful not to exhaust the available memory.

It is a good idea to schedule I/O-heavy operations like backups during low use periods to avoid increasing disk throughput that could slow down other applications. Scheduling high load operations like backups and data warehouse loads during low use periods, typically overnight, and staggering them to spread out the load is strongly recommended even if there is no apparent performance issue.

On older systems, each file system existed on a single disk. Under those circumstances, it was possible to spread out the load of heavy I/O operations in such a way that each disk could assume part of the load. With disk virtualization, these changes are typically not possible as the same disk is serving many file systems. One change that may be possible is to allocate more cache to a given file system through the virtualization setup. This can allow frequently used data to be served without having to access the disks and, in many newer virtualization systems, can even cache writes to improve performance further.

When tuning measures do not reduce throughput enough, it may be worth increasing the amount of memory in the system and increasing database memory parameters accordingly or moving to faster disks or disk controllers.

This typically represents a large and expensive undertaking, so it is important to consider tuning options first.

Monitoring Network Throughput

The network can be the hardest part of the Linux system to troubleshoot. To fully diagnose network problems, you need to consider each device between the two systems making the connection. This section will help with troubleshooting the network interfaces on the Linux system and give some direction for figuring out where else in the network to look.

Examining Network Throughput

Unfortunately, Linux does not include many tools for monitoring overall network throughput, but there are a few command line tools you should be aware of. For more long-term monitoring of network activity, you need to consider a tool like *ntop* or *mrtg* which will monitor and graph network activity over time. These tools are not included with all Linux distributions but may be installed as add-ons.

The *ifconfig* command gives information about the current state of network interfaces. If called without any arguments, it prints information on real and virtual interfaces currently in use on the system.

```
# ifconfig

eth0      Link encap:Ethernet  HWaddr 08:00:27:AA:75:F0
          inet addr:192.168.1.20  Bcast:192.168.1.255  Mask:255.255.255.0
          inet6 addr: fe80::a00:27ff:feaa:75f0/64 Scope:Link
          UP BROADCAST RUNNING MULTICAST  MTU:1500  Metric:1
          RX packets:43571 errors:0 dropped:0 overruns:0 frame:0
          TX packets:27461 errors:0 dropped:0 overruns:0 carrier:0
          collisions:0 txqueuelen:1000
          RX bytes:50651351 (48.3 MiB)  TX bytes:4509220 (4.3 MiB)
          Interrupt:10 Base address:0xd020

eth0:1    Link encap:Ethernet  HWaddr 08:00:27:AA:75:F0
          inet addr:192.168.1.30  Bcast:192.168.1.255  Mask:255.255.255.0
          UP BROADCAST RUNNING MULTICAST  MTU:1500  Metric:1
          Interrupt:10 Base address:0xd020

lo        Link encap:Local Loopback
          inet addr:127.0.0.1  Mask:255.0.0.0
          inet6 addr: ::1/128 Scope:Host
          UP LOOPBACK RUNNING  MTU:16436  Metric:1
          RX packets:12285 errors:0 dropped:0 overruns:0 frame:0
```

```
TX packets:12285 errors:0 dropped:0 overruns:0 carrier:0
collisions:0 txqueuelen:0
RX bytes:12578202 (11.9 MiB)  TX bytes:12578202 (11.9 MiB)
```

The output includes information on the amount of data received (RX) and transmitted (TX) including the total number of packets and any errors that were encountered. While ideally all the error numbers would always be 0, in reality it is not unusual for there to be some errors or dropped packets. If these numbers are very high or constantly growing, there may be a problem with the network interface or another device on the network.

By examining the values for RX bytes and TX bytes over time, you could calculate the amount of data being passed for the given time. Note that the virtual interface *eth0:1* does not have detailed information on throughput. Data passed over this virtual interface is recorded in the numbers for the physical interface *eth0*.

One common issue with network interfaces is packet collisions. Packet collisions happen when more than one device on a network try to send data at once over a connection that cannot handle it. If you are seeing packet collisions, as indicated by an increasing collisions number in *netstat*, you should consult with your network administrator to assure the Linux system duplex settings are appropriate for the network it is connected to. If all duplex settings are correct and packet collisions continue, there may be a network device starting to fail.

Other Monitoring Tools

There are a couple of other options for monitoring Linux performance which warrant mention. The first is provided as part of the GNOME desktop environment and is installed with Linux by default. The second one can be downloaded from Oracle.

The System Monitor

A graphical system monitor that shows an overview of system performance is included with Linux. It can be found in the GNOME desktop environment in the System menu under Administration->System Monitor. It can also be started with the command *gnome-system-monitor*, but an X Windows server needs to be available for the display.

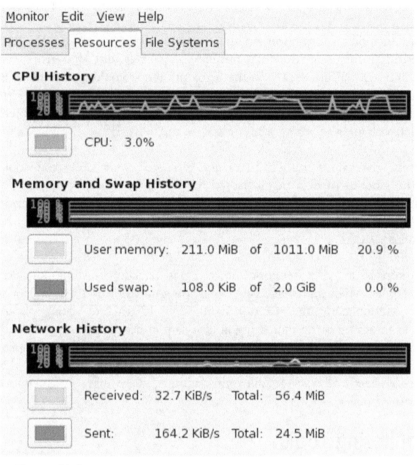

Figure 21.1: *The System Monitor Tool*

While it gives only a very gross overview of the system, it can be useful for getting a quick idea of what is happening on the system. Note that System Monitor only starts to graph system information after it is started. It is not possible to look back in time to an earlier point.

Oracle's OS Watcher

Oracle provides a tool called OS Watcher that collects and archives operating system performance information for future analysis. The OS Watcher utilities need to be downloaded separately from Oracle support. More information on the OS Watcher and download links can be found in Oracle support document ID 301137.1.

The OS Watcher includes two primary tools. The first is the watcher itself that gathers OS information. The second is the OSW grapher that creates graphs from the data gathered by the watcher. The first step to use the OS Watcher is to gather OS statistics over a period of time. Once you download and unpack the OS Watcher, change directories into the OS Watcher directory. There you find the *startOSW.sh* and *stopOSW.sh* scripts that are used to start and stop the OS Watcher.

The *startOSW.sh* script is typically called with two parameters. The first indicates how many seconds it should delay between gathering statistics. The second indicates how many hours statistics should be gathered for.

```
$ ./startOSW.sh 5 1

Testing for discovery of OS Utilities...

VMSTAT found on your system.
IOSTAT found on your system.
MPSTAT found on your system.
NETSTAT found on your system.
TOP found on your system.

Discovery completed.

Starting OSWatcher v3.0   on Fri Mar 19 08:37:05 EDT 2010
With SnapshotInterval = 5
With ArchiveInterval = 1
...

$ ./stopOSW.sh
```

> 🔔 The OS Watcher continually prints output to the terminal session where it was started. You can either redirect the output to a file with '>' or just plan to not use that terminal session until the OS Watcher has completed.

If you want to stop the OS Watcher before the originally indicated time period has finished, run the *stopOSW.sh* command.

Once you have gathered the statistics using the OS Watcher utility, you can use the *oswg.jar* java application to graph the information gathered. The graphs are displayed to the current X Windows server, so you need to have a working X Windows environment.

 Depending on what you have installed for Java, the default version may not be appropriate for the OS Watcher grapher. You can either install a newer version of Java or use the version installed with Oracle.

To launch the OS Watcher graphing tool, still from within the *osw* directory, call it using Java. The *-i* option is needed and you need to specify the location of the data created by the watcher. By default, the data is in the *archive* subdirectory where the OS Watcher was unpacked.

```
$ java -jar oswg.jar -i ./archive

Starting OSWg V3.0.0

Parsing Data. Please Wait...

Enter 1 to Display CPU Process Queue Graphs
Enter 2 to Display CPU Utilization Graphs
Enter 3 to Display CPU Other Graphs
Enter 4 to Display Memory Graphs
Enter 5 to Display Disk IO Graphs

Enter 6 to Generate All CPU Gif Files
Enter 7 to Generate All Memory Gif Files
Enter 8 to Generate All Disk Gif Files

Enter L to Specify Alternate Location of Gif Directory
Enter T to Specify Different Time Scale
Enter D to Return to Default Time Scale
Enter R to Remove Currently Displayed Graphs
Enter P to Generate A Profile
Enter Q to Quit Program

Please Select an Option:
```

After starting the grapher, you are presented with a list of options for graphing CPU, memory and disk information. You can also adjust the time period you wish to display in the graphs.

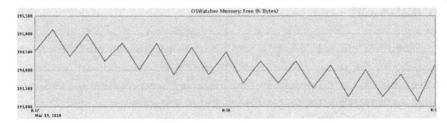

Figure 21.2: *The OS Watcher Free Memory Graph*

The OS Watcher consumes very little additional system resources and can generally be used without any noticeable impact on the system. Some DBAs even choose to have the OS Watcher start automatically and monitor the system continually for later analysis.

Conclusion

When performance issues are encountered, it is essential to look at what is happening on the system as well as in the database. Problems with memory, processor, disk and network quickly manifest themselves in database performance.

It is important to consider performance before there is a problem, rather than because of one. Some preemptive tuning can prevent performance issues in the future, and knowing what performance is like under normal circumstances can help in identifying bottlenecks when performance is poor.

Book Conclusion

To be an effective Oracle DBA, you need to be able to manage the system your databases run on, or at least understand how it is managed. In this book, you have seen nearly the complete system lifecycle, from installation of Linux to managing software, disk space, processes and much more.

Graphical tools have become commonplace for system level configuration tasks but command line skills are still essential and can often be more efficient than their GUI counterparts for many basic tasks. Command line tools also offer the opportunity to script complex, repetitive or seldom performed activities to simplify administration.

Having a well laid out system allows you to organize your databases in a flexible and durable manner. System resources can be monitored through system-provided tools to help identify problems and let Oracle make best use of the system.

An Oracle database itself is a large and complex product, but its functionality is dependent on the system being up and available. Whether you are managing the system yourself or working with a team of system administrators, the concepts and practices in this book should serve you well as you manage the database and the system.

Index

---

system-config-network command317, 320, 322

T

U

V

W

X

About the Author

Jon Emmons

Jon Emmons is an Oracle ACE with many years of full-time experience running Oracle in a UNIX environment. His Oracle experience is reinforced by his many years as a UNIX system administrator. Jon has published extensively about Oracle on his website which continues to receive acclaim from the Oracle community.

Jon's work experience includes both industry and education. In addition to his technical abilities Jon has also been called upon to teach a college course in database management systems.

CPSIA information can be obtained
at www.ICGtesting.com
Printed in the USA
LVHW101303080321
680874LV00012B/187